THE PHILOSOPHY OF EL1

One of the most important philosophers of recent times, Elizabeth Anscombe wrote books and articles on a wide range of topics, including the ground-breaking monograph *Intention*. Her work is original, challenging, often difficult, always insightful; but it has frequently been misunderstood, and its overall significance is still not fully appreciated. This book is the first major study of Anscombe's philosophical *oeuvre*. In it, Roger Teichmann presents Anscombe's main ideas, bringing out their interconnections, elaborating and discussing their implications, pointing out objections and difficulties, and aiming to give a unified overview of her philosophy. Many of Anscombe's arguments are relevant to contemporary debates, as Teichmann shows, and on a number of topics what Anscombe has to say constitutes a powerful alternative to dominant or popular views. Among the writings discussed are *Intention*, 'Practical Inference', 'Modern Moral Philosophy', 'Rules, Rights and Promises', 'On Brute Facts', 'The First Person', 'The Intentionality of Sensation', 'Causality and Determination', *An Introduction to Wittgenstein's Tractatus*, 'The Question of Linguistic Idealism', and a number of other pieces, including some that are little known or hard to obtain. A complete bibliography of Anscombe's writings is also included. Ranging from the philosophy of action, through ethics, to philosophy of mind, metaphysics, and the philosophy of logic and language, this book is a study of one of the most significant bodies of work in modern philosophy, spanning more than fifty years, and as pertinent today as ever.

Roger Teichmann is Lecturer in Philosophy at Oxford University, teaching at St. Hilda's College.

The Philosophy
of Elizabeth Anscombe

ROGER TEICHMANN

OXFORD

UNIVERSITY PRESS

OXFORD
UNIVERSITY PRESS

Great Clarendon Street, Oxford OX2 6DP

Oxford University Press is a department of the University of Oxford.
It furthers the University's objective of excellence in research, scholarship,
and education by publishing worldwide in

Oxford New York

Auckland Cape Town Dar es Salaam Hong Kong Karachi
Kuala Lumpur Madrid Melbourne Mexico City Nairobi
New Delhi Shanghai Taipei Toronto

With offices in

Argentina Austria Brazil Chile Czech Republic France Greece
Guatemala Hungary Italy Japan Poland Portugal Singapore
South Korea Switzerland Thailand Turkey Ukraine Vietnam

Oxford is a registered trade mark of Oxford University Press
in the UK and in certain other countries

Published in the United States
by Oxford University Press Inc., New York

British Library Cataloguing in Publication Data

Data available

Library of Congress Cataloging in Publication Data

Teichmann, Roger, 1963-
The philosophy of Elizabeth Anscombe / Roger Teichmann.
p. cm.
Includes bibliographical references and index.
ISBN-13: 978–0–19–929933–1
1. Anscombe, G. E. M. (Gertrude Elizabeth Margaret). I. Title.
B1618.A574T45 2008
192—dc22
2008000196

Typeset by SPI Publisher Services, Pondicherry, India.
Printed in the United Kingdom by
Lightning Source UK Ltd., Milton Keynes.

ISBN 978–0–19–929933–1 (Hbk)
ISBN 978–0–19–960335–0 (Pbk)

To Sarah

Contents

List of Abbreviations

ACTP	'*Analysis* Competition—Tenth Problem', in *MPM*
AIDE	'Action, Intention and "Double Effect"', in *HLAE*
AM	'Authority in Morals', in *ERP*
BF	'On Brute Facts', in *ERP*
CD	'Causality and Determination', in *MPM*
ERP	*Ethics, Religion and Politics: Collected Philosophical Papers of G. E. M. Anscombe*, iii (Oxford: Blackwell, and Minneapolis: University of Minnesota Press, 1981)
FAEH	*La filosofía analítica y la espiritualidad del hombre: Lecciones en la Universidad de Navarra*, ed. J. M. Torralba and J. Nubiola (Pamplona: Eunsa, 2005)
FP	'The First Person', in *MPM*
FPW	*From Parmenides to Wittgenstein: Collected Philosophical Papers of G. E. M. Anscombe*, i (Oxford: Blackwell, and Minneapolis: University of Minnesota Press, 1981)
HJC	'Hume and Julius Caesar', in *FPW*
HLAE	*Human Life, Action and Ethics*, ed. M. Geach and L. Gormally (St Andrew's Studies in Philosophy and Public Affairs; Exeter: Imprint Academic, 2005)
I	*Intention* (2nd edn.; Oxford: Blackwell, 1963, and Cambridge, Mass.: Harvard University Press, 2000—identical in format)
IS	'The Intentionality of Sensation: A Grammatical Feature', in *MPM*
IWT	*An Introduction to Wittgenstein's Tractatus* (London: Hutchinson, 1959)
KRHL	'Knowledge and Reverence for Human Life', in *HLAE*
MEC	'Memory, "Experience" and Causation', in *MPM*
MMP	'Modern Moral Philosophy', in *ERP* and *HLAE*
MOC	'Must One Obey One's Conscience?', in *HLAE*
MPM	*Metaphysics and the Philosophy of Mind: Collected Philosophical Papers of G. E. M. Anscombe*, ii (Oxford: Blackwell, and Minneapolis: University of Minnesota Press, 1981)
MT	'Making True', in R. Teichmann (ed.), *Logic, Cause and Action: Essays in Honour of Elizabeth Anscombe* (Cambridge: Cambridge University Press, 2000)
OMPCY	'Does Oxford Moral Philosophy Corrupt Youth?', in *HLAE*
OT	'On Transubstantiation', in *ERP*
PI	'Practical Inference', in *HLAE*
PJ	'On Promising and its Justice, and Whether it Need be Respected *in Foro Interno*', in *ERP*
PMC	'Parmenides, Mystery and Contradiction', in *FPW*
PPDM	'Prolegomenon to a Pursuit of the Definition of Murder', in *HLAE*
QLI	'The Question of Linguistic Idealism', in *FPW*

RP	'The Reality of the Past', in *MPM*
RRP	'Rules, Rights and Promises', in *ERP*
SAS	'On the Source of the Authority of the State', in *ERP*
TAA	'Thought and Action in Aristotle: What is "Practical Truth"?', in *FPW*
TBC	'Times, Beginnings and Causes', in *MPM*
TKEA	'The Two Kinds of Error in Action', in *ERP*
UD	' "Under a Description" ', in *MPM*
V	'La Verdad', in *FAEH*
WM	'War and Murder', in *ERP*

For articles, all page references relate to the volume in which the given article appears (or to the first-mentioned volume, in case of the article's appearing in more than one).

Introduction

Elizabeth Anscombe was one of the giants of twentieth-century philosophy, a bold and original thinker who wrote on a huge variety of topics. But her work is often difficult or puzzling, and an impatient reader will not get far with it. To read and reread her is undoubtedly the best way; a remark or passage which had at first seemed obscure can come to seem absolutely the right way of putting things. The difficulty of her writings is a fact, for all that, and one of the aims of this book is to present Anscombe's thought in as clear a way as is possible without falsifying or simplifying it. It should go without saying that there can be no substitute for reading Anscombe herself, and this book is not intended as such a substitute.

Part of the difficulty in reading Anscombe is in finding your bearings, and this has to do with her eschewal of System. A system or theory often makes things easier for the reader. Once you have grasped N's theory, you can frequently infer what N would have to say on some point by simply 'applying' the theory. But it can often be hard to predict in advance what Anscombe will say about some given thing. She is infuriatingly prone to take each case on its merits. There is a familiar philosophical, or meta-philosophical, issue here, to do with the pointfulness or otherwise of constructing generalizations. Wittgenstein considered prefacing the text of the *Philosophical Investigations* with the epigraph 'I'll teach you differences',[1] and Anscombe certainly shared Wittgenstein's belief that glossing over differences was one of the main sources of error in philosophy. But there is another reason for the lack of apparent systematicity in Anscombe's writings, and that is that her purpose in writing was typically to get somewhere in her own thoughts on some topic; she usually spends little or no time in providing a background, or in justifying her main 'assumptions', preferring to begin *in medias res*.

These same assumptions may be justified or addressed elsewhere in Anscombe's oeuvre—another reason why it helps to read her thoroughly. There are indeed manifold connections between her thoughts on different topics, and it is a further aim of this book to bring out these connections. Such connections do bind Anscombe's thoughts together into a system, if you like, but this is not a system concocted so as to be applied to particular problems. Rather it is a

---

[1] A quotation from *King Lear*, Act I, scene 4.

system itself constituted by a mature overview of those problems, the result of one mind's having actually tackled many particular and interrelated questions.

A third aim of this book is to engage with what Anscombe says, as opposed to merely expounding it. On the one hand this entails putting forward possible objections and counter-arguments, and on the other, developing or applying her ideas beyond the limits of her original discussions. On occasion I may even pursue Anscombe's thoughts in directions she would not have followed; if so, however, it ought to be clear that that is what I am doing. The ultimate purpose of the enterprise, after all, is the same as it is in philosophy generally, namely to achieve understanding. As Mary Geach has said of the difference between a philosopher and a sage, 'the way to show respect for a sage is to accept his teaching, but the way to respect the philosopher is to argue'.[2]

Gertrude Elizabeth Margaret Anscombe was born in 1919, the youngest child of Alan Wells Anscombe, a schoolmaster at Dulwich College, and his wife Gertrude Elizabeth (née Thomas), a headmistress. She was educated at Sydenham School, and was occasionally coached by her mother, who was a classical scholar. Already as a teenager Anscombe's intellectual curiosity was evident. Reading done between the ages of 12 and 15 led eventually to her being converted to Roman Catholicism,[3] and it was as a result of reading a book by a nineteenth-century Jesuit entitled *Natural Theology* that she became embroiled in philosophy. In that book Anscombe found a doctrine that she could not believe and an argument that appeared to her to be a *petitio principii*. The first was the doctrine that God knows what anybody *would* have done if, e.g., he hadn't died when he did; it seemed to the young Anscombe that 'there was not, quite generally, any such thing as what would have happened if what did happen had not happened'.[4] The second was an argument for the existence of a First Cause, and it was in repeated attempts to produce an improved version of the Jesuit's argument that Anscombe began on the path of active philosophy:

In two or three years of effort I produced five versions of a would-be proof, each one of which I then found guilty of the same error, though each time it was more cunningly concealed. In all this time I had no philosophical training about the matter; even my last attempt was made before I started reading Greats at Oxford.   (*MPM*, p. vii)

At Oxford Anscombe attended St Hugh's College. Greats, or *Literae Human-iores*, was and is Oxford's classics course, consisting of classical literature, history, and philosophy. Anscombe's attachment to philosophy in preference to the two other components of the course resulted in what must have been an unprecedent-edly unbalanced performance in Finals. The philosophy examiners wanted to give her a First, on the basis of her philosophy papers, but the ancient history examin-ers would agree to this only on condition that she showed a minimum knowledge

---

² *HLAE*, Introduction, p. xxi.   ³ Cf. *MPM*, Introduction, p. vii.   ⁴ *MPM*, ibid.

of their subject in a *viva voce* (oral) examination. Anscombe's performance in the *viva* was less than spectacular: she made a bad start and seems to have more or less dried up as a consequence. To the last two questions she answered 'No', these being 'Can you give us the name of a Roman provincial governor?' and (in some desperation) 'Is there any fact about the period you are supposed to have studied which you would like to tell us?' The examiners cannot have been well pleased, but somehow or other ended up being persuaded by the philosophers to agree to Anscombe's being awarded a First after all. As Michael Dummett writes in his obituary for Anscombe, 'For the [ancient historians] to have yielded, her philosophy papers must have been astonishing'.[5]

While an undergraduate Anscombe met Peter Geach, who was studying at Balliol, and whom she was to marry in 1941. After graduating, she was awarded a Research Fellowship at Newnham College, Cambridge. At Cambridge she attended the lectures of Wittgenstein, subsequently becoming a personal friend of his. She was later to be his main English translator and one of the three literary executors appointed by Wittgenstein himself, along with Rush Rhees and G. H. von Wright. After Cambridge, she returned to Oxford, to take up a Research Fellowship at Somerville College.

In 1948 Anscombe delivered a paper to the Socratic Club which criticized an argument of C. S. Lewis, the Christian apologist and author of the *Narnia* books, to the effect that naturalism is self-refuting. By 'naturalism' Lewis meant a doctrine according to which human thought can be fully explained by reference to natural causes. His argument had appeared in chapter 3 of the book *Miracles*. Lewis, the founder of the club, was present on the occasion, and was evidently aware that Anscombe's criticism had force. But it seems unlikely that he felt as irretrievably crushed as some of his acquaintances made out afterwards; the episode is probably an inflated legend, in the same category as the affair of Wittgenstein's poker. Certainly, Anscombe herself believed that Lewis's argument, though flawed, was getting at something important; she thought that this came out more in the improved version of it that Lewis presented in a subsequent edition of *Miracles*—though that version also had 'much to criticize in it'.[6] The story is nevertheless of biographical interest, as showing the confidence and intellectual acumen of the young Anscombe.

Anscombe remained in Somerville, becoming Lecturer and then Tutorial Fellow, and at the college got to know Philippa Foot and Iris Murdoch. With Foot in particular she formed a close personal and intellectual bond. Foot writes:

We were close friends in spite of my atheism and her intransigent Catholicism, and she remarked once that she thought we had never had a cross word. Very often we sat down in the SCR after lunch going straight into discussion of a philosophical topic suggested by her; and might be still at it when tea was brought in.[7]

---

[5] *The Tablet*, 13 Jan. 2001.   [6] Cf. Introduction, *MPM*, pp. ix–x.
[7] Obituary in *Somerville College Review*, 2001, p. 119.

Foot attended Anscombe's seminars on Wittgenstein's remarks on private language, etc., and

> as I then supported a conventional view on the subject I attacked her every week; always caused to think again but always there with new objections next time. Much later some remark of Norman Malcolm's made me think 'Good heavens, there may be something in what Wittgenstein says'. So I asked Elizabeth 'Why didn't you tell me?' to which she replied 'Because it is important to have one's resistances'. She obviously thought that a long period of strenuous objection was the best way to understand Wittgenstein. Although she was his close friend, a literary executor, and one of the first to recognise his greatness, nothing could have been further from her character and mode of thought than discipleship.[8]

Foot's assessment of Anscombe's relationship to Wittgenstein seems to me very accurate, and is worth recording in view of the oft-repeated description of Anscombe as a 'disciple' of Wittgenstein's. Wittgenstein himself was at the very least ambivalent about the idea of having disciples, and his whole way of doing philosophy was opposed to students' simply taking what their teachers said as truth: learning to do philosophy, he thought, meant learning to think for yourself. That Anscombe was capable of thinking for herself was apparent from early on, and it is no doubt that capacity that endeared her to Wittgenstein intellectually—plus her sheer intelligence, of course. Some followers of Wittgenstein have been content to repeat what he said in different ways, but Anscombe's philosophy is truer to the spirit of Wittgenstein's precisely in its *not* doing that.

One way in which Anscombe differed considerably from Wittgenstein was in her attitude to political and social evils. Wittgenstein was almost pathologically distrustful of people taking a moral stand in public; his preferred reaction to what he took to be social evils seems to have been one of quasi-fatalistic disgust, rather than an urge to do something about them. In 1946 he wrote in one of his notebooks:

> The hysterical fear over the atom bomb now being experienced, or at any rate expressed, by the public almost suggests that at last something really salutary has been invented. The fright at least gives the impression of a really effective bitter medicine. I can't help thinking: if this didn't have something good about it the *philistines* wouldn't be making an outcry.[9]

Wittgenstein specifies what kind of a 'good' he has in mind—'the end, the destruction, of an evil,—our disgusting soapy water science'. His only worry concerns 'what would come *after* this destruction'. The contrast with Anscombe could hardly be greater. While still an undergraduate she and a friend, Norman

---

[8] Obituary in *Somerville College Review*, 2001, pp. 119–20.
[9] Ludwig Wittgenstein, *Culture and Value*, ed. G. H. von Wright and Heikki Nyman, trans. Peter Winch (Oxford: Blackwell, 1980), 48e–49e.

Daniel, published a pamphlet, 'The Justice of the Present War Examined' (1939), arguing that the war in which Great Britain was engaged was not a just one, in particular because of an evident willingness on the part of her government to target civilians. And in 1956, when it was proposed that Oxford University should honour Harry Truman, the former US President, with a degree, she publicly opposed the proposal, again on the grounds of a government's targeting and killing innocent civilians. (Truman had ordered the dropping of atom bombs on Hiroshima and Nagasaki.) Anscombe was evidently one of those 'philistines' referred to by Wittgenstein. [10]

Wittgenstein and Anscombe differed in their attitude to the Bomb, and to war generally; but they also differed about public protest as such. It is of course a part of traditional Christian thinking that protesting at wickedness is something worth doing for its own sake: it is a case of being a witness to the truth. (The word 'martyr' comes from the Greek for 'witness'.) Later still, Anscombe spoke and acted in protest at legalized abortion and the activities of abortion clinics. She was altogether one of those people who earn the epithet of 'being outspoken', and her most indulgent friends would have to admit that her manner could on occasion be eye-openingly brusque. There were plenty of fellow philosophers who took offence at things she said to, or wrote about, them, and no doubt their reaction was sometimes justified. But if Anscombe erred here, she would probably have thought she was erring on the right side; in English academic circles, it is often more tempting to be silent, or to smile and pass on, when somebody says something outrageous or stupid than it is to stop the person in their tracks, since stopping them in their tracks will almost inevitably come across as upbraiding them. That policy, however, can lead to a kind of complacency, which Anscombe believed out of place in serious philosophy (cf. Ch. 3, pp. 116–17). And for an intelligent woman in a man's world, the advice 'Just smile and be nice' may be all too gratingly familiar. It should also be said that Anscombe was free of one very prevalent professional vice, that of modifying one's behaviour and manners according to the status of one's interlocutor. She could listen with as much seriousness to something said by a nervous undergraduate as to something said by a well-established professor, and be as encouraging to the former as she could

---

[10] Anscombe made her case for Truman's not getting the degree to the University members in Congregation, and the content of her speech is reproduced in a pamphlet she had published, 'Mr. Truman's Degree' (in *ERP*). An account of the episode can be found in Jonathan Glover's *Humanity: A Moral History of the 20th Century* (London: Pimlico, 1999), pp. 106–9. Glover writes: 'It is hard to warm to the response of those who heard Miss Anscombe and then voted in a way that left her in such a small minority. Just possibly, each person who voted against her may have had good reasons. But their silence and utter imperturbability now seem extraordinary. Was there too little time for discussion, because of the pressing issue of Greek New Testament in the Theology degree? Did no one think that this courageous and powerful speech deserved the compliment of rational opposition? Apart from Philippa Foot, where were the philosophers?'. Glover is right to wonder at the general silence and imperturbability of the Oxford dons, but there is some doubt as to whether there was a vote of the sort he mentions: according to one version of events, Anscombe was unaware of the procedural necessity of her asking for a vote after her speech, and so did not do so.

be annoying to the latter. This fact no doubt helps to explain the affection and esteem in which she has been held by her former students.

Anscombe was a person of enormous industry. She wrote articles and lectures, translated, gave tutorials, all while bearing and rearing seven children and running a household. Foot says of her life that it 'must have been one that only a woman of Elizabeth's monumental strength of mind, will and body could have survived';[11] and Dummett, after commenting that Anscombe 'had astonishing strength and powers of concentration', recalls the following typical incident:

After the *Philosophical Investigations* was published, she presided over a group to discuss it at her house. During that term, she had a baby, and I heard that the labour was extremely difficult. Assuming that the discussion group would be cancelled, I went round the next day with a bottle of wine for a celebration. I found Elizabeth in a dressing-gown and the discussion in full swing; she merely glanced at me, remarking that I was late.[12]

Over the years Anscombe travelled widely, giving lectures in many countries, including the United States, Canada, Poland, Finland, Austria, Germany, Sweden, Spain, and Australia. Her stock of philosophical acquaintances was quite international, and it may be that she found the intellectual atmosphere of a single university overly narrow. Anscombe was not alone in feeling out of tune with the mainstream Oxford philosophy of the 1950s and 1960s, which (like the Oxford philosophy of today) was to some extent governed by fashion; Dummett writes that 'in Oxford she was a largely isolated figure, fiercely opposed to Austin and to most that was going on among the philosophers at the university, but highly regarded in Somerville and by a similarly disaffected minority'.[13]

The 'similarly disaffected minority' included Dummett himself, who felt as sceptical as did Anscombe about many aspects of the 'ordinary language' school associated with J. L. Austin and his followers. Perhaps the doctrines of that school which aroused most resistance from Anscombe were those relating to sense-perception. She clearly felt that Austin and others had trivialized the discussion of this issue, or possibly just changed the subject. In this connection, it is worth quoting her description of the lectures of H. H. Price, to which she went as an undergraduate, before Austin had really hit the scene:

I went to H. H. Price's lectures on perception and phenomenalism. I found them intensely interesting. Indeed, of all the people I heard at Oxford, he was the one who excited my respect; the one I found worth listening to. This was not because I agreed with him, indeed I used to sit tearing my gown into little strips because I wanted to argue against so much that he said. But even so, what he said seemed to me to be absolutely about the stuff.   (Introduction, *MPM*, p. viii)

Her own major attempt to avoid the errors of both the phenomenalists and the ordinary language philosophers was to appear in 1965—'The Intentionality of Sensation', discussed in Chapter 4 of this book.

---

[11] *Somerville College Review*, 2001, p. 120.   [12] *The Tablet*, 13 Jan. 2001.   [13] Ibid.

Anscombe and Dummett shared more than a dislike of ordinary language philosophy. They both had a great admiration for the work of Frege, at a time when this was not very common. So did Anscombe's husband, Peter Geach; and if Frege's works now occupy a central position in the philosophical canon, that is largely thanks to the efforts of Dummett, Geach, and Anscombe, among others. [14] A joint venture of Anscombe and Geach was *Three Philosophers: Aristotle, Aquinas, Frege*. In *An Introduction to Wittgenstein's Tractatus*, Anscombe makes much of the Fregean background without which a proper understanding of the *Tractatus* is impossible. And in several of her articles she applies notions or theses of Frege's where these cast light on the issue, e.g. in 'The First Person' (cf. *MPM*, 23).

That Anscombe should have chosen the *Tractatus* as the theme for one of her books is another indication of how her philosophical interests were immune to fashion. In the 1950s and 1960s, followers of Wittgenstein were liable to regard his early work as having been more or less refuted by his later work, or at best as being less mature and less significant than the *Philosophical Investigations*. And it would have seemed the most natural thing for Anscombe to have written about the latter book, which after all she had translated into English. It may be that she felt that the *Investigations* was receiving enough attention already, and that philosophers were in danger of forgetting about the *Tractatus*; but she also clearly believed that there was much of value in the earlier book, even if some of its main ideas turned out to be philosophical dead ends. It is yet another case of her valuing some work or some philosopher not on account of its 'conclusions', but on account of its raising the right questions—its 'being absolutely about the stuff'.

Something similar can be said, I think, about her favourable reception, much later, of Kripke's influential *Wittgenstein on Rules and Private Language* (1982). In a review of that work, [15] she wrote:

Wrongness of exegesis, especially when exegesis is disclaimed, is not so grave a charge—even if Kripke somewhat belies the disclaimers.

What Kripke claims—namely that there is a serious sceptical argument—*that* is what is interesting and it is one thing we should be grateful to him for. It is Kripke's argument—I mean, he is its mother, even if it was begotten in him by Wittgenstein. [16]

Anscombe was pretty uninterested in whether Kripke had 'got Wittgenstein right'—indeed, she thought he had not. But for her the interest of Kripke's argument was independent of his qualities as an exegete. Moreover, the interest of his argument was independent of whether its conclusion was *true*; the point was that it opened up deep and important questions.

---

[14] Including of course J. L. Austin, who provided the now standard English translation of Frege's *Foundations of Arithmetic*.

[15] In *Canadian Journal of Philosophy*, 15/1 (Mar. 1985), 103–9.   [16] Ibid. 108.

In 1970, Anscombe took up a chair at Cambridge University, holding the same position that Wittgenstein had had. She was a Fellow of New Hall. My own acquaintance with Anscombe dates from not long after her arrival in Cambridge, when I was still a child; my mother (also at New Hall) had been taught by Anscombe as a graduate student in Oxford, and maintained the friendship in Cambridge. Over the years, I got to know the Geachcombes[17] very well, particularly the younger generation. As a philosophy student at Cambridge I went to Anscombe's lectures on causality, intention, Aristotle, and truth. Except on formal occasions, she lectured more or less without notes, her lectures being a kind of thinking in public, though of course not on topics that she hadn't thought a lot about already. Anscombe's lectures were as searching as her articles. She had the gift of coming out with remarks which at the time one might not fully see the point of, but which were sufficiently memorable to stick in one's mind, later to bear fruit. It was a kind of lecturing which would now be discouraged, if not forbidden, as having a value impossible to measure using common or garden yardsticks.

Anscombe retired in 1986. She had earlier suffered severe concussion as a result of falling off a horse, and about ten years later had to undergo emergency brain surgery after the car she was being driven in crashed into an oncoming vehicle driving on the wrong side of the road. These accidents, and her imperfect health, clouded her last years; but she continued philosophical work as long as she was able, and was sustained by the love of family and friends. She died in 2001, and was buried in a grave next to that of Wittgenstein.

The corpus of writings by Elizabeth Anscombe is very large and covers a wide variety of topics. A bibliography of her works may be found at the end of this book. There are the two books, *Intention* and *An Introduction to Wittgenstein's Tractatus*, plus (with Geach) *Three Philosophers*. Then there are the numerous articles, many but by no means all of which are to be found in the three volumes of her *Collected Papers*. The recently published *Human Life, Action and Ethics* (ed. M. Geach and L. Gormally) contains further essays; and other collections are due to appear.

I have attempted to present what seem to me to be Anscombe's most original and philosophically significant ideas, in a way that shows their interconnections and in a format that as far as possible constitutes a coherent 'narrative'. Most of her best-known writings are discussed, but so are several lesser-known pieces. Among the latter is a lecture she gave at the University of Navarre in 1979, 'La Verdad' ('Truth'). I am very grateful to José Maria Torralba for supplying me with a copy of the original English manuscript of that lecture, and also for the bibliography of Anscombe's works, which was compiled by him, with the help of Luke Gormally and Christian Kietzmann. I would also like to thank Professor

---

[17] The term was first coined by Arthur Prior, I believe.

Cora Diamond, Sir Anthony Kenny, and Professor Anselm Müller for helpful comments on earlier drafts of Chapters 2 and 3, and an anonymous referee for Oxford University Press for very useful comments on an earlier draft of the whole book. Finally, my thanks to Peter Momtchiloff at Oxford University Press for his encouragement and help, and to Bonnie Blackburn for copy-editing the manuscript and compiling the bibliography.

R.T.

St. Hilda's College
Oxford

1

Intentional Action

Sometimes it can seem as if a philosopher and a topic were made for one another. Such is the case with Elizabeth Anscombe and intention. Anscombe is one of the most versatile of philosophers, and one aspect of this versatility is her capacity to see multiple philosophical strands. Intention is a topic bristling with such strands. In the philosophy of mind, intention appears to be a bridge connecting the mind and the body; it also provides an especially interesting case of first-person authority; as for metaphysics, there is the question whether intentions are causes; knowledge of one's future actions is a theme for epistemology; concerning expressions of intention there are various questions to be asked as to truth, error, and so on; deliberation about actions constitutes a special kind of reasoning (practical reasoning); and in ethics and legal philosophy, problems about intention and agency are of enormous significance.[1] Mind and body, first-person authority, causation, knowledge, truth, reasoning, ethics: matters coming under each of these headings are dealt with by Anscombe in her work on intention. The strands are both picked apart and woven together.

These different aspects of the topic are interconnected: were you to concentrate on just one of them, your understanding of that one would only be partial. There are plenty of writings on intention that exemplify this sort of limitation. It takes a philosopher of Anscombe's range to give us the wood as well as the trees. What is remarkable is that she should have managed to do this in a work of a mere ninety-four pages. Not that *Intention* is the last word on the subject—there could be no last word, I suppose, in particular because of those very pathways into other domains that I have noted. But its combination of brevity and richness may well explain both why *Intention* is recognized as the seminal work that it is, and why its lessons are still under-appreciated and often misunderstood.

Anscombe introduces her subject under three heads:

(A) Expression of intention for the future (e.g. 'I'm going to buy some milk')
(B) Intentional action (e.g. my buying of some milk)
(C) Intention in acting, or intention 'with which' (e.g. *to buy some milk*).

---

[1] Anscombe's daughter, Mary Geach, reports that the impetus for the course of lectures which were to become *Intention* was Anscombe's involvement in the debate about whether Harry Truman should be given an honorary degree. Truman had ordered the bombing of Hiroshima and Nagasaki; under what descriptions were his actions intentional? See Geach's Introduction to *HLAE* (p. xiv).

The structure of the book essentially corresponds to these themes in this order. There are certain strategic advantages in this division and ordering, notwithstanding the fact that Anscombe characterizes her starting point by saying that 'there is [. . .] nothing wrong with taking a topic piecemeal' (*I*, 1). For example, it will turn out that the picture of intentions as inner states that cause actions is radically defective; and by putting off any direct discussion of phrases like 'the intention to φ' till we get to (C), Anscombe allows us to proceed unhampered by that picture. She is thus able to take such expressions of intention as 'I'm going to buy some milk' at face value, i.e. as about future actions, not present mental states. She is also able to include among intentional actions ones that are not informatively describable as 'actions done *with* such-and-such an intention' (and which are therefore unlikely candidates for being actions *caused* by such-and-such an intention)—namely, actions performed from some motive, e.g. the motive of revenge. This is not to say that she doesn't give a hearing to the adherents of the 'inner state' picture, even when discussing phenomena that are thus awkward for them. The point is that her approach to the phenomena is unencumbered.

In this chapter, I will deal with (A) and (B), leaving (C) for Chapter 2. I will, however, begin with (B) rather than with (A). As Anscombe saw, there is no compulsory entry point for this subject.

1. NON-OBSERVATIONAL KNOWLEDGE

1.1. Separately Describable Sensations

Anscombe begins her discussion of intentional action with an extremely simple and effective move. That is to remind us of how we can very often say straight off what someone is doing, when we are observing that person:

> I am sitting in a chair writing, and anyone grown to the age of reason in the same world would know this as soon as he saw me, and in general it would be his first account of what I was doing; if this were something he arrived at with difficulty, and what he knew straight off were precisely how I was affecting the acoustic properties of the room (to me a very recondite piece of information), then communication between us would be rather severely impaired. (*I*, 8)

This phenomenon displays several key features: (a) 'What X is doing' here picks out *one* (or a few) of the many true descriptions of X's observable behaviour; (b) insofar as we can report what X is doing under some particular description, we can also very often report an intention of X's—namely, to do that thing, under that description; (c) X himself will be able to say straight off what he's doing; (d) what X would say he's doing will typically be the same as what we would say he's doing.

(a) introduces Anscombe's famous notion of an action's being intentional under a description. We shall have more to say about this in the next chapter. (d) is worth a moment's consideration, being an example of the sort of empirical fact that underlies the possibility of a language-game, by enabling 'agreement in judgements'.[2] It is an empirical fact that people can say what they're doing, and that others can say the same thing of them. But we must be careful here: given the existence of the language-game, it is a criterion of X's building a wall that X says he's building a wall. (After all, all that he may ever end up *doing* is buying some bricks, digging a trench, and mixing some cement—for he may be prevented from finishing his job.) So the connection between what a person does and what he says he's doing is not purely contingent. The harmony between word and deed is not guaranteed in each particular case, but it must hold generally, or at any rate in enough cases. If people too often said bizarre things about what they were up to (e.g. 'I'm writing a symphony', said by the man with the bricks), then the practice of giving an account of what one was doing would break down. And 'bizarreness' is here largely determined by what observers can make sense of. The account given by the person himself and the account given by other people hold one another in check, as it were.

Others can say what someone is doing by observing him. A person can say what he's doing straight off—without observing himself. This sort of non-observational knowledge is the linchpin of Anscombe's account of intentional action. Now the fact that a person can say straight off what he's doing does not yet give us a sufficient condition of some personal event's being an intentional action. One can know straight off that one has hiccupped, for example. So intentional actions will be at best 'a sub-class of the events in a man's history which are known to him *not* just because he observes them' (*I*, 24). (The point of 'just' here is this: you *can* observe your intentional actions, and indeed know things *about* them on the basis of observation. But you do not need to observe yourself to know that you are intentionally φ-ing.) This subclass will be further determined by the fact that the question 'Why?', in the relevant reason-giving sense, has application to the personal events in that subclass. What the relevant sense of 'Why?' is, and what it is for the question 'Why?' to have application, are matters we shall come to; first, let us examine Anscombe's notion of 'events in a man's history which are known to him *not* just because he observes them'.

Strictly speaking, the phrase applies to the peristaltic movement of the gut: for although you might well know about that, it's probably not through having observed it that you do. But Anscombe does not mean to include such things among the events in a man's history which are known to him not just because he observes them. We might try to exclude peristaltic movement of the gut by adverting to the fact that someone will only know about it (if he does) because of

[2] See Ludwig Wittgenstein, *Philosophical Investigations*, trans. Elizabeth Anscombe (Oxford: Blackwell, 1953), paras. 241–2.

background knowledge—knowledge acquired at school, from books, etc. This latter knowledge appears to be based on observation, of teachers, books, or what have you. So we could for present purposes lump together (a) things known through observation of them, and (b) things known through observation of other things (e.g. teachers). We need not address the question whether (b)-style knowledge is based on inference; the point is to delineate a class of observation-based knowledge about events in a person's own history. The complementary class will be that of events in a person's history which are known to him *not* just because he observes them—or anything else.

We still need to say something about what *observation* is. A natural explanation of observation is: looking, or listening, or smelling, or feeling (as in feeling with your fingers), or ... If I know I am developing a mole on my arm, then it will typically be because I have looked at it and seen it; and this seems a paradigm case of observation-based knowledge. So non-observational knowledge would, for our purposes, be knowledge of X that is neither acquired through looking (etc.) at X, nor acquired through looking (etc.) at anything else.

This account of (non-)observational knowledge is not Anscombe's, however. Her account makes use instead of the notion of 'separately describable sensations'. She introduces this notion by reference to knowledge of the position of one's limbs, which she regards as non-observational:

E.g. a man usually knows the positions of his limbs without observation. It is without observation, because nothing *shews* him the position of his limbs; it is not as if he were going by a tingle in his knee, which is the sign that it is bent and not straight. Where we can speak of separately describable sensations, having which is in some sense our criterion for saying something, then we can speak of observing that thing; but that is not generally so when we know the position of our limbs. (*I*, 13)

What is it for a sensation to be separately describable? Anscombe gives the following illustration:

If you speak of 'that sensation which one has in reflex kicking, when one's knee is tapped', this is not like e.g. 'the sensation of going down in a lift'. For though one might say 'I thought I had given a reflex kick, when I hadn't moved' one would never say e.g. 'Being told startling news gives one that sensation': the sensation is not separable, as the sensation 'like going down in a lift' is. (*I*, 15)

Now it cannot be that Anscombe is simply pointing out that e.g. being told startling news just never *is* accompanied by the sensation of giving a reflex kick, or of any sensation like it. The point seems rather to be this. In a world without lifts (not hard to conceive of), people might still have 'that sinking feeling', a feeling that could, and would perforce, get described or picked out without reference to going down in a lift; while in a world without reflex kicks, it isn't conceivable that people should have that same sensation we now call 'the sensation of giving a reflex kick'. And this is because the *concepts* 'reflex kick' and 'sensation of giving a reflex kick' are too tightly tied together. The claim being made is not undermined by the fact that one can be mistaken as to whether one had given a reflex kick—for it is a claim about concepts, not about knowledge. The conceptual point comes out in the fact that you couldn't *say* 'I just had that sensation of giving a reflex kick', nor say anything tantamount to that, if there were no such thing as a reflex kick.

What is the point of explaining what observation is in terms of separately describable sensations? How is such an explanation to be preferred to one that simply alludes to looking, listening, feeling, and the like? The answer to these questions emerges when we turn to our main topic—intentional action. If we want to apply the conception of observation as looking (etc.) to intentional activity, we shall face a dilemma concerning which of two criteria we should use: (a) that of whether preventing looking (etc.) tends to prevent the activity; or (b) that of whether one would justify one's account of what is going on by alluding to what one sees (or hears, or . . .).

For example, when I know that I am writing a letter, is my knowledge based on my looking, or feeling, or whatever—or is it not so based? Well, when I write a letter, I certainly do look at the paper, my pen, etc. But that on its own isn't enough to show that I only know I am writing *because* I am looking. To show this, it seems necessary to add that I would find it hard to continue letter-writing if I were blindfolded; for connected with this will be a decreasing certainty as to whether I am in fact succeeding, if I continue to try. (The ink might run out without my knowing it—or my handwriting become illegible.) And a decrease in certainty surely amounts, eventually, to a loss of knowledge.[3] On the other hand, if asked 'What are you doing?', my answer, 'Writing a letter', isn't an answer that I would ordinarily back up by saying 'I can see that I am'. By criterion (a), my knowledge that I'm writing is observation-based, while by criterion (b), it is not.

Now a philosopher influenced by Gricean notions of conversational implicature might try to explain *why* 'I can see that I am' is a strange way to back up 'I am writing a letter' in the following manner: since almost the only way a person can know she is writing is by looking and seeing, she will almost certainly fail to provide any information by saying 'I can see that I am'—so that there is a conversational 'rule' against saying such a thing. According to this view, 'I know I'm writing because I can see that I am' would not be *false*, but only conversationally inappropriate. Hence (b) would not, as it stands, give a suitable criterion for whether knowledge is observational; but it would manage to give such a criterion if, instead of requiring that one *would* justify one's account of what is going on by alluding to what one sees (etc.), it required only that one

---

[3] What of the view that if there is an 'appropriate causal chain' linking my looking with my knowledge that I'm writing, then my knowledge is based on my looking? We shall see in Ch. 4 why this sort of invocation of causality achieves nothing beyond what is achieved by such everyday tests as 'What happens if he's blindfolded?'. See Ch. 4, §1.3.

could—truthfully—justify one's account by alluding to what one sees (etc.). Of course, there is only any point in adopting this Gricean amendment of (b) if we have some independent reason for claiming that 'I know I'm writing because I can see that I am' is in fact true. The evidence from what people ordinarily say does not, *ex hypothesi*, support that claim. So it seems that another criterion must be operating which might support the claim—criterion (a), presumably.

But in fact 'I know I'm φ-ing because I can see that I am' cannot in general be true for intentional φ-ing. This can be seen from such a case as that of building a wall. Until the wall is built, it would not be right to say that you can see that you are building a wall, as opposed to digging a trench (for example). Nothing in what you see favours the answer 'Building a wall' over 'Digging a trench'. So if your ability to answer 'What are you doing?' straight off is the same sort of ability whether you are writing or whether you are building a wall—which surely is the case—then 'I can see that I am' must be an inappropriate answer *not* just for Gricean reasons. Criterion (a), then, cannot be adequate as a criterion of observation-based practical knowledge, since according to it you know you are writing because you can see that you are. But if we consequently adopt the unmodified version of criterion (b) of what it is for practical knowledge to be based on observation, we appear to be adopting Anscombe's criterion, that of whether there are separately describable sensations. For the reason why you couldn't justify your statement that you are building a wall (as opposed to digging a trench) by saying 'I can see that I am' is that nothing *in the appearances of things* favours 'Building a wall'. After all, you are in fact building a wall, let us say; and your activity is visible; but this does not give us 'So it can be seen that you are building a wall'. 'Seeing', in this context, connects with 'appearances', i.e. with appearances as you could describe them or depict them. And for Anscombe, describable appearances amount to describable sensations (e.g. visual).

Anscombe can extend these considerations to cases of observation-based knowledge of the sort I described as paradigm—e.g. knowledge that you have developed a mole. This knowledge counts as observation-based knowledge, not just because you can't tell that you have a mole if you are blindfolded, but because you can describe what you see in a way that backs up your claim that you have a mole—i.e. by describing the appearances. (I am assuming that 'observation-based' means the same in 'Knowledge that you have a mole is observation-based' as it does in 'Knowledge that you're building a wall is *not* observation-based'.)

So far, then, there seems to be a good case for explaining observation in terms of separately describable sensations, and for characterizing knowledge of what one is doing as not based upon observation. Anscombe's conception of 'sensations' here is one according to which they enjoy what she elsewhere calls subjectivity:[4] the person who describes her visual sensations—i.e. describes how things look to her—has a certain kind of authority as to the veracity of her

[4] See Ch. 4, p. 145.

description, without this entailing that the vocabulary of the description is in any sense 'private'. We find her more fully developed thoughts on sensations and appearances in 'The Intentionality of Sensation' (to be discussed in Ch. 4). For now it is worth noting that the taking seriously of 'appearances' puts Anscombe in a different camp from many of her contemporaries. She herself alludes to this fact in a footnote (*I*, 49):

I think these facts [about describable visual sensations, etc.] ought to make people less contemptuous of phenomenalism than it has now been fashionable to be for a good many years; I have heard people jeer at the expression 'seeing an appearance' on the grounds that it is incorrect speech. It does not seem to me to matter whether it is incorrect speech or not; the fact remains that one can distinguish between actually seeing a man, and the appearances' being such that one says that one is seeing, or saw, a man; and that one can describe or identify 'what one saw' on such an occasion without knowing e.g. that one really saw a reflection of oneself or a coat hanging on a hook.

The impatience with the issue of what is 'incorrect speech' shows how Anscombe differs from what are often called ordinary language philosophers. At the same time, she is not recommending the reinstatement of sense-data, or anything like them. There is, as so often, a third way; and in 'The Intentionality of Sensation' she was to chart that way.

However, Anscombe's reliance in *Intention* upon the notion of separately describable sensations is not without its problems. The main problem, I think, is that it is doubtful whether *bona fide* observation reports rely on sensations that are any more separately describable than those sensations which accompany movement, posture, and action. Is the conceptual connection between 'sensation of giving a reflex kick' and 'reflex kick' any more tight than that between 'visual appearance of a dog' and 'dog'? In what sense is the visual appearance separately describable, and not the sensation? Anscombe might reply that one can, for instance, draw what one sees, imitate what one hears, and so on: visual and other appearances are representable non-linguistically, and to that extent their connection to concepts (whose paradigm use is in linguistic representation) is less tight than for sensations of the sort under discussion. Moreover, can't we after all talk of colours, shapes, movement, and so on?—whereas there is no analogous vocabulary available for talking about so-called kinaesthetic sensations.

When discussing perception, there is often a danger of concentrating too much upon sight. Human vision is such that we have fairly sophisticated ways of visually representing things, both where the representation is linguistic and where it is non-linguistic. But observation can employ other sense modalities than sight. Knowledge through smelling is observation-based knowledge; but (i) it is unclear what a non-linguistic representation of an olfactory appearance could be, and (ii) our vocabulary for smells is thoroughly bound up with the concepts of things smelt (roses, burning, dampness, etc.). So olfactory sensations seem to be in the same boat as sensations of posture and movement, when it comes to not being separately describable—awkwardly for Anscombe. And as for vision, there are limits on how far our descriptions of things seen can go without mentioning objects. Colours, shapes, and the like are not always so easily invoked, and the only or best way of describing a visual appearance may well be as the appearance of a certain kind of object, on occasion.[5]

When it comes to knowledge of one's posture, movements, or intentional actions, the important point seems to have to do with the *ungrounded* nature of such knowledge. One can report these things straight off, in the sense that one's reports will not be based on, or derived from, anything.[6] But this much surely can also be said (*pace* the sense-datum theorists) of many observation reports, such as 'There's a face at the window'. Anscombe's notion of separately describable sensations is meant to enable us to put such observation reports in a distinct category; but the notion seems a problematic one. In order to understand why she saw the notion as useful, or even indispensable, it might help to put Anscombe's discussion into a broader context. Philosophers had long recognized that there is a sense in which one is an authority about one's intentions, at any rate insofar as, typically, one's own statement of what one intends counts for more than what another person would say on the subject. This first-person authority, however, is enjoyed equally when it comes to what one is *doing* ('I am building a wall', etc.); and it betokens a misguided, Cartesian diagnosis of the facts to insist that the second kind of authority, since it concerns 'public' events, must be derivative from, and less secure than, the first kind (which the Cartesian will regard as concerning 'private', mental events). Now it is in the writings of the later Wittgenstein that we find a persuasive alternative to the Cartesian account of first-person authority; and in those writings, among a number of strands of thought on the subject, possibly the most arresting and influential strand compares present tensed first-personal psychological statements to primitive, or non-linguistic, expressions or avowals—as opposed to descriptions or reports, true or false, of 'the mental facts'. Thus, 'I'm in pain' is famously compared to a groan.[7] Anscombe agreed with Wittgenstein that 'authority' was not in general a matter of any privileged access to one's own mental goings-on, having to do more with the *lack* of grounds for one's utterances than with a special kind of grounds; but she was averse to treating many of the first-personal utterances of the sort under discussion as avowal-like rather than report-like. The concepts of truth and falsity, and also therefore of knowledge or the lack of it, would seem to have a proper application to a person's statements about her actions; also, therefore, to her

---

[5] See P. F. Strawson, 'Perception and its Objects', in Jonathan Dancy (ed.), *Perceptual Knowledge* (Oxford: Oxford University Press, 1988), 92–112.

[6] Items of general or background knowledge, including items that concern 'events in one's own history', are not consciously inferred from anything, and there is little reason to think that they are subconsciously inferred from anything. But we might still say that they are grounded, in the sense of having had grounds, e.g. 'Teacher told me'.

[7] Wittgenstein, *Philosophical Investigations*, e.g. para. 244: 'Here is one possibility . . .'.

statements about (i.e. expressions of) her intentions—the two classes of statement belonging in the same boat. These things really are described or reported in the first person, and avowals or natural expressions are not the right model. Thus:

> a cat's movements in stalking a bird are hardly to be called an expression of intention. One might as well call a cat's stalling the *expression* of its being about to stop. Intention is unlike emotion in this respect, that the expression of it is purely conventional [. . .] Wittgenstein seems to me to have gone wrong in speaking of 'the natural expression of an intention' (*Philosophical Investigations*, para. 647).   (*I*, 5)

What really shows that the concepts of truth and of knowledge have application to X is that there is such a thing as intelligible error about X. A groan cannot be emitted in error, though of course it can be a feigned or insincere groan; and maybe the same goes for 'I'm in pain'. But, as we shall see, Anscombe thought that an expression of intention could be straightforwardly false, though perfectly sincere—sincere falsehood making for error, or what we might as well call error in this context. And what goes for expressions of intention goes more obviously still for statements about what one is actually doing, and more obviously again for statements about one's posture or movements. Indeed, the evident kinship between statements about what one is doing and statements about one's posture or movements naturally prompts the thought that non-observationality is the key to both phenomena, given especially that the notion of an avowal cannot be that key. This kinship shows in two ways: first, that others can very often say or observe, just as well as you can, the position/movements of your body, but also what it is that you're doing—second, that statements about what you're doing very often involve, rely on, or commit you to claims about your posture or movements.

Although the kinship between one's intentional actions and one's posture or movements is real enough, non-observationality as Anscombe characterizes it does not, I believe, provide the key to both phenomena. There is a way of explaining the ungrounded nature of reports of what one is doing that does not invoke the problematic notion of separately describable sensations at all—namely, by appeal to what I shall in §2.1 be referring to as 'Theophrastus' principle'. This explanation will not carry over to the putatively ungrounded nature of reports of one's posture, or of one's involuntary movements. Hence it will leave hanging the question what, if anything, distinguishes the directness of these latter reports from the directness of *bona fide* observation reports. But before I turn to Theophrastus' principle, I will say a bit more about the connection touched on in the last paragraph, the connection which links knowledge and the possibility of intelligible error.

1.2. 'Knows' vs. 'Can Say'

Anscombe writes:

> [A]lthough there is a similarity between giving the position of one's limbs and giving the place of one's pain, I should wish to say that one ordinarily *knows* the position of one's

limbs, without observation, but not that being able to say where one feels pain is a case of something known. This is not because the place of pain (the feeling, not the damage) has to be accepted by someone I tell it to; for we can imagine circumstances in which it is not accepted. As e.g. if you say that your foot, not your hand, is very sore, but it is your hand you nurse [. . .] and so on. But here we should say that it is difficult to guess what you mean. Whereas if someone says that his leg is bent when it is straight, this may be surprising but is not particularly obscure. He is wrong in what he says, but not unintelligible.   (*I*, 14)

Anscombe is here in agreement with Wittgenstein, that knowledge presupposes or involves the possibility of intelligible doubt or error (in clear contrast to the Cartesian view of knowledge as *ruling out* the possibility of doubt or error). The criteria for where a pain is include both behavioural criteria—nursing, flinching or limping, pointing to the part, etc.—and also a linguistic criterion: saying (e.g.) that one's big toe hurts. If these criteria came apart too often, the concept of the location of a pain would be undermined or radically altered; and if, on a given occasion, the linguistic criterion is in conflict with behavioural criteria, the overall phenomenon will be hard to make sense of—in fact, Anscombe argues, the person's utterance itself will be hard to make sense of. (This doesn't entail that the behavioural criteria always trump the linguistic, by the way.) Given this role for statements about where one's pain is, they cannot be statements of knowledge.

When it comes to intentional action, by contrast, there is room for intelligible error. 'I am pinning the tail on the donkey', said by a blindfolded child, may be mistaken for obvious reasons. Hence we can speak of *knowing* what one is doing—as we can speak of knowing the position of one's limbs. Does the same apply to expressions of intention? The answer seems to depend on whether these are couched in the future tense or in the present tense with a verb like 'I intend'. 'I will now pin the tail on the donkey' can prove to be mistaken (and so be false, according to Anscombe), whereas the same doesn't apply straightforwardly to 'I intend to pin the tail on that donkey'. Of course, a subsequent failure to pin the tail on the donkey has to be admitted as *relevant* to the earlier statement of intention, however it is phrased, and that relevance cannot be accounted for if we take the statement as simply reporting a 'present state of mind'. (More of this in §2.2.) Nevertheless, 'What is your intention?' is clearly a different question from 'What will you do?', and Anscombe might well have said that, whereas an answer to the latter can express genuine knowledge, an answer to the former cannot (where the form of each answer is tailored to the form of its question).

You know what you are doing, and you know the positions of your limbs; but you *can say*—you do not know—where your pains are. With this distinction in mind, let us now look at what Anscombe has to say about what she calls 'mental causes'. The concept of non-observational knowledge is applied by Anscombe, not only to what one's body is doing (e.g. jumping), but also to the fact that something (e.g. the leap and loud bark of a crocodile) is *making* one's body do that (*I*, 15). One knows *that* the crocodile's bark made one jump in the same non-observational way that one knows that one jumped. The cause—the crocodile's bark—is a 'mental cause'. The effect of a mental cause can be an involuntary action, thought, or feeling, but it can also be a voluntary action: Anscombe illustrates this with someone's saying 'The martial music excites me, that is why I walk up and down' (*I*, 16).

The question I wish to raise is: does a person *know* that he jumped because the crocodile leapt and barked, or is it only that he *can say* this?

It is perfectly true that what we *don't* have here is any sort of knowledge of causation based on observation, including observation of past instances. Consequently, if we are to call it knowledge of causation at all, and if we are to follow Anscombe in her account of non-observational knowledge, then we must invoke separately describable sensations, or rather the lack of them. As with posture, etc., the troublesome contrast is with observational knowledge—this time of causation. Hume thought that there could be no such knowledge, but Anscombe herself famously threw doubt on Hume's assertion, in particular in her 'Causality and Determination'. In that article she argued that Hume, among other things, was employing an overly restrictive (atomistic) model of perception, and that there can be no objection to saying that one sees the knife cutting the bread, hears the cat purring, feels the biscuit crumbling at one's touch. Are we to say that this kind of perceptual knowledge is based on observation? It is not based on or derived from sense-data, but then neither is perceptual knowledge of objects and events. If we follow Anscombe, the question we shall need to ask is whether there are any separately describable sensations of causation—i.e. of cutting, purring, crumbling, and so on. If there are, then knowledge of causation *is* here based on observation, but if there are not, it is not, and mental causation won't be distinguished from other kinds by the fact that knowledge of it is not based on observation.

Well, you can on the face of it depict non-linguistically a man cutting a loaf of bread, just as you can depict the loaf of bread itself; and if the latter amounts to depicting an appearance, why not the former? Of course, Hume would say that 'strictly speaking' your picture is only of a man holding a knife inserted in a loaf—and that if it is a movie, all that is 'strictly speaking' depicted are some back-and-forth movements of the knife-holding hand followed by (with some overlap . . .) a slice of bread coming away from its loaf. But let us say that Hume is labouring with a wrong model of perception, so that we can in fact speak of separately describable sensations in connection with seeing a loaf being cut. Even so, one might ask, 'Can't you *depict* being made to jump by the bark of a crocodile?'—i.e. won't whatever goes for the loaf-cutting go just as well for being made to jump, *pace* Anscombe?

'I know it was the crocodile's bark that made me jump, and my knowledge is not associated with any separately describable sensations.' If we are tempted to think that being made to jump by the bark of a crocodile is depictable, that is probably because we are thinking of depicting someone else's jumping at the bark of a crocodile; whereas what Anscombe claims that I know straight off is that *my* jumping is caused by the bark. Try to depict *this* (in imagination?), and you arrive at no separately describable sensations other than those of the crocodile's barking—so it might be said. In which case, the non-observationality of knowledge of mental causation looks as if it boils down to the non-observationality of knowledge of the effect: a bodily movement, action, thought, or feeling. But the enquiry seems to have become rather nebulous—and this is largely because it is unclear how the notions of depiction and of separately describable sensations, already somewhat plastic, are to be applied to causation, whether external or internal.

Anscombe is surely right in thinking that the things she gives as examples of mental causes are known *directly*, in some important sense. And the phenomenon she has picked out is of considerable philosophical interest,[8] largely because of its constituting a counter-example to the dominant Humean account of causation (see Ch. 5, pp. 182–3; and cf. pp. 178–9). But it does not seem to me that much light is shed upon it by consideration of separately describable sensations. Rather, the possibility raised by my earlier question may have something going for it: perhaps the right thing to say is that a person *can say* what made him jump (cf. can say where his pain is), rather than that he *knows* what made him jump. The overall account could go, very roughly, as follows. We can get people to do things (especially involuntary things) by certain means, and we see certain things as making them do such things; children are taught to cite causes of why they do such things, in appropriate contexts, i.e. where *we* should cite those causes (it is this taught ability that would need most explaining); this learnt ability is an ability to do something spontaneously, i.e. straight off; and a person's citing a (mental) cause of why he has done something becomes a criterion of its having been a cause. If on a given occasion someone's version of what mental cause made him do something were in conflict with what others would have confidently said caused him to, then the case would resemble that in which the linguistic and non-linguistic criteria for where a person's pain was came apart (see above, p. 19)—as opposed to resembling the case where a person got it wrong what position his limbs were in, or got it wrong what he would do in the shop across the road, a bus being about to knock him over. In other words, intelligible error about mental causes appears hard to come by, and this suggests a certain account of *why* one has an ability to say straight off what a mental cause was, an account that might lead us to prefer 'can say' to 'knows'.[9]

We shall have more to say about mental causes in §3.1. But it is time now to turn to one of Anscombe's best-known but least understood ideas, with the help

---

[8] Despite her own statement that the phenomenon in itself is 'of very little importance' (*I*, 18). Of course it all depends what one means by 'in itself'.

[9] Of course, if we are unhappy with the Wittgensteinian account of knowledge, we could simply advert to the fact that there is no such thing as intelligible error about mental causes—in contrast to 'external' causes.

of which, among other things, the puzzle of non-observational knowledge will be put to rest.

2. PRACTICAL KNOWLEDGE

2.1. Theophrastus' Principle

Intentional actions, as Anscombe says, are among the events in a person's life which he knows about not on the basis of observation; but I have suggested that a clear light is not cast upon this fact by reference to separately describable sensations. Illumination is to hand, however, in the form of a principle that applies both to expressions of intention and to one's descriptions of what one is doing; its application to the latter supplies the clue to the phenomenon of non-observational knowledge of one's actions. The principle in question is first adumbrated by Anscombe in §2 of *Intention*:

> In some cases the facts are, so to speak, impugned for not being in accordance with the words, rather than *vice versa*. This is sometimes so when I change my mind; but another case of it occurs when e.g. I write something other than I think I am writing: as Theophrastus says (*Magna Moralia*, 1189b 22), the mistake here is one of performance, not of judgment.   (*I*, 2–3)

The same principle is later illustrated by means of a famous example:

> Let us consider a man going round a town with a shopping list in his hand. Now it is clear that the relation of this list to the things he actually buys is one and the same whether his wife gave him the list or it is his own list; and that there is a different relation when a list is made by a detective following him about. If he made the list himself, it was an expression of intention; if his wife gave it him, it has the role of an order. What then is the identical relation to what happens, in the order and the intention, which is not shared by the record? It is precisely this: if the list and the things that the man actually buys do not agree, and if this and this alone constitutes a *mistake*, then the mistake is not in the list but in the man's performance [. . .]; whereas if the detective's record and what the man actually buys do not agree, then the mistake is in the record.   (*I*, 56)

The principle is applied to expressions of intention for the future in the example of the shopping list, and to descriptions of one's present actions in the previous example of writing. I shall refer to the principle as Theophrastus' principle.[10]

---

[10] The *Magna Moralia* were traditionally numbered among Aristotle's works; they have been attributed (though not with any certainty, as Anscombe remarks) to Aristotle's student and younger colleague Theophrastus. In the passage to which Anscombe refers, the mistake is attributed to the action, and not to the understanding, on the ground that there is no room for deliberation: one knows perfectly well how to spell the word which one is accidentally misspelling. Anscombe extends the idea of a mistake in action to cases which can involve deliberation, as in the shopping example. So for more than one reason, the label 'Theophrastus' principle' does not embody any historical claim.

Some philosophers[11] have taken note of these remarks of Anscombe's, and have applied the phrase 'direction of fit' to the phenomenon she drew attention to, a phrase not actually found in *Intention*. However, most of these philosophers have themselves used the idea of direction of fit in a way quite alien to Anscombe's original purpose. Thus it has been made out that beliefs and desires are to be distinguished from one another by their having a different direction of fit with the world, where this amounts to the claim that a belief is 'meant to' fit the world, while the world is 'meant to' fit a desire. There are three respects in which such a view, in its typical form, is un-Anscombean. First, it makes mention of classes of mental state (for want of a better word), rather than classes of utterance; second, it refers to desires, rather than to intentions (and if intentions are mentioned, they tend to get lumped with desires, e.g. as 'conative' states); and third, the item which the belief/desire is meant to fit, or which is meant to fit the belief/desire, is *the world*—rather than the performance of an action.

The thought that the world is meant to fit my desires might betoken a kind of megalomania; more charitably, it might only indicate a philosopher's tin ear. If there is any sense in using 'meant to' this way, it doesn't seem to be the same sense in which it is alleged that my beliefs are meant to fit the world. The latter claim does at least give a sane indication of where to locate the problem when I get things wrong—i.e. with me. For Anscombe, when I don't do what I said I would do, and this and this alone constitutes a mistake,[12] then 'the mistake is in the performance'. A parallel can be drawn with orders: a mistake in performance occurs when a person obeys an order wrongly (e.g. accidentally turning right at the order 'Left turn!'), where obeying an order wrongly is to be distinguished from ignoring, disregarding, or disobeying it (cf. *I*, 57). And the fact that the concept of a *mistake* applies unequivocally now to speech-acts and now to actions, and in both cases does so where there is a discrepancy between speech-act and action—this fact is a reflection of how in the language-game speech and action are intertwined (a familiar Wittgensteinian theme).

As noted, Theophrastus' principle applies to the present as much as to the future. An answer to 'What are you doing?' (e.g. 'Pinning the tail onto the donkey') might be wrong, and might therefore imply a mistake; if so, the mistake is in the action. But what about the case where the answer is 'I'm replenishing the water supply', and where, unknown to the agent, there is a hole in the water pipe, so that no water reaches the tank? Isn't the mistake here in the statement,

---

[11] See e.g. Mark de Bretton Platts, *Ways of Meaning: An Introduction to a Philosophy of Language* (London: Routledge and Kegan Paul, 1979), pp. 256–7; Lloyd Humberstone, 'Direction of Fit', *Mind*, 101/401 (1992), 59–83; Daniel J. Velleman, 'The Guise of the Good', *Noûs*, 26 (1992), 3–26; R. Langton, 'Intention as Faith', in J. Hyman and H. Steward (eds.), *Agency and Action* (Royal Institution of Philosophy suppl. vol. 55; Cambridge: Cambridge University Press), 243–58.

[12] The point of the qualification is to exclude (a) cases where I *couldn't* do what I had planned or said I would do, so that the statement of intention involved an 'error of judgment', and (b) cases where I simply change my mind. See *I*, 56.

and not in the action? Anscombe takes the view that there is no mistake, either in statement or in action. She describes the statement in such a case ('I'm replenishing the water supply') as *falling to the ground* (*I*, 56–7). How are we to decide the matter?

Now if there is anything wrong with the statement, it is clearly not simply that the agent has misreported things. In discovering the hole in the pipe, he will not correct his statement and proceed as before; he will more likely try to fix the hole. An action is meant to fit its intention, and this applies to an action given under a 'wider description' as much as to one given under a 'narrower', more direct, description. From this I think we should conclude that there *is* reason to talk of a mistake in the action; after all, the action may be criticized as futile or unsuccessful, in essentially the same way as a bit of shopping is unsuccessful if one omits to get an item on the shopping list. Theophrastus' principle, I would therefore argue, does apply to such cases. In a sense Anscombe could agree with that proposition—at any rate, such cases would not, for her, count against the principle, since it states only that where there *is* a mistake, the mistake is in the action. However, in what follows I will take Theophrastus' principle as applying in a more substantial sense to present actions given under wider descriptions.

An answer to 'What are you doing?' may be wrong, but on the other hand it may be right, and indeed it usually is: and in this case we can speak of practical knowledge, knowledge of what one is doing. Now as we have just seen, an action's being successfully performed frequently involves results that are 'at a distance' from the starting point (which starting point we *might* identify with a bodily movement), and whether these results actually occur is something only settleable by observation. (This shows how elastic our concept of the present needs to be here: 'what you are doing now' may be something which spans a certain amount of time.) How, then, can someone know straight off that he is e.g. replenishing a water tank, given that *whether* he is in fact doing so depends on things quite outside him (such as the pipe's not having a hole in it), and is something that can only be verified through observation?

There are two ways of knowing here, knowing straight off and knowing on the basis of observation; and as Anscombe says, this can tempt us to conclude that 'If there are two ways of knowing there must be two different things known' (*I*, 53). But the second way of knowing is certainly a way of knowing that I do in fact replenish the water tank; so it seems that the object of the first way of knowing must be something 'inner', such as an act of will, something whose occurrence is not to be settled by observation. All I really know is that I will such-and-such to happen. The dual vocabulary of what is *done* versus what *happens* reinforces the temptation to think this way: all I really *do* is will something.[13] Which means that willing is a kind of thing that I do, and intentional action is to be

---

[13] Cf. 6.3737 and 6.374 of Wittgenstein's *Tractatus*; discussed by Anscombe in *IWT*, 171–2.

thought of along the lines of internal willings producing external happenings. The Cartesian and causalist pictures are here combined in one very seductive, but fatally flawed, picture.

Anscombe has some telling remarks to make on the subject of willing, including the following:

the only sense I can give to 'willing' is that in which I might stare at something and will it to move. People sometimes say that one can get one's arm to move by an act of will but not a matchbox; but if they mean 'Will a matchbox to move and it won't', the answer is 'If I will my arm to move in that way, it won't', and if they mean 'I can move my arm but not the matchbox' the answer is that I can move the matchbox—nothing easier. (*I*, 52)

Nothing easier than to move a matchbox or to write your name. And typically you will know straight off (without observation) that you are doing such things. But to return to our earlier point, how is this possible, if whether you *succeed*, e.g. in writing your name, is something only settleable by observation? The issue is not about certainty; we are not asking how you can be justifiably certain that you're writing your name when it is still uncertain whether you *will* have written your name. This last question arises also for other kinds of knowledge than practical knowledge, and is to be answered by adducing general facts about certainty, justification, and knowledge. Rather, the issue is how one and the same thing can be known without observation and yet require observation to be known. If we speak of two ways of knowing, that can suggest a parallel with different sense modalities: thus seeing and touching are two distinct ways of knowing what something's shape is. They are both ways of knowing because 'By looking' and 'By feeling' are both answers to the question 'How do you know? ... '. But *ex hypothesi*, that question receives no answer when it comes to knowing straight off what you are doing: and that is precisely what accounts for the paradox, that knowing what, or whether, you're writing is something that *requires* observation, and yet does *not* require observation.

The conception of knowledge that is forcing itself upon us when we find ourselves bemused by the paradox is that of contemplative (or theoretical) knowledge, according to which '[k]nowledge must be something that is judged as such by being in accordance with the facts'. If all knowledge is contemplative knowledge, then

if there are two knowledges—one by observation, the other in intention—then it looks as if there must be two objects of knowledge [e.g. an action and a willing]; but if one says the objects are the same [i.e. an action], one looks hopelessly for the different *mode of contemplative knowledge* in acting, as if there were a very queer and special sort of seeing eye in the middle of the acting. (*I*, 57)

The solution of the difficulty lies with Theophrastus' principle. Knowing what you're doing is not any species of contemplative knowledge. Your knowledge of what you are shopping for can be expressed in a shopping list; and the same list, if compiled by the detective, would also express (his) knowledge of what you had shopped for. Theophrastus' principle in effect distinguishes the different functions of the two lists; and we might speak also of the different functions of the corresponding knowledge claims. We can do this, note, without having to classify an answer to 'What are you doing?' as an avowal, in a Wittgensteinian sense; though it is true that such an answer will in many cases count as a criterion of what you are doing—e.g. if the answer is 'Building a wall'.

Linguistic training enables me to say straight off what I am doing—the training is successful to the extent that my utterances are generally in sync with my actions. I need no grounds for these utterances. If *doubt* arises as to whether I am in fact doing what I say I am doing, then I will need to resort to observation, or to asking others. But doubt is the exception, not the rule, and lack of doubt is the default position. For others, if I say I am φ-ing, then that counts as grounds for them to say that I am φ-ing; but of course it may be perceptibly evident that I am not φ-ing, and this will trump what I say.

An answer to 'What are you doing?' in effect gives one's intention, and this is more clearly the case when the description of the action encompasses results at a distance from what might be called the immediate action. 'What are you doing?'—'I am building a wall'. In this case, the same answer could just as well have been given to the question, 'Why are you digging that trench?', in which case it would give a reason, as well as describe an action. The reason why I do not need grounds for my statement that I am doing such-and-such is not just that I have been trained in a certain sort of spontaneous utterance; it is that the function or role of the action description I give is that of blueprint for my action: my action is meant to fit it, not *vice versa*. Non-observational knowledge of one's actions, Theophrastus' principle as applied to those actions, and the stating of one's intentions thus all connect with one another.

2.2. Expressions of Intention

Having looked at Anscombe's account of practical knowledge (knowledge of what one is doing), we are now in a good position to consider what she has to say about expressions of intention. As we saw, Anscombe takes it that 'I am building a wall' really is about an observable action in the world, not about some inner intention, volition, or willing. The same goes for an expression of intention like 'I am going to visit Paris next month': its subject matter is a proposed visit to Paris. The temptation to say that what is *really* reported here is a present mental state arises in large part from the fact that it can seem puzzling that a person should have confident belief or knowledge of the future, including of their own future actions. The distinction between practical knowledge and contemplative knowledge (see p. 25, above) helps provide a solution to this puzzle. But it is worth considering in more detail what is wrong with the view that an expression of intention is about a present mental state.

Anscombe presents the following dilemma for a proponent of the view. Either the putative state of mind bears only a contingent relation to subsequent action, or it bears some sort of non-contingent relation to subsequent action (*I*, 2). The first horn of the dilemma is unbelievable—it is not a mere happy accident that people's intentions generally get carried out, nor is it something established by induction, as it is established that people who were abused as children often go on to abuse their own children. This is connected with the fact that an expression of intention can only be picked out, in some language, by its having a systematic connection with subsequent action; it will only *count* as an expression of intention if there is that connection. (Contrast 'being abused as a child'.) It makes no sense to suppose that there might be creatures for whom the intention to eat an apple was generally followed, not by apple-eating nor attempts at apple-eating, but by jogging.[14] The second horn of the dilemma takes the present state of mind as having the sort of necessary connection to subsequent action we have just taken note of. But what now is the point of using the phrase 'present state of mind', beyond recording the fact that the expression of it is present tensed and relates to a person's psychology (whatever that means—perhaps it has to do with the person's 'authority')? One does not have to be a dyed-in-the-wool Humean to be suspicious of a state of mind's having such a necessary connection with the future—that is, if there is any weight at all being put upon the word 'present', in 'present state of mind'.

It might be added to this that one just does not find within oneself any such events as willings or volitions. Questions such as 'How long do they take?', 'What do they feel like?', 'How many occurred just then when I put the kettle on?', are simply unanswerable, which they really should not be, if willings (etc.) are to be taken as reportable states of mind. If you do look inside yourself, you may find various things, such as images, internal exclamations—even trains of thought on topics quite removed from the topic of what you're actually doing (*I*, 6, 17). None of these deserves the title of 'willing an action'.

If an expression of intention is about a future action, should we see it as a (reliable) *prediction* of that action? Not any reliable prediction of something I will do, in a broad sense of 'do', counts as an expression of intention: 'I am going to be sick' does not, for instance (*I*, 1–2). Perhaps we should then say that an expression of intention is a prediction of a future *intentional* action, to be performed by oneself. This of course would leave us with the

---

[14] Some philosophers have attempted to argue for the possibility of such bizarre cases, more or less by saying 'I should know whether I can conceive of such-and-such, and I jolly well can'. David Lewis is a notable example: his imaginary case of 'mad pain' involves a creature in whom pain typically goes with doing mental arithmetic while crossing the legs and snapping the fingers—see Lewis, 'Mad Pain and Martian Pain', in Ned Block (ed.), *Readings in Philosophy of Psychology*, i (Cambridge, Mass.: MIT Press, 1980), 216–22. He writes: 'my opinion that this is a possible case seems pretty firm' (ibid. 216). Absent any additional argument, the phrase carries with it the suggestion that introspection (or 'intuition') can be used as a means of determining what is possible—an interesting view for a realist about possible worlds to hold.

question 'What is an intentional action?'; but in any case, the suggestion will not do as it stands. For one can predict that one will do something intentionally without thereby expressing the intention of doing it, as: 'I am going to drink a glass of water at some point this month.' Such a statement is an expression of knowledge of one's own habits, a kind of self-knowledge, not an expression of intention. It is in fact an expression of contemplative, not practical, knowledge, in Anscombe's terms.—This point, by the way, will make trouble for behaviourist or functionalist accounts of intention. A behaviourist or functionalist will say, roughly, that an intention to φ is a disposition to φ intentionally; and this view is shown to be wrong (or at best, radically incomplete) particularly by its failure to distinguish an expression of intention from an expression of self-knowledge of the kind just mentioned, the latter being, if anything is, a report about one's disposition to φ intentionally. [15]

'But how can an expression of intention be about something wholly future? For the intention might be thwarted, and then the statement will have been about *nothing*.'—The worry here is the same as the ancient worry: how can there be false judgement? For a false judgement is about what is not, and so appears not to be a judgement at all. The problem arises from a reading of 'about' according to which it signifies a relation between existents. We shall be dealing with this problem later on in this book; [16] for present purposes, we may note that if there is a problem here, it afflicts future-tensed statements generally. But even without the picture of statements as being about things, in a demanding sense of 'about', there is a question as to whether future-tensed statements can have a truth-value when uttered. Anscombe is of the view that they cannot; rather, they become true or false when the thing predicted either happens or fails to happen. This goes for expressions of intention like 'I am going to visit Paris' as much as it does for any other future-tensed statements. Now this might seem an odd thing to say, given the sort of comparison with orders and shopping lists which we saw Anscombe making in the last section. For you wouldn't call an order or shopping list *true* if it got carried out.

Of course the comparison with orders and shopping lists is only a comparison; expressions of intention are a distinct category, and hence perhaps one for which the notions of truth and falsehood are not inappropriate.—But wasn't the point of the comparison precisely to indicate how 'the facts' will typically not impugn the statement, but rather *vice versa*? If, in the case of an unfulfilled intention, the expression of intention isn't at fault, doesn't that mean that it isn't *false*?

---

[15] Rosalind Hursthouse has pointed out how causal theories of intentional action in general suffer from the defect of taking expressions of intention as manifesting 'contemplative knowledge'. She spells out the ramifications of this defect in 'Intention', in Roger Teichmann (ed.), *Logic, Cause and Action: Essays in Honour of Elizabeth Anscombe* (Cambridge: Cambridge University Press, 2000), 83–105.

[16] See Ch. 5, pp. 166–7, and Ch. 6, §1.1. Anscombe's discussion of intentionality is also relevant here; see Ch. 4, §1.1.

Anscombe thinks not. She regards an expression of intention as capable of giving information, just as any prediction might—and to be informed is to be informed of something true, or at least of something that will be true. If I tell you that I am going to be at the pub at 8 p.m., then, armed with this information, you can decide to be there also at that time. If I turn out not to be at the pub when I said I was going to be, then you were misinformed. In this respect, an expression of intention is clearly unlike a typical order. It is also, to be sure, unlike a straight prediction (or estimate, in Anscombe's terminology); but *that* difference has not to do with informativeness and truth-aptness, but with what expressions of intention and orders *do* have in common—their being subject to Theophrastus' principle, and their being justified in a certain sort of way (of which more anon).

The informativeness of expressions of intention is nicely illustrated by Anscombe with the following example:

when a doctor says to a patient in the presence of a nurse 'Nurse will take you to the operating theatre', this may function as an expression of his intention (if it is in it that his decision as to what shall happen gets expressed) and as an order, as well as being information to the patient; and it is this latter in spite of being in no sense an estimate of the future founded on evidence, nor yet a guess or prophecy; nor does the patient normally *infer* the information from the fact that the doctor said that; he would say that the doctor *told* him. This example shews that the indicative (descriptive, informatory) character is not the distinctive mark of 'predictions' *as opposed* to 'expressions of intention', as we might at first sight have been tempted to think.   (*I*, 5)

As well as illustrating the informative character of expressions of intention, Anscombe's example happens also to show how you can express the intention that someone else do something. We should not insist that, because the person himself is not the one who's meant to fulfil the terms of the utterance, that utterance must be an order or request, rather than an expression of intention. After all, you can *want* another person to do something, despite the fact that 'the primitive sign of wanting is *trying to get*' (*I*, 68). We may note that this kind of intention constitutes an awkward case for the causalist: for if the doctor's intention is to be the efficient cause of the nurse's taking Smith to the operating theatre, it will have to operate in a pretty indirect manner—which apart from anything else will raise all sorts of worries about 'deviant causal chains'[17].

Expressions of intention and orders have been several times compared. Another point of similarity is expressed by Anscombe thus:

The reasons justifying an order are not ones suggesting what is probable, or likely to happen, but e.g. ones suggesting what it would be good to make happen with a view to an objective, or with a view to a sound objective. In this regard, commands and expressions of intention are similar.   (*I*, 4)

---

[17] For more on this notion, see Ch. 4, pp. 142–3.

The question 'Why?' has a different application to orders and to expressions of intention from that which it has to estimates of the future. 'That pot plant is going to die soon'. 'Why?' 'It hasn't been watered for a month'. (Or: 'Its leaves are withering'.) Contrast: 'I am going to visit Paris.' 'Why?' 'So as to get out of London for a bit.' This sense of the question 'Why?' is also the one at issue when the question is asked in connection with a present intentional action; as, 'Why are you tearing up that essay?' For Anscombe, it provides the clue to the distinction between the intentional and the unintentional.

3. THE QUESTION 'WHY?'

Anscombe partially delineates the special 'reason-demanding' sense of the question 'Why?' by pointing to cases where the question is refused application, where such refusal can be expressed by one of three ripostes: (a) 'I didn't know I was', (b) 'I observed that I was', and (c) 'I didn't mean to'. If asked irately by one of the audience at a promenade concert why you are standing on her toes, you may reply apologetically that you were unaware that you were doing so—in which case it will be her word that initially informs you of the fact for which you feel the need to apologize. You might observe that same fact, either before being told, or after; but if you need to observe or be told that you are φ-ing, then your φ-ing is not intentional, and (a) and (b) can be taken together, as both ruling out non-observational knowledge. This of course connects with the characterization that we have already given of intentional actions, as a subset of those of one's doings of which one has non-observational knowledge.

'I didn't mean to' may be said of something one didn't know one was doing. But it can also be said when one *does* know, without observing it or being told, that one is doing something—say, hiccupping. In this case, the question 'Why?' is refused application for the reason that

the action is somehow characterised as one in which there is no room for what I called mental causality. This would come out if for example the only way in which a question as to cause was dealt with was to speculate about it, or to give reasons why such and such should be regarded as the cause. (*I*, 25)

Anscombe here distinguishes a case like hiccupping from one like jumping at the bark of a dog. In the latter case, one can give a mental cause (the dog's bark), i.e. a cause that one knows to be such *not* on the basis of observation. (As we have seen, there is certainly an important phenomenon here, even if it is one hard to give a precise account of.) The cause of one's hiccupping, by contrast, is something about which one must speculate, or rely on one's general knowledge, etc.

But may not an intentional action—putting on one's socks, say—be an action for which 'there is no room for mental causality'? And if asked for the *cause* of such an action, in the sense of efficient cause, wouldn't one have to speculate about it? As, 'I'm not sure—something to do with neurones firing in the brain ... '. As Anscombe herself writes, the question 'Why?' has not the special reason-demanding sense 'if the answer is evidence or states a cause, including a mental cause' (*I*, 24). So our problem is to say how an intentional action can be such that speculating as to its efficient cause is ruled out; only by doing this will we have explained what it is for the question 'Why?' to be granted application, and not refused it.

I think that what Anscombe is getting at, in the quotation a couple of paragraphs back, must be this: if, having e.g. hiccupped, you are asked 'Why did you do that?', the only way in which you can *take* the question is by speculating as to cause, or adverting to general knowledge, and so on. This clearly doesn't go for intentional actions, for you can take the question 'Why?' as asking for a reason. But it won't do simply to characterize the special sense of 'Why?' by saying that answers to it will have to be non-speculative, etc.: for one thing, the notion of speculation is too vague (I don't usually need to *speculate* as to the cause of my tripping up); for another, there may turn out to be room for speculation when it comes to intentional actions, if subconscious motives and the like are to be admitted; and finally, of course, I don't need to speculate as to cause if my action (intentional or unintentional) has a 'mental cause'. Hence an account of the special sense of 'Why?' that refers solely to cases where the question is refused application looks inadequate, and a more positive characterization is needed—which indeed Anscombe gives, in provisional form, in section 16: 'the answer may (a) simply mention past history, (b) give an interpretation of the action, or (c) mention something future' (*I*, 24). We shall come to (c) in Chapter 2. Let us first deal with (a) and (b). Cases falling under (a) need to be distinguished from ones involving mental causes; and it will be convenient to discuss (b) alongside (a).

3.1. Motives

Often it is enough to explain why you have done, or are doing, something to mention a bit of past history. 'Why are you feeding your neighbour's cat every day?' 'I promised to.'—'Why are you sending the Principal a Christmas card?' 'She sent me one.' And Anscombe's own example: 'Why did you kill him?' 'He killed my brother.' In many such cases, you do not have an independently describable intention with which you perform the action. One may, it is true, be able to cite what looks like an 'intention with which'; thus, in the last example, one could say, 'I killed him in order to have my revenge'. But as Anscombe notes, we need to ask, 'What is an act of revenge?' (*I*, 20; and cf. *I*, 65–6). And the answer is: 'It is an act performed to harm another, because that other has done one some harm.' In other words, the concept of revenge involves the reason which is given by the phrase 'Because he harmed me'—and so that phrase expresses one's reason more directly than does the phrase 'In order to have my revenge'.

The motive of revenge is called by Anscombe a backward-looking motive. Other motives of this kind include gratitude, remorse, and (sometimes) pity. She contrasts backward-looking motives with 'motive-in-general', giving as an illustration of the latter one's signing a petition out of admiration for its promoter (*I*, 20). Motive-in-general is often expressible in English using the words 'out of' or 'from'; you can do things out of friendship, out of spite, from a sense of dignity, and so on. According to Anscombe, to give a motive of this sort is to say something like 'See the action in this light': it is to give an *interpretation* of the action (see (b), above). As with backward-looking motives, giving a motive-in-general is not equivalent to giving an 'intention with which'. 'In order to retain his dignity' does not really give an independently describable aim of the person who decides to ignore a crude insult, for example, and a less misleading and more direct phrase would be 'Out of a sense of dignity'. For the *concept* of dignity involves, among other things, seeing certain situations as demanding certain responses, etc.

As already mentioned, the bits of past history that serve as reasons in the case of backward-looking motives look very much like mental causes: one can cite either in answer to the question 'Why did you do that?', and in each case one's answer is given 'straight off'. Moreover, as the example of the martial music which makes one march up and down shows, a voluntary action can have a mental cause—so it is not their association with voluntary actions that distinguishes motives from mental causes. But the sense of the question 'Why did you do that?' is pretty obviously different, according as the answer to it cites a motive or a mental cause. So how are we to distinguish them? Anscombe's answer is that *the ideas of good and of harm* are involved in a certain way in backward-looking motives (as with revenge: I harm him because he harmed me), this being something that 'comes out in the agent's elaborations on his answer to the question "Why?"' (*I*, 22). Now such an account will strike many a philosopher as simply arbitrary; and this fact itself shows up a deep philosophical—one might almost say cultural—divide, between such philosophers and a philosopher like Anscombe. The complaint would go roughly as follows: 'Surely if there are *any* past facts giveable as reasons for present or proposed actions, then no restriction can be placed on what past facts an agent might give as reasons? An agent might not be interested in good or harm particularly; and in any case, how can such "concrete" notions possibly enter into a proper account of such an abstract concept as *motive*, which connects with practical rationality as such, not just with the practical rationality of creatures with particular interests?'

The view that there are no *a priori* restrictions on what a person might intelligibly want, or have an interest in, is one that can be attributed to Hume and to his followers, and which has had a huge influence on moral philosophy since Hume. The view most opposed to it, attributable for instance to Philippa

Foot in her most recent writings,[18] is that there are in fact restrictions on what a person might rationally want or have an interest in—practical rationality being conceptually connected with the notions of human good and harm. Anscombe's position is in between these two (though closer to Foot than to Hume). But, because the issue is so important, I will postpone discussion of her view till later on,[19] as she does herself at this point in *Intention*, writing: 'Whether in general good and harm play an essential part in the concept of intention it still remains to find out. So far they have only been introduced as making a clear difference between a backward-looking motive and a mental cause' (*I*, 22–3).

To conclude this section on motives I will make three general points. First, an intentional action performed from some motive, be it backward-looking or general, is not an action performed with any independently describable intention; and this appears enough to refute the view that intentional actions are ones caused by things called 'intentions', which items would have to be (in the relevant sense) independently describable. Second, it's worth pointing out that the argument concerning independently describable intentions is of a kind that we find elsewhere in Anscombe's philosophy. Take her discussion of institutions like that of promising. As we shall see,[20] Anscombe demonstrates how the giving of reasons like 'Because you promised' or 'Because it's mine' (and a host of others) presupposes the forcefulness of a more basic linguistic move, employing such modals as 'must', 'meant to' and 'can't'; for the *concept* of (e.g.) a promise involves the idea that if you promise to φ you have to φ, and this *for no independently describable reason*. (Thus, you don't supply such a reason if you say, 'Because if you *don't* φ, you will commit a wrong—namely, that of breaking your promise'. To give this as a reason for not breaking your promises is to court circularity, in the same way as the phrase 'In order to have revenge' courts circularity if proposed as giving the intention behind my harming X because X harmed me.)

Third, it is significant that Anscombe distinguishes motives from mental causes particularly by reference to 'the agent's elaborations on his answer to the question "Why?"'. One might naively feel that such a distinction ought to be 'real' or 'ontological', in a way that has nothing directly to do with how an agent elaborates on his answers to questions. Won't the difference between 'She jumped because the crocodile snapped' and 'She poked out her tongue because the crocodile snapped' be a difference in what is going on in the agent's head or mind, after all?—maybe a difference to do ultimately with what causal routes are activated in her central nervous system?

The picture of motives, intentions, and mental causes as inner processes or states which can be more or less accurately reported to those around one is a picture that has already been thrown into doubt by this stage in our discussion. As to this, of course, Anscombe is continuing the work of Wittgenstein, and her

---

[18] See e.g. *Natural Goodness* (Oxford: Oxford University Press, 2001), ch. 4.
[19] Ch. 2, §3.1.   [20] Ch. 3, §2.2.

method, like Wittgenstein's, is to direct our attention to the different kinds of language-game that we find, as these embody different kinds of human concern. It is thus quite natural for her to allow that the distinction between motive and mental cause is not a hard and fast one. She writes:

> we should often refuse to make any distinction at all between something's being a reason, and its being a cause [. . .] [H]ow would one distinguish between cause and reason in such a case as having hung one's hat on a peg because one's host said 'Hang up your hat on that peg'? [. . .] Roughly speaking—if one were forced to go on with the distinction—the more the action is described as a mere response, the more inclined one would be to use the word 'cause'; while the more it is described as a response to something as *having a significance* that is dwelt on by the agent in his account, or as a response surrounded with thoughts and questions, the more inclined one would be to use the word 'reason'.   (*I*, 23–4)

(The distinction referred to here is that between 'cause' and 'reason'; but the passage follows on from Anscombe's discussion of mental causes and backward-looking motives, and insofar as we would ascribe a motive to the hat-hanger, that motive can indeed be given, by some such phrase as 'From politeness'—the *reason* being given by 'Because my host asked me to'.)

Citing motives and giving reasons go together; and the reasons for our responses are related especially to the significance we attach to what it is we are responding to. Not anything can be intelligibly given as a reason, and not any feature of a situation can be intelligibly described as significant. But explaining the significance, both of situations and of actions, by reference to good and harm is a paradigm case of significance-ascription. So my third point relates back to what was said earlier about the difference between motive and cause: that difference boils down to a difference between language-games, as these latter embody various interests and concerns (themselves complex and overlapping)—and human interests and concerns are paradigmatically related to *good* and *harm*.

3.2. Reasonless Actions: The Merely Voluntary

So far we have considered two types of answer to the question 'Why did you do that?' (or 'Why are you doing that?'): the first type of answer being one that refuses application to the question, the second type being one that gives a motive. The main kind of positive answer to be discussed will be that which gives the intention with which one acted, or is acting. This topic will be the starting point of the next chapter; but before we get to that, there is another type of answer to consider, one which it is tempting to regard as refusing application to 'Why?', but which according to Anscombe should not be so regarded. This type encompasses two main forms:

(a) 'For no particular reason'
(b) 'I don't know why I did that'.

Answers of this type do not make out that the action in question was un-intentional in the way in which, say, tripping up, singing out of tune, or let-ting the cat out of the bag are unintentional (or usually are). But the epi-thet 'intentional' may seem inappropriate; and in fact here we come across a distinct category of action, that of the voluntary, including the 'merely' voluntary.

Variants of (a) include 'I just thought I would', 'It was an impulse', and the like. The action in question might be doodling, or cracking one's finger joints, or jumping over a puddle. Anscombe says that (a)-type answers do not refuse application to 'Why?', any more than the answer 'None' refuses application to the question 'How many coins do you have in your pocket?' (*I*, 25). (Though she does not say so, she would presumably count e.g. 'I have no pockets' as an answer that does refuse application to this question.)

There is more than one version of the (b)-type answer. The first, which might be supplemented by the self-directed question, 'Now why did I do that?', Anscombe applies to certain actions that one 'discovers' one has done, such as 'put[ting] something in a rather odd place' (*I*, 26). A second version of (b) that I will mention applies to actions where you assume that you *had* a reason, but have now forgotten what it was—as when you find yourself looking in a drawer, but have forgotten what it is you are hunting for. Here, the self-directed question is liable to be, 'Now what am I doing?'. And there is yet a third version of (b), distinguished from the first two by the fact that one doesn't *find* that one has done something, and which is the sort of statement someone comes out with 'as if to say "It is the sort of action in which a reason seems requisite". As if there were a reason, if only he knew it; but of course that is not the case in the relevant sense' (*I*, 26). Anscombe supplies no examples of actions fitting this bill,[21] but maybe perverse or gratuitously vicious actions would be good examples. As the bride leaves the room in tears, her brother is asked why he had to bring up that anecdote from their childhood: he can only reply, 'I don't know why I did that'.

If Anscombe is right, we could call actions where (a)-type or (b)-type answers to 'Why?' are appropriate 'reasonless actions'. Like actions done from backward-looking or general motives, reasonless actions would be ones that are not performed *with* some intention. It may be that some of them would count as intentional; but if not, then at any rate as voluntary. Since we are speaking of actions performed with no intention, 'voluntary' can no more amount to 'caused by an intention' than can 'intentional' itself. As for 'caused by a volition', enough doubt has already been cast upon introspectible present states of mind, of the sort that volitions (a.k.a. willings) are standardly taken to be, for that possibility to appear attractive.

---

[21] Perhaps not surprisingly, given that she goes on, 'I myself have never wished to use these words in this way'.

But (it might be said) doesn't it need to be established more conclusively that so-called reasonless actions are in fact reasonless?—that they are not done with any intention in mind?

If we were to posit a reason for what I will call (a)-type actions, such as doodling, what reason would serve? Here are two possibilities: 'Because I felt like it', and 'For the pleasure of it'. The former 'mentions a bit of past history', in Anscombe's phrase, while the latter appears to give a 'further intention'. Taking the second first: there is indeed a long tradition in philosophy of saying that many, if not all, of our actions are performed with the further intention of getting pleasure. But it is of course a fallacy—one certainly committed by many in the tradition just spoken of—to infer from the fact that one finds doodling pleasurable that one doodles in order to get pleasure. And with such thoughtless or semi-automatic actions as doodling, talk of pleasure or fun looks quite peculiar in any case, especially since many such actions are ones done *while* doing something else, such as talking on the phone.

What about the alleged reason, 'Because I felt like it', or 'Because I just wanted to'?

> Say I notice a spot on the wall-paper and get out of my chair. Asked what I am doing I reply 'I'm going to see if I can reach it by standing on my toes'. Asked why, I reply 'I want to, that's all' or 'I just had the idea'. [. . .] [I]f an idea of something I might do inspires me to set out to do it, or to make up my mind to do it, not with any end in view, and not as anything but itself, this is 'just wanting' to do it.   (*I*, 91)

'I just want to', said of a future action, and 'I just wanted to', said of a past or maybe present action, are statements giving a certain kind of mental cause: the thought or idea of a certain action has inspired the person to set out to do it. But if that is so, then such statements do not give *reasons*. The question 'Why?' is not refused application, according to Anscombe, but is nevertheless answered by giving a cause, as with our earlier example, 'The martial music excites me, that is why I walk up and down'. The cause is an idea or thought, or similar—something that comes into one's mind, as we say; it is not a state of wanting, nor is it a feeling of desire (typically). On the other hand, 'I just want to', said of a *present* action, is not used to indicate a mental cause of the sort we have been discussing (*I*, 90–1). This statement really is about wanting. But it still does not give a reason—nor yet a cause. The phenomenon of wanting will be one of the main topics of the next chapter, so I postpone discussion of it for now.

So 'I just want to', said of a future action, and 'I just wanted to', said of a past or present action, are statements giving a certain kind of mental cause. But given that what is cited *is* a cause, how can we say that 'Why?' is not refused application by these statements?—Perhaps the idea is this: there is a mental cause of the person's 'setting out', or 'making up her mind', to do something, not just of her doing it; and what this means is that the person can say (or could have said) 'I am going to φ'—e.g. 'I am going to see if I can reach it by standing on my toes'—the latter being a *bona fide* expression of intention. But the question 'Why?' could also be asked of such a putative expression of intention. And since the answer would be 'I just wanted to', we would again face the question of why that answer does not refuse application to 'Why?'. If it did refuse application to 'Why?', the alleged expression of intention would of course appear not to be an expression of intention after all.

In short, it is unclear why Anscombe takes (a)-type statements as not refusing application of 'Why?', given that they are indeed reasonless. But it is surely true that a distinction needs to be drawn between things like reaching for a spot on the wallpaper, on the one hand, and things like jumping at the bark of a dog, on the other. The former are voluntary, the latter involuntary. We shall come back to this.

There is perhaps more of a temptation to think that there must be intentions in mind when it comes to (b)-type actions than when it comes to (a)-type ones. This goes especially for the second of the three versions (see p. 35, above), at any rate if we include your *past* intentions in the picture: if you find yourself looking in a drawer, you might well say something like, 'The reason I came over here and opened the drawer must have been to find something'. Of course, this still leaves us with the present action of continuing to peer into the drawer; though even there you could on occasion give a reason, namely: so that it will come back to you what your previous reason or intention was. Hence it is at any rate not obvious that such actions (either opening the drawer or continuing to peer) do in fact deserve the title 'reasonless'. What about 'putting something in an odd place'? Such actions are performed thoughtlessly, and seem to be cases of minor irrationality; the odder the place, the more irrational. Putting a cup of tea in the fridge, as a friend of mine once did, seems to be a case of being on automatic pilot, since it is likely that in this case opening the fridge door (e.g. to get milk) simply triggered an action often performed after fridge-opening (i.e. putting a thing held into the fridge). 'Automatic pilot' and 'triggering' are causal-explanatory notions, even if they have something of the promissory note about them. It thus looks as if one could give a causal, and speculative, answer to 'Why?' in this case; but if so, given that there is no reason to be given in answer to the question 'Why?', one would seem to be refusing application to that question in its reason-demanding sense. But here, in contrast to where an action is performed because one 'just wanted to', there is at least some case for saying that the action in question is involuntary, rather than voluntary, so that one would expect 'Why?' to be refused application.

As for cases like that of the gratuitous anecdote (if I am right that that is the kind of scenario Anscombe has in mind), surely it might occur to us to posit a subconscious intention, such as that of hurting or embarrassing the other person? Anscombe claims that when someone in such a situation says 'I don't know why I did that', 'it is not the case in the relevant sense' that there was any intention, 'even if psychoanalysis persuades [the agent] to accept something as his reason' (*I*, 26). But it is not quite clear what her ground is for this claim. And she is certainly in a position to allow for the existence of subconscious intentions, being careful to delineate the class of intentional actions as ones where the question 'Why?' *is given* application. That this phrase is not short for 'is given by the agent' is evident from the fact that Anscombe allows animals to act with intentions (*I*, 86). Hence if we ascribe a subconscious intention to someone, e.g. in the case of the gratuitous anecdote, *we* supply an answer to 'Why?', and the question is thus given application.[22] But of course the fact that ascribing a subconscious intention is not ruled out does not supply us with a reason for actually ascribing such an intention; and where there really is nothing to be gained from the action, the hunt for a subconscious intention, Anscombe may argue, simply betokens the prejudice that there *must* be an intention.

For Anscombe, neither (a) nor (b) refuses application of the question 'Why?' (as do such answers as 'I didn't know I was'); but it does not follow that 'Why?' is *given* application. I have raised the question whether the third species of (b)-type actions are in fact reasonless; but the following remark, made by Anscombe in connection with such actions, seems worth quoting, as being applicable to whatever actions *are* in the relevant sense reasonless (e.g. (a)-type actions): 'the question "Why?" has and yet has not application; it has application in the sense that it is admitted as an appropriate question; it lacks it in the sense that the answer is that there is no answer' (*I*, 26). There is no more need to insist on hard and fast distinctions here than there was with 'reason' and 'cause' (see above, p. 34). Merely voluntary actions are not fully-fledged intentional actions, and we should be prepared to see both similarities and differences holding between the two kinds of action.

'But', it may be objected, 'why *shouldn't* we say that "Why?" is refused application by (a), and perhaps by (b)? How can this be wrong, if we are going to call the associated actions reasonless?' The essential difficulty, as mentioned earlier, is to distinguish reasonless actions from such involuntary doings as jumps and spasms, doings whose explanations, authoritative or speculative, cite causes. If asked 'Why did you do that?' when one had jumped, one might reply 'The dog's bark made me'. How is such an answer different from the (a)-type answer 'I just wanted to'? If asked 'Why did you do that?' when one had moved spasmodically, one might reply 'I don't know'. How is *that* answer different from a (b)-type answer? Even with an (a)-type action such as doodling there seems to be room for speculating about causes—as, 'I don't know; perhaps it's that some pent-up physical energy needs to find a channel', or, 'Perhaps there's

---

[22] It should be said, though, that given the primary function of 'Why?', namely to elicit the sort of answer to which Theophrastus' principle applies (i.e. to elicit a blueprint for action), there is a priority of the second-person version of the question over the third-person version of it—and a related priority of human over animal, and conscious over subconscious, intentions.

an evolutionary advantage in being observably awake'. (The cause hypothesized in the latter answer is not a straightforward efficient cause, of course.) In short, there seem to be no good grounds for denying that the only way the agent can take the question 'Why?' in all these cases is as asking after causes—to use the locution mentioned earlier (p. 31).

One clear difference between a spasm and some doodling has to do with being under the agent's control. You can't help moving spasmodically, whereas you can help doodling. But what is meant by the phrase 'can/can't help'? And does it mark a general distinction between the voluntary and the involuntary?—That something you did was something you could or couldn't help is one of those things that you can say straight off; and this seems to show that the matter has not to do with whether what was done had a cause or not, a cause, that is, of the kind about which you need to speculate (or rely on general knowledge, etc.). Nor is there any question of a 'mental cause', either with spasms or doodlings. 'I could have helped, i.e. desisted from, doodling' is not, in fact, an empirical statement akin to, 'I could have got there in time (if I had caught the bus)'. 'How do you *know* you could have helped doodling?' is a silly question, and the answer 'By induction from past experience' an equally silly answer.

It is natural to think that the phrase 'could have desisted' is short for 'could have desisted IF so-and-so', where 'if so-and-so' tends to be filled in as 'if I had wished to'. Of course, if you had desisted from doodling, then it follows that you would have wished to: but this is because *desisting from doodling* is the name of a kind of voluntary action, unlike say *faltering in one's doodling*. So let us replace 'desisted from' by 'stopped', the latter being one of those verbs that can name (or be a constituent of the name of) either a voluntary or involuntary action. 'I could have stopped doodling if I'd wanted to' does look like an empirical proposition. But if it is taken as an empirical proposition, then it is uncertain, or as uncertain as many an empirical counterfactual. Maybe a minor stroke would have induced a pointless continuation of the doodling, etc., etc.[23]

It seems rather that your ability to say straight off that you could have helped doodling amounts to your knowledge that doodling is one of those things (i) which can be stopped when one is told to stop, and started when one is told to start; (ii) an intention to do which can be announced; (iii) which can be done for a reason—and so on. These features distinguish doodling as a kind from spasmodic movements as a kind. The fact that they do so could perhaps

---

[23] In philosophical discussions of free will, the focus has often been on the phrase 'could (not) have done otherwise'; and just as with 'could (not) have helped it' (or ' . . . have stopped'), the result of interpreting the phrase as a straightforward empirical hypothesis is to introduce an inapposite species of uncertainty. Harry Frankfurt has argued for the irrelevance of 'X couldn't have done otherwise' to the issue of whether X was responsible for his action, and it is noteworthy that he interprets the statement as an empirical one. This enables him to employ a number of more or less sci-fi thought experiments to illustrate the irrelevance. See his 'Alternate Possibilities and Moral Responsibility', in *The Importance of What We Care About* (Cambridge: Cambridge University Press, 1988), 1–10.

be called an empirical fact, but one of such basicness that a person who was ignorant that doodling had those features would surely be a person lacking the concept of doodling. A given piece of doodling will count as voluntary because it belongs to this kind, even though no one commanded it, no intention to doodle was announced, no reason for doodling can be given, and the rest of it. The default position is that it is voluntary: it will count as such unless something definite prevents its being voluntary (e.g. my taking your hand and forcing it to 'doodle').[24] The reverse point applies to spasmodic movements and tics. These *can* be feigned, of course; but the concept of a feigned tic is parasitic on that of a tic, and even if we described a tic in terms that didn't entail involuntariness ('tic' perhaps carries that entailment), it would belong to a *kind* of movement that typically lacks features (i) to (iii). The default position is that a tic or sudden jerk is involuntary.

But what about e.g. dropping a plate, and similar actions of the sort that can be either voluntary or involuntary? Dropping a plate as a *kind* of action may be said to satisfy (i) to (iii) from the last paragraph, plus whatever further appropriate conditions for voluntariness we add; so in virtue of what is a given plate-dropping involuntary? We might observe that involuntary plate-dropping is unintentional plate-dropping, where the question 'Why?' is refused application along the lines already adumbrated (see pp. 30–1, above). But at this point in our enquiry that observation would seem to beg the question. If you drop a plate and lack a reason for doing so, you will probably say, 'I didn't mean to', in answer to 'Why?', whereas if you doodle without a reason, you will probably say, 'For no particular reason'. But how are these answers different?—and why should only the first be considered as refusing application to 'Why?'?

Doodling is something that people 'just do'. The same does not go for dropping plates. The person who in answer to the question why she had dropped a plate said 'For no particular reason', or 'I just felt like it', would be scarcely intelligible—one would either doubt her sincerity or worry about her state of mind:

Answers like 'No particular reason'; 'I just thought I would', and so on are often quite intelligible; sometimes strange; and sometimes unintelligible. That is to say, if someone hunted out all the green books in his house and spread them out carefully on the roof, and gave one of these answers to the question 'Why?' his words would be unintelligible unless as joking and mystification. They would be unintelligible, not because one did not know what *they* meant, but because one could not make out what the man meant by saying them here. [. . .] [W]e are not 'excluding a form of words from the language'; we are saying 'we cannot understand such a man'.   (*I*, 26–7)

We have already encountered Anscombe's use of the distinction between intelligible and unintelligible, e.g. in connection with somebody's saying that his elbow

---

[24] For more on this important locution—'so and so, unless something prevents it'—see Ch. 3, §2.1, pp. 91–4.

hurts while nursing his foot, limping, and so on (see p. 19, above). In her use of this distinction we may discern a lesson taken to heart from Wittgenstein's philosophy of language; namely, that an expression does not 'carry its meaning around with it', that although a sentence may have linguistic meaning in the sense of being useable (it is not 'excluded from the language-game'), it does not follow that *any* use of the sentence counts as making sense. A hammer is a tool with a use; but if you found someone waving a hammer around his head, you would find him perplexing, and would want to ask, 'Why are you doing *that* with *that*?' In the linguistic arena, the analogous question is, 'What are *those* words meant to be doing in *this* context?'

The temptation to think that 'No particular reason' *must* be an intelligible answer to 'Why?' does not only come from the implicit assumption that if a sentence is ever well behaved it is always well behaved. There are two other possible sources of the temptation. The first is the idea that 'psychological' statements in general, and ones like 'I did that for no particular reason' in particular, must enjoy first-person authority. The second is the Humean view, already mentioned, that a rational person can have any desire, preference, or whim. The first of these is indeed related to the idea that a well-behaved sentence carries its meaning around with it. But in any case all three ideas (assumptions, pictures) are steadily undermined, both in *Intention* and elsewhere in Anscombe's philosophy.

Part of the usefulness of the intelligible/unintelligible distinction, as we have seen, is in its enabling us to bolster the difference between voluntary and involuntary. Plate-droppings as a kind fulfil the conditions for voluntariness—but where a given piece of plate-dropping was not ordered, done for a reason, or whatever, it won't follow that it can still be classed as merely voluntary (as doodling can). For plate-dropping, unlike doodling, is not an example of normal everyday human behaviour. The person who says he dropped a plate for no particular reason will, on the face of it, be unintelligible: that form of words is only appropriate where an action is the sort of thing that people just do. What makes for intelligibility has to do with the natural history of human beings, and relates to various things, such as what is pleasurable, what is not difficult to do, what occurs frequently—and, one might simply add, what is natural.

What of the person who gets up and tries to reach a spot on the wallpaper? Asked after the event why she did that, the person replies 'I just wanted to', and this, I am assuming, is an (a)-type answer, comparable to 'For no particular reason'. But is trying to reach a spot on wallpaper a thing people 'just do'? A habit of reaching for spots on walls would look more like a symptom of obsessive compulsive disorder than like a hobby. But the action has another description: 'trying to do something to see if you can'. And under that description it perhaps *is* one of those things that people just do—though to be sure, not every action that might satisfy this bare description could count as normal or natural. Still, the action of trying to reach a spot on wallpaper is, we might say, natural *under this description*. We shall have more to say about that locution in the next chapter (§1.2).

There remain all sorts of actions which occupy the grey area between involuntary and voluntary: swallowing, shifting position, opening your eyes having closed them while listening to music, laughing politely, pulling a face at a bad smell. It is not just that pulling a face can sometimes be voluntary, sometimes involuntary—it is that on many occasions, it can be indeterminate which of the two it is. My inclination is to say that this indeterminacy applies to (b)-type actions like putting a cup of tea in the fridge. Putting a cup of tea in the fridge belongs to a *kind* of action that satisfies the general conditions for voluntariness—you can start or stop when told to, etc. But it is not like doodling, any more than is spreading books on a rooftop: putting cups of tea in fridges is not something that people just do. Nor, on the other hand, is it quite like dropping a plate unintentionally, for the reason that we can see it as a deviant form of a perfectly normal intentional action (putting milk or whatever into the fridge). Absent-minded behaviour is akin to somnambulistic behaviour. The latter does count as definitely involuntary, I suppose; but the former, just in virtue of being wakeful, is harder to classify as such.

That it can be indeterminate whether an action is voluntary or involuntary is further evidence against the view that voluntariness consists in the occurrence of a special kind of mental event or state—such as a volition, trying, or whatever. For such a state should presumably either be present or not. Nor is it really an option to say that it might be indeterminate whether a given mental state *was* a volition, say. Would the indeterminacy be reportable by the subject through introspection?—if so, would that imply a scale of 'volitiousness', enjoyed to a greater degree by some mental states than by others, so bringing with it a grey area?—if not, what would the indeterminacy consist in? Such questions may be left to those who are happy to get embroiled in them.

2

Practical Reason

1. FURTHER INTENTIONS

1.1. The Centrality of Further Intentions

At the start of *Intention*, Anscombe introduced her subject under three heads: expressions of intention, intentional action, and intention in acting. In the last chapter, we looked at the first two of these; it is now time to turn to the third, and in particular to what Anscombe calls 'further intention with which'. The further intention with which someone acts is often that which he would tell us of, in answering the question 'Why?' by mentioning something future: the third sort of positive answer to that question, after (a) mentioning past history, and (b) giving an interpretation (*I*, 24). But the 'further intention with which' may not involve anything future. 'Why are you scribbling on that poster?' 'So as to give Tony Blair a moustache.' In this case, the pictorial vandalism is not something that happens *after* the scribbling; but we may still say that 'giving Tony Blair a moustache' mentions something further.

If I mention some further state of affairs in answer to the question 'Why?', I may or may not thereby mention myself as agent, or at all. 'Why are you putting cheese in that trap?' 'So that the mouse will be lured into it.' But whatever answer I give, the state of affairs that I mention will be one that I can be said to aim at, and this is signalled by the phrases 'so that', 'in order to', and the like. Typically, what I do will be done as a means to the end given by my answer to 'Why?'—which end, as we shall see, may itself be a means to a further end.

In some modern discussions of intention, it is the phenomenon of action-explanation that is taken as philosophically central. This as it were puts the third-person stance before the first-person stance; or if the two stances are to be on a par, that will only be because, on such an account, one can explain one's own actions by mentioning one's intentions in just the same way as another person can (though one can perhaps do so more reliably than another person). Anscombe's discussion, as we saw in Chapter 1, does proceed for some way by concentrating on the second of her three headings, intentional action; but the features of intentional actions which interest her are especially those which are revealed via the first-person stance. Non-observational knowledge of actions is a person's knowledge of his own actions; Theophrastus' principle applies to first-person accounts of what one is doing; and the question 'Why?', which is used to delineate the class of intentional actions, is primarily asked *of* the agent, not *about* him.

A third-person conception of intentional action would be one according to which there could be a concept of intentional action without there being such things as expressions of intention for the future, or of 'further intention'. Such a conception must be shared by many of those philosophers who put action-explanation centre stage. It is a conception that Anscombe explicitly argues against in §20. She takes certain marks of the concept *intentional*, and asks whether those marks would survive in a concept where the possibility of expressions of further intention was lacking. She concludes that those marks would not survive, and that any resultant concept would not deserve to be called a concept of the intentional.

The argument of §20 is rather obscure; what follows is something of a paraphrase.

Three salient marks of the intentional which might appear to be independent of further intention, and which therefore might be alleged as sufficient for a purely third-person concept of intentional action, are these: (a) intentional actions are intentional under some descriptions and not others; (b) intentional actions may be so in virtue of a backward-looking or interpretative motive; (c) intentional actions are voluntary. For a 'reduced' (third-person) concept of intention, (a) would amount to no more than that there are various descriptions of what a person is doing which he knows to apply to what he is doing. Of course, the descriptions you know straight off to be true of what you're doing do not necessarily coincide with those under which your action is intentional, as things are; so the 'reduced' sense of 'intentional under a description' would appear to have a different extension from the actual sense. But in any case, 'intentional under description D' can only have the sense it actually has where there is such a thing as practical deliberation, in which a series of action-descriptions corresponds to a piece of means–end reasoning, in a way we shall be looking at shortly—all of which relies upon 'further intention with which'.

Turning to (b), we are back with the problem of distinguishing motives from 'mental causes'. 'One can argue against motives—i.e. criticise a man for having acted on such a motive—but a great deal of the point of doing so will be gone if we imagine the expression of intention for the future to be absent . . .' (*I*, 31–2). The kind of criticism that is possible of motives is (as things are) quite distinct from the kind of criticism that is possible of mental causes—e.g. of the causes of one's fear, or of one's fearful behaviour. If, in answer to 'Why did you kill X?', you reply, 'Because he killed my brother', you are not just saying something along the lines of 'X's killing of my brother made me feel murderous towards X'. Criticism of the latter might go, 'You really should have your feelings more under control'. Rather, you are bringing your grounds into the same logical space as forward-looking reasons, and hence into potential conflict with such reasons.

You can thus be criticized for your weighing of reasons, or for not having weighed up reasons where you should have: 'All right, X did kill your brother, but all the same you should have reflected that in killing X you would be orphaning four children.' But all of this would be impossible without forward-looking reasons and further intentions.

What about voluntariness (mark (c))? In §3.2 of the previous chapter, I spoke of certain conditions of voluntariness, as that a voluntary action can be done or stopped on command (pp. 39–40). For a 'reduced' concept of the voluntary, we have to imagine these conditions to hold in the absence of expressions of further intention. But, as with motives, the *point* of the distinction between voluntary and involuntary would seem then to disappear. Doodling is unlike fainting in that it can (e.g.) be done or stopped on command; but the interest of this has to do with such facts as this: that there is a connection between criticizing an action of φ-ing and telling the agent to stop φ-ing. To criticize an action of φ-ing is to criticize the actual or supposed answer to 'Why are you φ-ing?'—a positive answer to which will give either a motive (already discussed), or a further reason.[1] Another such connection is referred to by Anscombe in the following passage:

If they [certain actions] are subject to command they can be distinguished as a separate class; but [in the absence of further intentions] the distinction seems to be an idle one, just made for its own sake. Don't say 'But the distinction relates to an obviously *useful* feature of certain actions, namely that one can get a person to perform them by commanding him'; for 'usefulness' is not a concept we can suppose retained if we have done away with 'purpose'.   (*I*, 33)

It is these connections between the conditions of voluntariness and forward-looking reasons that give point to the idea that 'For no particular reason' doesn't refuse application to the question 'Why?'. The merely voluntary, as we saw, is a close cousin of the intentional.

All in all, then, to subtract the possibility of further intentions from the concept of intentional action would radically affect the contents of (a), (b), and (c), in such a way as to produce a concept with quite a different point, if not a pointless concept. In asking what is essential to intentional action, you are at least in part asking what is essential to the concept *intentional action*; and if imagining a certain mark of that concept away means imagining a concept with quite a different point, or with no point at all, then the imaginary concept cannot be called the *same* as our actual concept. (In this respect, concepts are to be compared with tools, as Wittgenstein said; a tool's function belongs to its essence.) It follows that the mark in question—that of the possibility of expressions of further intention—is essential to the concept *intentional action*. What I have called a third-person conception of intentional action is thus thrown into doubt.

---

[1] Of course, you can also ask someone to stop φ-ing when they are only φ-ing unintentionally; and part of the interest of 'subject to command' will admittedly relate to such cases.

For completeness it might be as well to defend what I have been taking for granted, that the existence of further intentions and the possibility of *expressions* of further intention are mutually entailed. One can, of course, attribute further intentions to human beings and other creatures in the absence of any expressions from them of those intentions. But if there were no such thing as an expression of further intention, what would such attribution amount to? What would we be attributing to the agent? We have already encountered the problems with the answer 'A present state of mind' (see Ch. 1, pp. 26–7): any such state of mind would have to have an internal connection to a subsequent state of affairs, for a purely causal connection (e.g.) would put intentions in the same camp as any other states of mind with more or less predictable outcomes, such as certain moods or emotions. But an internal connection to subsequent events (a) makes the phrase '*present* state of mind' either redundant or misleading, and (b) shifts the focus to the subsequent events themselves, so that the attribution of a further intention turns out, in effect, to be a prediction. In the absence of expressions of intention, what kind of prediction would it be?

In some cases, it would have to be a prediction that the agent will intentionally do something, since a prediction that the agent will be sick, for example, needs to be excluded; which will set us hunting for marks of the intentional. But we will also have to deal with further intentions as to what is to *happen*. I put some cheese in the mousetrap, and you ascribe to me the intention that a mouse be caught in the trap. Predicting that a mouse *will* be caught in the trap is clearly neither necessary nor sufficient for the ascription of the further intention—so what is being predicted? Maybe: that I will feel (or show signs of) satisfaction if a mouse is caught, and feel (or show signs of) disappointment if no mouse is caught. I might of course die before a mouse comes along; in which case a subjunctive conditional is needed: 'Were a mouse to be caught, he would smile and rub his hands, while if not ... ' (retrospective ascriptions of further intention would then often require counterfactual conditionals: 'Had a mouse been caught ... '). But what is '(a sign of) satisfaction'? To define satisfaction in terms of the relevant intention would in this context be viciously circular. We are left with a certain kind of pleasure; but it is an empirical matter what things, and how many, could produce this feeling of pleasure. I put the cheese in the mousetrap, a mouse comes along . . . then pirouettes, does a somersault, and stands on its head. I show signs of obvious pleasure. But of course it won't follow that my intention in putting the cheese in the trap was that a mouse should perform such antics.[2]

1.2. 'Under a Description'

When a person is doing something intentionally, there will be a class of descriptions of what she is doing, C1. A subclass of C1 will be the class of those

---

[2] Cf. Wittgenstein, *Philosophical Remarks*, iii, paras. 21–2.

descriptions that the person knows to be true of her action—C2. Some of the descriptions in C2 will be ones that the person knows straight off ('without observation') to be true of her action, and these belong to a subclass of C2: C3. Finally, there are those descriptions of the action under which it is intentional, and these will belong to a subclass of C3: C4.

The members of C4 will typically form a series, a series that can be elicited from the agent by repeatedly asking 'Why?'. Here is Anscombe's scenario:

> 'Why are you moving your arm up and down?'—'I'm pumping.' 'Why are you pumping?'—'I'm pumping the water-supply for the house.' 'Why are you beating out that curious rhythm?'—'Oh, I found out how to do it, as the pump does click anyway, and I do it just for fun.' 'Why are you pumping the water?'—'Because it's needed up at the house' and (*sotto voce*) 'To polish that lot off'. 'Why are you poisoning these people?'—'If we can get rid of them, the other lot will get in and ...'   (*I*, 38)

In this example, the descriptions of the person's action are all descriptions under which it is intentional, and they form a main series, together with a small parallel one-member series ('beating out that curious rhythm'). Moving the arm up and down is a means of operating the pump; operating the pump is a means of getting water to the house; getting water to the house is a means of poisoning the inhabitants ('a small group of party chiefs, with their immediate families, who are in control of a great state'); and so on. The final answer to a series of 'Why?' questions will give what may be called *the* intention with which the person is doing what she is doing: the end or goal at which she is aiming.

As we saw in Chapter 1, the questions 'Why are you doing that?' and 'What are you doing?' are frequently interchangeable. The answer to either question will typically give a description of the action that is 'wider' than the description which the enquirer can see for himself to hold of the action, this latter description being implicit in the 'that' of 'Why are you doing that?' (e.g. 'moving the arm up and down'); and each answer in the series of answers to 'Why?' will typically give a wider description than the previous answer. A wider description will often entail things, e.g. effects, that are at a distance from the agent. Thus 'I am replenishing the water-supply' entails 'Water is getting into the water-tank' (assuming a tank to be the receptacle). In answer to 'Why are you pumping?' one could either reply, 'I am replenishing the water-supply', which employs a wider action-description, or, 'So that water gets into the water-tank', which simply mentions the intended effect. Which answer is appropriate depends roughly on how much a matter of course it is that the effect in question should come about (*I*, 39–40). This explains why in the pumping example, the final answer to the series of 'Why?' questions is not going to be 'I'm bringing down the government', but rather 'So as to bring down the government'—or even just 'So as to help bring down the government'.

When one gives a wider action-description, one may employ an imperfective form of verb, e.g. 'I am building ...'. An interesting feature of language here is that employment of the imperfective form does not entail the corresponding perfective form. Thus, you might be interrupted in building a wall, so that the wall never gets built, but it will still be true that you were building a wall. This point doesn't only apply to action-verbs: a tree might be falling down, but be stopped by a passing giant, so that the perfective form ('The tree fell down') won't be appropriate. The reason that the imperfective form of a verb doesn't entail the corresponding perfective form is that the perfective form entails some kind of end-result—e.g. there being a wall, or the tree's striking the ground. Why is the same verb appropriate in a context where the end-result is entailed (the perfective case) and in one where it is not entailed (the imperfective case)? Clearly, because we see certain processes as teleological: we see a process as making for, or tending towards, a certain result, even if that end-result doesn't come about. Where the verb is an action-verb, this teleology relates to Theophrastus' principle. As we saw,[3] Theophrastus' principle explains why a person can know without observation that he is, e.g., building a wall, despite the fact that whether a wall gets built can only be settled by observation. Of course, you can know that a tree is falling down without having to observe its striking the ground, simply because it can *be* falling down without ever striking the ground—the imperfective form doesn't entail the perfective form. This goes for action-verbs too, in a sense; but an action-description such as 'building a wall' only applies in the first place because of the person's aim, i.e. what he would give in answer to the question 'What are you doing?'. It is this actual or hypothetical answer that determines the 'end-result' (subconscious intentions aside). After all, it may be that nothing observable in what is being done warrants 'building a wall', rather than, say, 'digging a trench'.[4]

There is a certain kind of puzzle associated with the idea of an action's having a number of descriptions, a puzzle discussed by, among others, Judith Jarvis Thomson.[5] If Boris shoots Andrei, and Andrei dies later in hospital, we may say that what Boris did was intentional under two descriptions: 'shooting Andrei' and 'killing Andrei' (the latter description would be relevant if Boris were to be charged with murder). The two descriptions, accordingly, apply to one action for Anscombe: they could both be elicited as answers in the course of a single series of 'Why?' questions. But if Boris shot Andrei at noon on Monday, while Andrei died at noon on Tuesday, there would seem to be a problem about when the killing occurred. If the shooting is (the same act as) the killing—and we seem to be committed to this—then the killing occurred at noon on Monday. But how is this possible, given that Andrei was alive at noon on Monday, and for some hours later? 'Boris killed Andrei at noon on Monday; six hours later, Andrei asked for water' sounds like a piece of nonsense.

---

[3] Ch. 1, pp. 24–6.

[4] For a very interesting discussion of the perfective/imperfective distinction as applied to action-verbs, see M. Thompson, *Life and Action* (Harvard University Press, forthcoming), Part II, ch. 4.

[5] J. J. Thomson, 'The Time of a Killing', *Journal of Philosophy*, 68 (1971), 115–32.

Anscombe's own response to this puzzle[6] is to say that the different descriptions of an action may come true of it at different times. Thus, at noon on Monday, the description 'killing of Andrei' would not yet be true of Boris's action—it would come to be true of it on Tuesday. So at 12.15 on Monday it would not be right to say, 'Boris has killed Andrei', while to say this at 12.15 on Tuesday would be to say something correct. This seems fine. But isn't there still a problem? For after Andrei's death, we can avail ourselves of the description 'killing of Andrei', and of the sentence 'Boris killed Andrei', and this in itself is enough for us to be able to construct the piece of nonsense just mentioned, if we can also regard whatever (now) goes for the shooting as going for the killing—specifically, that it occurred at noon on Monday. Anscombe appears to take a 'piece of nonsense' like the above as at worst an amusing way of putting things; thus she writes:

It is indeed not particularly odd to say 'The widow stuck a knife into her husband', though it may amuse one to reflect that this might be paraphrased as 'The thereby widowed lady stuck a knife into her husband'. This would be precisely parallel to 'The thereby act of killing Jim caused the gun to go off' [. . .] [I]t was because John caused the gun to go off that Jim died, and this somehow makes the proleptic definite description of his act [i.e. one applied by anticipation in view of what happened later] sound inappropriate and out of key. But there is no logical difficulty ...   (*UD*, 214)

The oddity referred to in this quotation—the sounding inappropriate and out of key—is compounded if we allow a sentence containing an act-description ('John's killing of Jim') to be rephrased as one containing the sentence of which the act-description is a nominalization ('John killed Jim'). Anscombe does allow this, and consequently seems happy with the sentence 'B died after A killed him' (*UD*, 215).

Oddity aside, however, would 'Andrei died twenty-four hours after Boris killed him' even be *true*? This is hard to swallow; and I don't think that Anscombe needed commit herself to it. For as she herself says, when criticizing Davidson's famous argument from adverbial modification: '[T]he adverbial modification that suits one verb may not consort well with another, and yet the two verbs may occur in different descriptions of the same action. Then you can't really break the connection between the adverbial phrase and the verb' (*UD*, 218). Maybe specifications of time or place are examples of adverbial phrases that cannot be safely disconnected from their verbs or verb-nominalizations. Anscombe in fact denies this (*UD*, 219), but gives no reason for doing so. And surely the case is strong that if any adverbial modifications are untransferable in the way she describes, then temporal modifications are, at least on occasion. The existence of Thomson's puzzle itself provides such a case. 'At noon on Monday' cannot safely be transferred from 'Boris shot Andrei' to 'Boris killed Andrei'.

With some verbs, the questions 'When?' and 'Where?' don't even have any answer at all, at any rate if they mean 'Precisely when/where?'—and this not

---

6 In *UD*; see *MPM*, 214–16.

because of fuzzy event-boundaries, but because the sense of the given verb does not bring with it a way of deciding such questions. Take the question 'Where?' as applied to 'George Bush was elected president'. What is the answer? In the USA, of course. But *where* in the USA? In all the polling stations? In the polling stations in which a majority of Republican votes were cast? In the counting rooms? At the place where the ceremony of his admission to office occurred? In all of these? Arguing the pros and cons here would be a pointless exercise, the sort that brings philosophy into disrepute. 'When did the killing of Andrei take place?' may lead to a similarly pointless debate.

Some of our difficulties, to be sure, stem from the fact that talk of one action with various descriptions is not wholly assimilable to talk of one object with various descriptions. But Anscombe's point about untransferable adverbial phrases has an analogue for objects: an adjectival phrase cannot always be disconnected from a given object-description. A tip left on a table for the waitress in a café may be a quantity of metal; but we cannot go from 'That tip isn't very generous' to 'That quantity of metal isn't very generous'. And the point about indeterminacy of temporal or spatial location, as applied to such events as Bush's election, also has an analogue for objects: a question like 'Where is Oxford University?' may even, as Ryle said, constitute a category-mistake, unless an answer like 'In England' is all that's wanted. (We could decide to restrict 'object' to spatially locatable things, but this just leaves us with spatially unlocatable things deprived of an epithet, and still to be given an account of.)

With objects, as with actions, it is possible to construct a series of wider and wider descriptions, with more and more being entailed, presupposed, or involved in each description. (This characterization of 'wideness' is of course sketchy.) But the construction of such a series has a point when it comes to actions, with no analogue for objects. The series, as we have said, can be elicited by repeatedly asking 'Why?' of the given action—but it also corresponds, in reverse, to the practical reasoning, actual or implicit, of the agent. This will be the topic of the next section.

2. PRACTICAL REASONING

2.1. Means and Ends

The final answer in a series of answers to the repeated question 'Why?' gives the overall aim or goal of the agent. A statement giving that goal can also serve as a starting point, a premiss, in a piece of practical reasoning, the subsequent steps recapitulating the answers in our original series but in reverse order—culminating in a conclusion that employs the action-description in the initial answer, e.g. 'pumping', or the corresponding verb ('pump'). The starting point of the practical reasoning is something wanted—e.g. that the government be overthrown. The subsequent steps give means: thus the first step might give a means of overthrowing the government, the next step giving a means for achieving that means, and so on.

We could if we liked lay out the reasoning implicit in Anscombe's example thus:

Aim: To overthrow the government.
P1. If the party members die, the government can be overthrown.
P2. If they drink poisoned water, the party members will die.
P3. If the water in their tank is poisoned, the party members will drink poisoned water.
P4. If I get this water into their tank, the water in the tank will be poisoned.
   .... .
Conclusion: So I'll pump this pump.

The relation of means to end may be one of cause to effect, but it may not; and the means may be a condition that is either necessary or sufficient (in the circumstances) for the end—or it may be neither necessary nor sufficient. Anscombe gives this example: I want to get my camera, so I go upstairs. Going upstairs may not be necessary, for I may be able to get my camera by asking my friend to get it for me. Nor could my going upstairs be called a sufficient condition. We might call it 'sufficient in those circumstances [i.e. along with my then going into the bedroom, walking to the mantelpiece, picking up the camera, etc.]', and by this phrase intend (a) that the total set of conditions was sufficient, and (b) that my going upstairs was a non-redundant member of that total set ('non-redundant' so as to exclude, say, my scratching my nose *en route*). My going upstairs would then count as an INUS-condition, in Mackie's phrase.[7]

Mackie intended INUS-conditions to be the same thing as causes, or causal conditions—and this brings us to the view of the means–end relation as a species of the cause–effect relation. As to Mackie's account of causality, the idea that there is always a 'total set of conditions' sufficient for a given effect is a mere item of faith, and is criticized as such in Anscombe's 'Causality and Determination'.[8] And there are other problems with Mackie's account. But whatever theory of causation one adopts, the means–end relation cannot be seen as a species of the cause–effect relation, for the simple reason that there are plenty of cases where the means is neither a cause nor a causal condition of the end: for instance, if (feeling rebellious) I drive the wrong way down a one-way street in order to break the law. My driving would here be a formal cause, not an efficient cause, of the law's being broken.

---

[7] J. L. Mackie, 'Causes and Conditions', *American Philosophical Quarterly*, 2 (1965), 245–64. INUS: Insufficient condition that is a Non-redundant part of an Unnecessary and Sufficient condition.   [8] See Ch. 5, §2.1.

If means–end reasoning cannot, as such, be understood in terms of causality, nor in terms of necessary or sufficient conditions, how then is it to be understood? Anscombe writes:

In order to make sense of 'I do P with a view to Q', we must see how the future state of affairs Q is supposed to be a possible later stage in proceedings of which the action P is an earlier stage [. . .] I shall not try to elaborate [this] vague and general formula [. . .] For of course it is not necessary to exercise these general notions in order to say 'I do P so that Q'. All that it is necessary to understand is that to say, in one form or another: 'But Q won't happen, even if you do P', or 'but it will happen whether you do P or not' is, in some way, to contradict the intention.   (*I*, 36)

As her discussion reveals, Anscombe is focusing on what makes such an utterance as 'I do P so that Q' an *intelligible* one. In some contexts, saying 'I do P so that Q' will be unintelligible, e.g. if it is clear that if you do P, Q won't happen; and one can roughly delineate conditions of intelligibility by excluding whatever makes for unintelligibility. We have already encountered Anscombe's employment of this approach, and noted the Wittgensteinian rationale for it.[9] We might, however, wish to exclude her condition, that it must not be the case that Q will happen whether you do P or not. For the set-up may be such that if you don't do P, somebody else will, in which case Q will come about whether or not *you* do P. Such set-ups are of particular interest because of what they show about personal responsibility. It is often given as an excuse for doing something bad that somebody else would do it if you didn't, and this excuse would seem unassailable were we to adopt Anscombe's condition; indeed it would allow one to say: 'I admit I shot Casey in the head, but I didn't do so *in order* that Casey should die, since I knew that O'Brien would have killed him if I hadn't.' If this form of self-exculpation works, then the individual members of any malicious mob can get away with murder.[10] It is certain that Anscombe would want to rule out this mode of reasoning.

Why is 'I am doing P so that Q, but Q won't happen' an unintelligible statement? Isn't a person an authority about what further intentions he happens to have? And mightn't he have a further intention that Q should come about, while also finding within himself the belief that Q won't come about? Perhaps this would be strange and unusual, but couldn't it for all that be the case? The picture here is one of a present state of mind, which the person knows of and can report: the Cartesian picture that we already encountered once or twice in Chapter 1. Anscombe is surely right that saying 'I am

---

[9] See e.g. Ch. 1, pp. 40–1.
[10] In response to this, a consequentialist (e.g.) might allow that one does indeed intend Q if one does P in such a case, but then claim that it is *all right* to intend Q (given that Q would happen anyway). This would still give *carte blanche* to the mob members—*une carte même plus blanche*, in fact. Maybe if you didn't do P, someone else would do it, but in a nastier way than you? If this is an excuse, you're all right so long as the person next to you in the mob is even more vicious than you are. For more on these issues in relation to consequentialism, see Ch. 3, §4.1.

doing P so that Q, but Q won't happen' is not like reporting a nonsensical dream:

A man's intention in acting is not so private and interior a thing that he has absolute authority in saying *what* it is—as he has absolute authority in saying *what* he dreamt. (If what a man says he dreamed does not make sense, that doesn't mean that his saying he dreamed it does not make sense.)   (*I*, 36)

The intelligibility of a statement of further intention is constrained by what others can make sense of. The person's own statements have a criterial weight; but they must fit in a certain way with what others might predict, and might conceive of as predictable, both as to the person's behaviour and as to its outcomes.[11] As Anscombe puts it, we must be able to *see* how the future state of affairs Q is supposed to be a possible later stage in proceedings of which the action P is an earlier stage. Some 'proceedings' strike us as unified, as patterns (in both senses of that word), others do not; and this fact is what regulates intelligibility here. It is also, by the way, what enables us to teach and learn such primitive causal concepts as *push, cut, squash*, etc., whose importance for the general topic of causality Anscombe brings out elsewhere.[12]

Constraints on intelligibility analogous to those mentioned in the last paragraph apply also in the case of trying. If you know that you cannot get unaided to the moon, then you cannot (e.g. by flapping your arms) *try* to get to the moon—'I am trying to get to the moon' is here unintelligible. Descartes said that the human will was infinite,[13] and by this appeared to mean that there was nothing that you could not will to do, even though your capacities are finite, and known by you to be finite; and we see here just the picture of willing as private and interior which Anscombe is attacking.

Another related point concerns statements about what you are going to do—those expressions of intention for the future that we looked at in §2.2 of the last chapter. 'I am going to φ, but shall not φ' is a sort of a contradiction, and 'I intend to φ, but shall not φ' is no better off. These statements are akin to Moore's paradox, as exemplified by 'I believe that it is raining, but it isn't raining'. If 'I intend ...' and 'I believe ...' were ways of reporting present states of mind, we should not have anything that could be called paradoxical or unintelligible, merely something that was (possibly) strange and unusual. After all, your state of mind is one thing and the weather is another—and the same goes for your present state of mind and your future actions.

Anscombe discusses 'I am going to φ, but shall not φ' in the final section of *Intention*, where she calls a statement of this form 'a contradiction of a sort'. But she goes on to point out that a reflective agent will be aware that there's many a slip 'twixt cup and lip, and that in some circumstances the possibility of being

---

[11] Cf. Ch. 1, p. 12.   [12] In *CD*. Cf. Ch. 5, p. 178.
[13] Descartes, *Meditations*, Med. IV.

prevented from doing something is a very real one, while in others, the possibility of one's not sticking to one's intention is likewise very real.

[I]f one is considering the fact that one may not do what one is determined to do, then the right thing to say really *is* 'I am going to do this...unless I do not do it'. [. . .] It is for this reason that in some cases one can be as certain as possible that one will do something, and yet intend not to do it. [. . .] [A] man could be as certain as possible that he will break down under torture, and yet determined not to break down.   (*I*, 93, 94)

If one can be as certain as possible that one will do something, and yet intend not to do it, doesn't this mean that one should, in such a case, say: 'I intend not to φ, but I shall φ'? And wouldn't this be the same as 'I am not going to φ, but I shall φ'? But aren't these 'contradictions of a sort'?

'I won't manage to remain silent under torture, but I intend to' seems to be different from 'I won't manage to get to the moon unaided, but I intend to'. There is at least something employable as a means towards one's end, in the first case: namely, steeling oneself, holding the idea of resistance before one's mind, etc. So one can at least try to remain silent. But not even flapping your arms could be called a means of getting to the moon, for anything is as good as anything else when it comes to doing that—you might as well shut your eyes and intone 'Luna, luna'. Anscombe says that you could be as certain as possible that you will break under torture; but just as things may not turn out the way you expect in ways that thwart your ends, they may also turn out otherwise than you expect in ways that help you. It is at least *possible* that the torturer will be interrupted—or that you will actually forget the names of your accomplices—or that you will surprise yourself. And 'possible' doesn't here mean just 'logically possible'. It is not in the relevant sense possible that you'll get to the moon by flapping your arms.

'Why are you steeling yourself?' 'So as to resist the torture.' If one added: 'but I won't manage to', wouldn't this be to give up one's intention? Any straight expression of belief about what will happen seems in fact to be out of place. And there would be something absurd in applying a criterion of belief, such as what odds the person would give that so-and-so will happen. A criterion like that is meant for more everyday, or anyway calmer, situations. In such an extreme situation as that of torture, the question 'What does he think is going to happen?' ('Does he believe that he will break?') may have no real answer. Perhaps it is significant that Anscombe does not actually envisage a person's saying or thinking 'I intend to φ, but I shall not φ', only mentioning the form 'I am going to do this...unless I do not do it'.

There are a variety of psychologically interesting cases here. A full discussion of the issues would cover the topic of hope, especially the kind which is called 'hoping against hope'. Also worth mentioning are those *motives*, like honour or the love of truth, which can lead people to do things they know will fail. When Polish cavalrymen galloped towards the advancing German tanks in 1939, the motive must often have been sheer patriotism, or glory—motives which were manifested in (maybe in some sense 'requiring') actions whose proper descriptions certainly did involve ends, such as stopping the tanks. But the question 'Why is he charging towards those tanks?' would not have been completely, or even aptly, answered by saying 'So as to help stop their advance'. A more fundamental answer would be 'From a sense of patriotic duty', or some such. To be killed in action, and hence to fail to achieve one's objectives in one sense, can in another sense be to succeed gloriously. As we saw in the last chapter, what Anscombe calls 'interpretative motives' are quite different from intentions with which one acts.[14] For these reasons, it won't really do to ascribe to the Polish cavalrymen the thought 'We intend to stop the tanks, but we shall not stop them'.

2.2. Theoretical Reasoning and Practical Reasoning

We have been looking at the constraints on intelligibility when it comes to statements of further intention, and statements giving means to one's ends. Delineating such constraints casts light upon what is involved in means–end reasoning, and hence upon what is involved in practical reasoning. I said that means–end reasoning could not, as such, be elucidated by reference to causality; but of course the cause–effect relation is central to such reasoning, and may even be taken as giving the paradigm for the relation of means to ends. But if we look at a bit of practical reasoning laid out as above (p. 51), and then ask 'What *makes* this a piece of practical reasoning?', it is tempting to reply simply: 'It is just like theoretical reasoning, but with a special starting point and a special conclusion.' The reasoning itself involves a series of conditionals, the mirror image of which would, in theoretical reasoning, allow the repeated use of *modus ponens*; the logical relations between the steps (P1, P2, etc.) being just those that you would get in a piece of theoretical reasoning. The truth of the several conditionals—if they are true—may have to do with the cause–effect relation, but it is their being conditionals that is important for the validity of the reasoning, and hence for its being that kind of *reasoning*.

Practical reasoning can indeed appear like the mirror image of theoretical reasoning.[15] This relates to the fact that the series of answers to 'Why?' is the mirror image of the corresponding piece of practical reasoning, for the former series can easily be converted into an argument: 'I am pumping this handle; if I pump this handle, poisoned water will get into the tank; if water gets into the tank, they will drink it ... Therefore, the government will be overthrown.' Anscombe holds that what distinguishes practical from theoretical reasoning is the different uses to which certain logical structures can be put. One and the

---

[14] See pp. 31–3.
[15] The point is made by Anthony Kenny; see his 'Practical Inference', *Analysis*, 26/3 (1966), 65–73.

same structure of conditional propositions can be used, either (a) to derive a conclusion from a supposed truth, or (b) to derive a course of action from a supposed aim. If our concern is (a), we will lay out the structure in one way, while if our concern is (b) we will lay out the same structure in a different way, one that is a sort of mirror image of the first way.

In her article 'Practical Inference',[16] she illustrates this idea by contrasting *three* different uses to which one and the same logical structure can be put: the practical, the investigatory, and the theoretical. The respective aims of these three modes of argument can be given thus:

1. To attain: spectacular plant growth
2. To investigate: why there is spectacular plant growth
3. To prove: that there will be spectacular plant growth.

There are then two premisses:

P1. If plants are fed with substance X, there will be spectacular plant growth.
P2. If substance X is in the soil, the plants will be fed with it.

With the practical aim (1), and the two premisses, we may derive the conclusion: To put substance X in the soil. With the investigatory aim (2), and the two premisses, we may derive the conclusion: To examine the soil so as to check whether substance X is present.

The practical and investigatory conclusions correspond to the starting point of the theoretical argument, which is standardly put down as a premiss: 'Substance X is in the soil.' And the theoretical conclusion, 'There will be spectacular plant growth', corresponds to what were the starting points, and aims, of the practical and investigatory arguments, (1) and (3).

This is how Anscombe presents it. She could alternatively have taken the theoretical aim as: To find what follows from the proposition: that substance X is in the soil. In that case, the 'aim' and the 'starting point' would be (in effect) identical for each of the three modes of argument; but the *content* of the theoretical aim would of course differ from the contents of the other two aims. None of this affects the force of Anscombe's point, which is that what distinguishes these modes of reasoning is not that each has a special subject matter, but that each puts a certain logical structure to a particular use.

We have given the starting point in a piece of practical reasoning as 'something wanted'. This is importantly different from giving the starting point as a premiss of the form 'I/we want such-and-such'. A premiss of this form *may* figure in a practical argument, and Anscombe illustrates this with an example of Anselm Müller's:

Anyone who wants to kill his parents will be helped to get rid of this trouble by consulting a psychiatrist.

---

[16] *PI*, in *HLAE*. I have slightly altered Anscombe's example.

I want to kill my parents.

If I consult a psychiatrist I shall be helped to get rid of this trouble.

NN is a psychiatrist.

So I'll consult NN.   (*PI*, 115)

Here one does not identify with one's parricidal want, but rather treats it as something to be deliberated about—it is one of the facts of the case. By contrast, the 'thing wanted' is: to get rid of the trouble. One's reaching the conclusion, 'So I'll consult NN', *shows* that one wants this; that one argues as above, reaching the decision that one does, is a criterion of wanting. Hence 'I want to get rid of the trouble' is not needed as an additional premiss. In the same way, the premiss 'Substance X is in the soil', in the earlier bit of theoretical reasoning, was adequate on its own; we do not need 'I believe that substance X is in the soil'. When the theoretical argument is actually used by someone, so that premisses and conclusion get asserted, this *shows* that the person believes the premisses. His arguing in that way is a criterion of belief. These facts confirm the point that theoretical and practical reasoning make use of the same material (the same logical structures). The latter is not about wants, desires, etc., any more than the former is about beliefs.

Here is another piece of practical reasoning, imitating an example of Aristotle's, from the pages of *Intention*:

Vitamin X is good for all men over 60

Pigs' tripes are full of Vitamin X

I'm a man over 60

Here's some pigs' tripes.   (*I*, 60)

Let's assume the conclusion to be: 'So I'll have some of what's here.' In that case, what would the thing wanted be? What would be the *aim* of the agent—the starting point of the practical argument? Presumably, 'To have what's good for me'. But what sort of an aim is that? Does it mean 'To have something that's good for me'?—or again, 'To have everything that's good for me'? The latter is an insane aim.[17] So let us assume that the person's aim is the former one. Now very often, if you want to eat something that's good for you, you needn't eat the thing before you that's good for you; you could go elsewhere and eat something that's good for you. So the aim together with the premisses do not necessitate the conclusion, if this means ruling out any alternative conclusion. In this respect, practical reasoning is unlike theoretical reasoning. But given that practical reasoning is a sort of mirror image of theoretical reasoning, this 'non-necessitating' feature of the former is explicable: a theoretical conclusion can be deduced from more than one set of premisses, and the conclusion of a

---

[17] Cf. 'It is necessary for all men over 60 to eat any food containing Vitamin X that they ever come across', and 'Do everything conducive to not having a car crash' (*I*, 60, 58).

practical argument corresponds to a premiss in a theoretical argument. Thus, the theoretical conclusion 'I will eat something good for me' can be deduced from Anscombe's propositions, above, plus the premiss (A) 'I will have what's here [i.e. pigs' tripes]'—or from those propositions plus a different premiss (B), 'I will have some Vitamin X pills, available from the chemist down the road'. (The propositions about pigs' tripes would then be redundant, of course.) The two different theoretical premisses (A) and (B) correspond to different conclusions in pieces of practical reasoning.

But what sort of an aim is 'To have something that's good for me'? It is surely an odd one to go out into the world with. Is it even the aim of a person who helps himself to certain foodstuffs when standing in a lunch queue? If so, then it will very likely be an aim that only occurs to the person when confronted with the foodstuff; he might indeed say, as he reaches for a plate of tripes, 'I think I'll have something that's good for me'. But of course he wouldn't while doing this say 'I think I'll have something or other that's good for me'; the 'something' that he is after is really *this* thing. The tripes themselves appear to him under the aspect of *food that is good for me*. To reiterate our earlier point, what *shows* that his aim is to eat something that's good for him is the agent's taking certain propositions as leading to 'So I'll have some of this'. He need not have in any way formulated or inwardly produced the thought 'I will have something that's good for me'. And his taking the plate of tripes shows (in this context) that he has drawn that conclusion, from propositions he believes true: it is what it *is* to draw that conclusion here. This is why it is natural to say, as Aristotle did, that the conclusion of a practical argument is an action; but trying to φ is as good a criterion of having drawn the practical conclusion 'So I'll φ' as actually φ-ing is, so I have preferred not to speak that way, and nor does Anscombe.

2.3. Heteronomous Action: The Ironical Slave

Both the person who takes the plate of tripes and the person who merely tries to can be said to have drawn the conclusion 'So I'll have some'. So can the person who says or writes 'So I'll have some' when treating the practical premisses as a classroom example. [18] This last person sees what action there would be reason to do, given the truth of the premisses and a certain (natural) aim, while the first two people aim to perform that action for those reasons and with that aim. In virtue of what is it true that the third person *does* see what action there would be reason to do, etc.? Partly, that he says or writes the conclusion; also, that he can explain the argument, or explain it well enough. But for him, the argument is 'idle', having no practical application.

There is a fourth kind of case mentioned by Anscombe, which we may call the case of the Ironical Slave. The Ironical Slave draws a practical conclusion from

---

[18] Cf. Aristotle, *Nicomachean Ethics*, 1147[a]27–8; and *I*, 60.

premisses that include a statement of a 'thing wanted', but where what is wanted is wanted *by someone else*. He is not given an order. The reason for obeying an order may indeed be in terms other than its being a means to an end one has oneself—in particular, when the reason is simply 'Because he told me to'. But the Ironical Slave is in a certain sense more autonomous than that: he determines on a course of action himself. It is just that his reasons for doing what he does are, in effect, somebody else's reasons. Thus, I might say to you that this message is to get to N by four o'clock, and that unless you take it to him, it won't get to him by that time.

I then hand you the message with nothing more said, whereupon you carry it to N. (Such is our relationship.) [. . .] Asked for the grounds of your action, you point to *my* grounds, as a man may point to his orders.

You are then speaking as one who had a certain role, but whose own objectives do not yet come into the picture. [. . .]

Just as, without believing it, I can draw a [theoretical] conclusion from your assertions, so our ironical slave can draw a conclusion in action from the specified objective and the assertion made by his master.   (*PI*, 136, 137, 139)

Of course, a person *might* have as his objective that the other person's objectives be promoted. But Anscombe insists that there need here be no such objective, any more than there need be the objective of avoiding punishment or of earning praise. The role of the one acting is then that of subordinate. And this does not mean that he has as his aim 'to act as a subordinate', for acting as a subordinate just *is* acting for reasons that are not your own, but another's. It is like doing something 'in order to have revenge': revenge just *is* acting for certain backward-looking reasons. 'To act as a subordinate' does not give an independently describable aim, any more than does 'in order to have revenge'.[19]

But if the person who reached for the pigs' tripes showed what he wanted in so acting, without his having had to think or say 'I want to eat what's good for me', shouldn't we likewise say that the Ironical Slave, in taking the message (in those circumstances), shows what it is he wants—namely, that N receive the message? No. For the criteria for what someone wants, in doing something, connect in a certain way with the reasons that they can or can't give. If asked, 'Do you yourself want N to receive the message?', the Ironical Slave would probably reply 'I don't really care'.[20] And the reason is that if he replied 'Yes', the further question 'But why do you want *that*?' would be impossible for him to answer without being *ad hoc* (we can suppose that he knows nothing of what's in the message and nothing about N); and yet it is a question that demands an answer, and to which 'I just do, that's all' is not a proper answer. By contrast, if we asked the man

---

[19] See Ch. 1, pp. 31–2.
[20] For a discussion of this sort of reply, and of the criteria of truthfulness of such replies, see *Intention*, sec. 25.

in the lunch queue whether he wanted to eat what was good for him, in taking the tripes, he would be able to answer 'Yes'. He might indeed be stumped if we went on, 'But why do you want *that?*'—but this is because 'X is good for me' counts in itself as a reason: it already mentions a 'desirability characterisation', in Anscombe's phrase. (More of which anon.)

The Ironical Slave acts intentionally. He can answer a series of 'Why?' questions:

'Why are you catching the bus?'
'To get to Albert Street.'
'Why are you going to that street?'
'To visit N.'
'Why are you visiting N?'
'To give him this message.'

What is the last answer in the series of answers? Is it: 'To give N this message'? Or is there a further answer, an answer to the question 'Why are you conveying this message to N?', namely: 'My master wants him to get it'?

Now Anscombe *could*, I think, allow this last reply as one which the Ironical Slave would give, if it is possible to understand that reply as simply enabling the enquirer to see 'what the situation is'—rather than as giving a reason, of the sort that corresponds to a premiss in a practical argument mirroring the series of 'Why?' questions. An analogy might be made with certain cases involving belief. Imagine that Sally's flatmate, John, is putting on his coat to leave. Sally is on the phone to her friend, Sue, and she tells Sue that John is about to leave, adding, 'He's going into town'. Their dialogue continues:

'Why do you think that?'
'Because he's going to the chemist.'
'What makes you think he's going to the chemist?'
'He's coughing a lot.'
'But why do you think he's coughing a lot?'
'Because I can hear him.'

(Sue is strangely inquisitive.)

You can infer 'John is going into town' from 'John is going to the chemist', hence the latter can serve as a reason for believing the former. The same goes for 'John is going to the chemist' and 'John is coughing a lot'. (Both inferences would be facilitated by background knowledge, of geography and psychology respectively.) But you cannot in the same sense infer 'John is coughing a lot' from 'I can hear John coughing a lot'. Either this last already involves the assertion that John is coughing a lot, and so would not give a reason for belief to anyone who might wonder whether he is coughing a lot—or it is some sort of 'sense-datum report'. The problems with the latter notion are notorious, and I will not go into them here. Suffice it to say that if 'I can hear him coughing' were a sense-datum report, then the inference to 'He is coughing' would be problematic, as being an inference to a proposition that is essentially unverifiable. For the only possible verification would have to be in terms of the sense-datum report itself and ones like it, and if inference and verification thus collapse into one, we are left with an unstomachable phenomenalism.

I am not saying that P can only provide a reason for believing Q if Q is inferable from P. 'I was taught that Q' can, in many situations, provide a sufficient reason for believing Q, both for the person saying it and for the person to whom it is said, without the need for background knowledge, e.g. of the reliability of one's teacher. But there is an explanation for this: the practice of education requires that, in certain contexts, being told something counts as a reason for believing it. No such explanation will apply to a statement like 'I can hear him'.

So what is 'Because I can hear him' meant to achieve? What it achieves, surely, is to tell the enquirer what the situation is: that you are in a privileged epistemological position, able to give direct reports about John, in particular in terms of sounds produced by him. (You could say that you 'find yourself able' to give such reports, though that way of putting it is a little quaint.) In telling Sue that she can hear John coughing a lot, Sally does indeed give Sue a reason to believe that John is coughing a lot, which she might express by saying, 'Sally said that she could hear John coughing a lot'—or alternatively, 'Sally was in a position to hear whether John was coughing a lot, and she said that he was'. But these do not give *Sally's* reasons for belief.

Analogous remarks, it could be argued, go for the Ironical Slave's final answer to 'Why?'—if it is his final answer—'Because my master wants it'. Just as 'I can hear John coughing' does not serve as the basis for Sally's belief that John is coughing, so 'My master wants N to receive this message' does not serve as the starting point of a practical argument whose conclusion is 'So I'll take N the message'. If this is right, then the *real* final answer to the series of 'Why?' questions, given that the unity of the series is meant to reflect the practical reasoning of the agent, will after all be 'To get this message to N'. This gives the overall aim of the Ironical Slave, the 'thing wanted'. But for Anscombe, it is not the slave himself who wants this thing.

It may be useful to compare the Ironical Slave with someone who has been *trained* a certain way. Take a child who has been trained to fold her napkin after she eats, so that she does so even when alone—though she won't be particularly put out or upset if she can't fold it, or forgets to. The point of folding her napkin (if it has one) hasn't been explained to her, and she hasn't been told that any bad consequences will flow from not folding it. One day, the girl's chair is so positioned that in order to ensure a proper 'approach' to the napkin on the table, the child needs to shift the chair in a certain way, which she does. Why does she shift the chair? So as to be at the right angle to her napkin. Why be at that angle to her napkin? So that she can fold it. That is her overall aim. Is it something that she can be said to *want*? Folding her napkin, even in this situation, may be something as automatic as holding onto the banister when going down stairs—and 'automatic' does not mean 'unintentional' or 'reflex'. It goes against the grain to say that a person holds onto the banister because she *wants* to, especially if there is no question of her losing her balance; and surely we might feel the same way about napkin-folding. The phrase 'thing wanted' would then appear inapposite, given that nobody else can really be said to want the napkin folded. 'Specific objective' would do better, or just 'end'.

And yet couldn't the child give a reply to 'Why do you want to fold your napkin?', were we to ask that question, a reply that gave a desirability characterization?—namely: 'Because you're meant to'. If she did give such a reply, it would be possible to connect wanting with reasons, just as we did in the case of the tripes-eater. But what if she didn't feel like giving any such reply? She might just shrug; or she might say, 'I always do'—a reply which can hardly be said to give a reason. Then again, if she said, 'I just want to', wouldn't that be a perfectly good reply? After all, doing the things you were brought up to do is a natural and normal thing, like whistling or doodling.[21] There is a question now whether her 'I just want to' really gives us grounds for saying that the child *wants* to fold her napkin, for as an idiom it seems to be very like the simple answer 'For no particular reason'. But let us for the sake of argument take the answer as an expression of wanting, sufficient in itself as an answer to 'Why?' because doing the things you were brought up to do is a natural and normal thing. If we now return to the Ironical Slave, we shall note that delivering a message to N by four o'clock is not as such a normal or natural activity, hence the appropriateness of the question 'Why?' in that case, and the inadequacy of the answer 'I just want to'. If the slave had been *ordered* to take the message, he could have answered 'Why?' by saying 'Because I was told to' (cf. 'Because you're meant to'); but he has not been ordered. If there is a reply to 'Why?' in this case, it is, as we saw, 'Because my master wants it'. Anscombe, I have suggested, must construe such an answer as simply conveying what the situation is, rather than as giving a proper reason; for if it did the latter, the 'thing wanted' would appear to be that the master's wants be satisfied, and we are taking it that such a want need not be attributed to the slave. But if 'Because my master wants it' simply conveys what the situation is, why isn't that also true of 'Because I was told to'? Alternatively, if the latter can count as giving a reason, why can't the former?

A moment ago I said that the practice of education requires that being told something counts, in certain contexts, as a reason for believing it. A parallel fact holds of orders. The language-game of giving and receiving orders *goes with* its counting in certain contexts as a reason for doing X that you were ordered to do X. Within a practice involving orders, people must be able to understand

---

[21] Cf. Ch. 1, pp. 40–1.

'So-and-so ordered it' as giving a sufficient answer both to 'Why should I do that?' and, correlatively, to 'Why are you doing that?'. By contrast, 'So-and-so wants it' does not in itself count as a sufficient answer to 'Why?'. That a person wants something does not give a reason for procuring it, not even a reason for the person himself. (This connects with the point that a practical argument will not include 'I want ...' as one of its premisses.)

Of course in reality, if a master said to his slave, 'I want N to receive this letter', that utterance might well have the force of an order; but we are trying to imagine a case *not* like that. Maybe a Hanger-On would have served our purpose better than an Ironical Slave. And if a Hanger-On says, 'I'm taking this message to N; the Big Cheese wants him to get it by four o'clock', we learn, in Anscombe's phrase, that *such is their relationship* (the relationship between the Big Cheese and the Hanger-On). It is a relationship in which the Hanger-On does what the Big Cheese wants, not necessarily what he himself wants.

Since Hume, many philosophers have taken it that all voluntary actions are done because the agent wants something or other. Wanting to chew your food might, as Hume would say, be a calm want, with little force or vivacity—but a want it is, nevertheless. And if it seems odd to describe someone at dinner as wanting to chew his food, a Gricean might account for this oddity by appeal to the blinding obviousness of the remark, and to the conversational rule against stating the blindingly obvious. The Gricean gambit establishes very little on its own; after all, a philosopher who tried to account for the oddity of saying 'I am located just behind my eyes' by calling it blindingly obvious would have some work to do. The proper use of the gambit is alongside more positive argumentation, and such argumentation is certainly required when it comes to the view that all voluntary action is accompanied by wanting. We mustn't forget how natural it is to say such things as, 'I didn't *want* to go to the funeral, but I thought I'd better'. A philosopher may reply, 'Ah, so you *did* want to go: for you wanted to do what you thought you ought to do'; but is it so clear that the philosopher is right and the other person wrong?

One thing to watch out for here is a trap laid by the English language itself. The denial of 'He wants to chew his food', i.e. 'He doesn't want to chew his food', illogically signifies a want not to do something, rather than the absence of a want. So it can seem that in denying the want-to-chew, we are landing ourselves with the even stranger want-not-to-chew. But of course that appearance is deceptive.

The temptation to regard all voluntary action as explicable by reference to the agent's wants arises in large part from construing wants as inner causes, whose presence can then be used to distinguish the voluntary from the involuntary. Enough has been said in the last chapter concerning this kind of causalism. Wanting, like intending, is to be understood more by reference to the space of reasons than by reference to hypothetical causal stories. The point can be illustrated by the first-person plural case: in the context of practical reasoning, the 'thing wanted' may be wanted by a group of people, who could then say, 'We want ... ', where this cannot be understood as expressing a conglomeration of individuals' wants, and to that extent cannot be seen as a psychological-causal report. Examples might be: 'We want to form a team', or 'We at Blah plc want to apologize for the company's mistakes [and are therefore obtaining the addresses of our inadvertent victims]'. The methodological solipsist[22] will only tie himself in knots if he tries to understand such statements in terms of an 'I want ... ' attributable to the several group members, in particular because (e.g.) forming a team and apologizing as a company are not actions performable by individuals. What makes a group want a want is its role, actual or potential, in practical arguments, such arguments being public both in their manifestation (in boardrooms and other places), and in the standards of reasoning by reference to which alone they can be called arguments, or trains of thought, at all. And what goes for group wants surely goes for individual wants. 'I want' and 'We want' employ the same concept.

In the next section we shall further examine the limits on wanting, and on what things can be wanted.

3. THE ENDS OF ACTION

3.1. Wanting

'The primitive sign of wanting is *trying to get*', writes Anscombe (*I*, 68). In human behaviour there are further signs of wanting, in addition to the primitive one of trying to get—such as trying to bring about, planning to bring about, planning to get, etc. These marks of wanting allow us to see how wanting is different from wishing or hoping or the feeling of desire; and it also puts limits upon what can be wanted. 'The range [of wantable things] is restricted to present or future objects and future states of affairs' (*I*, 67). You can wish that you had drunk less beer last night, but you can't want to have drunk less, since what has already happened cannot be changed. Michael Dummett has famously argued for the conceptual possibility of affecting the past;[23] if he is right, then Anscombe's restriction on the range of wantable things holds only empirically and contingently. But presumably it holds even so.

Are there any other restrictions on what can be wanted? Typically, what you want is something that you have some idea of when you say 'I want ... '; for how could you try to get something (or bring it about, or whatever) if you had no idea of what it was you were trying to get? It would surely be like trying to get to

[22] As personified by J. Fodor; see his 'Methodological Solipsism as a Research Strategy in Cognitive Science', *Behavioral and Brain Sciences*, 3 (1980), 63–73.

[23] Michael Dummett, 'Bringing about the Past', in *Truth and Other Enigmas* (London: Duckworth, 1978), 333–50.

the moon unaided when you believe that you can't get there unaided. But can't someone say, 'What is it I want? I feel strangely ill at ease'? Such uses of 'want' only exist because of the fact that the dissatisfaction in question can often be retrospectively granted an object—e.g. if the person goes on to exclaim, 'I know! I want some noise about me; this silence is oppressive'. Wanting something without having an idea of what it is you want is like having a name on the tip of your tongue: as Wittgenstein saw, we classify such phenomena in the way we do because of the subsequent exclamations and avowals that often follow, and seem to consummate, them.[24] In the case of 'I want ... ', if such subsequent utterances did not occur as they do, the phenomenon in question would be that of objectless 'wanting'—which is not really wanting at all, but rather something like a vague feeling of dissatisfaction.

So an object of wanting has to be taken as attainable by the person who wants it, and likewise has to be conceptualizable by that person. But apart from these restrictions, can't one want anything at all? Many philosophers have thought so, and have consequently taken it that 'I want X' isn't the sort of statement that needs explaining or making intelligible. For a philosopher of an empiricist bent, 'I want X' is a report of a certain inner state; if one knows *what* inner state the person refers to by 'want X', then no further explanation is necessary of what he means. In the same way, if one knows what inner state a person refers to by 'pain', then no explanation of his statement 'I am in pain' is necessary. But in addition to this empiricist picture of mental states, there is, in the case of wanting, a kind of individualism, even existentialism, associated with the view that anything can be wanted: 'What I happen to want is my affair; I don't need to explain myself to anyone.' For R.M. Hare,[25] one chooses one's moral principles, and the choice thus made is at bottom an expression of a basic preference, or wanting—basic in being unsusceptible of further justification or criticism. You can be taken to task for internal inconsistency (which is meant to include hypocrisy), but not for any given preference you happen to have. In particular, you can't be taken to task on grounds either of rationality or intelligibility. The ethical implications of such a view are quite radical, and Anscombe's interest in the topic of wanting is largely motivated by the desire to give a clear account of wanting, suitable for an adequate ethics.

But is not anything wantable, or at least any perhaps attainable thing? It will be instructive to anyone who thinks this to approach someone and say: 'I want a saucer of mud' or 'I want a twig of mountain ash'. He is likely to be asked what for; to which let him reply that he does not want it *for* anything, he just wants it. It is likely that the other will then perceive that a philosophical example is all that is in question, and will pursue the matter no further; but supposing that he did not realise this, and yet did not dismiss our man as a dull babbling loon, would he not try to find out in what aspect the object desired

---

[24] Cf. Wittgenstein, *Philosophical Investigations*, p. 219.
[25] See e.g. R. M. Hare, *Freedom and Reason* (Oxford: Clarendon Press, 1963), Part I.

is desirable? Does it serve as a symbol? Is there something delightful about it? Does the man want to have something to call his own, and no more?   (*I*, 70–1)

In this example, the thing putatively wanted is a material object, a saucer of mud. (The want is general, not particular: any saucer of mud will do.) But Anscombe's point applies to any object of wanting. 'I want to walk to Istanbul', or 'I want the person living at No. 46 to wear green tomorrow', cry out for explanation as much as does 'I want a saucer of mud'.

We saw in the last chapter that the reply 'For no particular reason' is an adequate answer to 'Why are you doing that?' when—very roughly—the activity in question is a natural or normal one for human beings, or maybe for human beings of a certain kind (to which the agent belongs). Similar remarks go for the answer 'I want to'. For an activity that is not, as I have been putting it, normal or natural, a reason is needed both for the activity and for wanting to go in for it, if the activity is to count as voluntary or sane, in the following sense: if no reason can be given, then we must ask, 'Why say that the person *wants* to do this at all, rather than that he is doing it compulsively or instinctively or robotically or randomly?' We can say a similar thing in relation to putatively wanted material objects, for insofar as the primitive sign of wanting is trying to get, the concept of getting is not a starkly behaviouristic one:

But cannot a man *try to get* anything gettable? He can certainly go after objects that he sees, fetch them, and keep them near him; perhaps he then vigorously protects them from removal. But then, this is already beginning to make sense: these are his possessions, he wanted to own them; he may be idiotic, but his 'wanting' is recognisable as such.   (*I*, 71)

Anscombe further imagines a man who expresses the want for a pin, is given one, and promptly puts it down and forgets about it:

It is not at all clear what it meant to say: this man simply wanted a pin. Of course, if he is careful always to carry the pin in his hand thereafter, or at least for a time, we may perhaps say: it seems he really wanted that pin. Then perhaps, the answer to 'What do you want it for?' may be 'to carry it about with me', as a man may want a stick. But here again there is further characterisation: 'I don't feel comfortable without it; it is pleasant to have one' and so on.   (*I*, 71)

What is essential is that the thing wanted, be it material object or action or state of affairs, should be something characterizable by the person as somehow desirable. The person should be able to give some desirability characterization of the thing wanted, in Anscombe's phrase. The range of possible desirability characterizations is very wide, but for these too there is a requirement of intelligibility. 'Because it's a Tuesday' does not without further explanation show why some proposed action is desirable. And while 'For the fun of it' is something that *can* show why something is wanted, it will not do so (without further explanation) if the something is, say, standing with your mouth open for ten minutes. Behind such requirements for intelligibility there is, to repeat, the question: 'Why call this thing/activity/state of affairs something *wanted* by the person?', and related questions, such as: 'Why call this *getting* an object?' and 'Why call that *fun*?' None of these questions is properly answered by saying, 'Because the person himself calls it that'.

These remarks elaborate what was said in the previous section: wanting, like intending, is to be understood more by reference to the space of reasons than by reference to hypothetical causal stories—or, for that matter, by reference to introspectible inner states.

In the context of practical reasoning, the thing wanted is your *end*. An end may be a means to a further end, of course; though we have talked of a practical argument as having a single starting point, namely the 'thing wanted', a subsection of a practical argument can itself be taken as a practical argument, with its starting point being an end (e.g. 'To replenish the water tank', instead of 'To overthrow the government'). But there is a sense in which there is just one practical argument with a single starting point, an overall end. For Anscombe, the overall end is that which has a desirability characterization, i.e. an answer to 'What for?' that doesn't give a further end, but is a sufficient answer in itself by virtue of presenting the end as somehow desirable.[26]

The role of the phrase 'somehow desirable' relates, as we have seen, to the *intelligibility* of a claim that something is wanted. Can that role also be played by the phrase 'good in some way'? Can 'desirable' and 'good' be interchanged in this context? According to Anscombe, they can. As she points out, 'What do you want that for?' is pretty much the same question as 'What's the good of that?' And she writes: '*Bonum est multiplex*; good is multiform, and all that is required for our concept of "wanting" is that a man should see what he wants under the aspect of some good' (*I*, 75). In this, Anscombe is following Aquinas.[27] 'Seen under the aspect of some good' is to play the same role as the phrase 'seen as being somehow desirable'.

But doesn't 'It's good' just give one desirability characterization among many? Or rather, don't the family of statements involving 'good' do so? As: 'Pigs' tripes are good for men over 60', 'A good parent gives his children gifts on occasion', 'Yoga is a good way to relax', and so on? We can agree with Anscombe that *ethics* is not yet in question: that practical reasoning is not as such an ethical

---

[26] It follows, arguably, that the Ironical Slave is not fully rational, since his final answer to the series of 'Why?' questions is either 'To get the message to N' or 'Because my master wants it'—neither of which gives us a desirability characterization. But his master will presumably be able to supply such a characterization in connection with getting the message to N, in which case the Slave's action will enjoy a sort of derivative rationality.

[27] See e.g. Aquinas, *Summa Theologiae* Ia–IIae. i. 7, c. 'In the abstract, human beings agree in desiring goodness, for all crave to become complete and perfect. [. . .] Sinners turn away from the object in which goodness is truly found, but not from goodness itself, which they mistakenly seek in other things' (Thomas Aquinas, *Theological Texts*, selected and translated by Thomas Gilby (Oxford: Oxford University Press, 1955), 111).

phenomenon, that desirability characterizations involving words like 'should' or 'suits' are not *ipso facto* ethical in nature (see *I*, 64), and that the same goes for the characterization 'good'. But even so, the concept *good* would appear not to be the same as the concept *desirable*, in Anscombe's sense. Does 'I don't feel comfortable without it' (her example) relate in any obvious way to some *good*? The title of Iris Murdoch's novel *The Nice and the Good* surely alludes to a real distinction, between goals as well as between types of person.

In 'Good and Evil',[28] Peter Geach points out that 'good' typically functions as an attributive adjective, where an attributive adjective F is such that 'A is an F so-and-so' cannot be re-expressed as 'A is F and A is a so-and-so'. Example: 'Jack is a good cricketer' cannot be re-expressed as 'Jack is a cricketer and Jack is good', for if it could, the addition of 'Jack is a gardener, but not a good gardener' would allow the inference to 'Jack is good and is not good'. 'Good', like 'normal', 'big', and other adjectives, is not detachable from the noun that follows it: a thing cannot simply be good, it must be good *qua* something-or-other. The same goes for 'good for': Vitamin X cannot just be good, or good for you—it must be good for some specific category of thing or creature. A good G will typically be a G that performs the function, or role, or job, of Gs well (or maybe better than average). And something that is good for Gs will typically be something that is conducive to, or a constituent of, the proper functioning or welfare or flourishing of Gs. Finally, something, e.g. bodily health, can be called a good for Gs if it simply encompasses a certain family of things that are good for Gs.

On such an account, the reason why *bonum est multiplex* is that there are many kinds of thing that can be good specimens of their kind, and that can function well or thrive. Even a single person can have a number of roles: parent, neighbour, employer, cricketer—and so can be good (or bad) in various ways, and can do well (or ill) through various influences. Now it is true that if a role itself involves certain practical ends, then there will be a conceptual connection between what a person in that role wants and what is good in, or for, such a person acting in that role; for to have that role is to be aiming at certain ends, i.e. treating them as what one wants. If a batsman doesn't want to score any runs, and acts accordingly, then (except in rather recherché conditions of the game) he will lose at least some entitlement to being called a good cricketer. And 'I'm going in to bat now, and I want to score no runs' is, without further explanation, hard to make sense of. This conceptual connection between what a G wants, in pursuing the role of a G, and what is good for a G, goes some way to explaining why 'It's good for me as a G', or 'It suits me as a G', serve to give desirability characterizations: for in the light of that conceptual connection, these statements must give sufficient reasons for wanting a thing.

But there are now three questions to press: (i) Where a person can be a good G, and where things can be good for Gs, does it follow that 'G' denotes a role with

---

[28] Peter Geach, 'Good and Evil', *Analysis*, 17 (1956), 35–42.

certain practical ends? (ii) If the answer to (i) is No, for some 'G', how in *that* case can 'It's good for me as a G' serve to give a desirability characterization? (iii) Even if 'It's good for me as a G' serves always to give a desirability characterization, for every 'G', is it also the case that every desirability characterization describes an end as somehow good?

As to the first question, the important apparent counter-example is 'human being' or 'person'. Human beings can thrive, can do well *qua* human beings; but the concept 'human being' does not itself involve practical ends in the way that, say, 'teacher' does. If in life you aim at things inimical to your good as a human being, then naturally, if you are successful, you will end up being less of a good human being, or end up living a life less good for a human being. But if such behaviour is self-stultifying, it is not self-stultifying in the way in which that of the perverse cricketer was.

The answer to (i) does seem to be No. What then of question (ii)? A desirability characterization brings an end to 'What for?' questioning. If 'It's good for me *qua* human being' brings an end to such questioning, the reason may have to do with its being normal and natural (to say the least) for human beings to pursue what is good for them. This would put such a reply somewhat on a par with the answer 'For no particular reason' when the question is 'Why are you doodling?'. The latter exchange doesn't relate to any practical (means–end) *reasoning*, only to bare voluntary action; but the criteria of intelligibility, and of sufficiency as an answer, seem to be similar to those pertaining to the answer 'It's good for me *qua* human being'.

But how similar? We can conceive of human beings who never doodled—even human beings who never played music or wore clothes. But can we conceive of human beings who never pursued what they took to be good for them? It is tempting to think not—but why? Such creatures would very likely die out, but species *have* died out because of being ill-fitted to survive, so we can hardly appeal to the Theory of Evolution if we wish to call such people inconceivable. If there are grounds for such a claim, they surely relate to what is presupposed by the possibility of ascribing wants to people at all. To interpret or make sense of the behaviour of a creature requires one to assume a certain form of life, in Wittgenstein's phrase, a form of life sufficiently like that of actual human beings. One has to be able, e.g., to see some behaviour as that of *trying to get an apple*. The 'assumption' here is not a working hypothesis, but at bottom a set of basic responses; and if none of the behaviour of a group of creatures simply *strikes* us as this or that (trying to get an apple, being in pain ...), then the concept of wanting something or other will not get a foothold, any more than it does in the case of kettles or oak trees. And it seems likely that notions of what is good for certain creatures, of what enables them to fare well, and of what they need, will underpin a lot of our basic responses to and interpretations of their behaviour. Think of the connections between *hunting, catching, eating, food*, and *nourishment*. Wants, ends, and needs are here interwoven in a single phenomenon. We can see so-and-so as *hunting* because of what in a broad sense 'surrounds' it, this being what enables us to see the activity as having a *telos*, i.e. the predator's catching its prey; we can see that as *catching* (as purposeful in the way that catching is) because of what the predator then does with its prey; of the various things the predator does with its prey the important one is *eating*, on account of the natural history of such animals, and of animals generally (natural histories being largely framed in terms of what animals need); we call that *eating* because ... and so on.

Maybe Anscombe has something of this sort in mind when she writes:

[T]here is some sort of necessary connection between what you think *you* need [as opposed to what you think something else needs], and what you want. The connection is a complicated one; it is possible *not* to want something that you judge you need. But, e.g., it is not possible never to want *anything* that you judge you need. (*MMP*, 31)

My example of hunting connected an animal's wants with its needs, rather than with what it *took* to be its needs. But in the context of the interpretability of behaviour, this difference is less than it seems. For animals, there is almost no distinction at all; and when it comes to human beings, though people can be wrong about what they need and what is good for them, it is what they are trying to get and what reasons they would give for trying to get it that are important for interpreting their actions—'interpretation', it might be said, is of the whole gamut of behaviour, linguistic and non-linguistic. And of course it couldn't be that people were by and large radically mistaken about what was good for them.

If there is this, somewhat looser, connection between what a human being wants and what is good for human beings, then one can see how 'It's good for me as a human being' will be a statement apt for bringing an end to 'What for?' questioning. (After all, the questioner must partake sufficiently of your own form of life to be talking to you in the first place.) Let us take all this as supplying at least a partial answer to question (ii).[29]

We are left with question (iii). What of those desirability characterizations that appear not to relate, as such, to what is good? Prime examples are: 'Because it's pleasant', 'For the pleasure of it', 'For the fun of it'. To be sure, there are constraints of intelligibility on such statements: they do not make sense in all possible situations. But still, there are extremely common pleasures that serve no practical ends and make no obvious contribution to human flourishing, such as going on funfair rides or ensuring that one's furniture is polished. Worse still, there are very common pleasures that are actually inimical to the human good of others and/or of oneself, such as the pleasures of cruelty and dissipation.

---

[29] Philippa Foot likewise argues that 'It's good for me as a human being' necessarily counts as an adequate answer to 'What for?', by making out that the concept of a good reason for action is partly determined by what is good for us. See *Natural Goodness* (Oxford: Oxford University Press, 2001), ch. 4, esp. pp. 62–5.

Anscombe certainly doesn't take pleasure to be a sort of intrinsically good mental accompaniment to all those things that are found pleasant or pleasurable—something 'like a particular tickle or itch' (*I*, 77):

Nor should an unexamined thesis 'pleasure is good' (whatever that may mean) be ascribed to me. For my present purposes all that is required is that 'It's pleasant' is an adequate answer to 'What's the good of it?' or 'What do you want that for?'   (*I*, 77–8)

We may accept that 'It's pleasant' gives a desirability characterization, i.e. counts as an adequate answer to 'What for?'. After all, as far as the interpretation of behaviour goes, the concept of pleasure presumably has as tight a connection with that of wanting as does that of what's good for a creature. Our problem is whether 'It's pleasant' presents something 'under the aspect of some good'.

Well, a life without pleasure, it might be said, is not a good life; children deprived of all pleasure when growing up will be maladjusted, unhappy, and quite probably psychologically disturbed. 'But for a *good* life, shouldn't the pleasures be only innocent pleasures?' The question can be answered in the same sort of way as can the question 'For a character trait to be a *virtue*, shouldn't it result only in good actions?' This latter question seems to make problems, e.g. for the character trait of courage, since courage can be employed for evil ends. But in classifying a trait as a virtue, we have to assume a surrounding of 'proper functioning', i.e. of other virtues; and in classifying pleasure as part of a good life, we similarly have to assume a surrounding of other good life components, including good or innocent ends. This is not cheating, as can be seen when we reflect on the nature of biological concepts: in biology, a kidney has certain functions, and a kidney with such-and-such features can only be classified as a good, well-functioning kidney if we assume a healthy surrounding for it. For it may function badly, and even have bad effects, when working alongside other organs which are defective. The biological analogy is appropriate given the sort of naturalistic account of 'good' adumbrated above, an account that Anscombe would endorse.

On the other hand, if a life with little or no pleasure is liable not to be a good life, isn't the same true of a life with little or no pain, physical or mental? This could either mean a life where physical injury, etc. fails to produce pain in the person—such people tend to die young—or alternatively an extremely sheltered and cosseted life—this being a recipe for producing a spoilt, soft, and morally flabby individual. Of course, 'It hurts' can still count as an undesirability characterization, so to speak, because of the necessary connection between pain and *not* wanting. But couldn't pain, or rather the right kind and amount of pain, count as a human good, just as much as pleasure, or rather the right kind and amount of pleasure? Many admirable characters in history have been moulded by suffering. The doctrine is a Spartan-sounding one, and against the grain of the times, but it is not absurd.

Against this it might be pointed out that the *function* of pain is to signal that something is wrong, for instance that a part of the body has been injured; while the function of pleasure (at any rate of physical pleasure) is, if anything, to signal that things are as they should be. The pleasures of food, sex, warmth, etc. are obvious examples. But this way of putting things is liable to lead us to classify pleasure as a sensation, in the sense in which physical pain is a sensation, and such a classification is surely misleading, as Anscombe and others have argued.[30] Perhaps we should say that the function of the pleasurable sensations associated with certain bodily states and activities is to signal that things are as they should be. But this still leaves untouched all those pleasures that are not those of bodily states and activities, about which it would be ludicrous to claim: the function of the pleasurable sensations is, etc. The only *sensations* you have when rock-climbing or reading about the Wars of the Roses may not be pleasant sensations at all, but either neutral or painful.

What seems fairly clear from all this is that if 'It's pleasant' gives an adequate reason for wanting something, it is not because pleasure is good for you in the sense in which food or motherly love is good for you. (The same is true if we substitute 'activity in which pleasure is taken' for 'pleasure'.) We saw above why 'X is good for me' might be thought of as a desirability characterization, but the reasons for that don't carry over to the case of 'X is pleasant'.

Let us look a little closer at the concept of a desirability characterization. We have, in effect, taken the phrase as meaning any answer to 'What do you want that for?' which is sufficient in itself, and so forestalls any iteration of the question unless the enquirer is being irrational or frivolous. But surely such answers are very various in kind? Consider 'I was told to'. As has been noted, this sort of answer just counts, in certain situations, as providing a sufficient reason for doing something; consequently, it will very often suffice as an answer to 'What do you want [to do] that for?' Or again, in the context of a game of chess, 'So as to win' would seem to bring an end to 'What for?' questioning. Certainly, 'What do you want to win for?' is an odd question, and while it *might* be possible to answer, 'I enjoy winning' (in which case we could perhaps say that pleasure was the end), a more pertinent reply, but one which deflects rather than answers the question, would be, 'You're meant to try to win!'—which as Wittgenstein would say is a grammatical note.

Another reply that deflects 'What do you want that for?' rather than answering it is the Ironical Slave's 'My master wants it' (see above, p. 60). If Anscombe is right, the Ironical Slave does not himself want the letter to be delivered, and need not in any real sense want that his master's wants be satisfied. 'My master wants it' brings an end to 'What for?' questioning, by conveying what the situation is, as I put it. But it is doubtful whether this sort of thing was envisaged by Anscombe when she coined the phrase 'desirability characterization'; and it seems clear that

---

[30] See e.g. Gilbert Ryle, 'Pleasure', in *Collected Papers*, ii (London: Hutchinson, 1971), 325–35.

such an answer does not present the objective of taking a letter to N under the aspect of some good.[31] Indeed, 'I was told to' and 'So as to win' could only be said to present ends under the aspect of some good in an attenuated sense, i.e. by virtue of the fact that their counting as good reasons rests upon the facts, respectively, that it is useful that orders get obeyed (in that situation), and that playing chess is pleasant (for many people)—rather than by virtue of the facts, respectively, that it's good if *this* order is obeyed (which you might be unable to vouch for), or that it's good if *I* win the game (why not the other player?).

There seem in the end to be three interconnected, but non-equivalent, notions. An answer to 'What do you want that for?' can: (a) serve as an adequate reply, or one that forestalls further iteration of the question; (b) serve to present an end as somehow desirable (making it intelligible why the agent should want it); (c) serve to present an end as somehow good (for the agent or for something else), or as somehow connected with something that is good. If these three notions were equivalent, then we should have reason for saying that wanting, quite generally, aims at the Good. They appear not to be. But maybe there is some other sense in which wanting aims at the Good. This will be the topic of the next section.

3.2. The Good and the True

For Anscombe, right thinking in ethical matters is not a case of thinking in conformity with canons of practical rationality; though naturally, if someone's ethical thinking violates such canons, that may result in an erroneous ethical (practical) conclusion, just as unsound theoretical reasoning may result in a factually erroneous conclusion.

One of her reasons for thinking this is quite simple. It is that not all right ethical thought is a case of reasoning at all, and not all ethically evaluable actions embody the conclusions of practical arguments—in particular, those actions that are the immediate and spontaneous manifestations of virtues: '[H]uman goodness suggests virtues among other things, and one does not think of choosing means to ends as the whole of courage, temperance, honesty, and so on' (*I*, 78). But there is a deeper reason as well, one which, while distinguishing questions of goodness from questions of sound practical reasoning, at the same time is meant to indicate why the ultimate *aim* of practical reasoning is goodness. The goodness of an end, and of an action aiming at an end, is like the truth of a proposition:

This is the great Aristotelian parallel: if it is right, then the goodness of the end and of the action is as much of an extra, as external to the validity of the reasoning, as truth of the premises and of the conclusion is an extra, is external to the validity of theoretical reasoning. *As* external, but not *more* external.

[31] Cf. above, n. 26, p. 67.

We know that the externality is not total. For truth is the object of belief, and truth-preservingness an essential associate of validity in theoretical reasoning. The parallel will hold for practical reasoning.   (*PI*, 146)

The question whether an action or end is in fact good is like the question whether a belief is in fact true. Someone can be faulted for believing something false, despite the fact that his reasons for thinking it cannot be impugned. The 'fault' just is that the belief is false, in such a case, and the person's rationality is not called into question. Analogously, someone could think an end good that was not in fact good, though his reasons for thinking so could not be impugned. This would be the case if those reasons themselves rested upon blamelessly false beliefs (as, that the liquid in this bottle is water, not poison).

But what about generic ends, such as health, knowledge, affluence, power? If it is wrong to regard power over others as something worth pursuing in life, what sort of error is this? For me to treat it intelligibly as an end of mine already shows that I can see it under the aspect of some good, according to Anscombe; so my error seems to consist in the end's not in fact partaking of that good—or alternatively, in that good's not being a good that can take precedence over certain other goods, in the way that I must take it to be if I am to make power an end of mine. In the first case, I might anticipate deriving pleasure from having others in my power, but turn out to be quite wrong: I discover that, after all, 'uneasy lies the head that wears a crown'. Or I might not even discover this. (Perhaps I keep on thinking that sooner or later I will feel the buzz.) In the second case, though I do indeed derive real pleasure from my power, I wrongly believe that this pleasure is a greater good for me than, say, the good of my being able to love and be loved by those around me. In the last section, I threw doubt on the notion that pleasure could be seen, as such, as a good. But even if this doubt is well placed, we can still distinguish two sorts of error; the second error will now consist in not realizing that 'It's pleasant', as applied to the wielding of power, is *outweighed*, as a reason for action, by, e.g., 'You will be less able to love or be loved by those around you'. If we follow Anscombe, our task (in delineating the second kind of error) will be to explain what it means for one good to be greater than another; while according to my alternative account, our task will be to explain what it means for one sort of reason for action to outweigh another.

The first task admittedly has a more tractable look about it. Let us once again turn to biology for a parallel. Where 'Power will give me pleasure' embodies the first sort of error, it will be like 'Monkey glands will give me health and strength'. Where I allow the pleasure of power to take precedence over other good things, thus falling into the second sort of error, it will be rather like concentrating all my efforts on eating healthily, hence forgetting about the need to exercise properly. If the latter mistake derives from an ignorance of the relative importance of diet and exercise, it could be called a factual error, in the same category as the error about the monkey glands: the false belief may or may not arise from unsound reasoning. The error may, however, result directly from obsessiveness, or wishful thinking, or some such, in which case my reasonableness is impugned.

Our question is: In the case of ethics, is an error about the ordering of generic ends (about which generic ends take precedence over which) a factual error?—or an error of rationality?—or both, or neither? To answer this, we need to look closer at what the 'ordering' of ends consists in.

It is a fallacy—one sometimes attributed to Aristotle—to argue from the premiss that every purposive action has an end to the conclusion that there is an end that every purposive action has. But maybe, for all that, there *is* some overriding end, some single end at which all purposive human action aims. If there is no such end, it might seem as if human ends cannot be ordered, and this is indeed Anscombe's opinion. She writes (note the 'only if' in the second paragraph):

But may not someone be criticizable for pursuing a certain end, thus characterizable as a sort of good of his, where and when it is quite inappropriate for him to do so, or by means inimical to other ends which he ought to have?

This can be made out only if man has a last end which governs all [...] . An action of course is good if it is not bad, but being inimical to the last architectonic end would prove that it was not good. (*PI*, 147)

The question whether there is such an architectonic end 'would belong to ethics, if there is such a science' (*I*, 76). Ethics, if there is such a thing, is a science, insofar as it deals, like biology, with facts, rather than with practical rationality as such.

On the face of it, it looks as if the answer that Anscombe would give to our earlier question must be: An error about the ordering of human ends is an error of fact, not an error of rationality.[32] And, she would add, we can only talk of facts or of error here on the assumption that man has an ultimate end.

The second of these claims can be challenged. I will turn to it in a moment. As for the first, I think we must say: 'It depends what you mean by *error of rationality*.'

In showing someone why some belief of his is false, you will typically adduce certain facts which count against it. The person could of course deny or doubt these facts, in which case further facts will need to be adduced in support of *them*. At some point, it may be possible for you actually to point to something, e.g. something visible, in support of what you say; but then again it may not. Whatever the situation, if you fail in the end to convince the other person that his original belief is false, then the main possible causes of this would seem to be: (a) because you have reached something which you take yourself to know, though

---

[32] By which is meant either practical or theoretical rationality. Cf. n. 1, p. 76 of *I*: 'Following Hume, though without his animus, I of course deny that this preference [of a greater good over a lesser one] can be as such "required by reason", *in any sense*' (my italics).

not on the basis of a reason you can then and there give (e.g. a piece of general knowledge, such as that Canberra is the capital of Australia), which putative fact the other still denies; *or* (b) because the complexity and difficulty of the issues prevent either or both of you from attaining the clear view necessary for a right judgement; *or* (c) because of a disagreement about what counts as a good or sufficient reason for believing something. In the case of (a), you probably could, if inclined, look for indirect support from other beliefs, or more direct support, e.g. from a book; so that if you found such support, and if the disagreement persisted, we might end up with (b) or (c). But you might either not look for, or not find, such support. However, where the disagreement *does* in the end resolve itself into either a (b)-style or a (c)-style disagreement, then it seems we can say the following. With a (b)-style disagreement, confused or unclear thought is responsible; with a (c)-style disagreement, the reasonableness of one of the parties is in doubt. There might of course be situations containing elements of both (b) and (c). Two qualifications need to be made to the statement just made about (c)-style disagreement: first, it may just be that A thinks that p is more likely than not, while B thinks that, all things considered, he'd rather bet on not-p (i.e. neither person is very firmly attached to his belief, the issue occupying a bit of an epistemic grey area); second, the disagreement may be of a radical kind, indicative e.g. of differing 'world views'. Whether in these two cases the reasonableness of one of the parties must be in doubt is a difficult question. The case of difference of world view, in particular, deserves consideration in its own right, and we shall be examining it more closely in Chapter 6.

Consider now a disagreement about generic ends. You say: 'Honesty should come before short-term monetary gain'—I deny this. Other things being equal, let us say that short-term monetary gain is indeed a good, at any rate for those like me who are far from rich, so that here we have a disagreement about the ordering of goods. How are you to show me that I am in error? Surely by adducing any, and any number, of a huge range of facts, some abstract, some concrete; and by means of various supplementary moves, including 'How would you like it if … ?' and 'What if everybody put monetary gain before honesty?'. It would be largely a case of filling in detail, in the hope that eventually I would *see* that I couldn't just go on saying 'But still, why not be dishonest if that way I can make some money?'.

Could our disagreement be to any extent an (a)-style disagreement, relating to disputed facts? It could: I might, for example, deny certain historical or biographical facts, to do with how people assessed their own or others' lives, or to do with how successful certain people's projects were, or whatever. Ignorance or inexperience might account for my denials. But of course my inclination to make such denials could well be the result of prejudice, or of a kind of self-serving wishful thinking common in such cases (e.g. if I have a particular incentive for dishonesty). My thinking on the subject would thus be not all that it should be. And in fact it is easy to see how our dispute is liable to boil down to a (b)-style or (c)-style disagreement. In the end, we would be likely to have a disagreement due either to confused and unclear thought, or to different notions of what counts as a good reason for believing something—or (if those of a non-cognitivist bent require proof that *belief* is involved) about what counts as a good reason for saying something. In this context, a good reason for saying/believing something can also function as a good reason for doing (or not doing) something—'The potatoes have been delivered to you', which, as we shall see in the next chapter, can serve both as a reason for thinking that you owe the grocer £5, and as a reason for paying the grocer £5, given certain background facts.

Perhaps there are some irresoluble ethical disagreements, irresoluble because it is unclear how to weigh up all the reasons *pro* and *contra*. But not all ethical disagreements can be of this sort. At any rate, if they are, then there is no rational point in ethical argumentation *qua* argumentation (as opposed e.g. to: '*qua* brow-beating'), and we are doomed to radical subjectivism or nihilism. The falsehood of such doctrines is not our present concern, so I will assume that ethical argumentation does have a point. What we seem to have established is this: that persistent disagreement about generic human ends will very often be a sign that one of the parties suffers from faulty thinking, in a broad sense. Confusion in the face of difficult and complex questions is very natural, and scarcely culpable, one might say.[33] And in this context, one who fails to see what counts as a good reason may also scarcely deserve the epithet 'irrational'. But it should be clear by now that 'Error of fact or error of rationality?' presents too simple a dichotomy.

In giving reasons why honesty should come before short-term monetary gain, do we at any point reach a single rock-bottom reason, concerning an architectonic end for man? There seems no reason to suppose so. 'Filling in detail', as I put it, will of course mean describing human life or lives, human interactions, human arrangements, and so on, but all this falls short of giving an ultimate end for human action. The same goes for filling in detail in defence of some non-ethical factual claim: we need not reach any foundational level (e.g. of sense-datum reports). If we do reach bedrock, in Wittgenstein's phrase, it will be at the level of 'framework propositions', propositions the acceptance of which is a presupposition of the discourse at hand. In ethics, there may well be such propositions. Candidates might be: 'Human beings are more important

---

[33] In *TKEA*, Anscombe argues that certain bad actions, A, are only imputable to agents ignorant that they are committing A when the 'ignorance is voluntary'. An important case of such ignorance's being voluntary is where it is both necessary and possible that the agent *find out* whether he would be committing A in doing something (A could be murder, for instance). And she writes: '[T]he possibility of knowledge may be lacking, because of the difficulty of the question', by which she means the difficulty of such a question as 'Would this be murder?'. Getting the answer to the question wrong in such a case would not be culpable, and A could not be imputed to the agent; even though the cause of his getting it wrong was his inadequate thought. It seems that she must say: 'You can commit murder, without murder's being imputable to you [i.e. without your being *guilty* of murder]'. See *TKEA*, 8–9.

than stones', and 'Knowledge is as such better than ignorance'. But there is no reason to think that among the bedrock propositions is any giving a final end for human life and action. Someone who denies that man has an ultimate end of action appears not to be the sort of radical sceptic, nihilist, nutcase, or member of an alien life-form that a denier of bedrock propositions will *prima facie* be.

But couldn't it be said that the ultimate end, for a human being, is flourishing, or *eudaimonia*? The end would be ultimate in this sense: that if a certain end or action could be shown to be inimical to your flourishing as a human being, that would *ipso facto* count as a reason against the end or action, one that outweighed any reason for it that did *not* relate to your flourishing. It may be that not every uncriticizable purposive action will aim at that end, nor yet (if successful) be a constituent of it, but this fact would not of itself undermine the concept of an ultimate end of human action. But what is *eudaimonia*? Isn't it just the sum of all the many and various human goods at which we can aim? If so, its status as a single end for human life would appear specious.

At this point, it may be instructive to return to the 'great Aristotelian parallel', between goodness and truth. The parallel goes thus: just as the object of belief is truth, so the object of action is goodness. We are at the moment taking this 'goodness' to be *eudaimonia*. But if the latter is a mere conglomeration of human goods, won't the parallel between goodness and truth break down? Well, maybe not. For Pilate's famous question might not be answerable by giving any single property, relation, or what have you, along the lines of: correspondence-to-a-fact, or coherence-among-propositions. If truth is a protean notion, whose shape depends on the nature of the proposition being dubbed 'true', then there will be a sense in which truth, too, is a conglomeration. Wittgenstein showed that this applies to the notion of meaning, even to that of indicative sentential meaning; and there is good reason to think that what goes for indicative sentential meaning here will go also for truth. According to this way of thinking, 'is true' will amount, very roughly, to 'is to be asserted' — or to 'is as such worthy of assertion'. But the kinds of indicative assertion are many and varied. Reports, predictions, proclamations, rules, verdicts, expressions of intention, promises, metaphors, insults, jokes, and more all get expressed by means of indicative sentences, and while 'true' applies more naturally to some of these than to others, (a) this may be as much a matter of 'dispensable usage' as of anything,[34] and (b) the motley to which 'true' does naturally apply are still a motley, though doubtless bound together by family resemblances.

If 'is true', as applied to sentences, amounts roughly to 'is to be asserted', then as applied to beliefs it surely amounts to 'is to be believed'. (I skip over such questions as whether types or tokens are meant, whether 'is to be ... ' conveys permission or requirement, and so on.) The notion of believing looks to be as variegated as that of asserting. 'The object of belief is truth', like 'The object

---

[34] Cf. *I*, 3.

of assertion is truth', hides a teeming variety behind a façade of unity. But none of this makes problems for the great Aristotelian parallel—on the contrary. This will at any rate be so if we can read 'good' (as applied to actions) as not much more than 'to be done',[35] adding, in justification of this saying, that the grounds in virtue of which actions are to be done are not of a single kind—just as the grounds in virtue of which propositions are to be believed are not of a single kind. Establishing that an action is good, is to be done, very often involves weighing reasons against one another; and (it can be argued) the prime mode of weighing practical reasons consists in bringing facts about human goods to bear—and by goods we *now* mean such things as health, love, knowledge, courage, honesty, laughter, and the rest: those things which are good for human beings, are conducive to a life's being a good one for a human being.

Whether the variety of human goods constitutes a mere conglomeration depends on what sort of unity can be ascribed to a human life. Physical health comprises an enormous variety of factors, but counts as a unitary notion to the extent that its subject, the human organism, is a biologically unitary thing. Perhaps we can see a human life as similarly unitary, with its various activities, projects, and biographical aspects enjoying an interconnectedness analogous to that enjoyed by bodily functions, activities, and processes. If so, the parallel between *eudaimonia* and health will be quite close. If not, not.

Many of the themes of this section have been as much topics in ethics as topics in the philosophy of action. We shall have an opportunity to investigate them further in the next chapter, in which I will be considering Anscombe's moral philosophy.

3.3. Practical Truth

We have been discussing a parallel, between good action and true belief. But Anscombe thinks that there is more than just a parallel here. Following Aristotle, she sees good action as embodying 'practical truth', bad action—or one kind of bad action—as embodying 'practical falsehood'. The key phrase of Aristotle's, in explication of 'practical truth' (ἀλήθεια πρακτική), she takes to be: 'truth in agreement with right desire' (ἀλήθεια ὁμολόγως ἔχουσα τῇ ὀρέξει τῇ ὀρθῇ). Practical truth is the good working (εὐ), or the work (ἔργον), of practical intelligence.[36]

---

[35] Cf. *TAA*, 70. Anscombe, expounding Aristotle, takes the ἀκόλαστος (the licentious man) as thinking that the pursuit of pleasure 'is a good way to carry on'—where this is the same as thinking, of pursuing pleasure: 'that's the thing to do!' Of course, this equation of 'good' with 'to be done' gibes well with taking 'seen as somehow desirable' as equivalent to 'seen under the aspect of some good'; the notion would relate simply to what there is good reason to do, where good reasons serve to render an agent's wants intelligible. But it seems clear that Anscombe wants the 'goodness' which is the ultimate end of action to be the substantive goodness for human beings *qua* human beings whose analogue is physical health.   [36] See *Nicomachean Ethics*, book 6, 1139ᵃ30.

A necessary condition of an action's embodying practical truth is that the premisses of the practical reasoning behind it be all true (and the conclusion too, if this is to be a judgement: 'So I'll . . .'): 'It is practical truth when the judgements involved in the formation of the "choice" [προαίρεσις] leading to the action are all true; but the practical truth is not the truth of those *judgements*' (*TAA*, 77). Anscombe says of 'truth in agreement with right desire' (the same as practical truth) that it

is brought about—i.e. made true—by action (since the description of what he does is made true by his doing it), provided that a man forms and executes a good 'choice'. The man who forms and executes an evil 'choice' will also make true *some* description of what he does. He will secure, say, if he is competent, that such and such a man has his eyes put out or his hands cut off, that being his judgement of what it is just to do. But his description 'justice performed' of what he has done will be a lie. He, then, will have produced practical falsehood.   (*TAA*, 77)

Will all bad actions be cases of practical falsehood? No; for a person can be swayed or ruled by passion or desire (ἐπιθυμία). In that case, the person's wanting is not rational wanting, and so is not a wanting of something *as good*. But where what is wanted is wanted as good, but is not in fact good, the action arising from the want embodies falsehood. Such falsehood may or may not be culpable. Culpability here relates to ignorance or confusion:[37]

It appears to me that *only* when we get to questions where it is difficult to know the truth, or questions as to facts which the agent can't be expected to have found out, is there any chance for the wanting of what is judged a means to doing well to be right when the judgement itself is wrong.   (*TAA*, 77)

(This passage relates to right (and wrong) *wanting*, but in the context supplies the needed rationale for our distinction between the two kinds of falsehood in action: culpable and blameless.)

Where what is wanted is wanted as good, and is in fact good, the action arising from the want embodies practical truth. Acting thus is, as Anscombe liked to say, 'doing the truth'. And she insists that the predicates 'true' and 'false' apply to actions 'strictly and properly, and not merely by an extension and in a way that ought to be explained away' (*TAA*, 77).

Anscombe's main purpose in discussing practical truth was to expound the views of Aristotle; and some of what she says should be read with the qualification, 'If Aristotle is right, then ... ' in mind. But it is quite clear that she takes Aristotle to be very largely right, certainly as to the usefulness and importance of the notion of practical truth. So: can actions (in particular good ones) be called true in a quite literal sense? Given the explanation of 'practical truth' that has been given, an objector might say, 'But surely what is true is the agent's *judgement* that a certain proposed action would be good, e.g. by being just?—or alternatively,

---

[37] See above, pp. 75–7, and n. 33, p. 77.

the judgement that a specific action performed by him is or was good?' To this, Anscombe would reply that in acting, the agent makes certain descriptions (of what he does) become true. Another way of putting this would be to say that the agent makes certain propositions, about what he does, become true (e.g. 'Smith treats Jones justly'). But however we put it, the key notion is that of making true, and this notion does apply literally to actions, not to judgements.

But of course, as Anscombe herself points out, any action will make all sorts of things true. What is needed for practical truth is that what is aimed at by the agent is what he actually does: that the description of what he aims at is the same as the (or a) description of what he does. The description of what he aims at could occur in a statement by the agent, as: 'I will act justly', or 'My action will be a just one'. If his action then *is* a just one, shouldn't we say that it was his statement that was true, not his action? This is compatible with saying that, in acting justly, the person makes the proposition 'I will act justly' true. *His action makes what he said true*—so 'true' applies to what he said.

'I will act justly', 'I will treat Jones justly', etc., are expressions of intention. And, as we saw in Chapter 1, such statements are governed by Theophrastus' principle: when there is a discrepancy between statement and action, and this alone constitutes a mistake, then the mistake is in the action, not in the statement. 'The mistake is in the action'; maybe another way of putting that would be to say, 'The action is false'. If so, then, correlatively, an action in accordance with expressed intention would be true. Could this be the notion of practical truth and falsehood that we are looking for?

Well, Anscombe herself is happy to call the expression of intention true, when the intended action gets performed (see Ch. 1, pp. 17–18). This by itself would not rule out our calling the action true also; maybe both statement and action can be true—or false, as the case may be. With an action, the concept of falsehood would get explained via that of a mistake, of something at fault; while if Anscombe is right, the falsehood of an expression of intention does not in itself constitute something at fault in the statement. Nevertheless, for many kinds of statement, if not for expressions of intention, there surely is a sense in which falsehood is a sign of the statement's being at fault, and perhaps the falsehood (and truth) of such statements could provide a paradigm for the falsehood (and truth) of actions.

The notion of practical truth, however, is not meant to apply to any case of executed intention. Rather, it is 'truth in agreement with *right* desire': the action must not only 'fit' the desire (Theophrastically), the desire must itself be right, i.e. good. For a desire to be good is for it to aim at what's good—that is what desire is *for*, so to speak. Anscombe appears to be sympathetic to Aristotle's view that man's rational faculty has a function: 'For as seeing can be seen to be what the eye is for, so understanding—the enjoyment of the truth—can be seen to be what the mind is for' (*TAA*, 75). 'The enjoyment of the truth' will cover not only theoretical truth (belief), but practical truth (action). Both kinds of truth are constituents of *eudaimonia,* and both are aimed at by human beings insofar as they are rational:

Apart from being ruled by passion (this is what I want, even if it is no good) 'doing well' is what anyone wants in some obscure and indeterminate way. One could call it that part of blessedness [εὐδαιμονία] for which one's own action is essential.   (*TAA,* 76)

In the end, the question whether 'true' and 'false' apply to actions 'strictly and properly' may not be so important. Or rather the thing to say might just be that there are significant similarities between the application of those predicates to actions and their application to beliefs, similarities that are enough for us to say that 'true' and 'false' are not being used equivocally in the two cases. (Compare descriptions, like 'black cat': these can be true, *of* objects. Is 'true' being used in a special sense here?) In the last section, I suggested that truth was a protean notion, even as applied only to indicative sentences and beliefs. Maybe it is sufficiently protean to embrace actions also, if we want it to. The motive for doing so would not come from ordinary usage, to be sure; the philosopher who speaks of practical truth may be saying, 'See things this way'.[38]

---

[38] This remark, however, can hardly be applied to Anscombe, who would probably reject the idea that truth is a protean, as opposed to genuinely transcendental, notion—a transcendental notion being one that 'runs through' all the categories (thought, action, will, being, etc.). We shall return to these themes in Ch. 6; see pp. 196–8.

3

Ethics

In the Introduction to *ERP*, Anscombe writes: 'In general, my interest in moral philosophy has been more in particular moral questions than in what is now called "meta-ethics" ' (*ERP*, p. viii). The dichotomy between 'first-order ethics' and 'meta-ethics' is not a hard and fast one, and I doubt if Anscombe would have thought it was. Certainly, a number of her papers straddle both kinds of approach; and it is largely thanks to her writings, and those of some others of her generation, that a concomitant of the idea that the dichotomy *is* hard and fast now looks to have been something of a shibboleth—namely, the conception of philosophy as impotent to address first-order moral issues at all. This has surely been good news, both for the discipline called philosophy and for anyone who wants to reflect rationally on the important questions of life. That said, a rough and ready distinction can be made, and the focus of the present chapter will be Anscombe's meta-ethics—her moral theory.

There are quite a few philosophers who, if asked about Anscombe's moral philosophy, will answer in a way that shows that they regard as an unfortunate intellectual hindrance her having been a Roman Catholic.[1] Two things need to be said about this. First, because the moral framework of her thought is at odds in certain important respects with that of modern secular liberalism, the reaction I have mentioned can in many cases be put down to the complacency that any established ideology produces in some of its adherents. For a lot of people, the values of individualism, egalitarianism, democracy, sexual freedom, religious scepticism, tolerance, etc. etc., have a more or less axiomatic status, and a philosopher who seriously challenges any of them is liable to be classified as eccentric or worse. But Socrates' idea of the philosopher as gadfly surely has something going for it. Complacency is never good, even if it attaches to views that, luckily, are true—and, if nothing else, the inconsistencies to be found among the medley of views constituting the modern Western ethos indicate that not all of those views can be true.

The second thing to point out is that, although Anscombe clearly *did* stick pretty strictly to Catholic teaching, she also believed, like Aquinas, that church teaching about ethical matters could be rationally argued for, and she made

---

[1] Although it shouldn't be necessary, I will insert a disclaimer here for the sake of a certain kind of reader: I am not a Catholic myself.

it her business, when addressing non-Catholics, to present such arguments. If
you oppose her views, you will need to address those arguments; and if as well
as arguments in the traditional sense you find in her writing appeals, parables,
polemics, and more—well, maybe that is actually what serious ethical discussion
looks like, and always has looked like. But in any case, the 'Catholic' aspect
of Anscombe's moral philosophy is one that is really not so evident in the
more meta-ethical pieces. If we were to mention influences at all here, then we
would probably have to cite Aristotle, Wittgenstein, and Hume: Aristotle for the
direction of his thought, Wittgenstein for his philosophical method, and Hume
for his ability to raise important and hitherto unnoticed questions.

The contribution of the gadfly is more urgently needed in ethics than, say, in
epistemology, insofar as ethics itself is more needed than epistemology. (I don't
mean by this that ethicists are more needed than epistemologists, but rather that
the ethically unexamined life is worse than the epistemologically unexamined
one.) Anscombe's moral philosophy is certainly motivated in large part by the
desire to point out what is wrong with prevalent ideas, and to sting in the way
that a gadfly is meant to sting. Of 'War and Murder' she writes: '[It] is written in
a tone of righteous fury about what passed for thinking about the destruction of
civilian populations' (*ERP*, p. vii). Lest anyone think her incapable of self-doubt,
here is how she goes on: 'I don't much like it, not because I disagree with its
sentiments but because, if I was torn by a *saeva indignatio*, I wish I had had the
talent of Swift in expressing it.'[2]

Whether or not she had Swift's talents of expression, Anscombe's critical
acumen cannot be doubted. I will in this chapter be presenting her moral
philosophy via her critique of certain dominant or influential trends of thought.
This is in fact as good a way as any of presenting her positive ethical views, which
perforce manifest themselves in the playing out of the critical argument.

1. THE OBJECTS OF THE CRITIQUE

The three main objects of Anscombe's critique that I will consider are these: the
fact/value distinction, a legalistic conception of morality, and consequentialism.

A student of English-speaking moral philosophy is usually introduced early
on to the idea that there is a 'fact/value distinction'. The history of this idea
can be traced back to Hume, and at the heart of it is Hume's psychology,
according to which what Hume called 'reason' is necessarily impotent either to
produce or to justify human actions. (That Hume tended to conflate the issues
of production and justification is significant.) The faculty of reason produces
beliefs about what is the case; its impotence is the impotence of those beliefs.

---

[2] It seems to me, however, that 'War and Murder' is at any rate more temperate in its language
than e.g. 'Modern Moral Philosophy' or 'Mr. Truman's Degree'.

Actions are to be seen as issuing from passion or sentiment; later Humeans supply various alternative terms here, including emotion, desire, pro-attitude, etc. Reason, Hume famously said, 'is and ought to be the slave of the passions'; by which he meant (though the phrase 'ought to be' appears inexplicable) that while the passions determine a person's ends, reason can only tell her how to achieve those ends—i.e. it determines means. Rational justification or criticism can relate only to what is reason's domain, hence they cannot touch what ends a person has, the things she 'happens to want'. This is the point behind Hume's saying that a want or desire is an 'original existence'. You cannot, according to any standard of *reasoning*, infer or derive a want from things you know or believe, Hume thought; though believing something may indeed *cause* you to start wanting certain things—which fact of course requires some qualification of the claim that of reason and passion, it is the former that is impotent to produce action.

The relevance of all this for morality is clear. Morality, or at least a part of morality, has to do with action, and with the question 'What should I do?' as it is encountered in real life. If Hume is right, this question may always be answered by: 'It depends on what you want.' The further question 'What should I want?' Hume and his followers take to be nonsensical, unless it means 'What should I want to go for as a way (means) of achieving my goal?'. When it comes to ends, what you want might be strange, it might conflict with what others (e.g. 'we') want, it might cause people to hate or revile you—but it cannot in itself embody error or irrationality.[3] As far as our aims in life go, there is not the sort of objective standard of right or wrong that there is for our beliefs, for which the objective standard is truth.

The twentieth-century descendants of Hume—emotivists, subjectivists, prescriptivists, projectivists, *et al.*—held on to the basic tenets of Hume's moral psychology. Their developments of his ideas were primarily linguistic in character; that is, theories were advanced about the special function or meaning of 'moral language', in line with the moral psychology. Moral statements were 'evaluative', and to be sharply distinguished from statements that expressed beliefs and so were capable of being true or false—these statements being dubbed 'factual'.

The idea of a fact/value distinction, and the various kinds of moral subjectivism or non-cognitivism that go with it—these constitute the first main object of Anscombe's critique. The next object of her critique to mention is what I shall call a legalistic conception of morality. As we shall see, the historical roots of this

---

[3] In 'Of the Standard of Taste', Hume argued for the existence of aesthetic norms, saying that the opinions of those with discernment, without prejudice, etc., simply count as trumping the opinions of others. It is possible to take what Hume says about aesthetics as applying equally to ethics, and to take Hume as having thought so. It seems to me, however, that despite what various sympathetic exponents of his philosophy have claimed, Hume's basic subjectivism about wants and preferences is fairly clear. Anscombe's attack on the fact/value distinction is in any case independent of whether Hume himself can be credited with having espoused it.

conception, if Anscombe is right, lie in our Judaeo-Christian heritage (at any rate if we are talking of the Western form of that conception)—rather than in the works of a specific philosopher or philosophers. But one might mention the work of one philosopher as vividly typifying a legalistic conception: namely, that of Immanuel Kant.

So what is a legalistic conception of morality? It is the view that the basic moral concept is that of obligation or duty. The question 'What should I do?' is then regarded as a 'moral' question only if it means 'What am I obliged to do?'. Even here we must be careful to exclude such senses of 'obliged' as: 'legally obliged', 'obliged by custom', 'obliged by the rules of the practice', and so on. 'Obliged', 'should', 'must', 'ought'—all such terms are deemed to be capable of having a special 'moral' sense, and 'You morally ought to φ' is typically taken as having a special overriding character. To act wrongly is to break the moral law, a law which binds more strongly than any actually promulgated law, and against the standard of which any actually promulgated law (as well as any action) may be judged right or wrong.

The third object of Anscombe's critique is a certain tendency of thought, a tendency she dubbed 'consequentialism'. This term is now usually applied to any moral theory according to which the rightness or goodness of an action is determined solely by the value of its actual consequences (though this definition does not quite fit 'rule consequentialism'). However, when she introduced the term, Anscombe meant something rather different from this—which explains why she counts Ross and Prichard as consequentialists but not Mill, a classification that is the reverse of what would now be the customary one.[4] The tendency of thought that Anscombe had in mind relates to deliberation, intention, and responsibility. For a consequentialist, rational deliberation essentially takes the form of weighing up all the pros and cons of a possible action or actions and deciding on the action whose pros most outweigh its cons: this will mean weighing up the values of the different possible consequences of actions. 'Consequences' is to be construed widely. It may include 'intrinsic features' of the action, such as being a promise-breaking, or being *prima facie* wrong; but the significant thing is that it will include not only consequences intended by the agent but also ones foreseen by him—even such 'consequences' as somebody else's doing something. Finally, moral responsibility, for the consequentialist, is assigned not primarily according to a person's intentions, but according to the foreseen or foreseeable consequences of the person's action.

---

[4] This is pointed out in Cora Diamond's 'Consequentialism in Modern Moral Philosophy and in "Modern Moral Philosophy"', in David S. Oderberg and Jacqueline A. Laing (eds.), *Human Lives: Critical Essays on Consequentialist Bioethics* (Basingstoke: Macmillan, 1997), 13–38. Diamond provides a very useful explanation of what Anscombe *did* mean by 'consequentialism' and of why the notion is an important one. She also argues, with Anscombe, that Mill avoids the charge of being a consequentialist, at least according to one very natural interpretation of his views. For Anscombe's classification of Ross and Prichard, see *MMP*, 33 n. 4.

2. THE 'FACT/VALUE DISTINCTION'

2.1. Humean Themes

Hume's psychology of action has survived well. In its modern incarnation, it is known as the 'belief/desire model',[5] according to which the proper explanation of any intentional action will cite a belief and a desire, where these are typically taken to be mental states existing prior to and/or simultaneously with the given action, and such as to cause it. That such a model of intentional action is suspect is one of the themes of the previous two chapters. But for present purposes, what most concerns us in the belief/desire model is the thesis that you neither explain nor rationally justify any action by reference only to the agent's beliefs.

Consider now the eater of pigs' tripes from Chapter 2 (p. 57). The practical argument that was spelt out on his behalf ran thus:

Vitamin X is good for all men over 60
Pigs' tripes are full of Vitamin X
I'm a man over 60
Here's some pigs' tripes
So I'll have some.

That the man draws the practical conclusion 'So I'll have some' *shows* what he wants: namely, to eat something good for him. But the only propositions to which he need point in justification of his conclusion are those appearing in the argument, which (as we saw in Ch. 2) do not include the premiss 'I want to eat something that's good for me'. So the tripes-eater can justify his practical conclusion by appeal to what he believes, about Vitamin X, tripes, men over 60, and so on. For one justifies a conclusion by appeal (a) to the truth of the premisses, and (b) to the validity of the reasoning. Given what he wants, the man's conclusion does indeed follow from the premisses, in the non-necessitating way characteristic of practical inference. Thus (b) is satisfied; and we are assuming that (a) is also. What goes for justification goes likewise for action-explanation: one could explain the action of the tripes-eater by citing his beliefs. Since these beliefs include one involving a desirability characterization (in the first proposition), both justification and explanation by reference to such beliefs will be perfectly adequate.

I cannot object to the tripes-eater's account of his action that I myself do not want to eat what's good for me, even if I too am a man over 60. Of course, if I am

---

[5] Adherents of the model include Donald Davidson, Michael Smith, and Simon Blackburn. See Davidson, 'Actions, Reasons and Causes', in *Essays on Actions and Events* (Oxford: Clarendon Press, 1980), 3–21; Smith, 'The Humean Theory of Motivation', *Mind* 96 (1987), 36–61; Blackburn, *Ruling Passions: A Theory of Practical Reasoning* (Oxford: Clarendon Press, 1998), ch. 4.

a man over 60 in the same situation and with the same beliefs as our hero, I may decide not to have the pigs' tripes, simply because I don't want to eat what's good for me. And this shows in what sense it is true that it depends on what a rational person happens to want whether he does X or Y, and also whether he is justified in doing X or Y. Now something analogous holds of beliefs: it very often depends on what else a rational person believes whether or not he infers P from some set of premises, and likewise whether he is justified in inferring P from them. Of course, if we are dealing with a deductively valid argument, the conclusion will follow regardless of what else the person happens to believe. But in real life, many disputed conclusions do in fact turn out to depend on what background beliefs different people have, so that in these cases it could be said that 'it depends on what you believe' whether you infer P. Nevertheless, if somebody's background beliefs were to be inserted into the original set of premises, we could in principle decide on the rationality of their inferring P simply by considering the total set of beliefs, and nothing else—at any rate, if the argument is a purely deductive one (a relatively uncommon case). And no practical argument has *that* feature.

It does not follow from this either (i) that a practical argument requires a premise of the form 'I want X' if its conclusion is to follow, or (ii) that appeal to a set of propositions cannot suffice to justify a practical conclusion. There is a parallel case worth mentioning here: that of rules of inference. As Lewis Carroll's tortoise taught us,[6] the premises of a deductively valid argument entail their conclusion without benefit of additional premises stating 'logical laws' (e.g. that of *modus ponens*)—and this despite the fact that there is a sense in which the conclusion only follows in virtue of those laws' holding, so that one could say, 'It depends on what logical laws you adhere to whether you infer P'. Thus the analogues, for rules of inference, of theses (i) and (ii) would be clearly false. *Modus ponens* does not need to appear as a premise, and a conclusion of an argument utilizing *modus ponens* is entirely justified by appeal to the premises as they stand. Of course, it might be argued, you would be irrational (or linguistically incompetent) not to accept *modus ponens* as a rule of inference. And the Humean denies that anything similar holds of wants: no desire is rationally compulsory. But how exactly is this claim relevant either to (i) or to (ii)?

It is true that if appeal to a set of propositions is ever to suffice in justifying a practical conclusion, then there must be standards of justification and criticism that apply to background wants or aims, much as the standards of rationality and of truth apply to background beliefs, or as the standards of harmony, etc., apply to rules of inference. We saw in the last chapter that 'I just want it' is rarely an adequate, or even intelligible, answer to 'Why do you want that?'; what is generally required is a desirability characterization, such as 'It's good for me'. I suggested (pp. 72–3) that there are various kinds of answer that can play the role that desirability characterizations play, that of forestalling the further question 'But why

[6] Lewis Carroll, 'What the Tortoise Said to Achilles', *Mind*, 4/14 (Apr. 1895), 278–80.

do you want *that*?'. And the existence of language-games in which that question is thus forestalled is enough to throw the Humean view into doubt, and that in two ways. First, there do appear to be standards of rationality or reasonableness applicable to wants as such. Second, appeal to a set of beliefs will often be adequate justification of a practical conclusion. For giving a desirability characterization is expressing a belief one has—e.g. that Vitamin X is good for one.

Hume took the iteration of 'But why do you want *that*?' as coming to an end only with 'I just do'—e.g. 'I just do want health'.[7] He could with equal justice have said that the iteration of 'But why do you believe *that*?' comes to an end only with 'I just do'; after all, if in answer to that question one produced another assertion, the question could be asked again, and we wouldn't have reached the end! The obvious thing to point out is that the person who accepts *no* answer to 'Why...?' as supplying an adequate reason—and 'I just do' is not a reason-giving answer—has not grasped what counts as a good reason in the discourse in question. Either that, or there is no such thing as a good reason in the discourse in question.

Why would Hume not accept an answer like 'It's good for me' as adequate and final? Presumably because the person is conceivable who doesn't want to have what's good for him, i.e. who doesn't treat 'It's good for me' as supplying a reason for him to do something. Actually, as Anscombe points out, it's not so easy to conceive of someone *never* wanting what he took to be good for him (see Ch. 2, pp. 69–70). So we are talking of sometimes not wanting what you take to be good for you. But of course the person is also conceivable who sometimes doesn't treat a proposition as a reason for believing something which patently *is* a reason to believe it. What Hume needs to show is that a *rational* person is conceivable who etc. etc., and he needs to do this in a non-question-begging way.

Actually he needs more than this; for a person who doesn't treat 'It's good for me' as a reason (on this occasion) for his doing X isn't thereby a person who is entitled to regard it as an inadequate reason for *another* to do X. Perhaps avoiding something good for you, with no ulterior benefit in mind, is perfectly rational; perhaps it is a bit irrational—but not accepting 'It's good for me' as a justification of another person's action looks to be definitely irrational (or perverse, or frivolous). A desirability characterization simply does count as such a justification. To say 'But it shouldn't' is to invoke an imaginary, and non-existent, higher standard of rationality. Moreover, a rational person must also accept 'It's

---

[7] D. Hume, *Enquiry Concerning the Principle of Morals*, Appendix I, §5. In line with other empiricist philosophers, Hume takes pleasure and pain to be man's guiding principles of action, so that the final answers to 'Why?' are either 'I just do want pleasure', or 'I just do want to avoid pain'. Thus, in Hume's imagined dialogue, the desire for health gets explained either by the person's saying 'Because sickness is painful', or by his saying that health enables him to earn money, which is 'the instrument of pleasure'. But for Hume it is a merely empirical matter that answers such as these are most likely to be final: a final answer, 'Because money can often be carried in one's pockets', would be just as intelligible as the others.

good for you', if addressed to him, as supplying a proper reason for wanting or doing something, even if he sees fit to ignore it on a given occasion.

These facts put constraints on what can reasonably be said or denied in concrete ethical disputes; and they surely mean that any out-and-out subjectivism in ethics is untenable.

The arguments I have so far outlined against the fact/value distinction derive from what Anscombe has to say about wanting and practical deliberation. The errors alleged of the Humean view thus relate to the philosophy of psychology; and Anscombe believed that philosophers (at least the ones she was addressing) should sort out their philosophy of psychology before even attempting ethics:

is it not clear that there are several concepts that need investigating simply as part of the philosophy of psychology and—as I should recommend—*banishing ethics totally* from our minds? Namely—to begin with: 'action', 'intention', 'pleasure', 'wanting'. (*MMP*, 38)

In the essay from which this passage comes, 'Modern Moral Philosophy', and earlier in 'On Brute Facts', Anscombe examines another version of the fact/value distinction, also due to Hume: the thesis often expressed as 'No ought from an is'. If 'Reason is the slave of the passions' is to be dealt with primarily by doing philosophy of psychology, 'No ought from an is' is to be dealt with primarily by doing philosophy of language.

It is in his *Treatise* that Hume famously introduces the idea of an 'is/ought' gap. In the passage in question,[8] Hume does not exactly propose a general thesis; but those who have followed in his footsteps would probably state the following: that a conclusion about what ought to be done cannot be validly inferred from premises none of which contains 'ought' or some synonym. The connection with Hume's first thesis is meant to be this: a statement about what *is* the case expresses a belief and so cannot in itself motivate actions, while a statement about what *ought* to be the case is 'action-guiding', i.e. its function is precisely to motivate actions. So statements of the first kind cannot yield statements of the second kind.

What Hume noticed was that the relationship between 'is' and 'ought' is not at all straightforward, and that the transition from is-statements to ought-statements is philosophically problematic. But to unravel the difficulties here we need to jettison, or anyway modify, two empiricist assumptions: (a) that an ordinary empirical truth should be in some way verifiable by the senses; and (b) that a proposition's meaning should be giveable by an analysis of it, unless it happens to be a 'simple proposition'. It is particularly (b) that Anscombe tackles, but the results of her investigation deprive (a) of any attractiveness it might have had.

By way of analogy, she considers the word 'owes'. We are to consider the following sort of scenario. Mrs Smith asks the grocer for a quarter of potatoes, and

---

[8] Hume, *A Treatise of Human Nature*, III. i. 1.

the grocer delivers them and sends her a bill for X pounds. These, it might be said, are the facts of the case. Can we now derive the conclusion: 'Mrs Smith owes the grocer X pounds'? Well, that conclusion would not seem to follow logically, since there might be other facts of the case that prevent its being true—as, that the grocer and Mrs Smith are acting in an educational film. But if they are acting in a film, it might be urged, the 'bill' won't really be a bill, but only a pretend bill. Maybe so; but what now is the difference between a bill and a pretend bill, or for that matter between ordering some potatoes and just pretending to? Is it that the person who pretends lacks a certain intention—namely, the intention actually to charge somebody for some potatoes? That does seem to be part of the difference; but we should note that 'charge' is another term like 'bill', and an intention to (really) charge someone is on the same level as the intention to send a (real) bill.

So if we try to analyse these concepts—'bill', 'order', 'charge', and the like—part of our analysis will apparently involve intentions that themselves have to do with bills, orders, charges, and the like. In order really to charge someone something, you must *intend* to charge her. A paradox looms here, and it is one we shall be looking at more fully later on. But even aside from such intentions, the proposal that the concepts in question are fully analysable is doomed. So, therefore, is the hope that 'Mrs Smith owes X pounds' might follow logically from mere statements of fact—at least, on a certain natural, and Humean, conception of what a statement of fact is. And this is because the class of additional circumstances that might *prevent* the conclusion from following is open-ended. In general, with such concepts as those under discussion, there is no way of giving all the negative conditions, of citing all the things that must *not* hold, if the concept is to apply. Consider the concept of 'supplying'. You don't supply potatoes if you leave them somewhere and they're then stolen; or if you leave them too far from the place you're meant to be delivering them to (and how far is 'too far'?); or if they have changed too much in transit, e.g. by rotting (but how much is 'too much'?); and so on.

There can be no such thing as an exhaustive description of *all* the circumstances which theoretically could impair the description of an action of leaving a quarter of potatoes in my house as 'supplying me with a quarter of potatoes'. If there were such an exhaustive description, one could say that 'supplying me with a quarter of potatoes' *means* leaving them at my house, together with the absence of any of those circumstances. As things are, we could only say 'It means leaving them ... together with the absence of any of the circumstances which would impair the description of that action as an action of supplying me with potatoes'; which is hardly an explanation.   (*BF*, 23)

That the concepts under discussion have this kind of open-endedness is connected with their being institutional concepts. We ought to note at once, however, that it is not only institutional concepts that have this feature. Here are two other sorts of concept with the feature: (i) laws of nature, and (ii) biological functions or norms. As we shall see,[9] Anscombe elsewhere argues that a statement of the form 'As cause Bs', intended as expressing a law of nature, very often amounts to 'If an A occurs and no B follows, there must be something that prevents a B from occurring'. But once again, there is no prospect of citing *all* the possible things that might prevent a B from occurring. Similarly, 'The eye is for seeing' is at least closely related to 'If an eye does not see, it is defective; i.e. there is something (which we call a "defect") that prevents it from seeing'. Certainly the sentence doesn't amount to 'Most eyes see'. Anscombe mentions the fact that '*man* has so many teeth [thirty-two], which is certainly not the average number of teeth men have, but is the number of teeth for the species' (*MMP*, 38). ('Most adults have thirty-two teeth' is likewise no good, having been false for centuries.) If you don't have thirty-two teeth, there'll be some explanation, as that the upper right molar fell out, or that your front canines never developed owing to ... something or other. The preventing factor may not even be observed or known; the important thing is that it is posited. But citing *all* possible preventing factors is out of the question.

We can typically indicate that there are no preventing factors by saying that conditions are 'normal'. A normal eye sees; in normal circumstances, injecting the patient with morphine will reduce the pain; delivering potatoes in the context above described will normally constitute supplying them to someone. But there is a difference between the institutional and non-institutional cases, corresponding to different senses of the phrase 'unless something prevents it'. If the morphine is injected (etc.), but the pain is undiminished, then something must have prevented the hoped-for effect. The hoped-for effect can be specified independently of the injection and the holding of normal conditions, and hence verified independently; so that we can find that the pain is still there, and from that infer 'There must have been a preventing factor'. But the supply of potatoes is nothing over and above certain facts obtaining, along with an absence of preventing factors. We could not *find* that the potatoes had not been supplied—we would have to infer that they had not been, having *found* that there had been some specific preventing factor. The 'must' in 'If the potatoes weren't supplied (given the initial facts), then there must have been something to prevent it' is a conceptual sort of 'must', and easier to give an account of than the 'must' in 'If X occurred and Y didn't occur, there must have been something to prevent it'.

It does not follow from what we have observed about normal conditions that 'The grocer supplied her with potatoes' entails, or involves the implicit assertion, that conditions were normal: 'Every description [of this sort] presupposes a context of normal procedure, but that context is not even implicitly described by the description. Exceptional circumstances could always make a difference, but they do not come into consideration without reason' (*BF*, 23). The default position is that conditions are normal—this is 'presupposed'. One does not need to ascertain that conditions are normal before being fully justified in using such a description as 'supplying potatoes'. This is not just because the job of ascertaining is, as a matter of fact, open-ended and hence uncompletable, so that we allow people to describe actions as supplyings even though 'strictly speaking' there is room for doubt. After all, since the rules of the institution (of buying and selling) are up to us, we could stipulate a finite and ascertainable set of possible preventing factors. Why, then, is the list of such factors open-ended? Why do our institutional concepts have this sort of shape?

Many other concepts are open-ended, of course. The concept *game* is a famous instance: what games have in common are various criss-crossing similarities, rather than a single property or set of properties common to all games. One cannot list all the combinations of properties that could constitute being a game, just as one cannot list all the factors that could prevent an action's being an act of supplying potatoes. In both cases, the reason why this doesn't matter is, roughly, that agreement in judgement, of the sort that underlies language use quite generally, is an empirical fact. We do, as a matter of fact, respond to new cases in the same way most of the time, and not because we each employ the same definition of a word, or have the same idea in mind (in any helpful sense of 'idea'). A newly devised activity that strikes you as a game will most likely strike me as one, too; and a circumstance that strikes me as undermining the description 'supplying potatoes' in a given case will most likely strike you the same way. At any rate, the only way of addressing disagreements on such issues is by appeal to perceived similarities or dissimilarities with agreed cases.

The open-endedness of institutional concepts relates to 'preventing factors'. That such concepts are usable relies on an important principle relating to possible disagreements: namely, that in a given case, the default position is that there are no preventing factors. The practices of buying and selling, ordering and supplying, and so on, require that we cross bridges only when we come to them, and this must therefore go also for the associated practices of describing actions as buyings, sellings, orderings, etc. The onus of proof is on the person who says there has been a preventing factor. Here is a clue to the defeat of much philosophical scepticism: doubt is allowed for in all these language-games, but to make his voice heard the doubter must be prepared to show us an actual abnormal circumstance.[10]

The transition from 'is' to 'owes' turns out to have the following features. A set of factual premises will not entail 'X owes Y such-and-such a sum', if 'entails' means 'logically guarantees'. For additional facts could show the conclusion to be false. But citing those same factual premises can nevertheless be a sufficient justification for asserting 'X owes Y such-and-such a sum'. We can indeed say that

[10] Cf. Wittgenstein, *Philosophical Investigations*, para. 84: 'But that is not to say that we are in doubt because it is possible for us to *imagine* a doubt.'

the truth of the conclusion *consists in* the truth of the premises, rather than in the truth of the premises plus the absence of preventing factors. In the same way, an action's being a supplying of potatoes may consist simply in its being a delivering of potatoes, which may consist simply in its being a leaving of potatoes outside a door. This connects with what it is appropriate to say, e.g. about temporal location: '*When*, one might ask, did he supply me? Obviously, when he left the potatoes; it would be absurd to add "and also when he did *not* send to take them away again"' (*BF*, 23). The relation of 'owes' to the concepts occurring in the factual premises (e.g. 'asked Y for a quarter of potatoes', 'delivered the potatoes', etc.) is a complex one, and not such as to enable us to analyse 'owes' in terms of those concepts, or in terms of any such concepts—unless we are allowed to insert 'in normal conditions'. For an explanation of how concepts like 'owes' work, philosophical analysis in the traditional sense is of little use. We have, rather, to attend (a) to the exigencies of the practices in which they are embedded, and (b) to the empirical facts of agreement in judgement.

Anscombe's discussion of 'owes' prepares us for what needs to be said about 'ought'. Now as we shall see, there is more than one kind of 'ought'. But in many cases, the transition from 'is' to 'ought' will turn out to be similar to that from 'is' to 'owes', in particular where the 'ought' is embedded in an institution or rule-governed practice—such as that of promising.

2.2. Promising and Practical Necessity

With her discussion of the transition from 'is' to 'owes' Anscombe has already gone some way to defusing the two main problems that Hume drew our attention to: (i) how a certain kind of conclusion can follow from merely 'factual' premises, in view of the apparent gap; and (ii) how an action-guiding conclusion can follow from premises none of which is in itself action-guiding. For 'owes' looks to be an action-guiding word, if any is. In the absence of (empirically specifiable) preventing factors, 'You owe me £10' entails 'You should pay me £10'. But (ii) is only answered in the sense that it will probably be agreed that an 'owes' statement does follow, in the way Anscombe describes, from certain premises. How it is *possible* for an action-guiding statement to follow from those premises in this way remains puzzling.[11]

Owing something is being under a certain sort of obligation; this is the reason why 'owes' is action-guiding. And *obligation* is clearly a crucial concept for ethics. Anscombe's investigation of this concept has a number of important consequences. These include: (a) that to understand how it is possible for an obligation to be created, we have to describe a certain pervasive sort of

---

[11] John Searle's famous 'How to Derive "Ought" from "Is" ', *Philosophical Review*, 73 (1964), 43–58 may be said to apply the argument of 'On Brute Facts' to promising, thus answering (ii) in the minimal sense; the 'puzzling' aspect of (ii) is left more or less unaddressed.

language-game; (b) that the notion of a special 'moral' variety of obligation is senseless; (c) that the notions of having an obligation to oneself and of self-legislation are senseless; (d) that what needs to be added to (a) if we are to explain how moral statements are action-guiding in a *special* way is not one of the senseless notions mentioned under (b) or (c), but rather certain facts about what human beings need, and of what is good for them.

It is to the institution of promising that Anscombe turns in order to arrive at an understanding of the nature of obligation. And once again, Hume provides her with her starting point. As she says at the very start of 'Rules, Rights and Promises': 'Hume had two theses about promises: one, that a promise is "naturally unintelligible", and the other that even if (*per impossibile*) it were "naturally intelligible" it could not *naturally* give rise to any obligation' (*RRP*, 97). Hume opposed 'nature' to 'convention'. His discussion points out that the key thing about a promise is its being expressed by means of a sign whose significance consists, not in any attendant act of the mind (a natural phenomenon), but in the conventional role it plays in society. Anscombe takes Hume to have noticed certain very important facts about the nature of promises, and a number of points made by her echo points made by Hume. But Hume, I think it fair to say, did not get right down to the bottom of the question. A sign of this is that, for Hume, the absurdity in the idea of there being promises antecedent to convention relates to the impossibility of changing one's sentiments at will: 'A promise creates a new obligation. A new obligation supposes new sentiments to arise. The will never creates new sentiments. There could not naturally, therefore, arise any obligation from a promise, even supposing the mind could fall into the absurdity of willing that obligation.'[12] But the real absurdity has not to do with any supposed intrinsic connection between obligation and sentiment. It does have to do—in part—with the impossibility of bringing an obligation into existence by a mere act of will. But in order to explain why this is impossible we need to go further than Hume did into the nature of the 'sign' by which one indicates a promise. And this is what Anscombe does.

What is it to promise something? It appears to be this: to make a sign, together with a description of a future state of affairs, where the consequence of doing so is that one has to bring that state of affairs about. ('Make a sign' must be construed broadly: sometimes the context of utterance has the force of a conventional sign.) But what does 'has to' mean here? A natural way to read 'X has to φ' is as meaning 'Such and such will eventuate if X does not φ', especially where 'such and such' is something bad. Thus, 'I have to take these pills every morning' amounts to 'If I don't take these pills each morning, I'll get ill'. The kind of necessity conveyed by the modal 'have to' in such a case is explained by Aristotle[13] as follows: the necessary is that without which good cannot be or come to be (cf. *PJ*, 15); and

---

[12] *A Treatise of Human Nature*, III. ii. 5 (Everyman's Library; London: J. M. Dent, 1911), ii. 221.
[13] See Aristotle, *Metaphysics* D, ch. 5, 1015ᵃ20–5.

in view of Anscombe's use of this notion and ascription of it to Aristotle, various philosophers refer to it as 'Aristotelian necessity'.[14]

So what bad thing will eventuate if one fails to bring about the state of affairs mentioned in the promise? Could it be this: that one will incur sanctions, suffer punishment? But that may well not be the case; and anyway, you're meant to keep your promises whether or not you'll be caught or get punished. Could it be this: that you will upset or annoy the recipient of the promise? But that also may not be the case; the recipient may have other things on his mind, or may have died (death does not nullify a promise). Moreover, we need to be careful not to conflate the making of a promise with the expression of an intention; and not carrying out your intentions, whether because you forget to or because you change your mind, may upset or annoy those who wanted you to stick to those intentions. The 'annoyance' caused by breaking a promise must be specified as a special kind of annoyance. 'Justified annoyance' seems right; but of course the justice of the annoyance, or of the complaint against the promise-breaker, relates to his having done something bad. But the act (or omission) will most likely not be something for which one would be blamed had one not made the promise. It may, e.g., be one's not babysitting for a friend one evening. Evidently, the bad state of affairs that typically eventuates if one breaks a promise is just that of one's having broken a promise. But this is circular, if we are trying to say what a promise *is*: 'Promising to φ is giving a sign such that you then have to φ, lest something bad eventuates—namely your not keeping your promise.' Just as with 'X owes ... ', we find that an *analysis* of the concept of a promise eludes us.

And this is not the only problem. In the last section, I mentioned the fact that with a range of institutional verbs φ, to φ requires that you take yourself to be φ-ing. But if 'X thinks he is promising' is part of the analysis of 'X promises', an infinite regress seems to result. The difficulty is not that in order to promise, X must have an infinite series of thought-episodes, for we could explain 'X thinks that ... ' as ascribing to X a certain sort of disposition (to speak in Rylean mode):[15] in the same way, it can be claimed that if you are thinking, then you think that you're thinking, and think that you think that you're thinking ... each of these steps corresponding, roughly, to the condition that if asked 'Do you think that you're (...) thinking?', you would reply 'Yes'. The difficulty, rather, is that the *content* of the thought, 'I am promising', remains unspecified. How could one teach someone what a promise is, and so how to make one, if that person would need first of all to know what it was to have the thought 'I am promising ... '? It appears that learning what a promise is must be impossible. But we clearly do learn what promises are. A paradox.

Both of the difficulties we have encountered are solved in the same way: by a change of philosophical tack. Rather than hunting for an analysis of 'promise', we need to examine the nature of the language-games in which such things as

---

[14] See e.g. Foot, *Natural Goodness*, p. 15.   [15] Cf. *PI*, 12.

promises occur, together with an account of how these language-games are taught and learnt. This is Anscombe's method. She begins by looking at the 'has to', in 'X has to bring about such-and-such state of affairs'. This modal turns out not to be an expression of Aristotelian necessity after all; rather, it expresses a special and primitive variety of necessity, found in all rule-governed practices, such as games:

> Think of the game played with very small children where several players pile their hands on top of one another. Then, if one of them doesn't pull his hand out from the bottom, you say 'You have to put your hand on top'; if he pulls it out too soon you say 'No, you can't pull it out yet, so-and-so has to pull it out first'. 'You have to' and 'you can't' are at first words used by one who is making you do something (or preventing you), and they quickly become themselves instruments of getting and preventing action. (*RRP*, 101)

'You have to' ('You're meant to', etc.) expresses a kind of necessity, and 'You can't' expresses a kind of impossibility. As usual, necessity and (im)possibility are interdefinable: thus, if it's necessary for you to φ, then it is not possible for you not to φ. The modal 'can't' is dubbed by Anscombe a *stopping modal*, 'have to' a *forcing modal* (*RRP*, 100). (A 'permitting modal', such as 'may', can be defined as the negation of a stopping modal.) Although Anscombe applies 'stopping modal' to cases of Aristotelian necessity as well as to ones embodying the sort of non-Aristotelian necessity we are looking at, [16] I will for purposes of clarity apply 'stopping/forcing modal' only to the latter.

If in the context of a game a child says '*Why* can't I do that?', we might answer 'Because it's against the rules'. But this answer will only be understood if the child is already acquainted with the idea of a rule. What is a rule? A rule may or may not be written down somewhere; but whether or not it is written down, what it says will involve (explicitly or implicitly) stopping or forcing modals. 'A player may not castle more than once'—or: 'The players take turns to move', i.e. neither player *may* move twice in a row, and each player *must* move (or resign) after the other has moved. And so on. Hence the meaning of stopping and forcing modals must be understood before one learns the concept of a rule.

Another kind of answer to 'Why can't I do that?' might be specific; e.g. 'Because your king is in check (so you can't move that pawn)'. Such answers cannot be used to explain the meaning of the modals. For an answer of this kind can only be understood as *giving a reason* by someone who already knows the modals: it involves grasping that (e.g.) you *have to* move your king when it's in check. It is true that a full grasp of the modals involves knowing that a modal is to be backed up with a reason, or as Anscombe calls it a *logos*, [17] such as 'Your king is in check'; but the significance of the *logos* cannot be grasped independently of the modal. Modal and *logos* are learnt in a package, as it were, and it is especially

---

[16] See e.g. *RRP*, 101: 'You can't move that, the shelf will fall down.'
[17] *RRP*, 102; also *SAS*, 142.

their interdependence that Anscombe sees as scuppering the idea that promises might be 'naturally intelligible' (*RRP*, 103). For *explanations* of the meanings of modals or of *logoi* are, in a crucial sense, impossible.

How then are stopping and forcing modals taught? They are taught by means of actions: actions of showing (I might move the child's king for him), or actions of being made to do something (in Anscombe's game I might take the child's hand and put it on top of the others'). As Wittgenstein said, 'In the beginning was the deed.'[18]

At the beginning, the adults will physically stop the child from doing what they say he 'can't' do. But gradually the child learns. [. . .] It is part of human intelligence to be able to learn the responses to stopping modals without which they wouldn't exist as linguistic instruments and without which these things: rules, etiquette, rights, infringements, promises, pieties and impieties would not exist either.   (*RRP*, 101)

As we see from this passage, Anscombe took the notion of stopping/forcing modals to have a very general application. She was surely right. In the last few decades, especially since Kripke reminded philosophers of the importance of Wittgenstein's remarks on rules and rule-following, much attention has been directed to the question of what a rule is. Anscombe's modals are of direct relevance here; and we shall see in Chapter 6 how they bear on the question that exercised Wittgenstein and Kripke, that of the nature of logical and linguistic rules.[19]

How do stopping/forcing modals help when it comes to promising? Our first difficulty was to say what a promise *is*, without running into circularity; and we are now in a position to do this. The bare bones of the account are as follows: to promise to φ is to make a sign, together with the specification of one's φ-ing, where the significance of this is that one now has to φ (or to φ later on). Since 'has to' is a forcing modal, not an Aristotelian modal, the question 'Has to φ, lest what happen?' is in a sense out of place (it was the apparent need to answer this question which landed us with the circularity). Not wholly out of place, however; for of course teaching people how to make and keep promises will be accompanied by sanctions of some sort in the case of promises' being broken—so that it could be said, 'You have to φ, lest you incur sanctions'. Such sanctions are not only needed at the stage of teaching, but also later on, since a person often has an incentive to break a promise. (The analogous thing doesn't go so much for games, unless they involve betting.) However, 'You have to φ, lest you incur sanctions' serves only to teach or enforce the rule; it does not express the rule,

---

[18] Wittgenstein, *On Certainty*, trans. Elizabeth Anscombe and Denis Paul (Oxford: Blackwell, 1969), para. 402 (quoting Goethe).

[19] That Anscombe gives her account of practical necessity (stopping modals plus Aristotelian necessity) in at least four articles—*PJ*, *RRP*, *SAS*, and *QLI*—is an indication of the general importance she must have attached to that account. For Saul A. Kripke's contribution, see his *Wittgenstein on Rules and Private Language: An Elementary Exposition* (Oxford: Blackwell, 1982).

nor explain the special meaning of the modal implicit in the rule: You have to keep your promise. For, as was said above, you're meant not to break a promise even if you're likely to get away with doing so.

We avoid circularity in our account of promising by describing, in the course of that account, how stopping and forcing modals work, i.e. by describing how they are taught and what the learner learns to do—namely, to respond appropriately to those modals, to use them as instruments for getting people to do certain things, to back them up with contextually given *logoi*, and so on. We describe what people actually do with these bits of language, and thus describe the function (meaning) of these bits of language.

The second difficulty we faced concerned the fact that in order to promise something, one had to be able to have the thought that one was promising. The solution of the difficulty lies in seeing what 'thinking you are promising' amounts to. A clue to this was already to be met with in our discussion of owing, supplying, etc., where we found that the default position is that there are no preventing factors. In the same sort of way, in the conduct of the language-game of promising, and of other games, the default position is that one who shows no signs of thinking that some preventing factor is present, and so who goes on in the normal way for a person who is playing the game, is to be counted a person who *thinks* he is playing the game:

[Playing the game] involves that you are acquainted with the game and have an appropriate background, and also appropriate *expectations* and *calculations* in connection with, e.g., moving this piece from point A to point B. To have these is to think you are playing the game. [. . .] If someone seriously thought he was only rehearsing [getting married], he would not afterwards *act* as if he thought he was married: if he did so, his plea that he 'thought it was only a rehearsal' would not be heard.   (*PJ*, 17)

At this stage of our enquiry, the answer to what might be called 'Hume's first question'—what is a promise?—has been sketched out. Some more needs to be said; but the best place to say it will be in answering his second question: how can one *create* an obligation for oneself? And more generally: how can an action-guiding statement like 'You have to φ', or 'You ought to φ', follow from, or come to be true because of, various facts about what people said to one another?

Of course, we might say that we've already explained how you can be obliged to move your king, and how the action-guiding 'You have to move your king' follows from various facts. But the relation of human action to ethics seems to be on an altogether different plane from that of human action to chess. If promising is *like* a game, still, for all that, it *isn't* a game. Here is one source of the inclination to posit a special 'moral' sense of 'ought', 'have to', 'cannot', 'must', and so on, a sense that is appropriate when it comes to promises, but not appropriate when it comes to chess. Unfortunately, this idea cannot be explained by claiming, à la Kant, that 'You must keep your promises' is a categorical imperative while

'You must move your king out of check' is a merely hypothetical imperative. For as Philippa Foot famously pointed out[20] in connection with the rules of etiquette, such rules are not in Kant's sense hypothetical: they do not apply only to those with certain aims or wants. The rules of etiquette and the rules of chess are non-hypothetical, and in both cases the reason has to do with the nature of stopping/forcing modals.[21]

We shall look in more detail at the notion of a 'moral ought' in the next section. For now, it is enough to observe that we need have recourse to no such notion in order to explain the *special* action-guiding nature of 'ought', in 'You ought to keep your promises'.

The question to ask is: *Why do we go in for promising?* And the answer is simply that the institution of promising is very useful for human beings. All sorts of enterprises and activities require that people can rely upon others to do certain things. You can indeed rely on others to do things if they love you or fear you, or if there exists some sort of tit-for-tat arrangement between you and them. But these sorts of situations are comparatively rare; the institution of promising vastly extends the range of situations of this type. (Here Anscombe's discussion is quite close to Hume's.)

Thus such a procedure as that language-game is an instrument whose use is part and parcel of an enormous amount of human activity and hence of human good; of the supplying both of human needs and of human wants so far as the satisfactions of these are compossible. It is scarcely possible to live in a society without encountering it and even actually being involved in it.   (*PJ*, 18)

The necessity expressed by 'You have to, since you promised to' is that of a forcing modal, internal to the practice of promising; but the necessity of going in for promising, and so of sticking to the rules internal to the practice—this is an Aristotelian necessity. Without promising, an enormous amount of human good would be impossible. Breaking one's promises 'will tend to hamper the attainment of the advantages that the procedure serves' (*PJ*, 18)—and the same goes, to a lesser degree, for eschewing all promising. Note the use of the verb 'tend to' here. An act-utilitarian will ask why he should keep a promise, if in the actual situation more good (of the very sort mentioned in our account of the purpose of promising) will result from breaking it than from keeping it. The answer must allude to actions of that *type* (promise-breaking), or if you like, to rules or dispositions or tendencies—in short, to the general as opposed to the particular. We shall be saying more about this in §4.2. For now, the point to be made is that it is the good of the institution of promising that explains how

---

[20] Foot, 'Morality as a System of Hypothetical Imperatives', in *Virtues and Vices and Other Essays in Moral Philosophy* (Oxford: Blackwell, 1978), 157–73.

[21] The argument here connects with what was said in the last chapter about what kinds of answers are adequate to the question, 'But why do you want (to do) *that?*', the context being a game or similar. See pp. 72–3.

it is possible for 'genuine obligation' to be created: 'And hence it comes about that by the voluntary giving of a sign I can restrict my possibilities of acting *well* and hence it can lead to my deserving, as well as receiving, reproach [if I break a promise]' (*PJ*, 19).

'You have to φ, lest you incur sanctions' expresses an Aristotelian necessity, since sanctions are something bad for the agent, indeed are designed to be. As we saw above, 'You have to φ, lest you incur sanctions' can be invoked in the teaching and enforcing of the rule about keeping your promises. But there is an additional Aristotelian necessity, concerning human good generally. It is because of this *additional* necessity that the reproach against a promise-breaker is said to be not only incurred but deserved; and because of it that we feel the 'ought' of promising to have a special force, lacking from the 'ought' of chess. For although playing chess does serve a purpose—that of yielding a certain kind of pleasure—it is not an instrument of human good as such in the way that promising, in all its many forms, is.

The overall purpose of the institution of promising—or, as we might put it more generally, of undertaking—accounts for some of the characteristic features of that institution:

For one thing, an undertaking must be made to someone else. But even that is not enough. For if I go to someone and say 'I undertake to stand on my head' and he replies: 'But I don't want you to stand on your head', then I have not undertaken anything. An undertaking must be received by someone else and in someone's interest. [. . .] 'being in someone's interest' here *includes* 'being in accord with his desire'.   (*PJ*, 15)

Also explicable is that feature of promises (and of many other institutions) which we mentioned earlier: the feature whereby if you are promising something, then you must think that you are. For the giving of a promise needs to be voluntary, and this can only be the case if you think you are giving it (*PJ*, 14). Why does the giving of a promise need to be voluntary? The answer to this relates both to the giving of promises and to the receiving of them. An institution that was like promising, but which had the rule that you are bound even by promises not voluntarily given, would be an institution open to obvious abuse, and hence would be an instrument of an enormous amount of human ill. The point applies most obviously to promises that are extorted: Smith, armed with a cosh, could get Jones to promise him all his worldly possessions, and Jones would then have to abide by his promise. But in this scenario, Jones would at any rate be aware that he was making a promise, or a 'promise'. Where the issue has to do with the rationale for one's being *aware* that one is promising, the sort of bad rule to consider is that whereby one would be bound even by promises one had unwittingly made. A girl who didn't speak English and who, in the context of a marriage ceremony, said 'I promise . . . ' (or said 'Yes' to the question, 'Do you promise . . . ?'), having been told that the words meant something else, or simply being too frightened to ask what they do mean—such a girl would be bound by her promise. And as with extortion, a rule that allowed this and cases like it would be a rule open to obvious abuse. As far as the receiving of promises goes, if a person could promise something involuntarily, there would often be a doubt as to whether she was even *able* to fulfil her promise; and in that case the receiver of the promise could not rely on its fulfilment.

'Because it's good for you' gives a desirability characterization. So does 'Because it's good for us human beings'. The latter is a perfectly good answer to 'Why should I keep my promises (or: this promise)?'; more precisely, the answer is 'Because the institution of promising is good for us human beings'. That this statement can give an adequate reason is surprising only to those under the spell of an egoistic account of human psychology. The language-game of giving reasons for one's actions, like all language-games, is a public thing, and so it is to be expected that what counts as an acceptable reason for action will not be something restricted to the agent's own good. After all, why would we have a concept of reason according to which a person's saying 'I did that solely for my own benefit, and regardless of other people' can only be met with 'Oh I see; well, I must admit that is a good reason'? Giving reasons for one's actions is giving an *account* of oneself—and this is not the same as describing one's own psychology.

Nevertheless, a person might play 'Because it's good for me' and 'Because it's good for us' off against each other: 'For this reason it is intelligible for a man to say he sees no necessity to act well in that matter [of keeping promises], that is, no necessity for himself to take contracts seriously except as it serves his purposes' (*PJ*, 19). The line taken by such a man is intelligible—given that he accepts 'Because it's good for us' as *a* reason. The mistake of such a man consists in a wrong ordering of goods. I have already looked at the question how a disagreement about the ordering of goods may be addressed (see Ch. 2, §3.2); and I suggested that at the bottom of a wrong ordering of goods there may be, if not unintelligibility, then at any rate confusion or less than total rationality. If it is an essential part of being a good human being, of leading a good life overall, that one's ordering of goods is right; and if taking 'Because it's good for us human beings' as a weighty reason for action is necessary for having a right ordering of goods (something demonstrable only to those with some aptitude for 'hearing' the arguments); then it follows that keeping your promises is good for *you, qua* human being. In that case another answer to 'Why should I keep my promises?' is available, once again citing an Aristotelian necessity: 'Because it's good for you *qua* human being'. You might of course be more interested in being a good money-making machine than in being a good human being, but apart from anything else this amounts to aiming at being good in one small area rather than being good overall—which *prima facie* appears to constitute a wrong ordering of goods.

3. THE LEGALISTIC CONCEPTION OF MORALITY

Anscombe's famous essay of 1958, 'Modern Moral Philosophy', puts forward three main theses.

The first is that it is not profitable for us at present to do moral philosophy; that should be laid aside at any rate until we have an adequate philosophy of psychology, in which we are conspicuously lacking.   (*MMP*, 26)

We have seen how Anscombe proposed that the lack she referred to should be addressed, namely by righting a wrong (especially Humean) view of reason, passion, wanting, and related notions. Her second thesis

is that the concepts of obligation, and duty—*moral* obligation and *moral* duty, that is to say—and of what is *morally* right and wrong, and of the *moral* sense of 'ought', ought to be jettisoned if this is psychologically possible; because they are survivals, or derivatives from survivals, from an earlier conception of ethics which no longer generally survives, and are only harmful without it.   (*MMP*, 26)

One thing that Anscombe clearly does *not* mean by this thesis is that 'ought', 'must', 'obligation', 'duty', 'right', and 'wrong' are all terms without a proper use within ethical discourse. Her point is rather that within that discourse, those terms do not have a special ('moral') meaning; and that ethical discourse is not to be characterized as discourse employing those terms with such a special meaning. Ethics is to be characterized by its subject matter: roughly, human flourishing, or various aspects of human flourishing. That is why ethics may be called a 'science' (*I*, 76).

In *MMP*, Anscombe took the *paradigm* case of obligation to be legal obligation, of the sort that can only exist within a legal framework—which itself involves the existence (e.g. past existence) of a legislator. She had not yet developed her thoughts on stopping/forcing modals; but from the following it seems clear that she thought of obligation as also arising in non-legal contexts, of the sort to which her theory of modals was to apply: 'Here [sc. in a divine law theory of ethics] it really does add something to the description 'unjust' to say that there is an obligation not to do it; for what obliges is the divine law—*as rules oblige in a game*' (*MMP*, 41; my italics). If we take *MMP* along with Anscombe's subsequent thoughts on modals, we may put the point as follows. Just as you may not castle twice in chess, you may not take another's property without his consent: the same modal, 'may not', occurs in both cases. It is the Aristotelian necessity of our having the institution of property that makes the second example a moral example, rather than any special 'moral' sense of the phrase 'may not'. (The stopping modals used in explaining property or promises are not a special 'moral' kind, any more than are the stopping modals used in explaining chess a special 'boardgame' kind.)

Moreover, there are various uses of 'should' and 'ought', other than as forcing modals, which, like such modals, might or might not occur within an ethical context. 'Should', for example, may be used in the course of one of those practical arguments about which Aristotle wrote, and which were the topic of Chapter 2 (esp. §2.2):

In thinking of the word for 'should', 'ought' etc. (δεῖ) as it occurs in Aristotle, we should think of it as it occurs in ordinary language (e.g. as it has just occurred in this sentence) and not just as it occurs in the examples of 'moral discourse' given by moral philosophers. That athletes should keep in training, pregnant women watch their weight, film stars their publicity, [. . .] that meals ought to be punctual, that we should (not) see the methods of 'Linguistic Analysis' in Aristotle's philosophy; any fair selection of examples, if we care to summon them up, should convince us that 'should' is a rather light word with unlimited contexts of application ... '   (*I*, 64)

The problem, Anscombe argues, is that '[t]he ordinary (and quite indispensable) terms "should", "needs", "ought", "must"—acquired this special ["moral"] sense by being equated in the relevant contexts with "is obliged" [. . .] in the sense in which one can be obliged or bound by law, or something can be required by law' (*MMP*, 29–30).

As the title of 'Modern Moral Philosophy' makes clear, the arguments expounded in that essay were aimed especially at the moral philosophy of the time, not at all moral philosophy ever done or to be done. This goes by the way for the third as well as for the first two theses, '[t]hat the differences between the well-known English writers on moral philosophy from Sidgwick to the present day are of little importance' (*MMP*, 26). I will be discussing this thesis in the next section. For now it needs only to be stressed that Anscombe's main target in *MMP* really was the then modern moral philosophy. What she has to say in connection with each of her three theses has two aspects: (a) the philosophical nature of a certain prevalent error or errors; (b) a historical sketch of how the error(s) came to have currency. The second of these belongs to the methodology of diagnosis, as well as being interesting in its own right. Just as Nietzsche's 'genealogy of morals' is intended to cast doubt on an ideology or way of thinking by laying bare its historical and psychological roots, so Anscombe's remarks under (b), especially with regard to her second thesis, are intended to help us to see the bankruptcy of prevalent notions within moral philosophy—and thus to help us to understand (a).

Did Anscombe think that the errors she was attacking were ones committed only, or mainly, by professional philosophers? Or did she regard the wider intellectual culture as also infected?—When it came to her third thesis, and the issue of consequentialism, I think it is pretty clear that Anscombe did have the wider culture in mind. But with her second thesis it is rather less clear. Alasdair MacIntyre, on whom *MMP* had a crucial influence,[22] took the second thesis

---

[22] See MacIntyre, *After Virtue: A Study in Moral Theory* (London: Duckworth, 1981); e.g. MacIntyre's acknowledgement of Anscombe on p. 51.

much further than Anscombe herself did, elaborating it and adding to it, and taking it to apply to Western culture quite generally. But whatever the merits of MacIntyre's view, a reader of *MMP* would do well to consider Anscombe's second thesis with the injunction in mind, 'If the cap fits, wear it', applying the injunction to himself and those around him.

The claim is that people are (or at least were, when Anscombe wrote) using a term like 'ought' *as if* there were a law, such that doing what you ought not to is breaking that law—but where in fact there is no such law. What is the evidence for the claim? On the one hand there is textual evidence: the work of various writers, such as Kant, Prichard, Hare, and Mackie, to name but four. The last, writing a couple of decades after *MMP*, argued against the reality of moral properties (as he put it) by assuming that such properties would have to be ones that somehow imposed obligations on people: to know that some such property inhered in some state of affairs, e.g., would be to feel, and in some sense *be*, compelled to do something—to bring an end to the state of affairs, for example. For Mackie, morality, if there is such a thing, must have to do with 'objective obligation', obligation independent of any legislators or practices, obligation that was somehow 'part of the fabric of the world', in Mackie's phrase.[23] The idea that morality must have this character is what Anscombe was attacking.

On the other hand, there is evidence in how people generally talk and argue. Anscombe speaks of how 'ought' may 'be spoken with a special emphasis and with a special feeling in these contexts' (*MMP*, 30), and of how the word in those contexts has 'become a word of mere mesmeric force' (*MMP*, 32). MacIntyre adds more detail to the picture, extending Anscombe's second thesis to include 'good', which term, in the mouths of modern intellectuals such as the Bloomsburyites, MacIntyre takes to have been as empty as Anscombe's 'morally ought', and for similar reasons. His evidence is the way people like the Woolfs, Lytton Strachey, Roger Fry, *et al.* wrote and talked. G. E. Moore's account of 'good' as a non-natural object of intuition suited such people perfectly, hence their adulation of Moore's moral philosophy; but

[a]n acute observer at the time [. . .] might well have put matters thus: these people take themselves to be identifying the presence of a non-natural property, which they call 'good'; but there is in fact no such property and they are doing no more and no other than expressing their feelings and attitudes, disguising the expression of preference and whim by an interpretation of their own utterance and behaviour which confers upon it an objectivity that it does not in fact possess.[24]

MacIntyre does not think the Bloomsburyites alone suffered from emptiness of moral discourse; they are merely a vivid example of a modern phenomenon.

Another piece of evidence that Anscombe makes use of is the fact that philosophers (and others) are so quick to accept the idea of an 'is/ought gap'.

[23] Mackie, *Ethics: Inventing Right and Wrong* (Harmondsworth: Penguin, 1977), p. 15.
[24] MacIntyre, *After Virtue*, p. 16.

For if the function of 'ought' is to invoke a moral law, a law independent of any particular sort of *content*—pure obligation, as it were—then it is not surprising that an 'ought'-statement cannot be inferred from factual premisses. Moreover, 'obligation' in the absence of actual laws or practices will in fact be an empty notion, and those in the grip of the picture of moral obligation will often dimly perceive this; so that they will find the 'is/ought' gap a very believable thing. And in fact Hume's assertion that an 'ought', used in *this* way, cannot be inferred from an 'is' turns out to be quite correct: 'This word "ought", having become a word of mere mesmeric force, could not, in the character of having that force, be inferred from anything whatever' (*MMP*, 32). Once again, Hume was noticing *something* real, according to Anscombe. She takes his 'no ought from an is' to encapsulate two correct ideas: first, that the transition is indeed problematic, in a way that she deals with in 'On Brute Facts' (see above, pp. 90–4); second, that where 'ought' is used in the sort of empty way indicative of a legalistic conception of morality, an 'ought'-statement cannot be inferred from anything whatever—not even other 'ought'-statements. In the same way, 'Socrates is grobulous' cannot be *inferred* from 'All men are grobulous' and 'Socrates is a man' (cf. *MMP*, 32).

This last thought—that 'morally ought' fails to mean anything at all in many of its uses—appears quite radical. Some of Anscombe's phraseology suggests a contradictory view, e.g. where she says that 'ought' and other terms 'acquired this special ['moral'] sense by being equated in the relevant contexts with "is obliged"' (*MMP*, 29–30; see above). That she speaks now one way, now another, may indicate that her response to the question 'Meaningful or meaningless? Sense or nonsense?' would simply have been: 'Say what you like.' Meaning, as Wittgenstein showed, is an extremely flexible notion, and there are pros and cons to ascribing meaning to 'morally ought'. Insofar as meaning is use, what we have is a confused sort of use, a use that involves conceptual idling, etc.—so that we perhaps have a case of 'confused meaning'. The important thing is to see the use for what it is.

The aspect of use that is really central is this: that all sorts of reasons for doing something are rejected as reasons. Reasons that cite what is needed (e.g. for a human being's health), or that cite established rules or customs, or that cite commands—none of these, it is alleged, touch the important issue, which is: what action am I morally obliged to do? For can't I always ask, 'But *ought* I to aim for what is needed, or what is dictated by rules, or what is commanded?' Now it is true that *often* one can ask some such further question, especially about commands, for instance. But a general dissatisfaction with all 'factual' reasons does raise the question: what can 'I ought to φ' amount to, if there can be no substantive reasons that fully support that judgement (nor, of course, reasons that count conclusively against it)? The situation is very like that which we encountered earlier with Hume, for whom the question 'But why do you want *that*?' was indefinitely repeatable (see above, p. 89). The result of not accepting any reasons as adequate answers to 'Why do you want that?' is to make the question itself futile and empty; and similarly, the result of not accepting any substantive reasons as adequate answers to 'Why ought I to do that?' is, on the face of it, to make *that* question futile and empty—and also that particular use of 'ought'.[25]

If it is thought that 'I ought to φ' is free-floating in this way, a natural response is to adopt some form of subjectivism, according to which moral statements simply express personal preferences, sentiments, or whatever, of the kind that are (following Hume) insulated from Reason. The legalistic conception, in other words, has a tendency to lead to subjectivism; and the attraction that subjectivism holds for many modern philosophers may be taken as further, indirect, evidence of the prevalence of the legalistic conception. Hare is perhaps the most obvious example, since his prescriptivism explicitly combined the legalistic conception (prescriptions, universalizability) with Humean subjectivism (moral prescriptions turn out to be based on personal preference). But subjectivism is not the only possibility. Mackie realized that the legalistic conception of morality is absurd, especially in his rather metaphysical version; but since he couldn't see what else morality could be than what the legalistic conception states it to be, he inferred that moral statements were simply mistaken, one and all. Thus was born the so-called 'error theory'.

In a moment, we will consider some responses that proponents of the legalistic conception might make to Anscombe's charge of emptiness. But before doing so, we should take a closer look at Anscombe's historical account; for if there is (or was) a prevalent empty use of 'ought' *et al.*, of the kind described, we must ask: How so? How did things come to this pass?

Anscombe's hypothesis is that the modern, legalistic use of 'morally ought' is a relic from a time when people believed in a divine lawgiver. More specifically, it is a relic from a conception of ethics she calls a 'law conception': 'To have a *law* conception of ethics is to hold that what is needed for conformity with the virtues failure in which is the mark of being bad *qua* man (and not merely, say, *qua* craftsman or logician)—that what is needed for *this*, is required by divine law' (*MMP*, 30). Now Anscombe herself is clearly an adherent of a law conception of ethics; but she does not think that having such a conception is essential for ethical understanding.[26] The reason for this is simple: God requires

---

[25] That one can always reject substantive reasons for a moral judgement is the gist of Moore's Open Question Argument, which argument is meant to supply the test for whether a 'naturalistic fallacy' has been committed.

[26] A number of Anscombe's readers have failed to see this. Thus Simon Blackburn describes Anscombe's position as 'a version of the Dostoevskian claim that if God is dead everything is permitted'. Anscombe nowhere rules out non-theistic uses of 'ought', 'obligation', etc. within ethical discourse; so Blackburn is off-target when he says that Anscombe must regard any talk of duties and obligations, such as the obligations of an academic to his university and his students (Blackburn's example), as 'using words with "merely" talismanic force'. This misunderstanding vitiates Blackburn's complaint that 'if I feel I must avoid [these words] because I have been told they are the private preserve of people who believe in divine law, then I have been hoodwinked and robbed' ('Against Anscombe', *Times Literary Supplement*, 20 Sept. 2005).

what is good because it is good—a thing is not good because God requires it. So one can grasp what is good without believing that God requires it, and indeed without believing in God at all. But one cannot, she argues, believe in being *obliged* not to steal, murder, lie, etc. without belief in a lawgiver, more specifically, belief in some not merely earthly lawgiver—for the desire to speak of obligation here is independent of whether any earthly authority has actually outlawed theft, murder, lying, etc. Since the Enlightenment, a law conception of ethics has gradually disappeared from Western thought, especially because of the rise of atheism and agnosticism. But the desire to speak of obligation remains: 'It is as if the notion "criminal" were to remain when criminal law and criminal courts had been forgotten and abolished' (*MMP*, 30).

Anscombe's historical account is a hypothesis, and to evaluate it properly would require a detailed examination of the ideas and beliefs of the last few centuries. That task is beyond the scope of this book, and Anscombe herself did not attempt it. A fuller historical account is to be found in Mac-Intyre's *After Virtue*, and that account has certainly not gone unchallenged. But as I have hinted, for Anscombe the real problem has to do with current errors of thought, especially within philosophy, and the historical hypothesis is meant merely to contribute to a diagnosis, of the kind that can aid understanding.[27]

But is she right? Is the notion of moral obligation in the absence of a divine lawgiver really altogether empty? The most profound thinker to have adopted such a notion was, of course, Immanuel Kant. For Kant, the moral life required autonomy, in the literal sense of making laws for one's own conduct; to be subservient to the laws of an external authority was to be heteronomous, to lack that freedom of thought and action necessary for moral choice. The power and authority that for centuries had been vested in kings, potentates, and God himself was placed by Kant in the hands of the individual. Philosophical expression was thus given to the aspirations of the Protestant Enlightenment, and Kant's writings helped sow the intellectual seeds of modern individualism.

In *MMP*, Anscombe is pretty brisk with Kant, but her main objection to his moral philosophy is quite clear:

Kant introduces the idea of 'legislating for oneself', which is as absurd as if in these days, when majority votes command great respect, one were to call each reflective decision a man made a *vote* resulting in a majority, which as a matter of proportion is overwhelming, for it is always 1–0. The concept of legislation requires superior power in the legislator. (*MMP*, 27)

---

[27] In his *Truth and Truthfulness*, Bernard Williams goes so far as to argue that a 'genealogical' account of a concept or way of thinking need not in general make any claims to historical truth. If he is right, a discussion of the accuracy of Anscombe's hypothesis would appear to be philosophically otiose. That said, it seems to me that there is at least a very large grain of truth in Anscombe's historical hypothesis. See B. A. O. Williams, *Truth and Truthfulness: An Essay in Genealogy* (Princeton: Princeton University Press, 2002), ch. 2.

For there to be a law, (a) it must be promulgated, (b) it must be enforced or enforceable. Enforcing a law means wielding sanctions against those who knowingly break it, i.e. punishing them—something that in general requires that the legislating authority have adequate physical power to do that, power superior to that of law-breakers. A law is not a request, nor yet a cooperative agreement. In fact, one cannot make requests of oneself, or make agreements with oneself, any more than one can legislate for oneself; but in the case of legislation, as Anscombe indicates, the main problem for Kant's view is that one cannot punish oneself for breaking one's own 'laws'. Of course, one can feel guilty at breaking one's own resolutions, but guilt is not something that one decides to impose on oneself, in the way that sanctions must by definition be deliberately imposed (so that they can also be threatened). To call guilt a sanction can only be to speak metaphorically.

What Anscombe says about legislation is very like what we found her saying about undertaking: 'an undertaking must be made to someone else' (*PJ*, 15; see above, p. 101). In both cases, we need to remind ourselves of the initial need that gives rise to the institution, and of what empirical facts are required for the existence and maintenance of the institution. (Hence the comparison with voting in the above quotation.) In the manner of Wittgenstein, Anscombe's method is to remind us of the actual role that a certain language-game plays within human life.

This is not to say that one cannot in *some* sense feel, and perhaps be, bound by a form of practical necessity. I have in mind in particular the sort of necessity that is naturally expressed through such locutions as 'I cannot possibly do that'. This 'cannot' is not a stopping modal of the sort that typically goes with the existence of a practice or institution. 'I cannot do that', in the sense I am talking about, is said by someone who will not even consider a certain course of action—for whom putative reasons in favour of the action will not even get a hearing. (The proposed action could, e.g., be that of killing off some group of people in order to remedy the problems brought on by overpopulation.) From such a statement one learns something of the speaker's psychology, of their habits of thought and feeling; and the necessity involved is that of psychological fact,[28] not that of a law. A proper account of it would be more Aristotelian than Kantian. As we shall see, Anscombe's own view of human virtue involves that a virtuous person take certain kinds of action as being 'off the agenda' in just this way.

If self-legislation cannot be a source of moral obligation, what other source might there be? One obvious candidate is *custom*. And given the role that Anscombe elsewhere assigns to custom, it is clear she herself sees custom as the source of obligation, of the kind that is expressed by stopping or forcing modals

---

[28] That the necessity is 'psychological' does not make it any less a case of literal necessity, as Williams has argued; see his 'Practical Necessity', in *Moral Luck: Philosophical Papers, 1973–1980* (Cambridge: Cambridge University Press, 1981), esp. 127–8. This justifies our saying that the agent not only feels, but is, bound by practical necessity.

and which is associated with the concept of a right: 'At the level of generation of the concept of a right, all rights are necessarily prescriptive and in this sense rights are wholly based upon custom' (*SAS*, 142). 'Prescriptive' here just means 'customary' (*SAS*, 134). Anscombe's point is that rights are necessarily based simply on custom in the first instance. Judicial institutions evolve, bringing new kinds of rights into existence; but the right to obedience of those creating or representing such institutions must be external and prior to the institutions themselves. It's not a *law* that you should obey the law. But if human custom is thus the source of rights, and of rights not yet requiring any lawmakers, doesn't this lend some support to the legalistic conception of morality (though admittedly in a way that makes the term 'legalistic' inappropriate)? After all, the concept of a right is surely a moral concept, unlike the broader concept of a rule.

This last claim, however, is false. In chess, one has the right to change a pawn on the eighth rank into a queen. What makes a right a 'moral' right is the nature of the background institution: there is a serious human need of promising, but no such need of chess. (See above, pp. 100–1.) It is because there is always a question to be asked as to whether a human practice is actually good or necessary for human beings that Anscombe gives short shrift to the idea that societal norms (a.k.a. customs) are as such a source of moral obligation, in *MMP*: '[J]ust as one cannot be impressed by Butler [for whom personal conscience is a source of obligation] when one reflects what conscience can tell people to do, so, I think, one cannot be impressed by this idea if one reflects what the "norms" of a society can be like' (*MMP*, 37).

Anscombe's own view, as so far expounded, looks like this: obligation, properly speaking, arises from either law or custom; in the first case, there must be a lawgiver with power to enforce the laws, and in the second case, there must be a society in which the modals 'cannot', 'may', etc. have the sort of role we have described. There will be a further question, as to whether the law or custom is good for human beings, whether there is an Aristotelian need for it; if the answer to this question is positive, we may speak of 'moral obligation', or better still, of what is *just* (*MMP*, 38–41).

The first half of this account may invite the thought that Anscombe is a positivist about obligations, duties, rights, and the rest. Bentham famously characterized talk of moral or natural rights (as opposed to legal or customary rights) as nonsense;[29] and must not Anscombe agree with him? Consider the question whether a slave-owner has a right to sell his slaves. For Bentham and Anscombe, the answer appears to be 'Of course he does'—though each philosopher can go on to criticize the institution which gives rise to such rights, and in not wholly dissimilar ways. Neither philosopher, it seems, will admit as

---

[29] He reserved the epithet 'nonsense on stilts' for inalienable or imprescriptible rights. See J. Bentham, *Anarchical Fallacies*, article ii.

sensible the further question: 'But does the slave-owner have a *moral* right to sell his slaves?' (Or at least, each will feel the need to rephrase that question in other terms.)

However, Anscombe's position is not in fact positivistic—at any rate, not in the way that Bentham's is. Her view is as follows. In learning that you cannot do X, where 'cannot' is a stopping modal, part of what you must understand is that it is not just *now* that you cannot do X: rather, you must acquire the habit of responding appropriately in this kind of situation (e.g. where your king is threatened by an opponent's piece). In this sense, stopping/forcing modals are based on custom—the behaviour of those who use and react to these modals *constitutes* custom; and it is this sense of 'based upon custom' that Anscombe has in mind when she says that rights are wholly based upon custom (see above, p. 110). The assertion of a right is the assertion of a 'cannot', or similar modal, which is meant to be responded to *as to a rule or custom*, and not just *now* (unlike an order, for example). The assertion of a right thus need not presuppose that there already is such a custom; though where there is in fact such a custom, assertions of rights will of course be possible as a result, and it will most likely be in the context of an already existing custom or rule-governed activity that a child first learns stopping and forcing modals.

If an actual custom need not exist for a right to exist, what grounds for assertions of rights can be given where there is no custom? Here is Anscombe's answer:

> If something is necessary, if it is for example a necessary task in human life, then a right arises in those whose task it is, to have what belongs to the performance of the task. [. . .] As: those who have and carry out the task of bringing up children quite generally perform a necessary task. It cannot be done without children's obedience. So those people have a right to such obedience.' (*SAS*, 145)

It is thus possible that two modals clash, one of actual custom, the other of actual need; and for Anscombe, the second kind may on occasion trump the first. After all, of any custom that gives rise to the assertion of modals we can ask, 'But why go in for that custom?'—and if no good answer can be given, the assertions are clearly undermined. The appeal to human needs 'gives us a way of arguing for a right without appeal to custom, law or contract; and similarly of arguing that some customary right is no right but is, rather, a customary wrong' (*SAS*, 145).

In her 'Prolegomenon to a Pursuit of the Definition of Murder', Anscombe goes further still, arguing that murder can be defined as 'unlawful killing', which phrase is meant to carry no connotations as to actually promulgated law (*PPDM*, 257–60). Her position by this stage (the article appeared in 1979) has clearly moved on from that of *MMP*. But although she now allows that something may be 'unlawful' although there is no law against it, she still requires the existence of a judicial system, and hence of a lawgiver. In claiming that one had been detained unlawfully, Anscombe argues, one may mean: 'I am wronged by having been locked up, and it is for you [sc. the courts] to punish the one who wronged me' (*PPDM*, 259). She even imagines a law that itself uses the phrase 'unlawful detention', saying in explanation of this that

[m]y suppositious statute therefore *looks forward* to the practice of the courts. It itself provides implicitly both that some detentions will need justification by legal entitlement, *and* that other detentions which are wrongs against the detained will now become possible matter for complaint ... "   (*PPDM*, 260)

So murder may be called 'unlawful killing', where this means killing (a) which wrongs the victim (is an act of injustice towards the victim), and (b) which it is the proper task of legislators to forbid and of law courts to punish. (But there is more to it than that: see the final paragraph of *PPDM*.)

A Benthamite might object to Anscombe's position, as involving a misleading use of words. 'Why not say that murder is unjust killing, which *should* be made unlawful?' Anscombe can allow this 'should': she, like Bentham, can take it as relating to what it is the task of legislators to do. Similarly: 'Why not say that parents *should* have the right to be obeyed by their children?' In this case, the 'should' will indicate an Aristotelian necessity, the necessity for a custom according to which a child 'must' obey her parents.

It might even be alleged that Anscombe's desire to talk of rights in the absence of customs, and of unlawful acts in the absence of laws, betrays just that hankering which proponents of the legalistic conception of morality feel, and which was the target of the second thesis of *MMP*. Her response to this allegation would, I think, be that proponents of the legalistic conception posit a legalistic sense of 'ought' in the belief that the concept they are dealing with has *no* connection with legal or custom-based practices and the empirical preconditions for such practices; whereas her account of 'right', 'unlawful', and related notions assumes that such practices must exist for those notions to get off the ground—and that the actual nature of such practices determines what kind of shape those notions can have. (So that, e.g., you cannot hold a right against yourself.) In a somewhat similar way, clocks must exist for certain temporal notions to get off the ground—'length of time', 'twice as long', etc.—though those notions can be applied to real or hypothetical situations in which there are, were, or could be no clocks (e.g. in a black hole).

4. CONSEQUENTIALISM

4.1. Intended and Foreseen Consequences

The question whether someone did something intentionally or not is central to many a deliberation as to responsibility. 'Was it the defendant's intention to kill the intruder, or only to wound him?'—the answer to this may determine whether a deed was murder or manslaughter. And in this respect the everyday notion of responsibility is just like the legal one. As we saw in Chapter 1 (p. 30), 'I didn't mean to' and 'I didn't know I was' are both standard ways of denying that one did X intentionally; they are also, of course, forms of excuse or self-exculpation. In general, you are responsible only for what you intend. Negligence is the obvious counter-example, and we shall look at that phenomenon presently.

If you know that Y will probably result from your doing X, does it follow from your intentionally doing X that you intend Y? Apparently not; after all, you might, while doing X, make strenuous efforts to prevent Y's occurring, or to minimize it, if it is an effect of degree. For instance, a surgeon carrying out an operation may know that there will be some post-operative pain, but she can hardly be said to intend that there should be pain, if she gives the patient prophylactic morphine. Most people would probably agree with all this. But there are many who will say that, as far as responsibility goes, the foreseen consequences of your actions are in the same boat as the intended consequences. On the face of it, this is inconsistent with the generalization just enunciated, that 'You are responsible only for what you intend', and inconsistent with a general reliance on 'I didn't mean to' as a form of excuse.

One form of the view that there is, as far as responsibility goes, a crucial difference between intended effects and merely foreseen ones is the view usually referred to as the Doctrine of Double Effect. In 'Action, Intention and "Double Effect" ', Anscombe uses 'Principle of Side-Effects' as the name of what people tend to call (and she herself had hitherto called) the Doctrine of Double Effect (*AIDE*, 224–5). I will follow her in this usage. In *AIDE*, Anscombe explains the Principle of Side-Effects with reference to killing, but for our purposes we may generalize, and state it thus:

(PSE) There are some things which, if aimed at either as ends or as means, necessarily render the action in question a bad action; but which, if brought about as a foreseen side effect of an action, do not necessarily render that action a bad action.

Not only does Anscombe think that there is, as far as responsibility goes, a difference between intended effects and merely foreseen ones; she thinks that a very important difference is that stated by PSE. But the defining error of consequentialism, as she characterizes it, is the denial of *any* difference—which of course entails a denial of PSE. In *MMP*, she mentions Sidgwick as having made the move of denying '*any* difference between foreseen and intended consequences, as far as responsibility is concerned'; and she suggests 'that *this* move on the part of Sidgwick explains the difference between old-fashioned Utilitarianism and that *consequentialism*, as I name it, which marks him and every English academic moral philosopher since him' (*MMP*, 36). [30]

---

[30] The move which Anscombe attributes to Sidgwick had in fact already been made by the father of 19th-c. Utilitarianism, Jeremy Bentham. (Cf. Bentham, *Introduction to the Principles of Morals and Legislation*, ch. 9, sec. 10) It is presumably J. S. Mill whom Anscombe particularly wishes to clear of the charge of consequentialism. See above, p. 86, n. 4.

What is that difference to which Anscombe here refers? It is this: a consequentialist, unlike an 'old-fashioned Utilitarian', denies the truth of absolutism,
absolutism being the view that there are some things that you must never do in
any circumstances (i.e. to do which intentionally is always to do a bad thing).
In other words, a consequentialist will *stop at nothing*: no course of action is
ruled out in advance of deliberating what to do. For Anscombe, it is this feature
of consequentialism that cuts it off so thoroughly from other modes of ethical
thinking that the differences between consequentialist philosophers look trifling
by comparison. In particular, consequentialism is incompatible with the ethical
tradition at the heart of Western culture, the tradition referred to by Anscombe
as the Hebrew–Christian ethic, according to which certain things are ruled
out absolutely—such things as killing the innocent, vicarious punishment, and
treachery (*MMP*, 34). But it is not only incompatible with that tradition. It
is also at odds with ancient Greek thought, for example (*MMP*, 41).

Anscombe suggests that the denial of absolutism is to be explained historically
by the assimilation of intended and foreseen consequences. And the former
denial does indeed follow from the latter assimilation. It does so with the help
of the idea that you can be at fault for not preventing something. Blameworthy
cases of not preventing something are cases of negligence, and the negligent
agent is naturally thought of as having been a cause, or causal condition, of the
undesirable outcome. ('Why did this patient die?' 'Because the doctor neglected
to treat his wounds.') The scenario to consider is one where if you don't do
X, you know that Y will occur, where Y is the sort of thing which (all will
agree) it would be bad to aim at. If the agent who knowingly allows Y to occur
may be regarded as we generally regard a negligent person, i.e. as having been a
cause of Y; and if knowingly causing Y is tantamount to aiming at Y (foreseen
consequences being in the same boat as intended ones), then it follows that if you
don't do X, and Y occurs, you are to blame for Y as much as if you had aimed
at it. But any action-kind alleged to be absolutely forbidden will be such that it
could on occasion play the role of X. If aiming at Y is also absolutely forbidden,
as is quite possible, then we end up with a contradiction. For a consequentialist,
the solution is to deny that there are any absolute moral rules, and to rely on
case-by-case weighing of consequences: 'If someone innocent will die unless I do
a wicked thing, then on this view I am his murderer in refusing: so all that is left
to me is to weigh up evils' (*WM*, 58).

For Anscombe, what we have is a *reductio ad absurdum* of consequentialism:
given that certain things clearly *are* completely ruled out (such as killing someone
innocent), a philosophy which must deny this is false. But this is not her only
complaint; for the assimilation of intended and foreseen consequences gives rise,
not only to a denial of absolutism, but to an inflated conception of personal
responsibility, according to which it becomes one's business to consider the
global 'effects' of one's actions, especially one's not-doings. Thus, the fact that I
could do something to try to help famine in Africa means that I am at least partly

responsible for people starving if I in fact do nothing. It would seem to be this sort of view Anscombe has in mind when she writes: 'Now this sounds rather edifying; it is I think quite characteristic of very bad degenerations of thought on such questions that they sound edifying' (*MMP*, 35). Of course, the person who gives generously to help relieve famine in Africa does well. So does the person who gives to beggars; but to regard 'Give to him that asks of you' as a maxim of *duty* is to turn a counsel into a precept, as Anscombe puts it elsewhere:

The turning of counsels into precepts results in high-sounding principles [cf. 'they sound edifying']. Principles that are mistakenly high and strict are a trap [. . .] Thus if the evangelical counsel about poverty were turned into a precept forbidding property owning, people would pay lip service to it as the ideal, while in practice they went in for swindling. 'Absolute honesty!' it would be said: 'I can respect that—but of course that means having no property; and while I respect those who follow that course, I have to compromise with the sordid world myself.' If then one must 'compromise with evil' by owning property and engaging in trade, then the amount of swindling one does will depend on convenience. (*WM*, 56)

This passage occurs in a discussion of pacifism. And Anscombe's beef with pacifism is very similar to her beef with consequentialism: each theory posits high-sounding but impracticable ideals, for falling short of which people will easily excuse themselves, and then proceed to rely on all that is left: convenience or 'calculation'. If I think it as much my duty to help the starving in Africa as to repay my debts, then (realizing the impracticability of devoting myself to Africa's starving) I will tend to find it excusable in myself that I fall behind on the repayments. Similarly, those who persuade themselves that all war is already a compromise with evil will be the more tempted to conclude, 'Well, if we must fight, we may as well do whatever it takes to win. War is war, after all!' And this sort of talk is indeed familiar.[31]

It might be objected that a proper consequentialist will not argue this way; he will, for example, feel just as bad about not helping Africa's starving as a person of probity feels about failing to repay his debts. If consequentialist thinking often or usually leads to self-serving calculations of 'convenience', that is a merely empirical fact. And can a theory be criticized for the bad effects it may have on people's thinking, even where the conclusions those people draw don't strictly follow from the theory? Aren't such effects themselves of the nature of unintended side effects? For a response to this objection, the following remark seems pertinent: 'I should contend that a man is responsible for the bad consequences of his bad actions, but gets no credit for the good

---

[31] A fairly recent example is quoted by Sabina Lovibond in her article 'Absolute Prohibitions without Divine Promises', in Anthony O'Hear (ed.), *Modern Moral Philosophy* (Cambridge: Cambridge University Press, 2004), 141–58 at 145 n. 18. The author is the journalist Polly Toynbee, who writes in the *Guardian* (7 Nov. 2001) that 'it is a kind of decadence to forget that only one thing matters—the right side must win'.

ones; and contrariwise is not responsible for the bad consequences of good actions' (*MMP*, 35–6). If propounding and adhering to a false ethical theory constitute bad actions, then the corrupting influence of one's pronouncements and adherences can indeed be laid at one's door, on this view. Anscombe does not actually argue for the principle she here states, and interestingly enough the effect of the principle is to put *certain* unintended effects in the same boat as intended ones, as far as responsibility goes. Nevertheless, it seems to have something going for it. If, for a joke, you tell Smith that you saw his girlfriend with another man, and he then goes home in a rage and beats her up, you surely bear some of the blame. The same does not so clearly hold if the story is changed so that what you tell Smith is actually true: the bad consequences of a good or permissible action are not your fault. (Assume in each example that you know nothing of Smith's violent tendencies.)

But can it be maintained that propounding and adhering to a false theory (e.g. consequentialism) are bad actions in themselves? That one does these things 'in good faith' would cut little ice with Anscombe: that excuse is of the same order as the excuse 'I followed my conscience', which she takes to be quite inadequate.[32] Nevertheless, it might be questioned whether mere falsehood is enough to render the associated actions bad, at any rate when the action is the propounding of a theory. Is propounding a false botanical or biological theory an intrinsically bad action? That would make an easy target of Aristotle, among other thinkers. But it is presumably relevant that consequentialism is (allegedly) a false *ethical* theory. For it can be argued that the propounding of an ethical theory is an expression of character, just as acting according to the tenets of such a theory is an expression of character—at any rate, if such propounding is habitual or characteristic. The 'character' in both cases (propounding and acting) will be the same—i.e. a bad one. And if the propounding can be seen as an expression of bad character, then it can surely be deemed an intrinsically bad action. In which case, the bad consequences of propounding a false ethical theory may, even if accidental, be laid at the door of the propounder.

We must after all remember that philosophical debate does not go on between theories, or between disembodied *dramatis personae* with names like 'the Utilitarian', 'the Deontologist', 'the error theorist', and so on. It goes on between real people; and a philosopher, just as much as (if not more than) a dinner-party companion, may be worthy of rebuke for propounding outrageous views, and for the possible corrupting effects of doing so, even if those possible effects were to be accidental. It is no excuse to say that you are riding the escalator of Reason wherever it takes you: if the escalator in question takes you into a barbarous place, that place is no less barbarous for your imagined mode of entry. Human sensibility should apprise you of the fact that you must have gone wrong somewhere. To insist in such a case that your proposal deserves

---

[32] See e.g. *MOC*.

a hearing is to forget that we all the time tacitly refuse a hearing to many among us, and that the right to a hearing may lapse. It is considerations such as these that lie behind one of Anscombe's better-known sayings: 'But if someone really thinks, *in advance*, that it is open to question whether such an action as procuring the judicial execution of the innocent should be quite excluded from consideration—I do not want to argue with him; he shows a corrupt mind' (*MMP*, 40).

Not many commentators have taken note of Anscombe's italicized phrase, '*in advance*'. She means, surely, 'in advance of giving any purported counter-example to the prohibition': for her, the absolute status of the prohibition is sufficiently clear that the onus is on one who denies it to make a case for denying it. If someone tried to mount a case, he would perhaps be listened to; but to take an initial attitude of scepticism or 'open-mindedness' towards the absoluteness of the prohibition is, for Anscombe, to manifest a mind corrupted by bad thinking. Some have taken Anscombe's attitude here to have been one of moral arrogance, but many of these same people would surely adopt just this attitude if the discussion turned, for example, to particular named people or groups of people. As: 'Well, but maybe it *would* be for the best in certain circumstances to round up and kill all the Irish gypsies? Maybe those circumstances actually obtain right now, as some have said? Shouldn't we at least discuss that?' It is probable that many philosophers who appear happy, in advance, to regard any course of action as possibly permissible are simply failing to imagine in vivid detail what the scenario in question would actually involve. In this respect, they would be succumbing to a general form of philosophical failure. But of course there are political and cultural pressures towards the sort of consequentialist thinking that Anscombe is talking about (some of which will be considered in §4.3), so that there is all the more reason to be on one's guard against laziness here—quite apart from the fact that, as has been argued, false ethical theorizing is likely to be more of an expression of character than, say, false epistemological theorizing.

As we have seen, Anscombe takes the denial of any difference between intended and foreseen effects (as far as responsibility goes) to be the source of much error in modern moral thinking. But she also thinks that there is an opposite error, to be found especially among Catholic thinkers: 'The denial of this [sc. The Principle of Side-Effects] has been the corruption of non-Catholic thought, and its abuse the corruption of Catholic thought' (*WM*, 54). The abuse she has in mind is that of taking intention to be a sufficiently private thing that an agent can 'direct' his intention away from certain effects of his actions, thereby bringing it about that he does not intend those effects. In combination with PSE, this view of intention leads to the idea that some actions are permissible which would not be permissible on a more robust understanding of intention. Where consequentialism inflates the domain of personal responsibility, this corrupt form of Catholic thinking reduces it. It relies on a notion of intentions as inner acts which Anscombe's work in *Intention* thoroughly explodes. Peter Geach mentions how this way of thinking can be used to excuse killing people in war, and quotes the following verse:

> Say I'm awfully aggressed:
> I pull the trigger—well I'm blessed!
> He hit the bullet with his chest!
> I'm glad I did my morals.[33]

As Anscombe says in *Intention*: 'while we can find cases where "only the man himself can say" whether he had a certain intention or not; they are further limited by this: he cannot profess not to have had the intention of doing the thing that was a means to an end of his' (*I*, 44).

You intend the things that you do as means to your ends, just as you intend those ends. But more than this needs to be said; and the issue of what things in general can be included in a person's intention, either as ends or as means, is crucial,[34] in particular for those espousing the Principle of Side-Effects. Could those who dropped the atomic bomb on Hiroshima have made out that it was only their intention to destroy the buildings and infrastructure of the city, and that the deaths of the city's inhabitants were merely foreseen side effects? That would sound like sophistry. Maybe there is no cut and dried set of principles enabling us to determine in all cases what effects can be laid at an agent's door as having been intended by him, but one or two conditions can be mentioned: e.g. the known certainty of an effect's occurring, and the 'closeness' of an effect to other effects that were intended. Both these conditions are proposed by Anscombe in *AIDE* (225, 223). The criticism that these conditions are somewhat imprecise is not in itself damning, for one could argue that their imprecision arises from the fact that they are meant to be interpreted case by case, in a way that we shall be looking at in the next section.

I said earlier that you are in general only responsible for things you intend. But you can also be held responsible for actions that were unintentional, but which arose out of culpable ignorance or culpable negligence. The commonsense idea is this: sometimes it's your *business* to find something out, or to attend (with due care) to some task. This notion of what is a person's business either gets inflated beyond all practicability by consequentialism ('My business is the human race'), or is dropped altogether by it. But as Anscombe puts it, there are in some situations things that it is both possible and necessary to find out, or to do.[35] 'Possible' means

---

[33] P. T. Geach, 'Intention, Freedom and Predictability', in Teichmann (ed.), *Logic, Cause and Action*, 73–81 at 75. The source of the verse is uncertain. Geach acknowledges Anthony Kenny, but Kenny has told me that he is unacquainted with it.

[34] The issue encompasses both an interpretative one—what sort of evidence (e.g. behavioural) is relevant to attributions of intention?—and what might be called a forensic one: what count as admissible reasons for, or accounts of, one's actions? Here ethics and psychology are *very* closely entangled.

[35] This way of putting things derives from Aquinas; see *Summa Theologiae* Ia IIae q. 6, art. 3.

'practicably possible'; 'necessary' relates, once again, to Aristotelian necessity. Anscombe imagines a man who marries for a second time without making any enquiries as to whether his first wife is still alive (presumably she has gone missing, or the couple have been separated for some time). The first wife is in fact alive.

'I acted in good faith in marrying Jane, for I did not know that my first wife, Mary, was still alive' could hardly be a successful plea if the speaker had no grounds for supposing his wife dead, but had acted on the assumption that his first marriage would never come to light. [. . .] He did not know those circumstances; nevertheless it was both possible and necessary for him to ascertain them ... (*TKEA*, 5)

It is necessary to try to find out if one's spouse is alive before remarrying, because of what one undertakes in marrying. Certain things can *become* one's business. Hence failure to do those things when the occasion arises makes one's ignorance culpable: not in itself, of course, but in connection with an intentional action (e.g. going through a marriage ceremony with Jane). For Anscombe, an action committed in this way can be said to be voluntary under the relevant description—under the description *bigamy*, for example. The sense of 'voluntary' in question is that of 'going along with' something by not doing anything to prevent it (cf. *I*, 89); the range of 'anything' depends on such practical considerations as what you know, what you have undertaken, how difficult it would be for you to prevent the thing, etc.

Hence responsibility relates to what is voluntary, as well as to what is intentional. As we saw in Chapter 1 (§3.2), some actions that are not intentional under any description can nevertheless be voluntary; and here we have another case of this. But if you can in this way be responsible for an action under its description as a voluntary action, won't that undermine the Principle of Side-Effects? For that principle states that one might *not* be responsible for the merely foreseen consequences of one's actions; but one surely does in some sense go along with the foreseen consequences of one's actions—i.e. these actions look to be voluntary under the description *producing such-and-such effects*. The obvious response to this is to say that you might or might not be responsible for your voluntary actions, and that this is precisely what PSE allows for. The unintentional bigamist of Anscombe's example fails to do what he should to guard against committing bigamy: he fails to make proper efforts to find out about his wife. On the other hand, there may be nothing that an SAS man who throws a tear gas canister into a hostage-takers' den can do to guard against hurting the eyes of the hostages, short of not throwing it at all. The identification of what it is both possible and necessary for someone to do must be a case-by-case matter. Once again, an understanding of psychological concepts—*intentional, voluntary*—turns out to be essential for doing moral philosophy.[36]

[36] Bernard Williams has made a case for laying at someone's door effects of his actions that were neither intended nor foreseeable, in certain circumstances—this being the phenomenon of what he

4.2. Absolutism

We have seen that Anscombe's main complaint against consequentialism is that it denies the truth of absolutism. But is moral absolutism so obviously correct? Isn't an adherence, come what may, to certain rules of conduct a sign of inflexibility and insensitivity to the particulars of a case quite at odds with the sort of practical wisdom (φρόνησις) described by Aristotle, whose account of the virtues Anscombe appears on the whole to be commending?

A *blind* adherence to certain rules would involve an inability to interpret and apply those rules in concrete situations; but an ability to interpret and apply a practical rule is a necessary part of properly grasping such a rule. This even goes for rules that have been given one by an authority:

Now there is indeed a sense in which only the individual can make his own decisions as to what to do, even if his decision is to abide by someone else's orders or advice. For it is he who acts and therefore makes the final application of whatever is said to him. [. . .] [D]oing what one is told is an interpretation and so with doing, however obedient one is, one can hardly escape being one's own pilot.   (*AM*, 48)

A rule of conduct will invoke a category or concept—'lying', say, or 'murder'—and anyone who follows a rule of conduct will need to ask, in any concrete situation, such a question as 'Would doing X be a case of lying?' They will need to *interpret* the rule in question. Many and various factors in a situation will be relevant to whether something would count, e.g., as lying; so following a rule, even an absolute rule, actually requires the sort of context-sensitive practical wisdom which Aristotle describes. What we have here, as Anscombe says, is the method of casuistry (from the Latin for 'case', as in 'case by case'), a method that is necessary for any sort of living by principles. Of the method of casuistry she says that 'while it may lead you to stretch a point on the circumference, it will not permit you to destroy the centre' (*MMP*, 36). (Both 'casuistry' and 'stretching a point' have received a bad press in the past, but the most that can be said against them is that abuses have taken place in their name.)

'But still,' it may be objected, 'even if Anscombe can allow flexibility in the interpretation of rules of conduct, doesn't she have to justify the assertion that some rules are absolute and exceptionless?' And it would not be indulging in an over-fanciful analogy to mention here the parallel issue of whether statements of natural or causal law are exceptionless. As to these, Anscombe takes the onus of proof to be on those who believe in exceptionless generalizations, while she

---

calls 'moral luck'. Under the relevant description, the act in question will be neither intentional *nor* voluntary. It is important for Williams's case that the act may be blameless 'in itself', for he is not merely stating the same common-sense principle that we have seen Anscombe state, concerning bad acts (pp. 115–116). But where the act *is* blameless, Williams would surely allow that neither is the agent exactly *to blame*. The phenomenon of moral luck certainly deserves attention, but unfortunately this would take us too far afield.

herself tends to the view that generalizations that are for the most part true are all that we have, and are all that we need.[37] What, then, makes (certain) rules of conduct different in this respect from laws of nature?

The clue might be thought to lie with the nature of rule-governed practices. A rule of a practice need not, and cannot, include reference to all possible preventing factors, as we saw above (pp. 91–3). Hence the statement of an institutional rule will be simple and unqualified, and in that sense 'absolute'. But preventing factors are possible; so although the statement of a rule will itself be simple—as, 'You must not break your promises'—a sane person will be able to see both (a) when the rule does not, after all, apply (this is where casuistry comes in), and (b) when it is all right to break the rule. The notion of 'preventing factors' is different, according to whether (a) or (b) is in question. But (b) is a real possibility, and Anscombe herself says as much in connection with both property rights and promises. Thus her absolutism is not meant to be defended by reference to the unqualified form of rule statements within practices.

So what is the source of Anscombe's absolutism? It is to Aristotle, once again, that we must turn. Whereas a consequentialist asks, 'Would doing X maximize good consequences?', a virtuous person in the Aristotelian mould will ask such a question as, 'Would doing X be just?' Wanting to ask that question, and counting it as being in X's favour that it is just (if it is), means having a certain character trait, a certain settled disposition of character. Anscombe's view is that the trait in question will involve ruling certain things out: '[I]t is clear that a good man is a just man; and a just man is a man who habitually refuses to commit or participate in any unjust actions for fear of any consequences, or to obtain any advantage, for himself or anyone else' (*MMP*, 40). Note the repeated use of 'any'. Elsewhere, considering the virtue of attachment to truth, Anscombe writes: 'Even if the convenient-looking falsehood does not rebound on you in the particular case, the habit of relying on falsehoods certainly will. As habits are created by practices, the wise one will therefore not want to engage in this practice at all' (*KRHL*, 66). (By 'habit of relying on falsehoods', Anscombe means such phenomena as that of *not wanting to know*—e.g. not wanting to know those awkward facts that put one's own opinions in a bad light. *KRHL*, 65.)

Here, it might be said, Anscombe's thought is not a million miles away from Kant's, insofar as the one who decides never to go in for something can be said to make it a rule not to go in for it. But this rule is not a Kantian maxim of reason: it is a turning away from certain things and following certain others. It is not open to a consequentialist to adopt such habits of thought and action, for according to him every practical decision must be made, as it were, afresh—at least if the agent has time and energy and can trust himself to think straight. The

---

[37] See Ch. 5, §2.1.

resultant (hypothetical) inability to develop, or indeed have, a moral character is what Bernard Williams has described as Utilitarianism's problem of integrity.[38]

But how are we to decide which rules of conduct are absolute? Kant took lying to be absolutely forbidden. Anscombe regards Kant as 'rigoristic' (*MMP*, 27)—though she probably agreed with him about this. In relation to Ross on the other hand, who seems to have taken an absolutist line on promise-keeping, Anscombe writes that 'people who are not maniacs know well enough' what sorts of undertakings may be broken in certain everyday circumstances (*PJ*, 15). She herself regards killing the innocent as quite ruled out. Philippa Foot cites torture.[39] Since the debates here will ultimately relate to what things a wise and virtuous person would want to turn her back on completely, those debates will have to include much detail from real life, the sort of detail that a wise and virtuous person will be prone to reflect upon and digest: detail to do with human needs, human psychology, human biology, human history and anthropology—and maybe more. In the case of murder, the 'hard core' of which concept is *the intentional killing of the innocent* (*MMP*, 262), Anscombe says: 'A sufficient consideration of it would comprehend "the whole man": the agency peculiar to man, his social being and possession of laws, his moral subjectivity and mystical value' (*PPDM*, 260).

4.3. Roots of Consequentialism

In her delineation of consequentialism, Anscombe held a mirror up, not only to English-speaking moral philosophy, but to the wider culture. That she herself looked at it in this way is clear from her answer to the question which forms the title of her 'Does Oxford Moral Philosophy Corrupt Youth?'.[40] Anscombe's answer was 'No', since she believed that the young already had the consequentialist views which Oxford moral philosophers were propounding: 'This philosophy is conceived perfectly in the spirit of the time and might be called the philosophy of the flattery of that spirit' (*OMPCY*, 167).

Many examples from journalists, politicians, academics, and others could be given to support the claim that intended and foreseen consequences are standardly lumped together, with all that that entails. Sometimes the consequences don't even have to have been foreseen or foreseeable: in politics, a good and feasible proposal which unluckily comes unstuck often damns its proponent's career. Actual consequences can matter more than intended ones. As Edmund Burke remarked: 'The conduct of a losing party never appears right: at least it never can possess the only infallible criterion of wisdom to vulgar judgements—success.'[41]

---

[38] B. A. O. Williams (with J. J. C. Smart), *Utilitarianism: For and Against* (Cambridge: Cambridge University Press, 1973), §5.   [39] Foot, *Natural Goodness*, p. 78.

[40] Anscombe was given this title for a talk she was to deliver on the BBC Third Programme. The talk was later printed in *The Listener*, 57 (14 Feb. 1957).

[41] Edmund Burke, letter to a member of the National Assembly, 1791, p. 7.

Turning to foreseeable, as opposed to merely actual, consequences, we find many who think that a Pope who declares condom use to be forbidden is *responsible* for the deaths from AIDS of those who might have avoided getting AIDS had they disobeyed the papal prohibition and used a condom (or as an acquaintance of mine put it: 'The Pope is just as bad as Pol Pot').[42] Yet others will see no distinction between a doctor who injects a patient with morphine so as to kill her, and one who does so to relieve pain, knowing that this will hasten her death—drawing a distinction here is thought of as 'logic-chopping'. These various ways of talking about justification and responsibility are not self-contained: they necessarily connect with some, and not other, directions of ethical thought.

What are the roots of this way of thinking? Anscombe does not examine these roots in the way in which she examines the roots of the legalistic conception of morality. There are probably a variety of impulses behind consequentialism. In what follows, I suggest some possible candidates.

We have already seen how a faulty philosophy of psychology can feed a faulty moral philosophy; hence a number of connections between the arguments of Chapters 1 and 2 and those of the present chapter. A prevalent theory of intention that was criticized in Chapter 1 was the causalist theory. Causalism is not only a theory held by professional philosophers; it is a naturally tempting way of thinking about intention, and indeed about the mind. And one might wonder whether causalism about intentions encourages the thought that intended consequences are not significantly different from other things that an agent brings about. For if an intention is just one of those states of a person that produces certain outer effects, akin to blood sugar levels or epileptic seizures, then it seems natural to say, 'Well, but isn't the important thing that this person somehow produces those effects? *How* he produces them isn't so important: there are all sorts of mechanisms that could be involved, of which intending is but one.' ('The main thing is that each doctor killed his patient, and in the same way'.) Intentions are probably alterable by means different from those adopted to alter blood sugar levels—behavioural conditioning rather than insulin—but the basic story will be the same. Such thoughts manifest something of an objective attitude towards a person, in Strawson's phrase;[43] though if I am right in associating them with consequentialism, they often go with an inflated view of personal responsibility—whereas, in the sorts of cases with which Strawson deals, adopting an objective attitude (e.g. towards a lunatic or small child) involves allowing that

---

[42] This is not to condone the papal prohibition, which itself appears to ignore the relevance of the Principle of Side-Effects: a woman who gets her husband to wear a condom with the intention of protecting herself from possible infection does not thereby intend contraception. It is the prohibition on contraception, however, which has been used to justify the blanket prohibition on condom use.

[43] P. F. Strawson, 'Freedom and Resentment', in *Freedom and Resentment and Other Essays* (London: Methuen, 1974), 1–25.

a person is *not* responsible for his deeds. If we turn from causalism to Anscombe's account of intention, we see how the latter, by contrast, in putting the question 'Why did you do that?' centre stage, can scarcely avoid making intention the crucial component of responsibility.

Another theme of Chapter 1 was the possibility of backward-looking and interpretative motives. A tempting, but false, view has it that all reasons for action cite states of affairs to be brought about by the action—i.e. that all practical rationality is a matter of means–end reasoning. A proponent of such a view will regard 'In order to get revenge' (e.g.) as the basic answer to a question like 'Why did you kill him?'. But as we saw (Ch. 1, pp. 31–2), the sense of 'In order to get revenge' in fact presupposes the force of such reasons as 'Because he killed my brother', and not *vice versa*.

The denial of genuinely backward-looking reasons for action is clearly at home in utilitarian theories, and may even be a necessary feature of those theories. Consequentialists, too, will find it hard to accommodate backward-looking motives. It was said above (p. 86) that a consequentialist may include among the consequences of an action such things as its being promise-breaking; but once Anscombe's point about backward-looking motives is admitted, there appears to be little sense in regarding such 'consequences' as a proper object of *calculation*. Breaking a promise is not an effect in the way that, say, breaking a window is. Of course, a person who is deliberating what to do can take account of the fact that in doing X she would be breaking a promise—and you can if you like call this 'assessing the value of one of the effects of doing X'. But an insistence on the model of *evaluating effects* looks to be quite unmotivated, and indeed misleading: *weighing reasons* (for and against) is surely a more apt notion to apply. As far as diagnosis goes, I am not sure whether a view about action ('All reasons for action embody means–end reasoning') encourages consequentialism in ethics, or the other way around—or both. In any case, the two species of error are common, and often go together.

Another possible source of consequentialist thinking is a certain feature of modern Western democracies: namely, the paternalism of government, whereby, for instance, it is the business of government to pass laws that will reduce deaths on the roads (e.g. by making the wearing of seat belts compulsory). Paternalism might or might not be a good thing; but it seems evident that a general acceptance of paternalistic laws has led to certain forms of reasoning becoming more respectable—as, 'People should wear seat belts (after all, a benign law requires them to); you didn't wear a seat belt; so you are as much to blame for your injuries as if you had jumped out of a high window'. But the rationale for introducing the law, for the politician, relates to the possibility of *generally* reducing injuries or deaths from car crashes by having people wear seat belts: it is not a rationale that involves the idea that eschewing a seat belt is somehow intrinsically irresponsible. (A statistical, probabilistic argument is all that is required in making a case for the law.) Of course, in a democracy, persuasive propaganda may be advanced in favour of a paternalistic law, and such propaganda will likely aim to present the government as one that looks after us rather than as one that tells us what to do. This aim may be served by making out that not doing X is really a failure in civic duty as such, not just a failure in obedience to the law. The charge relates not to one's intentions, but to possible consequences of one's actions or omissions, consequences that are indeed only foreseeable in the sense of being foreseeable *as possible*—since they need not even be likely to occur. And such ideas get swallowed and internalized by the citizens at whom they are targeted.

As I said, the point here relates not to the merits or otherwise of paternalistic laws. It relates to certain ways of thinking that pass muster in a society where such laws are in force and where the form of government itself (Western-style democracy) enjoys general prestige.

Although Anscombe distinguishes consequentialism from 'old-fashioned Utilitarianism', the two approaches clearly share quite a lot. And the political-legislative standpoint which I have alleged to be one source of consequentialist thinking has always been closely associated with utilitarianism. The aims of Bentham and Mill were as much political as philosophical, if not more so. For both utilitarianism and consequentialism, it is natural to treat the whole community as an object of hypothetical decision-making, in the sort of way that a politician or legislator may do. A politician may think: 'My task is to look after the community, to see that it flourishes as a whole. This means doing things on occasion that sacrifice individual people's interests.'

But if this is an appropriate thing for a politician to think, it is so because of the politician's task. Other people with other tasks (doctors, lawyers, parents, teachers, employers...) do not in general have a similar rationale for looking to the good of the whole community when making their decisions. Citing the general good as if it were an overriding consideration is, however, very common—as with those middle-class parents who send their children to a comprehensive school because they believe that such schools benefit from having such children, even when their own children will lose out by this decision. Part of what lies behind this must be the idea that political decision-making is a paradigm of moral decision-making in general; also the inflated conception of personal responsibility that comes from consequentialism.

But in any case, the politician's thought is not self-evidently a good one. Is it not in danger of leading to acts of injustice towards individuals? Perhaps that depends on what exactly is included in 'the flourishing of the community'. Many would argue (Anscombe included) that a community cannot be said to flourish in which certain individual rights are ignored or violated. Nevertheless, there is an interesting philosophical question here, as to the extent to which the community can be conceived of as an entity irreducible to its individual members. Anscombe would certainly allow talk of group rights, etc.—but in her writings on civil authority she shows a strong attachment to the rights of citizens. Thus, in 'On the Source of the

Authority of the State', the crucial question is: 'By what right do the agents of the state assume the rôle of carrying out the needful tasks of judgement and punishment of malefactors?' That the tasks are needful is not enough; a person or group has to have reasons, other than physical capacity, for why *they* should carry out the tasks—otherwise their acts will constitute assault, kidnapping, or extortion.

The view of the community as the sovereign object of political decision-making is not so much in danger of ignoring the distinction between intended and foreseen consequences as in danger of leading to various forms of injustice. It is thus as characteristic of utilitarianism as it is of consequentialism. But Anscombe's main complaint with modern moral philosophy is in the end that it commends and encourages forms of injustice. This charge, for her, is such a grave one that it renders the distinction between old-fashioned utilitarianism and consequentialism as inconsiderable as any other distinction among the moral theories that held sway from Sidgwick to Hare (and beyond).

5. CONCLUSION

It is sometimes said that the importance of 'Modern Moral Philosophy'—and even of Anscombe's moral philosophy as a whole—resides especially in its having triggered a renewed interest in the virtues as a philosophical topic. This is something for which Anscombe can indeed be thanked. But both the article and the moral philosophy clearly represent much more than this.

In this chapter, I have concentrated on Anscombe's critique of three main aspects of modern moral philosophy: the fact/value distinction, the legalistic conception of morality, and consequentialism. One thing that is notable about Anscombe's critique is how philosophy of mind, philosophy of language, a historical viewpoint, and a genuine involvement in concrete ethical issues are all present. Indeed, these features of Anscombe's moral philosophy are interdependent; and it can be argued that in any adequate moral philosophy, a similar interdependence will be evident. The case is similar to that of the virtues themselves according to Aristotle's theory of the unity (interdependence) of the virtues. R. M. Hare went in for philosophy of language, with his neustics and phrastics; but, if Anscombe is right, a false, Humean psychology can be seen to have lain at the bottom of, and vitiated, Hare's linguistic theorizing. Again, various philosophers have hunted for a source of 'objective obligation', or have simply taken that notion to be perfectly transparent—Kant, Prichard, Mackie, *et al.* The self-knowledge that a historical, genealogical viewpoint can give might have assuaged these philosophers' hankerings, or removed their complacency, as the case may be (though it might also have left a sense of emptiness in some of them).

In other words, in ethics it is Anscombe's philosophical breadth that is responsible for her philosophical depth. One should also mention her capacity—evident to all who knew her—of seeing the cant and intellectual nostrums of the time with something of an outsider's objectivity. Ideas that are in reality no more than myths or prejudices are prevalent in every period, and it is vital for a culture that it include people with an honest and sharp eye for those myths and prejudices. Such people may have their own blind spots—who does not?—but what they have to say is likely to be more significant and valuable than the contributions of those whose theories are designed to 'justify' propositions that already have the status of well-loved slogans.

4

Mind and Self

Anscombe tells us that there were two topics that aroused her interest in philosophy when she was still a teenager: causality and perception. The latter was a topic which she 'got hooked on without even realizing it was philosophy', as a result of reading a book by Fr Martin D'Arcy, SJ called *The Nature of Belief*. Having got hooked, Anscombe remained that way:

For years I would spend time, in cafés, for example, staring at objects saying to myself: 'I see a packet. But what do I really see? How can I say that I see here anything more than a yellow expanse?' [. . .] I always hated phenomenalism and felt trapped by it. I couldn't see my way out of it but I didn't believe it. It was no good pointing to difficulties about it, things which Russell found wrong with it, for example. The strength, the central nerve of it remained alive and raged achingly. It was only in Wittgenstein's classes in 1944 that I saw the nerve being extracted, the central thought 'I have got *this*, and I define "yellow" (say) as *this*' being effectively attacked.   (*MPM*, p. viii)

This last remark clearly alludes to those ideas of Wittgenstein's that came to be referred to as the Private Language Argument, ideas that are most fully expounded in the work that Anscombe was to translate into English, the *Philosophical Investigations*.[1] The influence of Wittgenstein upon Anscombe is perhaps nowhere more evident than in her writings on the philosophy of mind; but, as with all her work, the searching originality of what she has to say in these writings is incontrovertible. Moreover, while a number of philosophers in the 1950s and 1960s took Wittgenstein's (or Wittgensteinian) ideas to show up the complete bankruptcy of phenomenalism and the sense-datum theory, Anscombe believed that there was an important element of truth in what the empiricists had been trying to say—a baby that should not be thrown out with the philosophical bath water.

It is also worth noting how the problems in the philosophy of mind with which Anscombe grapples are very often problems connected with the first-person stance. Like Wittgenstein, she makes much of the first-person/third-person asymmetry of psychological verbs, and of the importance of that asymmetry. But it is 'I see ... ', 'I remember ... ', 'I think ... ' that she is primarily interested

---

[1] The article in which we find Anscombe most directly tackling themes from the Private Language Argument is 'The Subjectivity of Sensation', in *MPM*.

in—not 'He sees...', 'She remembers...', 'They think...'. (Though of course the two stances cannot be understood quite independently of one another.) And of course one of her most famous articles is about 'I' itself.

This fact is indicative of how far from being a behaviourist Anscombe is; for the tendency of behaviourists is to downplay the special features of the first-person stance, to minimize the difference between the first person and the third person. In Chapter 2 (§1.1), we encountered her argument that first-personal expressions of intention are central to the concept of intention, in a way difficult for behaviourists or latter-day functionalists to accommodate. As we shall see, something similar goes for other psychological concepts, such as that of perception. And this centrality of the first person is indeed connected with that grain of truth in phenomenalism which Anscombe is at pains to bring out.

1. PERCEPTION AND MEMORY

1.1. Intentional Objects

For the empiricists, the crucial question about perception was 'What do we directly perceive?' The question was crucial in particular because sense-perception was taken to be the basic and most important source of human knowledge. The things or facts (if any) that we perceive directly would be known more certainly than anything merely inferred from those things or facts. For Locke, Berkeley, and Hume, we are directly aware of the contents of our own minds (ideas, perceptions, impressions), and the question about sense-perception becomes one about the relationship between judgements concerning such contents and judgements concerning tables, chairs, and so on. By the time we reach Russell, the account of that relationship has become quite sophisticated—but the starting point is the same as it was for the earlier empiricists.

In the 1950s and 1960s, the empiricist account of perception came under concerted attack. J. L. Austin and other ordinary-language philosophers threw doubt on the very idea of sense-data,[2] and argued for the common-sense view that we see tables and chairs as directly as could possibly be wished. Sense-datum theorists had made much of the possibility of illusions, hallucinations, and so forth, arguing (a) that there must be *something* perceived in such cases, and then going on to say (b) that whatever is perceived in these cases must be the same sort of things as are perceived ordinarily. The objectors would typically only agree to both (a) and (b) in the case of misperception, where, however, they would insist that what is perceived is an ordinary physical object, not a sense-datum—so that when you mistake a cat in your garden for a fox, what you actually *see* is the

---

[2] See Austin, *Sense and Sensibilia* (Oxford: Clarendon Press, 1962).

cat. In general, these objectors would be suspicious of the idea of something seen (heard, etc.) that was authoritatively describable only by the perceiving subject.

In 'The Intentionality of Sensation', Anscombe aims to provide an alternative both to the sense-datum theory and to the accounts of its modern detractors, by revealing the different ways in which phrases like 'what you see', 'object of perception', etc. are to be understood. The distinction that most needs to be drawn, she argues, is between *intentional* objects of perception on the one hand, and *material* objects of perception on the other: 'Now "ordinary language" views and "sense-datum" views make the same mistake, that of failing to recognize the intentionality of sensation, though they take opposite positions in consequence' (*IS*, 13). (Anscombe alludes here, as she does in the title of her piece, to 'sensation'; it is sense-perception she mainly has in mind.)

The distinction between intentional and material objects is not like that between metal and stone objects: it is not a distinction between two *kinds of thing*. The reason for this is that 'object' is being used in its original sense, the sense it has in such phrases as 'object of desire' (*IS*, 4). If I desire a pair of satin boots, the object of my desire is: a pair of satin boots. Such an 'object' may not exist—i.e. there may be no satin boots anywhere. 'But how can I desire something non-existent?' The puzzlement expressed by this question arises because 'desire' is a transitive verb, so that it is tempting to think of it as like other such verbs—'possess', for example. If you *possess* a pair of satin boots, then those boots must certainly exist. It seems that we are misled by the surface forms of language: the grammatical object of the verb 'desire' (e.g. 'a pair of satin boots') may not have as its function the denoting of anything at all. If we insisted that it did have that function, we should have to posit a realm of non-existent, but somehow real, things, among them my pair of satin boots; 'existent' and 'non-existent' would then pick out two kinds of thing. Fortunately, we need resort to no such realm.

Various verbs behave like 'desire'. One such, says Anscombe, is 'intend'—and it is partly because that verb can serve as a paradigm here that she uses 'intentional', rather than the later term 'intensional' (*IS*, 4). The three marks of intentionality which she draws our attention to are then illustrated by examples involving 'to intend'; other verbs could equally have been used, such as 'think of', 'worship', or 'shoot at', three of Anscombe's own examples.[3] The marks of intentionality, as found in the case of 'intend', are these:

First, not any true description of what you do describes it as the action you intended: only under certain of its descriptions will it be intentional. [. . .] Second, the descriptions under which you intend what you do can be vague, indeterminate. [. . .] Third, descriptions under which you intend to do what you do may not come true . . .   (*IS*, 4)

---

[3] We could mention also 'want', the intentionality of which verb is discussed in *Intention*; see *I*, 69–70.

We have already encountered the first mark (Ch. 2, §1.2). Anscombe illustrates the second thus: 'You mean to put the book down on the table all right, and you do so, but you do not mean to put it down anywhere particular on the table' (i.e. one place is as good as another). The third mark is the one I have mentioned as producing puzzlement, in connection with 'desire'. And as Anscombe says, 'The possible non-existence of the object, which is the analogue of the possible non-occurrence of the *intended* action, is what has excited most attention about this sort of verb' (*IS*, 4).

The first mark of intentionality has a somewhat different application according as the thing in question exists or not (or as the action in question gets performed or not)—i.e. according as the third mark of intentionality is 'realized' or not. If I think of the Prime Minister, there will be true descriptions of him, such that I am not thinking of him under *those* descriptions—e.g. 'man now wearing a red vest'. But if I think of a ten-headed dog, the question as to what, if any, further descriptions apply to this dog is really the question, 'What descriptions, other than "ten-headed dog", do I have in mind, or would I acknowledge?'—rather than, 'What else is, as a matter of fact, true of this dog?'.

Intentionality has been defined as a feature of certain verbs. What then is an intentional object? It is simply the direct object of an intentional verb acting *as* an intentional verb (cf. *IS*, 6). We need to use this phrase, '*as* an intentional verb', for two reasons. First, so as to exclude 'nothing' as it occurs in 'She desires nothing': here, none of the three marks of intentionality is realized, and this is connected with the fact that the sentence just means 'There isn't anything that she desires'. So although 'nothing' gives the direct object of an intentional verb, it does not give an intentional object. Second, and more importantly, so as to exclude the *merely material* object of an intentional verb: a direct object given by means of a description which the subject of the verb would not acknowledge. ('Material object' will be explained in a moment.)

Consider: 'These people worship Ombola; that is to say, they worship a mere hunk of wood.' (cf. 'They worship sticks and stones.') [. . .] The worshippers themselves will not acknowledge the descriptions.   (*IS*, 9)

In 'They worship a mere hunk of wood', none of the three marks of intentionality is realized. Intentionality is connected with the first-person perspective (of the subject of the verb), and that perspective is absent where we use descriptions that are alien to it. So 'a mere hunk of wood' does not give an intentional object.

'Direct object' is a term from grammar; and this is why the subtitle of Anscombe's article alludes to a 'grammatical feature'. Intentionality of objects—specifically, of objects of perception—will turn out to be quite literally a grammatical phenomenon. And some of the puzzles about intentional objects are simply puzzles about direct objects in general. The main such puzzle which Anscombe mentions is this: 'ought we really to say that the intentional object is a bit of language, or may we speak as if it were what the bit of language stands for?' (*IS*, 6). The issue is not, as might at first be thought, a merely terminological one, and this can be seen from the fact that whether a *direct* object is a bit of language, or instead is what such a bit of language stands for, is likewise not a merely terminological issue. The problem is that there appear to be cogent arguments on both sides.

Anscombe's example is: 'John sent Mary a book' (*IS*, 6–8). The direct object of the verb ('sent'), we may say, is: a book. The absence of quotation marks in what I just wrote does not prevent our asking, 'Was the expression "a book" used or mentioned?'—or, in other words, does the expression 'a book' *give* the direct object, or *is* it the direct object? If it *gives* the direct object, the direct object itself would appear to be a book, not a bit of language; but the case against saying this is straightforward: if the direct object is a book, it must be some particular book. There is no such thing as a general book. But of course there may be no answer to 'Which book did John send Mary?', if 'John sent Mary a book' occurs in a joke or story, say, or (as here) in a philosophical example. Moreover, we could add, the direct object in 'John did not send Mary a book' is still: a book; and the question 'Which book?' is patently absurd here.

But there is just as plausible an argument against our saying that the direct object is a bit of language, i.e. the phrase 'a book'. We may begin by asking: How is the concept of a direct object to be taught and learnt in the first place? One who learns this concept must, when asked 'What is the direct object?', be able to reply: 'A book', and not: 'Mary'. ('Mary' is—or gives—the *indirect* object of the verb.) There is of course a convention in English that in such a context the direct object comes after the indirect object when no preposition is used; but one could not mention that convention when explaining the meaning of 'direct object'. For the reason why we can impute that convention to English (and not, perhaps, to some other language) is because we can *already* detect the direct object in the sentence 'John sent Mary a book', and in sentences like it. No doubt it is in virtue of the structural features of a sentence that a speaker of the language is able to discern what the direct object is, and indeed what the sense of the sentence is; but the capacities which the speaker must already have are linguistic, not metalinguistic. The speaker must know how to use words, not how to classify them. This shows up in how the concept of a direct object is in fact taught.

[T]he concept of a direct object [. . .] is learned somewhat as follows: the teacher takes a sentence, say 'John sent Mary a book' and says: 'What did John send Mary?' Getting the answer 'A book' he says: 'That's the direct object.'   (*IS*, 6)

Since there may be no such people as John and Mary, we can indeed take the teacher's question as equivalent to 'What does the sentence "John sent Mary a book" say John sent Mary?'—but the point remains that the teacher's question is not, nor could it be, a question primarily about words, about bits of language. No question starting 'Which words ... ?' would serve when teaching the concept of a direct object, unless it be a question like 'Which words pick out the *thing* that John sent Mary?'.

> [T]he question 'What does the sentence say John gave?' is fundamental for understanding either 'direct object' or 'direct-object phrase' as I am using those expressions ...   (*IS*, 8)

(She means, of course, the quoted question and questions like it.)

As Anscombe hastens to point out, she is not legislating against the usage of grammarians who say that an expression such as 'a book' *is* the direct object. Their concept of a 'direct object' is perfectly usable. What she is getting at is that this latter concept presupposes *a special way of using* such a phrase as 'A book', that way being illustrated in the imaginary dialogue between teacher and learner, above. The use of the phrase is special in that (e.g.) it precludes the question, 'Which book?'. But it is not a use of the phrase which can be assimilated to *bona fide* metalinguistic uses, such as ' "Book" rhymes with "cook" ', or 'The French for "book" is "livre" '.

After all, the teacher's counter-response to the learner's 'A book' could have been, 'And what might that show about John?'—planting the discussion firmly in the domain of (imaginary or real) people, gifts, and books, rather than of words and phrases. The learner doesn't know where the dialogue is going—maybe he is actually being taught about the possibility of altruism—and when he says 'A book' in answer to the first question, he is already using it in the special way Anscombe is talking about. 'Direct object' simply labels that kind of use, in effect.

The main lesson to be drawn (so far) is this: the dilemma we seemed to face earlier, as to whether the answer 'A book' should be construed as denoting (i) a phrase or (ii) what that phrase stands for (i.e. a book, if anything)—that dilemma is a false dilemma. So is the related dilemma, as to whether the answer involves use or mention, in the technical sense of those terms.

Do these remarks apply even where a direct-object-giving answer uses a paradigm referring term, such as a proper name? The teacher–learner dialogue might have gone thus: 'Whom does this sentence say the court condemned to death?' 'Socrates'. Now just as 'Which book?' was a senseless question, so is 'Which Socrates?'. For although it is tempting to answer, 'The teacher of Plato', this identification is not of course vouchsafed us by the sentence 'The court condemned Socrates to death', which could be used in connection with anybody called Socrates. In the teacher–learner dialogue, it is not being used in connection with anyone at all, and the process of teaching the concept *direct object* would succeed even if teacher and pupil were both completely ignorant of the classical world and its denizens.

'The sentence says that the court condemned x to death' will be recognized by many professional philosophers as an intensional or opaque context, and put in the same basket as 'Plato says that the court condemned x to death'. The modern discussion of such contexts can probably be traced back to

Frege;[4] for Frege, as for many others, the question to ask is, 'What does a term occurring in an intensional context refer to?' Frege's view was that the reference of a term in such a context was the term's 'customary sense'. Our considerations, however, indicate that in the sort of context we are considering, even a proper name like 'Socrates' does not refer—not to a person, nor to a word, nor indeed to a sense (for *which* sense should we choose?). Anscombe says of the 'special use' of such a phrase as 'a book', given in answer to a question like 'What does the sentence say John gave Mary?', that '*It* can name neither a piece of language, nor anything that the piece of language names or otherwise relates to, nor indeed anything else' (*IS*, 8). Although it is not completely clear from the passage whether what she says here is meant to apply to *any* direct-object-giving answer, it would in fact seem to apply even to answers employing proper names. Maybe what we should say is that the context 'The sentence says that . . . ' is neither one of pure indirect quotation, nor one of pure direct quotation, but is something in between.[5]

'Direct object' is not a name for a kind of entity, akin, say, to 'metal object'; though the grammar of 'direct object' has some of the same features as that of such a phrase as 'metal object'. This partial kinship has interesting consequences. Consider:

(D) The direct object is what the sentence says John sent Mary.

This is a true statement, and it has a true 'namely'-rider—namely: 'a book'. But it is clearly different in logical form from 'A book is what the sentence says John sent Mary'. This latter sentence amounts to: 'The sentence said that John sent Mary a book'; but (D) cannot be paraphrased as: 'The sentence says that John sent Mary the direct object'!

What this shows is that there is a way of taking 'The direct object is not a direct object' which makes this true; namely, by assimilating this sentence to 'The direct object is not a girl [e.g. Mary]'. (*IS*, 7)

Anscombe takes these considerations to have a bearing upon Frege's notorious paradox of the concept *horse* ('The concept *horse* is not a concept')—something we shall return to in Chapter 6 (pp. 207–10).

Just as 'direct object' is not the name of a kind of thing, neither is 'intentional object' (since intentional objects are a species of direct objects). And 'intentional object' has a *partial* kinship with such a phrase as 'metal object'. One logical

---

[4] See Gottlob Frege, 'On Sense and Reference', in *Translations from the Philosophical Writings of Gottlob Frege*, ed. Peter Geach and Max Black (Oxford: Blackwell, 1960), 56–78.

[5] J. E. J. Altham has pointed out that the divide separating direct quotation from indirect quotation is in any case less wide than many philosophers have thought, and that much direct quotation cannot be construed as involving mention (as opposed to a special kind of use) of words. His argument relies crucially on Anscombe's findings with regard to 'I', discussed later in this chapter. See Altham, 'Indirect Reflexives and Indirect Speech', in Cora Diamond and Jenny Teichman (eds.), *Intention and Intentionality: Essays in Honour of G. E. M. Anscombe* (Brighton: Harvester Press, 1979), 25–37.

or grammatical feature which is common to the two types of phrase is that of entering into identity-statements. We have statements like (M), 'That metal object is the very implement that was used by the murderer'; but also statements like (I), 'The intentional object of their worship is Ombola'. But the latter, of course, means much the same as 'They worship Ombola', as that statement would ordinarily be understood. Identity-statements do not always allow application of Leibniz's Law (the principle that if A is the same as B, then whatever is true of A is true of B, and *vice versa*); and in the present case, (I) together with 'Ombola is just a hunk of wood' will not allow the inference to 'The intentional object of their worship is a hunk of wood'. (Similar remarks apply to 'Ombola is just a figment of their imagination', etc.) This is because, as Anscombe says, 'An intentional object is given by a word or phrase which gives a *description under which*' (*IS*, 9).

The italicized phrase is familiar to us from our discussion of an action's being intentional under a description—see Chapter 2, §1.2. Failures of Leibniz's Law were mentioned there, in connection with 'Boris's shooting of Andrei' and 'Boris's killing of Andrei'. Perhaps in the end Leibniz's Law is to be taken as applying only to 'genuine singular terms'. But to say that would surely just be to give a criterion for what shall *count* as a genuine singular term. By this criterion, at least one of 'That tip' and 'That quantity of metal' would not be a genuine singular term (see Ch. 2, p. 50)[6]—and nor, of course, would 'Ombola'. The thing to take note of is that a term which by such a criterion is no genuine singular term can nevertheless enter into identity-statements. And if we insist that only genuine singular terms enter into identity-statements, we have simply given a criterion for what shall count for us as an identity-statement, thus arbitrarily restricting the sense of that phrase.

'A mere hunk of wood' gives what Anscombe calls the *material* object of worship, in our imaginary case. Another example is used to illustrate this idea: that of a man aiming a gun at what he takes to be a stag, the thing actually being his own father. 'A stag' gives the intentional object of his aiming, while 'his father' gives the material object. Now the identity-statement 'The stag was in fact his father' may well be deemed a loose way of speaking. (Perhaps the same is true of 'Ombola is a mere hunk of wood'.) 'The thing he took for a stag was in fact his father' looks better; but what was 'the thing he took for a stag'? Anscombe thinks we should take this phrase seriously. The reason is that we need a rationale for saying, e.g., 'He was actually aiming at his father'. It is not enough—though it may count as evidence—that the man pointed his rifle at the spot where his father was: you can after all point your rifle at a spot wide

---

[6] Alternatively, 'is generous' would fail to be a genuine predicate, so that Leibniz's Law would not come into question on *that* account. One way or another, it seems that Leibniz's Law serves to define certain logical categories (name, predicate, etc.); and the pointfulness of such definition must be relative to the purposes at hand. Our *present* purposes would not appear to be served by a too strict adherence to the Law.

of your target, if your aim is bad. 'The thing he took for a stag' is a promissory note for an intentional description (a description acknowledgeable by the agent) which is true of his father—as 'stag' is not true.

We can ask what he was doing—what he was aiming at—*in that* he was aiming at a stag: this is to ask for another description 'X' such that in 'He was aiming at X' we still have an intentional object, but the description 'X' gives us something that exists in the situation. For example, he was aiming at that dark patch against the foliage. The dark patch against the foliage was in fact his father's hat with his father's head in it.   (*IS*, 10)

Here we get the first hint of how Anscombe is going to introduce perceptual 'appearances', in a way that is free of the encumbrances of the sense-datum theory. An appearance, such as 'the dark patch against the foliage', is really an intentional object, supplied by a description giveable by the subject in answer to the question, 'What do you see?' But the verb in the question need not have been a verb of perception, nor any overtly 'psychological' verb: the question could have been, 'What are you aiming at?' The features of the verbs and their objects that are important for our enquiry have nothing to do with perception or psychology as such. We have already laid out those features by (a) giving the three marks of intentionality (above, p. 130), and (b) noting that the logic of 'intentional object' is the logic of 'direct object'. But perhaps what I just said about psychology should be qualified: for it may be that a proper account of psychological verbs will involve logical features of just the sort that are mentioned under (a). What may in fact be in question is the adequacy of certain traditional, e.g. empiricist, models of what a psychological verb (state, process, event) is.

   Our account of the relationship between intentional objects and material objects (in Anscombe's technical sense) has relied on the fact that intentional-object phrases can enter into identity-statements—as, 'That dark patch against the foliage is a hat'. But hasn't Davidson, reversing Quine's quip, asserted: 'No identity without entity'?[7] Must we not now ask seriously after the ontological status of these special entities, *intentional objects*? It is at this point that Anscombe's proposal that intentional objects are nothing but a species of direct objects saves us from much metaphysical heart-searching:

The answer to 'What is the direct object in "John sent Mary a book"?' is 'A book'. This is the right answer as much when the sentence is false as when it is true, and also when it is only made up [. . .] It is evident nonsense to ask about the mode of existence or ontological status of the direct object as such: or to ask what kind of a thing *a book* is, as it is thought of in answer to the question about the direct object.   (*IS*, 11)

The point still holds where we have an identity-statement proper—as 'Santa Claus is the direct object of this sentence'. Again, we could decide to withhold the title 'identity-statement' from such a sentence, on the grounds that 'Santa Claus'

---

   [7] D. Davidson, 'The Individuation of Events', in *Essays on Actions and Events*, 164.

is not a genuine singular term. But then Davidson's remark will be a fairly lame tautology. Whatever we *call* 'That dark patch is a hat', it looks as if an enquiry into the ontological status of the dark patch, and of intentional objects generally, will be as silly as an enquiry into the ontological status of direct objects.[8] We saw above that the problems about what a direct-object phrase stood for were to be solved, in effect, by saying 'Nothing', and attending instead to the special use of such phrases. Something similar goes for intentional-object phrases.

1.2. 'What is Seen'

How does all this relate to the debate mentioned earlier, between sense-datum theorists and ordinary-language philosophers? To begin with the sense-datum theorist:

He takes the expression 'what you see' materially. 'The visual impression is what you see', which is a proposition like 'The direct object is what he sent', is misconstrued so as to lead to 'You see an impression', as the other never would be misconstrued so as to lead to 'He sent her a direct object'.   (*IS*, 13)

Note that Anscombe is happy with the truth of 'The visual impression is what you see'. The sense-datum theorist's mistake, for her, is to take 'what you see' in the wrong way—as having the sense which it has in 'What you see is actually your father, not a stag'. This mistake is bound to lead to a nonsensical enquiry into the nature of what is seen—e.g. visual impressions. The ordinary-language philosopher is rightly suspicious of all this, but agrees with the sense-datum theorist in taking 'what you see' as having only a material sense, thus ignoring the perfectly genuine intentional sense which that phrase may also have, and which the sense-datum theorist is confusedly trying to remind us of.

For one thing, we cannot understand what the material object of perception is without recourse to intentional objects. What you see cannot just be whatever is before your opened eyes, for you may be totally hallucinated. Nor can it be whatever out there happens to be the cause of... cause of what? Whatever we insert here, the 'cause' of it need not be *what is seen*. This is largely because of the possibility of so-called deviant causal chains; but the hunt for non-deviant

---

[8] Some words and phrases occur only in intentional descriptions, being learnt in connection with the language-game of 'describing appearances'. An example is 'speck on the horizon': the question 'Is that a speck on the horizon, or does it just appear to be one?' is senseless. ('Is there a speck on the horizon?' is different—you may be hallucinating.) So we have two sorts of case to consider: (i) you can't enquire into the ontological status of a stag *qua* intentional object, though you can enquire into the ontological status of stags *qua* stags; (ii) you can't enquire into the ontological status of specks on the horizon, either *qua* intentional objects or *qua* specks on the horizon, though you can enquire into the ontological status of specks on the horizon *qua* Fs, where there is a true identity-statement available of the form 'That speck on the horizon is an F', and where 'F' is not the sort of expression that occurs only in intentional descriptions ('F' could be 'yacht').

causal chains could only have any direction at all courtesy of our already having a non-causal criterion to hand. From a neutral perspective, one causal chain is as good as another. 'Normality' is certainly not enough: in certain situations, illusion or hallucination is perfectly normal. More of this anon.

What Anscombe said about 'aims at' applies equally to 'sees'. We determine the material object of sight by lighting on an intentional description (acknowledgeable by the subject) which applies to something real. The vocabulary of any such description, as the ordinary-language philosopher says, is not 'private'—it is the public language that must be used. But 'describing what you see' has an affinity with 'describing how you feel': the scope for intelligible error is limited, and in that—post-Wittgensteinian—sense, there is first-person authority. 'But a dog can see a cat without being in a position to acknowledge an intentional description of the cat.' True; so the condition of acknowledgeability strictly applies only to linguistically competent human beings. Even so, it will be *under some description* that we think of a dog as perceiving a cat—as a cat, say, rather than as a mammal, or as a female. The reasons for this will I think have to do with how *we* interpret the dog's behavioural capacities for distinguishing things. We can see the dog as going after a cat partly because we ourselves see the cat as a player (and as a *cat*). But just as first-person expressions of intention are central to the concept of intention, and provide the conceptual anchor for talk of an action's being intentional under a description (see Ch. 2, §1.1), so first-person reports of what one sees are crucial to the concept of seeing, and provide the conceptual anchor for talk of the intentional objects of vision.[9]

It might be thought that Anscombe is taking the phrase 'what is seen' ('object of sight', etc.) to be *ambiguous*, according as it has an intentional or a material sense. Her view of perception would then appear to be a form of 'disjunctivism',[10] the view, roughly, that to see (e.g.) is either visually to perceive a public thing, or to have a private visual impression. There are three interrelated reasons for resisting this classification of Anscombe's position.

First: that a concept has distinguishable strands or aspects is not in general enough for us to call it simply ambiguous.[11] Referring to the case of an oculist testing for squint, she writes that he 'does not have to teach a new use of "see" or of "I see a (picture of a) bird in a nest" before he can ask "Do you see the bird in the nest?"'—the bird-picture and the nest-picture being in fact spatially separated' (*IS*, 13). What she then says of the oculist's use of 'see' applies to the various uses

---

[9] Anscombe addresses the objection to her notion 'intentional under a description' that animals lack language in ' "Under a Description" '; see *UD*, 209–10.

[10] The 'disjunctive' theory has been developed by Hinton, Snowdon, and others. See J. M. Hinton, *Experiences: An Inquiry into Some Ambiguities* (Oxford: Clarendon Press, 1973); P. Snowdon, 'Perception, Vision and Causation', in *Proceedings of the Aristotelian Society*, 81 (1980–1), 175–92.

[11] This point is of wider philosophical significance; thus, we are not driven by the quite different first-person and third-person uses of psychological verbs to call those verbs ambiguous. The interconnections between these uses constitute conceptual unity.

of 'see', including especially the 'intentional' use: 'There is indeed an important difference [from the "material" use]; though it is wrong to regard the uses which it marks as, so to speak, *deviant*, for our concepts of sensation are built up by our having *all* these uses.' The imagined charge of 'deviance' would be made by a 1950s ordinary-language philosopher, if by anyone—not by a latter-day disjunctivist. But Anscombe's more general point is that the different uses of, say, 'see' are not such as to justify talk of ambiguity, or of lack of conceptual unity, or of disjunction.

Second: the question whether a given intentional description is true of a real thing will often lack a determinate answer—so, therefore, will the question (in such a case) whether 'see' can be said to have a material object or only an intentional one. This is because cases of misperception, or partial perception, come in degrees. Anscombe gives the example of someone with defective sight seeing a shiny blur over there. 'That blur, we say, is my watch' (*IS*, 18). A watch, however, cannot be blurry. Still, 'it is a shiny thing and it is over there'. We may in the end conclude in favour of 'She sees her watch'; but it is clear that *how minimal* a description one is allowed to give and still be describing a real thing is not a hard and fast matter. It may be indeterminate whether a person is 'really seeing' something, especially if her defective eyesight is responsible for the vagueness of her report.

Third: you may use 'see' (e.g.) in a way that shows that you have not in advance decided whether it is to be taken in its intentional or its material sense. This would be evident from your being unprepared with an answer if asked, 'Which sense did you mean?' (*IS*, 19–20). And it is not as if there must be some fact of the matter, whether in a given case you intended 'see' to be taken materially or merely intentionally. Where a choice has to be made, one's retrospective decision can determine what one had meant; and this is enough to show that in the normal case, where no choice has to be made, there is no fact of the matter. Anscombe compares sense-perception with perception of pain-location, writing:

We may make a similar point about 'phantom limb'. I take the part of the body where pain is felt to be the object of a transitive verb-like expression 'to feel pain in—'. Then where there is, e.g., no foot, but *X*, not knowing this, says he feels pain in his foot, he may say he was wrong ('I did not see a lion there, for there was no lion') or he may alter his understanding of the phrase 'my foot' so that it becomes a purely intentional object of the verb-like expression. But it need not be determined in advance, in the normal case of feeling pain, whether one so intends the expression 'I feel pain in—' as to withdraw it, or merely alter one's intentions for the description of the place of the pain, if one should learn that the place was missing. (*IS*, 20)

Anscombe does indeed speak here of *altering* one's understanding of a phrase, and of *altering* one's intentions regarding a phrase, in cases where a choice has to be made as to the phrase's interpretation; and this may lead the reader to think that there was after all a fact of the matter as to what the person had meant, at the time when he used a phrase (namely: that he had meant the phrase to be taken 'materially'). But of course Anscombe also implies that a retrospective decision as to interpretation may be authoritative, even if it differs from what the person would have said earlier. The view of speaker-meaning implicit in these remarks is clearly akin to that argued for by Wittgenstein in various places.[12] If we accept such an account, then it does seem that we should agree that there is no reason to insist '*Either* material object *or* intentional object', in the normal case of a person's using a verb like 'see' (i.e. in the case where no choice as to interpretation has to be made).

For these reasons, it will not do to label Anscombe a disjunctivist. The same reasons, among others, count against her being classified as an 'adverbialist' in respect of intentional uses of 'see', etc.—an adverbialist being someone who regards the logical form of 'X sees an F' as renderable: 'X sees F-ly'.[13] She does indeed share with the adverbialist the view that where 'see' is meant to be taken as purely intentional, 'I see pink elephants' does not entail 'There are pink elephants'; or in her terms, that where 'see' is meant to be taken as purely intentional, I am not committed to withdrawing my statement if it is pointed out that there are no pink elephants. But, as we have seen, there may, in advance, be no fact of the matter whether I mean 'see' to be taken as purely intentional or not, and hence no fact of the matter whether the entailment holds or does not. Moreover, it is important for her overall account that the phrase that follows an intentional use of 'see' should in general be *capable* of allowing further identity-statements—as 'That dark patch is my father's hat'—something that would not be possible if the phrase were fundamentally adverbial ('I see dark-patchly'). For it is only via such identity-statements that we are able to determine the *material* objects of perception, where there are such. And what holds of 'I see pink elephants' holds of 'I see a dark patch': both are intentional-use statements, and their logical forms, if one may speak of such a thing, will not be radically different. Remember that even where 'I see pink elephants' is meant purely intentionally, this only means that it fails to entail 'There are pink elephants', not that it entails 'There are no pink elephants'.

But is Anscombe's account of the material sense of 'see' ('hear', etc.) adequate? The material object of perception is said to be determined by an intentional description true of something 'existing in the situation'. But what about so-called veridical hallucinations? I may give an intentional description of what I see: a large dog—this being a result of my taking a strong hallucinogen—but where there is in fact a large dog before me (i.e. in the place where I say I see a large dog). In this case, I surely don't see the actual dog, despite my giving an intentional description true of something really existing in the situation. Isn't the missing ingredient a *causal link*? When I see a dog (material sense of 'see'), mustn't the dog be causing me to be in the perceptual state I'm in?

---

[12] See e.g. *Philosophical Investigations*, paras. 633–63.

[13] Adverbialism about sense-perception is argued for, e.g., in M. Tye, *The Metaphysics of Mind* (Cambridge: Cambridge University Press, 1989).

Here we encounter the causal theory of perception. In the last half century or so, a large number of psychological and other concepts have been dealt with by invoking causality: perception, memory, knowledge, reference ... In Chapter 1, we had to do with causalism as regards intentional action, and reasons for rejecting that position were outlined there. It will be instructive to devote some space to causal theories of the mind, in particular of perception and of memory. What is Anscombe's attitude to such theories, and to the way in which causality is invoked by them?

1.3. Causality and the Mind

For the empiricists, direct knowledge was of one's own mental states. This starting point produced a form of epistemological problem: how can I distinguish between a 'true' state and a 'false' one? The question how a mental state could have content at all—could be *about* something—was a question whose nature and importance were only appreciated later; that a memory-state, say, had a certain content ('I had coffee for breakfast') could be taken more or less as a given, for the empiricist. The problem was to justify assenting to what the memory-state 'told' you. The best thing would be directly to compare the mental state with whatever it was about. But that would mean bringing a past event back, so as to compare the present memory with it. Analogously, if the mental state were a visual experience, it would mean comparing the objects before one with the experience. Both kinds of comparison being impossible, all that one could do was to distinguish different kinds of mental states by their intrinsic or introspectible properties: force and vivacity, or coherence with other mental states, or affectability by the will, etc., etc.

The picture of mental states as objects of our direct awareness was radically undermined by Wittgenstein. Sense-impressions (sense-data, appearances) had been presented as a paradigm instance of mental-states-directly-known; and we have just seen how Anscombe continued Wittgenstein's work with respect to such putative objects of awareness, while preserving the grain of truth in the sense-datum theory.

The need to distinguish true from false mental states arose from the main preoccupation of empiricism: to investigate the nature and scope of human knowledge. Modern causal theories may not have this epistemological preoccupation at their centre, but they do inherit the empiricists' form of question: What distinguishes a genuine (or 'true') state from a merely ostensible (or 'false') one? And there is certainly something in the idea that in order to say what seeing is, you have to be able to say how it differs from visually hallucinating. (But an enquiry into how it differs from hearing or feeling might also be philosophically enlightening.) Causality appears to do the trick. The dog causes you to see it; your breakfast is a cause of your now remembering it; more generally, a known fact is the cause of your knowledge of it. Each of these simple assertions encapsulates a causal theory of X.

But what is meant by 'cause'? And what does the philosopher who invokes this notion mean to *achieve* by invoking it?

We should clear our minds of all prejudice on the subject of causality in considering what we know here. Here is someone, let us say, who knows that such-and-such occurred. Let us suppose that this is a surprising fact—we want an explanation. How *has it come about* that this person knows that?—we ask. And then we are convincingly told: 'Well, he was there, he witnessed it.' The mystery is removed [. . .] This is an original phenomenon of causality: one of its types—whether or not anyone has yet classified it as such. No general theory about what causality is has to be introduced to justify acceptance of it. Nor does it have to be accommodated to any general theory, before it is accepted. [. . .] [W]e do not analyse memory in terms of causality. It is rather that what we call (personal) memory of a past time we also call an effect of the original witnessing of its events.   (*MEC*, 127)

Causality is indeed relevant to such phenomena as perception and memory. The fault of many a causal theory, for Anscombe, is that of putting the cart before the horse. It is not that we have an independently determined notion of 'cause' which can be invoked as the added ingredient in true seeing or remembering; rather, there are various familiar ways of determining that someone is really seeing or remembering, and these ways—precisely because of their role—serve to give paradigms of causal explanation. Anscombe mentions the case of someone's having been present at some event as a sufficient explanation of how they know something. Such knowledge would count as memory. 'Sufficient explanation' does not mean 'indefeasible explanation': further evidence might always turn up which undermined the claim to memory, as: that the person had been kidnapped in the intervening period, and brainwashed by hypnosis to think and say what had in fact happened. These sorts of tales are often presented as counter-examples to a philosophical account (here, of memory), or as possibilities which a proper account must strive to exclude. That notion of what the proper account should look like is what lies behind the quest for the Grail of non-deviant causal connection, something only to be found in true memory, true perception, etc. But we need to remind ourselves of the lesson of 'On Brute Facts'. That there are indefinitely many possible factors that would prevent P from being the case does not show either (a) that a person has to know that no such factors are present before being fully entitled to assert that P, or (b) that the only adequate explanation of 'P' must somehow embrace all such factors, in order to exclude them. (See Chapter 3, pp. 90–4.) What *can* in fact be said in such a case is that 'P' is not susceptible of analysis in terms of necessary and sufficient conditions, and by now philosophers should be neither surprised nor perturbed by such a result.[14]

---

[14] See C. B. Martin and M. Deutscher, 'Remembering', *Philosophical Review*, 75 (1966), 161–96 for an account which dutifully deals with a number of strange cases in the pursuit of necessary and sufficient conditions. 'Remembering' is also a classic exposition of the causal theory of memory.

We should also remember that the various familiar ways of telling whether someone really is e.g. remembering are more powerful than one might think if one is over-impressed by thought-experiments. Were the possibility to be aired that Smith might actually have been kidnapped, brainwashed, etc., we should probably (if we felt it worth our while) have a fairly easy time disposing of the possibility—by further quizzing of Smith, by asking his close friends about his movements during the intervening period, etc., etc. These facts help to assuage the sceptical worries characteristic of empiricist philosophy; but they also serve to flesh out how it is that the concept of remembering is actually usable, that a large measure of agreement attends its use, and so on—without there being any need for people to rule out sceptical scenarios when using it.

In the light of the above remarks, let us consider the case of veridical hallucination mentioned at the end of the last section. 'The person looking at a dog who reports seeing a dog might only be hallucinating.' Insofar as 'hallucinating an F' implies 'not seeing a real F', this amounts to: someone might appear to see a dog who doesn't really see it.[15] After all, having taken a strong hallucinogen isn't enough: you could do that and still actually see the dog before you (maybe you have a strong constitution). In that case, the hallucinogen in your bloodstream won't get to count as a cause, simply because the relevant *effect* (not seeing real things, seeing only non-real things) hasn't occurred. We need to know whether the effect has occurred or not; and it is this effect or the lack of it, rather than any cause, which is the crux of the matter. *Is* he seeing it? The ways to find out are various and familiar. Remove the dog, ask him what he sees now. Or stand in front of the dog, and ask him the same. Or simply: get him to describe the dog he sees. The first two of these help to show in what sense the dog, if he is really seeing it, *causes* him to see it.

A philosopher might say: 'A causal explanation is, or entails, a counterfactual conditional. What we must be after is a conclusion as to whether, had the dog not been there, the person would still have seen a dog. We are interested in his capacities as a truth-tracker with respect to dog-judgements. That is why everyday tests like removing the dog are suitable.' But is the persuasiveness of what we find when we remove an object and then ask someone what he sees really to do with what a merely *counterfactual* statement might have told us? Why does a counterfactual theory of causation have any attraction in the first place? We readily admit such a thing as 'If the dog hadn't been there, he wouldn't have seen a dog'; but what are our grounds for saying such a thing, and with such confidence? The answer to this surely has to do with the statement's connection with completely ordinary facts about what people can and can't say or do with respect to objects, according as those objects are in their presence or not. And what counts as 'in somebody's presence' is, in its turn, constrained by what the

---

[15] I ignore the case of someone simultaneously hallucinating a dog and seeing a real dog. (He would report two dogs, one supposes.)

person can and can't say or do, rather than by any physically describable set of conditions.

To see this last point, consider what would have to be included in the antecedent of our counterfactual conditional. 'If the dog hadn't been there...' Where is 'there'? 'In front of the person' isn't enough: he would still have seen the dog if it had been not directly in front of him but over to the side. 'Well, if it had been out of his field of vision, then he wouldn't have seen it.' Yes—but the field of vision is just the range of what you can see. The proposition is a tautology. 'If the dog had been so positioned that light could not be reflected from its surface directly into the eyes of the person, *then*...' This counterfactual would probably be true, if spelt out carefully enough. But it won't serve as a model for all cases of seeing. Light is not reflected from the sun, from shadows, from rainbows, from the sky, from the hole in your sock, from *muscae volitantes* [16]—yet we see all these things. This is not a piece of 'mere' ordinary-language philosophy. As Anscombe observed, our concept of seeing is made up of *all* these uses, and it would simply express a prejudice to claim that one case, the seeing of what Austin called medium-sized dry goods, is the only Proper case.

The variety of cases corresponds to the variety of senses in which something perceived can be said to cause the perception of it. Indeed, the concept of *cause* itself, permeating as it does not only the phenomenon of perception, but an enormous range of other things besides, manifests a variety daunting for philosophical enquiry. We shall see in the next chapter how Anscombe manages to give this variety its due, and to avoid all easy theorizing about 'the nature of causation'.

I said a moment ago that the question whether someone is really seeing something has more to do with what is true of that person than with any putative causes, what is true of him being determinable in various familiar ways. This fact connects with the second of the three reasons given above why Anscombe cannot be called a disjunctivist (pp. 138–40): if the descriptions a person gives of an object are too vague or distorted, it becomes doubtful whether he is seeing anything. A thing may be causing someone to describe what he sees (intentional sense of 'sees'), but that is not enough for him to 'really' see (material sense)—not because of any hypothetical deviant causal chain, but simply because to determine *what* he sees, we must have from him, or must be somehow able to attribute to him, an intentional description true (enough) of something existing in the situation. If we can't match his description to some best candidate, for example, we won't be able to say 'It is *this* that he sees'.

1.4. Memory vs. Perception

If Anscombe is right, perception cannot properly be understood without an appreciation of the distinction between material and intentional objects. But

---

[16] Floating specks, which are actually debris in the fluid of the eye. See *IS*, 19.

she takes this distinction to have no analogue for memory. Connected with this is the claim that remembering is not a kind of *experience*—unlike seeing, hearing, smelling, etc. Anscombe recounts how a deluded George IV said that he remembered leading a cavalry charge at Waterloo, though in fact he was never there; and she then contrasts memory and perception in the following way:

[T]hough what George IV thought he remembered need not have happened (in order for him to be using 'remember' correctly), nevertheless he himself could not *leave it open* whether the thing happened or not, whereas in contrast a man can leave it open whether what he sees is purely subjective or is really there. I mean 'subjective' in the sense that another could not check his seeing by looking himself.   (*MEC*, 123)

(Anscombe's bracketed phrase is not meant to imply that what George IV said would be *true*, only that he would not be misusing words.)

Of course, a person can doubt whether he is in fact remembering something, and another of Anscombe's examples can be used to illustrate this: that of Goethe's saying in his autobiography 'that he is going to tell of things belonging to his childhood, of which he does not know whether he remembers them or was told them' (*MEC*, 120). The difference to note is that between (a) one who says 'I remember that X happened', while leaving it open whether the thing did happen, and (b) one who says 'I seem to remember that X happened' or 'I may be remembering that X happened'. The person in (a), according to Anscombe, is misusing the verb 'to remember', but not the person in (b). The latter's use of 'seem to' (or 'may be') indicates doubt or hesitancy: it is an epistemic operator, as it were. In Goethe's case, the doubt concerns whether certain beliefs are in fact memories—which is a doubt about the origin of those beliefs. (A doubt of this sort could, but need not, give rise to a doubt as to whether the beliefs were true.) By contrast, one can say 'I seem to see flashing lights before me' without there being any question of doubt—for one may simply be describing appearances. Indeed, one could simply say, 'I see flashing lights before me', flashing lights being the intentional object of one's seeing. To see in this sense is to have a certain sort of experience: the concept of *experience* being connected with subjectivity, in the sense alluded to by Anscombe in the above quotation. It is essential to subjectivity in this sense that one can leave it open whether one's experience is veridical or not; this feature of visual experience provided the third of the reasons given above why Anscombe cannot be called a disjunctivist (pp. 139–40).

'Describe what you see' may ask for a merely intentional object; 'describe what you remember' never does this. But perhaps this is just a feature of our actual language? Couldn't a verb be coined for the subjective state which is common to real memory and 'false' memory, just as 'see' in its intentional sense can be used either by someone who sees real things or by someone who (e.g.) hallucinates them? Anscombe pursues this hypothesis, in order eventually to reject it, once again showing how important it is in philosophy to consider possible, as well as actual and ordinary, languages. The verb she coins for the putative subjective state is 'REMBER'.

Anscombe's case against the possibility of the verb 'to REMBER', and of the putative mental state it expresses, has a number of strands. There seem to be four key claims, which I have extracted from 'The Reality of the Past' (1950) and from 'Memory, "Experience" and Causation' (1974):

(1) Remembering must be prior to REMBERING (cf. *MEC*, 124)

(2) Use of the past tense must be prior to REMBERING (cf. *RP*, 108–9; *MEC*, 126)

(3) Remembering could not be: REMBERING plus a causal connection with the past event (cf. *MEC*, 127–30)

(4) There could be no special vocabulary for describing what one REMBERS (cf. *RP*, 107–8)

The question is: must a proponent of the subjective state of REMBERING deny one or more of these claims? If so, that would show that the proponent of REMBERING had gone wrong somehow. And Anscombe takes it that he must indeed deny some or all of 1 to 4. Now a philosopher who says that the contents of our minds are what we know directly may indeed be committed to the denial of some or all of 1 to 4.[17] And it is probably to such an empiricist-minded philosopher that Anscombe is addressing many of her arguments. But for our purposes it will be more interesting to consider the philosopher who would apply what Anscombe says about the intentionality of perception to the case of memory; that is, someone who does not take REMBERING to be some kind of epistemological building block or starting point.

Let us consider the analogues, for perception, of 1 to 3: (1′) the concept of seeing (material sense) is prior to that of seeing (intentional sense)—cf. *IS*, 13, bottom; (3′) seeing (material sense) is not to be explained as seeing (intentional sense) plus a causal connection—cf. §1.3, above. Proposition 2 doesn't really have an analogue for perception, unless it be that one's use of the *present* tense must be prior to one's having the concept of seeing (intentional sense)—presumably true enough. The motivations for asserting (1′) to (3′) would seem to carry over to propositions 1 to 3. Given these facts, a 'modest' devotee of REMBERING, understood on the model of intentional seeing, may accept 1, 2, and 3 with relative equanimity.

The analogue for perception of proposition 4, however, is definitely false. 'Special vocabulary' is my phrase, not Anscombe's; the sense of 'special' that I have in mind is that in which each sense modality has its special vocabulary: colours, shapes, etc., for vision, sounds for hearing, smells for smell, and so on. Such vocabularies help us when it comes to framing purely intentional descriptions of what we perceive; and to frame such a description is to 'describe

---

[17] Russell would be an obvious candidate; see *The Analysis of Mind*, ch. 9.

an experience'. Anscombe claims that no such special vocabulary could exist for the putative state of REMBERING; but that as a putatively subjective experience, REMBERING *ought* to be expressible using such a vocabulary. Hence there can be no such thing as REMBERING.

There are two claims in the offing here, to do with images. The first is that remembering does not in general require the having of images. The second is that where images are involved, these are not so much 'memory-images' as remembered (or misremembered) perceptual images. If REMBERING is to be a kind of experience, it would seem to have to be imagistic. It will not then be the 'core' of remembering as such. So whereas 'Describe what you see/hear/smell ... ' is always answerable using an intentional description, 'Describe what you remember' would only sometimes be thus answerable, if ever. And any answer that *was* given would in fact be a description of past perceptions, not a description of a present experience.

One can ask someone who remembers something to consider just what appearance he saw. But this is not drawing his attention to a memory-datum; it is trying to elicit a new memory—of a sense-datum. [. . .] If we look for a datum, then should we ask the rememberer to consider exactly what he is experiencing when he has the memory [. . .]? But he may not be able to produce anything that seems relevant if he has no image, and it is not necessary that he should have an image.   (*RP*, 108)

If a perceptual memory is a memory of a past experience (or 'datum'), does it follow that the memory is not itself an experience? Not straight off. But, Anscombe may point out, *what* you are describing, when asked to describe what you remember perceiving, is surely the past experience. Your description therefore cannot also be a description of a distinct, present, experience. But can it not? Could not one and the same description be employed, both for the perceptions that you take yourself to be remembering, and for the remembering itself? The fact that a special, e.g. visual, vocabulary is involved would not be enough to show that only seeing is being described; for one can *imagine* seeing something, and describe what one imagines, the vocabulary employed being visual. Two kinds of experience, viz. seeing and visual imagining, are both describable by means of the single vocabulary of vision. In describing what you are visually imagining, you describe what you *would* or *might* see; similarly, it may be argued, in describing what you are 'visually' remembering, you describe what you *did* see. If REMBERING lacks a special vocabulary, so too does imagining (in the sense of 'imaging'), which perforce borrows its vocabulary from one or another sense modality. But this surely shows that something can count as a subjective experience despite lacking a special vocabulary.

With seeing (intentional sense) and imagining (or 'imaging'), we may say that the experience or image that is had on a given occasion just *is* the seeing or imagining. (Or if you prefer, the having of the experience/image is the seeing or imagining.) But even where one experiences images in connection with remembering something, neither these images nor the having of them can *be* the remembering, according to Anscombe. Hence describing such images is not describing an experience of remembering (such an experience being our putative state of REMBERING).

> [I]t has often enough been remarked that one *need* not have a memory image when one remembers. But even if someone has one, and the memory image is just what he finds when he introspects to see what goes on 'when we remember', it *also* needs to be made clear that the memory image is not itself the remembering even on that occasion. One way of seeing this is to suppose the memory image replaced by an actual picture that one sees or draws. Referring an image to the past involves some belief; and it must be done by the person who has the picture before him, if to him it is even a false picture of the past.   (*MEC*, 122)

An image must be 'referred to the past' to count as a memory-image. But pastness cannot be a feature of an image, any more than it can be a feature of a painting. Anscombe takes it that some additional belief is required for an image to be about the past, e.g. 'This happened', or 'This did not happen'. (It is natural to say that of these two beliefs, only the former would render an image a memory image.) No such additional belief is needed for us to count an image as a visual image, of sight or imagination. For such an image is not 'referred to' anything, not even, in the case of seeing, to the present. One can respond to the demand that one describe what one sees by drawing a picture, a picture that is sufficient in itself, needing neither the belief 'This is the case' nor the belief 'This is not the case' to be tacked on. (The latter belief would be appropriate for cases of known hallucination.)

The point is essentially the same as was argued earlier, that you cannot, when giving a memory-report, *leave it open* whether it is true or not. The underlying reason for this turns out to be that *some* belief as to truth is necessary if the alleged experience is to count as being about the past, and hence as a memory experience. But can this be right? For we have already allowed the sensefulness of 'I may be remembering that X happened' (p. 145), and if memory images are allowed, could not someone likewise say in connection with such an image, 'This *may* have happened'? 'This may have happened' might indeed be said to express a belief, but it doesn't seem that such a belief could succeed in referring an image to the past, given that the belief could as well attend a piece of pure imagining. But perhaps an image gets to count as a memory image because the attendant 'This may have happened' amounts to 'I feel an inclination (possibly feeble) to believe that this happened'. After all, if you describe an image as one of memory, but happily say of it 'Of course, this didn't actually happen', won't that be because of reasons that *count against* believing it? In the absence of such reasons, you would have believed it—else, why not call it a bit of imagining? The inclination to believe that so-and-so happened is, it could be argued, the extra element in virtue of which a mere image can be said to be about the past.[18]

---

[18] Martin and Deutscher, in 'Remembering', deny that belief, or an inclination to believe, is what distinguishes a memory 'representation' from veridical imagining. They claim that a painter

'I see ...' in its subjective sense does not in the same way always go with an inclination to believe in a corresponding reality—not even a feeble inclination. Consider 'I see the bird in the nest', said at the oculist's, or 'I'm seeing double'. The same holds of other sense modalities—'There's a ringing in my ears', 'I have a bitter taste in my mouth', and so on.

Whether or not an inclination to believe is what determines the 'pastness' of memory images, Anscombe is surely right that such images or experiences must be referred to the past in virtue of *something*—and that there is no analogous requirement for perceptual images or experiences. The whole issue of reference to the past, and of how such reference relates to memory, will be discussed more fully in the next chapter. For now, let us conclude by noting some main strands in Anscombe's accounts of perception and memory.

First, there is the intentional/material distinction, a distinction which allows us to interpret 'object of perception' in such a way as to accommodate the subjectivity of perceptual experience without positing a realm of private objects. The truth in phenomenalism is thus salvaged. Second, there is the putting of causality in its place: causality is indeed relevant to both perception and memory, but not as an independently comprehensible added ingredient. Third, there is the insistence on an important disanalogy between perceiving and remembering, which centres on the requirement that any 'memory experience' be referred to the past, in virtue of something outside that experience.

Anscombe's work in the philosophy of mind deals with topics in addition to those of perception and memory, of course. Some of these were examined in the first three chapters: intention, motive, wanting, knowledge of posture and of action, etc. Elsewhere among her writings there are discussions of thinking, pretending, and enjoying. As I have indicated, it is particularly the first-personal use of these concepts that Anscombe is interested in: 'I intend', 'I see', 'I remember', and so on. So it seems appropriate now to ask, like Descartes, 'What then is this *I*?'.

2. THE FIRST PERSON

2.1. What am I?

The question 'What am I?' can be answered in multifarious ways. 'A dentist', 'An English person', 'A descendant of Scriabin', 'A human being', 'A mammal'. A number of these (assuming that the answers are all true) are things that you always

who paints what turns out to be a perfect likeness of a house seen in his childhood might be said to remember the house, even though he believes his painting to be a work of imagination; for them, the representation will be one of memory so long as its production has as its causal origin the house. But we could ask: what makes this picture a picture *of* the past house? If someone asked, 'What house is that a picture of?', the painter might reply, 'It is the house of Bilbo Baggins'; and his word surely goes. In general, causal origin cannot be equated with object of reference, or with intentional object.

were, and that you could not stop being, except by ceasing to exist altogether. Hence those things are essential to you. But philosophers have perceived a sense of the question 'What am I?' in which it cries out for a unique answer, an answer that would give something essential in a stronger sense of 'essential'. Similar remarks go for things with names. The possible responses to 'What is Prague?' include 'A city', 'A European capital', 'A place once visited by Mozart', 'A tourist resort' ... But there is a sense of the question that cries out for a unique answer, the canonical answer, as we might put it—the answer 'A city'. But what does it mean to call this answer canonical?

'Prague' is a name of a city, but it is also a name *for* a city.[19] To understand the word 'Prague', you have to know that it is a city, and what sort of thing a city is. Assertions about Prague are canonically verifiable or falsifiable by reference to facts about a certain city—facts in principle recordable in the form 'This city is F'. You don't need to find out whether the place visited by Mozart in 1791 is F, simply that a certain city is F. Which city? Prague, of course; and we jump out of any apparent circle here by adverting to the *use* made of the name 'Prague', a use connected with activities such as visiting, sending letters, and even the philosopher's favourite, pointing (from an aeroplane, perhaps). An actual verification of e.g. 'Prague is to the south of Moscow' will be an activity fitting in with these various activities in a certain way; and it is the totality of these activities, some having more weighting than others, which goes to determine that it is this particular city to which the word 'Prague' refers.

'Prague' is a name for a city—the sortal concept associated with the name is *city*. An answer to 'What am I?', in the special sense of that question, might be thought to lead to a similar claim. If the answer were 'A human being', for instance, the claim would be that 'I' is a term for a human being, and that the sortal concept associated with 'I' is *human being*. This would not on its own justify our calling 'I' a proper name, for it could be a sort of demonstrative. Demonstratives too require sortal concepts—'this' must always be understood as 'this so-and-so' (e.g. 'this human being') if it is to mean anything. But there might be reasons for thinking that 'I' isn't really a demonstrative either—that it is *sui generis*, neither name nor demonstrative. However, in answering 'What am I?' with a statement intended as canonical, we do seem to be saying at the very least that 'I' *refers* to something, a certain sort of thing, in the same sort of way as do 'Prague' and 'this chair'.

This very natural idea, that the function of the word 'I' (and any equivalent) is to refer to something, is what is denied by Anscombe in her famous paper 'The First Person'. The view that 'I' is a referring term leads, she argues, to insoluble difficulties: 'And this is the solution: "I" is neither a name nor another kind of

[19] The distinction is made by Geach; see P. T. Geach, *Reference and Generality: An Examination of Some Medieval and Modern Theories* (3rd edn., Ithaca and London: Cornell University Press, 1980), §34, p. 70.

expression whose logical role is to make a reference, *at all*' (*FP*, 32). But she does not deny that propositions like 'I am a human being' can be true; and more significantly, she allows the possible truth of such propositions as 'I am Elizabeth Anscombe' and 'I am this thing here'. These last, however, she claims not to be identity propositions (*FP*, 33), which of course is consonant with her denial that 'I' is a referring expression. How then does she arrive at such a position?

The key thought is this: that in referring to something by means of some expression, one must have some conception of that thing, in virtue of which it is *that* thing to which one refers. For instance, to be able to refer to a particular city by means of the expression 'Prague', one must associate a certain conception of that city with one's use of the name. The point is very similar to that which we encountered in §1, where we found Anscombe arguing that in order to determine the material object of somebody's seeing (or aiming, or worshipping...), it is necessary to have a description of some real thing that is acknowledgeable *by the person*—an intentional description (see pp. 135–6, 138 above). Such a description might be said to embody a conception of the thing.

The claim that reference must be mediated by a conception of the referent is clearly Fregean in spirit. 'Conception' is pretty well equivalent to Frege's term *Sinn* ('sense'). The problem as regards 'I' is that *if* one associates some conception of a referent with 'I', it appears possible that one might when using 'I' fail to refer to what one intended to refer to—for one's conception may fail to be true of the thing one had meant to refer to. It may even fail to be true of anything at all. But it appears that you can't be mistaken about the identity of the φ-er when you say 'I am φing', in the way in which you can be mistaken if you say 'John is φing', or 'That thing/person is φing'. The notions of mistaken reference and of reference-failure seem to have no application to first-personal statements. If 'I' were a referring expression, it would have to be immune to both mistaken reference and reference-failure; and this immunity can't be guaranteed by any conception. (In the next section, we shall consider an account of 'I' as referring expression that attempts to explain this immunity while doing without the notion of a conception.)

In fact, like Wittgenstein, Anscombe took the impossibility of mistaken or failed reference to show that there is no referring going on. The similarity with Wittgenstein is not complete, however, at any rate if we are considering the Wittgenstein of *The Blue Book*. In *The Blue Book* we encounter the distinction between two uses of 'I': the 'use as subject' and the 'use as object'. [20] With the former, there is indeed no possibility of error through misidentification—as, 'I am in pain', 'I know the answer', etc.—whereas with the latter, the possibility of such error has been allowed for, in Wittgenstein's phrase. There are, according to Wittgenstein, possible circumstances in which such a judgement as 'I am

---

[20] *Preliminary Studies for the 'Philosophical Investigations,' Generally Known as The Blue and Brown Books* (2nd edn., Oxford: Blackwell, 1969), pp. 66–7.

clenching my fist' is wrong, not because of the predicate's failing to apply but because of a misidentification of the subject. (One sees the fist in a mirror and mistakes it for one's own—someone else is clenching his fist.) Cases involving the use of 'I' as object, for Wittgenstein, 'involve the recognition of a particular person', and this is connected with the possibility of error through misidentification.

Anscombe's response to such examples of misidentification would, I think, be to say that any misidentification that does occur is not the responsibility of the first-person pronoun. Thus, one could indeed talk of having misidentified a certain *fist*—incorrectly attributing the description 'my fist' to it. It is the expression 'my fist' that embodies the misidentification, not 'I'. One may even misidentify a certain human body as 'my body', or a certain human being as 'the human being that I am'.[21] But to repeat an earlier point, the latter phrase does not involve an identity judgement, according to Anscombe—in which case it is not 'I' that embodies any misidentification.

For there to be misidentification, as opposed to a failure to say anything definite at all, there must, it seems, be some successful identification. Again, a comparison with intentional verbs is useful. 'He inadvertently aimed at his father' is true (say) because he really did aim at the dark patch against the foliage, something he could successfully describe as such. If I misidentify Tamsin as Jenny, I must at least be able to identify Tamsin successfully—not *as* Tamsin, of course, but (say) as the lady sitting on that bench. And even where there is a failure to identify anything at all, the would-be identifier must have *something* in mind, something which, if real, allows us to assess what he says for truth or falsehood, success or failure. Anscombe makes this latter point in connection with demonstrative reference, thus:

> Someone comes with a box and says 'This is all that is left of poor Jones'. The answer to 'this what?' is 'this parcel of ashes'; but unknown to the speaker the box is empty. What 'this' has to have, if used correctly, is something that it *latches on to* (as I will put it): in this example it is the box. [. . .] The referent and what 'this' latches on to may coincide, as when I say 'this buzzing in my ears is dreadful', or, after listening to a speech, 'That was splendid!' But they do not have to coincide, and the referent is the object of which the predicate is predicated where 'this' or 'that' is a subject.   (*FP*, 28)

These remarks about demonstratives show how 'this' and 'that' can fail of reference just as names can (e.g. 'King Arthur'), so that demonstrative reference serves no better as a model for the putative reference of 'I' than does nominal reference. If 'I' referred in the manner of 'this', it would need to be immune from both misidentification and reference-failure, and the only way to get such guaranteed reference would be by having a referent whose existence was indubitable. 'The thinker of these thoughts' seems the only possible contender:

---

[21] But surely not in all circumstances—see pp. 155–6.

here, *these thoughts* are what are latched on to, and the thinker of the thoughts is meant to be indubitable if the thoughts themselves are—unlike Jones's ashes and the box. How so? Because you cannot have thinking without a thinker. For proper reference, however, we need a sortal concept, and the question arises what sortal concept could be expressed by the term 'thinker'. It seems that this term could not be merely short for 'A such-and-such [e.g. human being] that thinks'—for the sortal concept involved in that case would be *such-and-such* (e.g. *human being*), and there would be no indubitability as to existence, and hence no guaranteed reference. The thinker of these thoughts must, in fact, be none other than the Cartesian Ego, whose very essence is to think: 'Thus we discover that *if* "I" is a referring expression, then Descartes was right about what the referent was' (*FP*, 31). But the Cartesian solution is no sooner stated than it is rejected: 'His position has, however, the intolerable difficulty of requiring an identification of the same referent in different 'I'-thoughts." The existence of the self may have been salvaged, but not its unity over time.

But hasn't Anscombe already gone too far down Descartes's road? Surely only a hyperbolic doubt could attach to the existence of my body, or of the human being that I am? Cartesian or hyperbolic doubt hardly seems a natural philosophical instrument for a student of Wittgenstein to be using. If I can be as certain of the existence of my body as Moore claimed to be of his two hands, then maybe 'I' can after all be understood demonstratively: as meaning 'this body', or 'this human being'. Armed with Moorean certainty, I can surely rule out the possibility of any misidentification or reference-failure.

If 'I' means 'this body', the demonstrative will need something to latch onto, e.g. a reflection in a mirror. Doesn't this introduce the possibility of misidentification on a given occasion (something Anscombe rejects for 'I', while Wittgenstein accepts it)? Yes, it does; but only if 'this' is allowed to latch on to anything, including such things as reflections in mirrors. If you only go in for what I shall be calling reflexive ostension, then the referent of 'this body' and what it latches on to will always coincide, in a way that precludes misidentification. This at any rate appears to be what Anscombe herself believes—as we'll see in a moment. What about reference *failure*? Can 'this body' fail to refer completely, as 'this parcel of ashes' can?

[I]magine that I get into a state of 'sensory deprivation'. Sight is cut off, and I am locally anaesthetized everywhere, perhaps floated in a tank of tepid water; I am unable to speak, or to touch any part of my body with any other. Now I tell myself 'I won't let this happen again!' If the object meant by 'I' is this body, this human being, then in those circumstances it won't be present to my senses; and how else can it be 'present to' me? [. . .] Am I reduced to, as it were, 'referring in absence'? (*FP*, 31)

The answer to this last question, of course, is meant to be 'No'. My use of 'I' is quite secure, unlike my use of 'this body'—which shows that the one cannot mean the other. (The similarity here with Descartes's mode of argumentation is obvious.) In the sensory deprivation tank, I do not have anything for 'this' to latch on to—any appearances or sensations. For all I know, I don't have a human body at all, or any other kind of embodiment or realization. And Anscombe means this quite seriously. In the sensory deprivation tank 'the possibility will perhaps strike me that there is none [i.e. no body of mine]. That is, the possibility that there is then nothing that I am' (*FP*, 34).

'There is nothing that I am' is a possibly-true statement; and this is meant to underline what was said earlier, that 'I am this human being', 'I am Elizabeth Anscombe', etc. are none of them identity-propositions. If '*A*' is a non-empty term in an identity-proposition '*A* is *B*', then 'There is nothing that *A* is' cannot possibly be true. Indeed, it is unclear whether it can have a meaning at all. But 'There is nothing that I am' is possibly-true. The qualification 'non-empty' is necessary because of propositions like 'Jupiter is Zeus', which is of course compatible with 'There is nothing that Zeus is', alias 'Zeus does not exist'. Now although Anscombe regards 'I' as a non-referring term, she does not take it to be like 'Zeus', for the latter is an expression belonging to the class of names, whose function is in general to refer. She does not, in other words, regard 'I' as an empty referring term. Hence the possible truth of 'There is nothing that I am' would, it seems, support the thesis that the function of 'I' is not to refer.[22]

The argument so far has been mainly negative, being directed against the view that the function of 'I' is to refer. Before considering possible rejoinders and counter-arguments, let us turn to Anscombe's positive views concerning the first person. In particular, if 'I am this body' (etc.) is not an identity-proposition, what sort of a proposition is it? Here is Anscombe's answer, as applied to 'I am this thing here':

It means: this thing here is the thing, the person (in the 'offences against the person' sense) of whose action *this* idea of action is an idea, of whose movements *these* ideas of movement are ideas, of whose posture *this* idea of posture is the idea. And also, of which *these* intended actions, if carried out, will be the actions.   (*FP*, 33)

A person 'is a living human body' (*FP*, 33). So the 'It means...' which begins this quotation is not an indication of synonymy or definition; for as we have seen, *what* I am (if anything) is a contingent matter, and 'I am this thing here' may be said by an alien or an angel—if angels occupy space. But whatever you happen to be, some explanation of 'I am this thing here' along the lines given will be possible. 'I am this human body (or person)' is contingent—but it is not something that I learn through observation.

---

[22] Anscombe distinguishes 'They worship nothing' from 'What they worship is nothing', on the grounds that the former would, unlike the latter, 'imply that no sentence "They worship such-and-such" will be true' (*IS*, 10). By contrast, 'There is nothing that I am' would appear to be intended as equivalent to 'I am nothing', since in the sensory-deprivation tank, what I am conceiving as possible is that *no* proposition 'I am X' is true. What about 'I am this thinking thing'? Perhaps *that* proposition is to be ruled out by adducing the absurdity of the Cartesian Ego.

'[O]bservation does not show me which body is the one [that verifies or falsifies my "I"-thoughts]. Nothing shows me that' (*FP*, 34). Anscombe derives this claim from those views of hers concerning non-observational knowledge that were outlined in Chapter 1 (§1.1). My knowledge of what position my body is in, what it is doing, what it will do, and so on, is not based on observation. The object whose state, as a matter of fact, verifies or falsifies 'I am sitting', 'I will go for a walk', etc. is this human body—but these 'I'-thoughts are 'unmediated agent-or-patient conceptions of actions, happenings and states' (*FP*, 36). But how exactly do we get from the premiss (a) that I do not observe or find out that I am standing, to the conclusion (b) that I do not observe or find out that it is *this* body that must be standing if my thought 'I am standing' is to be true?

What is it to know that it is *this* body that must be standing for my thought 'I am standing' to be true? The answer will surely depend on what 'this' latches on to, and how it latches. If I am pointing to a body that is being filmed on closed-circuit television, e.g. while standing in a queue at the bank, then it will only be by observation (of the TV screen) that I can know that 'this body' is the one which must be standing if I am to be standing. Anscombe seems to be thinking of uses of 'this body' that involve genuine reflexive ostension, as one might call it. If asked, 'Which body must stand for you yourself to be standing?', one might reply by pointing at oneself. But of course the question can be framed: 'Which body must you point at to be pointing at yourself?'—and it is unclear what answer would be adequate, since saying 'Why, *this* one', while pointing at oneself, seems to be a case of practical (non-theoretical) question-begging. Do I *learn* that it is 'this body' (pointing as I say so) to which I must point in order to be pointing at myself? Clearly not. But if pointing is merely a human action in the same class as standing up, etc., then it does look queer to say that I learn that it is this body that must stand for me to be standing. After all, in answer to 'Which body must stand ... ?' I could have replied 'This one!' while standing up. Here, presumably, would be a case of the referent of 'this' coinciding with what the demonstrative latched on to. The availability of such a response also serves to remind us how flexible the notion of demonstrative reference is and ought to be. And the fact that actions like pointing and standing up are known to the agent non-observationally provides a sort of foundation for the non-observational status of my knowledge that it is this body that must stand for me to be standing.[23] On the other hand, where 'this body' is accompanied by reflexive ostension, there seems to be no possibility of misidentification; which removes one reason for distinguishing 'I' from 'this body', though it does not remove another—namely, that 'this body' can *fail* of reference (as in the sensory-deprivation tank).

[23] Some will feel uneasy at the overtly linguistic and social dimension of these remarks. 'Can't I just *think* that this body is the one that must stand for me to be standing?' Maybe 'this body' latches on to something via an act of attending. But now ask yourself 'Which body must I attend to in order that I should attend to myself?' Answer (accompanied by the right act of attending): '*This* one!' Another *petitio principii.*

What about such statements as 'I am E.A.', 'I am a human being', or 'I am this human being'?

> These I-thoughts (allow me to pause and think some!) ... are unmediated conceptions (knowledge or belief, true or false) of states, motions, etc., of this object here, about which I can find out (if I don't know it) that it is E.A. About which I did learn that it is a human being.   (*FP*, 34)

What needs to be learnt or found out is: that such-and-such is my name, or that the kind of thing I am is a human being. Hence 'I am E.A.' and 'I am a human being' are not in the same category as 'I am this thing here'. But if the demonstrative 'this' needs a sortal, it might be objected, won't it need a concept that 'goes beyond' what I can immediately and unmediatedly say, in the way that the concept *human being* does? In which case, surely I *do* need somehow to learn that it is this body—this human body—that must stand if I am to stand? For I apparently need to learn what a human body is, and that this body is one.

You did learn that this body is a human body. But having learnt that, you do not need observation or extra information to say, on a given occasion, 'It is this body that must stand if I am to stand'. With reflexive ostension, the referent of 'this body' and what it latches on to coincide; though the capacity to perform such acts of reflexive ostension may well require my having learnt various sortal concepts in the past, in particular the concept *human being*.

Let's return to the question with which we began, namely 'What am I?' The answer 'A human being' is canonical, as 'A city' is the canonical answer to 'What is Prague?'; not because of a sortal concept attached to the word 'I', but because you are a human being who has learnt the use of 'I', so that it is facts about the human being that you are that verify or falsify your 'I'-statements and 'I'-thoughts. That it *is* 'facts about this human being' that verify or falsify your 'I'-propositions is contingent—but it is not something that you learn, in the sense in which you learn that you are a human being, or are female, or are called Elizabeth. One learns the truth of 'I am a human being', but not (in the same sense) the truth of 'I am this human being'. (Consider the reasons in favour of each statement that one might give, and the connections with other statements.) Finally, questions about the continuity of the 'I', in other words about personal identity, boil down to questions about the identity through time of the kind of things that we in fact are: human beings. Personal identity is simply human identity (*FP*, 34).

2.2. Referring Expressions

Objections can and have been made both to the negative and to the positive aspects of Anscombe's view of 'I'. As to the first, the main issue is whether *referring* must have the character which Anscombe says it must; if not, then the claim that 'I' is not a referring expression may founder. As to the second,

Anscombe detaches 'I' from any sortal concept, be it *human being* or *thinking thing* or anything else, and this can appear to take things too far. Does it really make sense to suppose that there might be nothing that I am?—or that the following is conceivable, as Anscombe alleges?

[S]omeone stands before me and says, 'Try to believe this: when I say "I", that does not mean this human being who is making the noise. I am someone else who has borrowed this human being to speak through him.' (*FP*, 33)

To begin with reference: isn't the fact that the logic of 'I' has much in common with that of names and other referring terms enough to show that 'I' should be classed with such expressions? For instance, from 'I am disgruntled' one can infer 'Someone is disgruntled'—just as one can infer this latter from 'Roger is disgruntled'. Moreover, from 'I am disgruntled' and 'I am Roger', one can infer 'Roger is disgruntled'—which inference *appears* to require our taking 'I' and 'Roger' as (in this context) co-referential, and 'I am Roger' as an identity-proposition, *pace* Anscombe. If inferential facts such as these were sufficient, when taken together, for us to call 'I' a referring expression,[24] that might seem to throw doubt on the claim that something else is needed on top—namely, the association of a 'conception' with proper uses of the term. And Anscombe does indeed take the 'inferential' account of the first person's referring status as implying the needlessness of any associated conception. It is this implication that she attacks.

An account of 'referring expression' which relies solely on inference-patterns and the like still needs to give us some sort of rule for determining, of a given expression, what its referent is on a given occasion of use—so it can be argued. Different *kinds* of rule will correspond to different species of referring expression. What sort of rule could be framed for 'I'?

[L]et me imagine a logician, for whom the syntactical character of 'I' as a proper name [i.e. as a referring expression] is quite sufficient to guarantee it as such, and for whom the truth of propositions with it as subject is therefore enough to guarantee the existence of the object it names. [. . .] [For such a logician,] 'I' is a name governed by the following rule: 'If X makes assertions with "I" as subject, then those assertions will be true if and only if the predicates used thus assertively are true of X.' (*FP*, 29)

The account which Anscombe ascribes to her imaginary logician is one which purports to give the reference of 'I' by alluding to the systematic way in which it contributes to the truth-conditions of sentences containing it. (It is not only imaginary logicians who would endorse such an approach, by the way.) Does the account thereby also purport to give the *meaning* of 'I'? Only if there is nothing more to the meaning than the reference. For if we do want to distinguish meaning (or sense) from reference, it will surely be the case, as Anscombe says

[24] A list of inferential properties that might be regarded as constituting a given term's status as a referring expression is given by Dummett, in *Frege: Philosophy of Language* (2nd edn., London: Duckworth, 1981), p. 59 ff.

in Fregean mode, that there is no path back from reference to sense (*FP*, 23)—so that a rule that merely determines reference could not also specify sense, if sense and reference are distinguishable. This would seem to hold for more or less any model of sense, or meaning.

Perhaps, then, sense and reference should not be distinguished in the case of 'I'. If this is the price to pay for a truth-conditional account of 'I', it may be a price worth paying. The account has various apparent advantages, after all, not least the one mentioned by Anscombe herself in the above quotation: that of explaining how, given that 'I' refers, its reference is guaranteed. But does it in fact explain this? There are two possible senses of 'guaranteed reference' to be considered (see *FP*, 29–30): (a) For there to be a statement or thought, 'I am F', it must be stated or thought by someone—the very person who must be F if the proposition is to be true. In other words, the subject of the proposition must exist for the statement or thought to exist, and this subject is the referent of 'I'; (b) One who says or thinks 'I am F' cannot be in error about who is F: there can be no error through misidentification (or through reference-failure). So the person one *intends* to refer to by 'I' will always be the person one *does* refer to (*FP*, 30). Now the truth-conditional rule for determining the reference of 'I' only gives us (a), and it thus allows for the falsehood of (b). But the philosopher who takes 'I' to be a referring expression is committed not only to (a), but to (b). So the truth-conditional account is inadequate, and cannot provide any reason for calling 'I' a referring expression.

Anscombe does not deny the *truth* of the rule 'If *X* makes assertions with "I" as subject, then those assertions will be true if and only if the predicates used thus assertively are true of *X*'. What she says of the rule is that it neither fully explains the function of 'I', nor amounts to a rule for determining reference.

But can't the truth-conditional account embrace (b) as well as (a)? This might be attempted along the following lines: 'To whom does Sarah intend to refer when she says "I am writing"? To herself, of course! She could hardly intend to refer to someone else—and that is because she is aware of the rule for "I".' However, as Anscombe points out, the use of 'herself' in which it will need to be true that Sarah intends to refer to herself when using 'I' is not that of an ordinary reflexive pronoun, but rather of what grammarians call the indirect reflexive pronoun (*FP*, 22). If Sarah is Mary's second cousin, though she doesn't know this, then when she says 'Mary's second cousin lives in Oxford', she speaks of herself (ordinary reflexive pronoun)—but she does not speak of herself in the way that she does when she says 'I live in Oxford'. This latter sense of 'to speak of herself' involves the indirect reflexive 'herself', which can only be understood by reference to its direct speech equivalent, 'I'. [25] If we say that Sarah *intends* to

---

[25] Anscombe gives credit to Hector-Neri Castaneda for 'discerning the indirect reflexive in English, which does not have a distinct form for it'. See Castaneda, 'The Logic of Self-Knowledge', *Noûs*, 1 (1967), 9–22.

speak of herself (in saying something), we mean 'herself' as an indirect reflexive. At any rate, we must mean it that way if we are at the same time trying to rule out the possibility of Sarah's misidentifying the subject of her assertion—which, for Anscombe, is the whole point of (b). The truth-conditional rule can only guarantee that Sarah (being aware of the rule) intends to refer to herself by 'I' if 'herself' is understood as the ordinary reflexive pronoun. This reading of 'Sarah intends to refer to herself' would be non-standard, amounting roughly to: 'Sarah intends to say that N is F, where she herself is N (whether or not she knows this)'—the clause after the comma coming within the scope of 'intends'. But worse than being non-standard, it would be a reading compatible with error through misidentification. [26]

Why, it might be asked, is an intention to refer necessary for actual reference? Aren't intentions and the like psychological facts, irrelevant to the essentially social phenomenon of linguistic meaning? The answer to this is that intentions are no more 'purely private' than linguistic meanings. And their relevance to meaning is obvious: we do need to know what a person intends or is after in order to know what she means, very often. On the other hand, a lack of intentions typically counts against meaningfulness. If a parrot were taught to say 'I am a parrot', it would not be telling us something about itself. But why not? Wouldn't its utterance conform to the truth-conditional rule? For us to deny that the rule applies here, we need to be able to deny that the parrot is *asserting* 'I am a parrot'. It lacks the background mastery of language necessary for real assertion, and such mastery is run through with intentions of divers kinds. But once the relevance of such background mastery is admitted, as it must be if we are so much as to apply the truth-conditional rule to the right sorts of creatures, we must be prepared to take note of aspects of that mastery that are essential to a creature's grasp of the first-person pronoun. For Anscombe, one such essential aspect is 'self-consciousness' (*FP*, 24–6). Self-consciousness is not consciousness of a self, as Hume and others have seen. But it is real enough. It is constituted by the capacity to have and express 'unmediated agent-or-patient conceptions of actions, happenings and states', and to have the intention that what one says or thinks be true of oneself (indirect reflexive). These things are only possible if first-person judgements are *not* in the business of 'picking out a particular person', i.e. if the intention that what one says be true of oneself is not the same thing as an intention to refer to (pick out) oneself. A sharp line must be drawn between the function of 'I' on the one hand and that of names and demonstratives on the other, and this line is best recorded by reserving the term 'reference' to the latter.

[26] Anscombe invites us to imagine an expression, 'A', whose function *is* wholly captured by the truth-conditional rule. Reports of the form 'A is F' will be made on the basis of observation (of one's own body), inference, testimony, etc.—they will not be 'unmediated agent-or-patient conceptions of actions, happenings and states'. They will thus be liable to error through misidentification. See *FP*, 24 ff.

Edward Harcourt has characterized this way of drawing the line as a 'non-standard way of delimiting the class of referring expressions'[27]—the allegedly standard way being in terms of inference-patterns and the like. He agrees with Anscombe that a line needs to be drawn between 'I' and names/demonstratives, this line relating to the lack of any associated conception for uses of 'I'. But this difference between 'I' and other singular terms he regards as insufficient ground for adopting Anscombe's non-standard definition of 'referring expression'. One might, like Harcourt, wonder why Anscombe felt that the aptest way of encapsulating her findings with regard to the first person was to deny that 'I' is a referring expression. It is, I think, the connection between reference and the intention to refer that is the basis of her 'non-standard definition'. And this connection is surely of considerable importance. The point is partly worth stressing because of the reliance that many present-day philosophers make upon causal theories of reference. If you have too simplistic a notion of the 'causal chain' that connects somebody's use of a name with an original baptism (say), you will tend to overlook those quite sophisticated linguistic capacities of speakers which distinguish them from parrots. Kripke, who probably did most to put causal theories of reference on the map, did in fact see the necessity of invoking the *intention to refer* in his account[28]—and it is a question whether that concession ultimately leads us away from causation, and towards *use*. If we investigate the use of 'I', Anscombe might argue, we find not an intention to refer so much as an intention that what one says be true of oneself. Given the special status of the indirect reflexive 'oneself', this finding is surely of the first importance.

The relevance of an intention to refer is related especially to questions of (mis)identification. If you misidentify Tamsin as Jenny, saying e.g. 'Jenny is laughing', then you intend to refer to that lady on the bench, but fail to do so; instead, you refer to a person not present (let's imagine).[29] It is this sort of situation that Anscombe claims to be impossible when it comes to 'I'. But the Wittgenstein of *The Blue Book* might here insist: if you look at a figure on closed-circuit TV and say, 'Oh dear, I am stooping these days', do you not intend to refer to the person on the screen, but fail to do so if it is in fact your neighbour in the bank queue? And why not go on: 'The person you actually refer to is yourself'? For it can't without begging the question be claimed that, since your use of 'I' is unsusceptible of error through misidentification, you don't refer to anything thereby. Anscombe must apparently say that 'I am stooping'

[27] Harcourt, 'The First Person: Problems of Sense and Reference', in Teichmann (ed.), *Logic, Cause and Action*, pp. 25–46 at 37. Harcourt (33–4) infers from Anscombe's 'no reference' account of 'I' the implicit claim that first-person propositions do not involve one-place predicates. This would indeed be a hard pill to swallow, but I think the inference may be too swift. Cf. 'Somebody is sitting', in which the predicate 'x is sitting' occurs, though 'somebody' is no referring term.

[28] See Kripke, *Naming and Necessity* (Oxford: Blackwell, 1980), pp. 96–7.

[29] Keith Donnellan would take issue with this; see his 'Reference and Definite Descriptions', *Philosophical Review*, 75 (1966), 281–304.

means something like 'The human body (or human being) that verifies or falsifies my I-thoughts is stooping', the subject of which sentence can in the relevant sense be regarded as a referring expression (leaving aside Russellian qualms). The suggestion would, I think, receive short shrift from Wittgenstein; but I will leave the matter there.

2.3. Embodiment

In the previous section, I discussed possible responses to the negative aspect of Anscombe's position in 'The First Person'—her denial that the function of 'I' is to refer. In this section, I turn to her positive claims about 'I', and in particular to those that imply the dissociation of any sortal concept from uses of 'I'.

As we have seen, Anscombe allows the truth of such statements as 'I am Elizabeth Anscombe', 'I am a human being', 'I am this thing here', etc. But the contingency of these statements is such that both of the following utterances *could* be true: 'There is nothing that I am', and 'I am not the person saying these words, but someone else'. The first possibility may occur to someone in a sensory-deprivation tank (*FP*, 34), the second possibility may be uttered by one possessed, such as a medium—were there to be such a person (*FP*, 33). The wedge of contingency driven by Anscombe between 'I' and a body is connected with those *ideas* which she mentions when she explains the sense of 'I am this thing here': '[T]his thing here is the thing [. . .] of whose action *this* idea of action is an idea, of whose movements *these* ideas of movement are ideas, of whose posture *this* idea of posture is the idea. And also, of which *these* intended actions, if carried out, will be the actions' (*FP*, 33). It might appear that in the sensory-deprivation tank, for example, one could refer to one's body, but only in its absence—via notions like 'the body of whose movement this idea is an idea of movement'. It seems that for Anscombe the existence of these ideas is no guarantee of the existence of any body, and that there is nothing else (to which one might advert while floating in the tank) capable of acting as such a guarantee.

Anthony Kenny has pointed out the problems surrounding Anscombe's use of 'this' and 'these' here. If the demonstratives are to be publicly comprehensible, it is hard to see how 'this idea ... ' could mean anything more than 'my idea ... ', just as 'this headache' conveys little more than 'my (present) headache'. And for an audience, the idea or headache to which Smith refers as 'my idea' or 'my headache' derive their identity-conditions from the identity-conditions attaching to Smith himself: it is Smith's behaviour or speech which will enable us to say such things as 'that idea (headache) is no longer present to consciousness'. As Kenny puts it:

What is *this* idea of action? As Professor Anscombe uttered these words in her lecture, perhaps she had a mental image of herself waving an arm, or had the thought 'I will wave my arm'. [. . .] 'This', in her mouth, in that context, was simply tantamount to 'my'. [. . .] To say 'my body is the body of whose action my idea of action is an idea' is not to say anything that could possibly be false; and 'this body is my body' is equally truistic if 'this body' means 'the body uttering this sentence'. We individuate people's ideas of action by individuating the bodies that give them expression.[30]

The point is not dissimilar to the one made earlier, in explanation of what Anscombe might have meant in claiming that I do not learn or observe that I am this thing here (see above, pp. 155–6). That claim had to be understood as relating to reflexive ostension—e.g. pointing to oneself as one says 'this'; which fact is enough to render 'I am this thing here' a statement that could not possibly be false, just like 'My body is the body of whose action this idea of action is an idea'. And just as it does not alter things if we posit a private form of ostension to go with 'this thing here' (see p. 155, n. 23), it also fails to help matters if we posit a private form of ostension to go with 'this idea of action'. This is largely because the needed notions of private ostension and private reference are deeply problematic ones, for familiar Wittgensteinian reasons. How, after all, is it to be determined *which* body is the one whose movement is the intentional object of 'this idea of movement'? Nothing intrinsic to the idea itself would determine the intentional object; indeed, Anscombe's own remarks on such themes[31] surely indicate that she would have little truck with private intentional objects. (Remember that 'private' is not the same as 'subjective' in her sense; see p. 145.)

But couldn't Anscombe make her point about the sortal-independent nature of 'I' without appeal to *ideas*? Isn't the thought-experiment about the sensory-deprivation tank enough to show that I might be in a position to doubt that I had a body, just as Descartes found himself able to doubt whether he had a body by consideration of the possibility that he was dreaming, or was being deceived by an Evil Demon? If Anscombe's argument is in effect no different from Descartes's, then it is as liable to all the objections that have been levelled against Descartes's over the years. Here is not the place to rehearse those objections. But her argument is surely not just a variant on that of the First Meditation. It is, as we have seen, intended to show that 'I' cannot amount to 'this body'—there being nothing in the sensory-deprivation tank for 'this' to latch on to. But even if this is admitted, there may be reasons why 'I am something', or 'I am embodied', are non-contingently true, reasons that are compatible with the non-equivalence of 'I' and 'this body', and more generally compatible with the thesis that 'I' is not a referring expression. These reasons would have to do with the preconditions of there being such an expression as 'I': preconditions concerning how the expression is taught and learnt, how any given first-personal judgement may be verified or falsified, and so on. Anscombe writes of her first-personal judgements (or 'I-thoughts') that she 'probably learnt to have them through learning to say what she had done, was doing, etc.—an amazing feat of imitation' (*FP*, 34).

---

[30] 'The First Person', in Diamond and Teichman (eds.), *Intention and Intentionality*, 3–13 at 7.
[31] e.g. concerning 'memory images'; see p. 148.

The capacity to say 'I kicked the ball', 'I am leaving', 'I am nervous', and so on, is acquired—like all such linguistic capacities—through imitating those around one. *Imitation* is as protean a notion as *same* (as in 'do the same thing'); the imitation in question is directed and constrained by what others say to one and about one. Smith's I-thoughts have to be sufficiently in sync with others' judgements about Smith if he is to count as having mastered the sense of 'I'.[32] And others' judgements about Smith are necessarily tied to the identity of the thing that Smith is: an embodied human being. Hence Smith's use of 'I' is also tied to the identity of that same embodied human being. 'What am I?', like 'What is Prague?', is susceptible of a canonical answer, even though (or even if) 'I' is not a referring expression—namely: 'A human being'. This conclusion is not really so foreign to Anscombe's view of things, as we have seen (pp. 154–6). Although impressed and influenced by Descartes, she never comes near to embracing his dualism of mind and body.

[32] Cf. Ch. 1, p. 12.

5

Time and Causality

What is metaphysics? The origin of the word is notoriously unhelpful: in an early catalogue of Aristotle's works, the *Metaphysics* comes after the *Physics* (*meta* = after). 'The study of being *qua* being' is how Aristotle characterized what he was doing in the *Metaphysics*, but the phrase is only really comprehended once one has already settled a bit into Aristotle's mode of thought. It does not serve as a starting definition, in the way in which 'theory of knowledge' serves as a starting definition of 'epistemology'.

Paradigmatically metaphysical topics include time, causality, properties, events, identity, substance ... Claims made when dealing with such topics have often invoked *necessity*: 'A cause must precede its effect', 'Two objects cannot occupy the same place at the same time', 'The past cannot be changed', and so on. Those philosophers who have, over the centuries, grappled with metaphysical problems have given varying accounts of what sort of necessity is at issue[1] and of how we can come to know these allegedly necessary truths, if indeed we can. Philosophers, on the other hand, who are suspicious of necessity, or of prevalent notions of necessity, tend to carry that suspicion over to metaphysics itself. Two main instances of this are Hume and Wittgenstein. Perhaps the *tour de force* of Hume's philosophy is his searching critique of the idea of necessary connection, as that idea appears in our thinking about cause and effect. His psychological and reductive account of this idea is well known, and is a classic attempt to debunk (or at any rate thoroughly tame) a metaphysical problem. Wittgenstein too, in his treatment of certain questions, looks for the source or sources of our belief in necessity—if indeed 'belief' is the right word; but the sources he finds are more

---

[1] A recent example of this is to be found in the theories of Putnam and Kripke, as put forward in Hilary Putnam, 'The Meaning of "Meaning"', in *Collected Papers*, ii: *Mind, Language and Reality* (Cambridge: Cambridge University Press, 1975), 215–71 and Kripke, *Naming and Necessity*. The effect of the publication of these theories was to reintroduce 'metaphysical necessity', 'real essence', etc. into many philosophical discussions. A number of philosophers, however, appeared not to have noticed Kripke's and Putnam's original arguments for their claims of necessity, which were based on premises in the philosophy of language—as a glance at the two quoted titles confirms. The opposition of many philosophers to a linguistic treatment of metaphysical questions at any rate gains no support from Kripke or Putnam. Often such opposition seems to be not much more than a sort of resentment at the fact of the 'linguistic turn', philosophy of language threatening to spoil the giddy fun of metaphysics. 'No-one shall expel us from this paradise!', as Hilbert said about set theory.

varied than Hume's. There is also in Wittgenstein rather less confusion as to whether a claim of necessity is being explained (e.g. by reference to other notions), shown to be unfounded, denied, or proclaimed senseless. But the debunking attitude to metaphysics is certainly there—as at para. 116 of the *Investigations*: 'What *we* do is to bring words back from their metaphysical to their everyday use.'

In Anscombe's work in metaphysics we find her, like Hume and Wittgenstein, sensitive to the importance of claims of necessity, and of the need to give some non-table-thumping account of them. In 'The Reality of the Past', she examines, among other things, the proposition 'The past cannot change', enquiring into the meaning of this claim and into the kind of impossibility asserted by it. In 'Causality and Determination', she detects an unmotivated claim of necessity that underlies a great many discussions of causation, discussions that are largely influenced, ironically enough, by Hume's famous theory. And in 'Times, Beginnings and Causes', she criticizes another of Hume's arguments, the argument to the conclusion: 'There is no necessity that a beginning of existence should have a cause.' In all these discussions, Anscombe does not bring a pre-baked Theory of Necessity to bear on a given problem, so much as see what a claim of necessity amounts to *there*, and assess it and its ramifications.

Time and causality are intimately connected topics, and each is connected in various ways with other philosophical subject matters. Causality, in particular, crops up in epistemology, philosophy of mind, ethics, and more. We have already had occasion to take note of this fact in previous chapters. What Anscombe has to say about causality thus connects with what she has to say on a number of other topics.

But let us begin with time, and with one of Anscombe's earliest papers: 'The Reality of the Past' (1950).

1. THE REALITY OF THE PAST

1.1. Meaning and Memory

Metaphysical discussions frequently make mention of reality, of what is real, and so on—and discussions of time are no exception. It is as commonplace now as it ever was for philosophers to assign reality and unreality, in varying distributions, to past, present, and future, and to events that have occurred, are occurring, or will occur. McTaggart argued that time itself is unreal; proponents of the 'tenseless' view of time may say that future or past events are as real as present ones; while St Augustine regarded only what is present as real. If J. L. Austin's allegation is correct that 'real' is, or ought to be, short for 'real such-and-such' (e.g. 'real cream', 'real money'),[2] then all these philosophers would seem to be

---

[2] Austin, *Sense and Sensibilia*, 69.

misusing the term. But even if an unqualified sense of 'real' does exist, it is far from obvious what it is, and metaphysical assertions containing it have a habit of resembling either truisms or blatant falsehoods. Thus, 'Only what's present is real' is harmless enough, if you are allowed to add, 'And what's future *will be* real'; while if the claim is taken to deny a truth-value to all but present-tensed propositions, it is absurd. One who holds the 'tenseless' view, on the other hand, courts only minor controversy when he says that future events are real (after all, the sun will rise tomorrow); but he risks sounding unbalanced if he adds, 'they aren't really *future*, though, since the future isn't real'.

These remarks can hardly be said to apply to Anscombe's paper 'The Reality of the Past'. In it we find, among other things, an exploration of what 'real' amounts to in the assertion that the past is real—but this assertion is to be understood as one that nobody sensible could deny, rather than as a debatable metaphysical thesis. Anscombe's starting point is a very compelling form of puzzlement, expressed in the question: How it is that we can so much as talk or think about the past? We can only talk about the past if our statements about the past have meaning—so our question can be rephrased thus: How is it that statements about the past have meaning? (*RP*, 103).

The problem arises because we are inclined to think that for a statement to have a meaning, it must be *about* something, and 'being about' expresses a sort of *relation*. On this side, bits of language—on that side, the things signified by the bits of language. If it's a statement, then what it signifies (is about, describes, etc.) might be a state of affairs, or a fact. But that won't do: a false statement has a meaning. Perhaps *it* signifies a merely possible state of affairs. That sounds odd, however, since in general a merely possible F isn't a something at all, any more than a non-existent F. 'Merely possible' entails 'non-actual', and although some philosophers have posited a realm of non-actual but existent things, the urge to do so pretty clearly derives from just that picture of meaning as relational which we ought to be questioning. Of course, if nothing will turn you away from that picture, you can always concoct suitable *relata*—maybe the word 'the' signifies the abstract entity *definiteness*—but the activity appears childish. False statements cannot be dealt with so easily nor so quickly.

The problem of falsehood is an ancient one, being expressed by the Greeks in the question, 'How is it possible to think what is not?', and the persistence of the problem is a sign of the persistence of the picture of meaning as 'being about'. As Anscombe points out at the beginning of *RP*, the problem about past-tensed statements is similar to the problem of false statements, since there seems to be nothing there for a past-tensed statement to be about, even when true—for what's past is no more. 'But what's past is real!' may come the objection. And after all, can't we say that 'Meg went to London yesterday' is about a real event, Meg's visit to London? But calling Meg's visit to London a real event—as opposed to imagined or fictitious, presumably—looks suspiciously like saying 'She really *did* visit London'. It is to say that 'Meg visited London' is true, not false. Part of the puzzle, however, is precisely to do with how past-tensed statements can be true. We cannot explain the truth of a certain sort of statement by appeal to what's real, since what counts as 'real' is too tightly connected here with truth. Indeed, the issue of whether past events are real or not can be side-stepped entirely, by allowing, for the sake of argument, that they *are* real (whatever that means), and then posing the question: How do some statements of the language we speak manage to signify these bits of reality, as opposed, say, to certain present bits of reality (e.g. memories, traces, etc.)?

It is this latter problem that Anscombe addresses. She does so, naturally enough, by imagining how the past tense might be taught to somebody:

Let us imagine that someone is taught (1) to say 'red' when a red light is switched on before him, 'yellow' for a yellow light, and so on; and (2) next to say 'red', 'yellow', etc., when lights of the appropriate colours *have* been switched on but are now off.   (*RP*, 103–4)

Take the word 'red' in this language. If we take this word as having a single meaning, conveyed by both teaching processes together, (1) and (2), then its meaning is equivalent to that of the English sentence 'There either is or was a red light on'. Or we could regard 'red' as having two, related, meanings (uses), corresponding to (1) and (2). Since nothing hangs on it, let us adopt this second way of speaking. The person who has been taught (2), and utters the word 'red' in the right situation, uses the word on that occasion to mean 'A red light was on'. But what is the 'right situation'? It seems to be a situation in which there is no red light on. (1) and (2), in other words, appear to conflict.

Imagine a spectator who finds (2) unintelligible, since the learner is not corrected for saying 'red' when there is no red light, but this is accepted. It is as if the learner were taught first to act according to a certain rule and then to break the rule.   (*RP*, 104)

The analogy between past-tensed statements and false statements is clear: to teach someone (2), having taught them (1), looks like teaching them to assert redness in the absence of redness, as it were. It is tempting to say that things appear this way only if you are 'looking in the wrong place' for the relevant state of affairs—in the present, rather than in the past (*RP*, 104). But if there is a 'right place' to look for a red light, shouldn't the learner actually be looking there in order justifiably to say 'red' in the case of there having been a red light? And shouldn't the teacher, somehow or other, be getting him to look there—rather than somewhere else, for example? 'It seems possible to show someone what to mean when one wants him to say "red" [i.e. "is red"] with meaning, but impossible to show him what to mean by "was red"; for how does one get his attention directed to what he is to speak of?' (*RP*, 105). It seems that one can show someone what to mean by 'is red', or what one means by 'is red', because one can exhibit, and point to, a red thing. Such explanation of meaning is ostensive; and it is extremely tempting to think that ostensive explanation of meaning must have a privileged status. You can explain an expression's meaning using words that are already understood, but what about the meanings of *those* words? These too could be defined in terms of other words, but this process cannot go on for ever; and when it comes to learning a first language, it cannot even start—for a child has no words at its disposal. Hence (the argument goes) there must be a basic way of explaining a word's meaning, without using other words. Presumably, one uses the word in a situation where it is correct to use it, hoping that the learner picks up on what it is about the situation that makes it the sort where it *is* correct to use the word. For the learner to do this, he must *perceive* the relevant feature of the situation. This already privileges sense perception; but perhaps more significantly, the very natural further step presents itself, of taking the relevant feature of the situation to be the meaning of the word, or to be what the word with that meaning points to or signifies. This is a version, or aspect, of the picture of linguistic meaning as 'being about'. The problem with 'was red' is that there is no feature of the learning situation which could serve as what the expression is meant to be about. In other words, the meaning of 'was red' cannot be explained ostensively; but nor of course can it be explained (to one learning the past tense) by means of other words, for those words will either presuppose a grasp of the past tense, or they will face exactly the same problem as does 'was red' itself, that there is nothing in the situation for the teacher to advert to—nothing that might distinguish 'was' from 'is not'.

It should be noted that the problem we face is not obviously avoided if we adopt a model of meaning as use, in preference to the model of meaning as 'signified situational feature'. If a person's grasp of 'was red' manifests itself in his using the expression correctly, and if this means using it *in the right situation*, then we must once again ask: but what is the 'right situation'? Nothing perceptible in the situation itself will fit the bill. But a person's grasp of the meaning of an expression, or system of expressions (such as past-tensed statements), is surely something that must be detectable by others, detectable, that is to say, on the occasion(s) of use. This seems to amount to saying, in the end: the criteria for the warranted use of 'was red' must lie in the present, not in the past. With the further assimilation of truth and warranted assertibility, the position arrived at will be recognized by many as being that of the anti-realist, whose account of tensed statements is persuasively outlined by Michael Dummett in *his* article, 'The Reality of the Past' (1969).

A solution to our difficulties beckons. It is a solution that you might try to avail yourself of whether you view meaning as giveable by ostension, or as manifested in use. The solution is: memory. 'It seems that memory must be the key to the problem; that it is memory that gives one the essential meaning of the past tense; that it is like an eye that can look in the required direction, or like sight that corresponds to visible space.' (*RP*, 105). If the learner remembers that a red light was on, and hears the teacher say 'red', won't he be able to associate the word with what he remembers? It's true that the teacher can't point to, or directly indicate, what it is that 'red' is to be associated with—but she can surely count on the learner making the association for himself. This would be a modified ostensive account. As for an account that appeals to meaning as use, can't a person's use of 'red' be detectably correct insofar as those around him remember that a red light was on? With a past-tensed sentence, verification *is* remembering, it might be said. On both accounts of meaning, it seems that the 'right situation' for uttering a past-tensed sentence can be taken to *include* the past, since the past is after all available to us, through memory.

Now it is of course true that for someone to learn how to use the past tense, he must be able to remember things. Moreover, it is *because* he can remember things that he can use, and learn to use, the past tense. Problems only arise if we try to invoke memories as somehow giving the sense of 'was red', etc.—as explaining or justifying the existence in a language of past-tensed forms. For if this is our aim, then we cannot avoid circularity in our account, for the reason that the concept of memory involves or presupposes the concept of the past. This is the case whether we take remembering to be a kind of knowing (i.e. as precluding falsity), or to be a kind of experience (true or false, veridical or non-veridical). In the first case, true memory is distinguished from apparent memory by virtue of the fact that *X did happen*; that is, the past tense has to be used in order to say what memory is (*RP*, 105–6). This on its own would only point to our account's being incomprehensible to those who lack mastery of the past tense; but both in this case and in the case where 'remembering' may be either veridical or non-veridical, the *content* of the relevant experience has to be explained using the past tense, in the following sort of way: '(It seems to me that) X happened' (cf. *RP*, 106–9). This content must amount to a judgement, rather than to a mental image, for example. The point needs to be made lest it is proposed that one simply *has* a memory-image, and (being thoroughly acquainted with it) can derive the sense of 'was' from the intrinsic character of the image. We saw in the previous chapter (pp. 148–9) how an image needs to be somehow 'referred to' the past. A picture of a man falling off a horse may express 'He fell off', 'He is falling off', 'He will fall off', 'He may fall off', or even 'He did not fall off' (cf. Ch. 6, pp. 194–5)—and no extra element, not even Russell's 'feeling of familiarity', could fix 'He fell off' as the unique content.

Do similar problems beset the future tense? How would one teach 'will be red' in Anscombe's set-up with different-coloured lights? Once again, there seems to be nothing in the teaching situation to which the teacher can advert. Suppose she says 'red', meaning to convey a third possible sense for that word, namely 'A red light will be on'. Given that the red light is still off, isn't she once again contradicting her initial rule, given by (1)? 'No', we say; 'for the teaching situation includes what is yet to happen. This shows in what *does* subsequently happen: the red light comes on, and the teacher says something like "You see?", or "There!".'

This is all perfectly true. And one thing that it shows is that the faculty needed if one is to learn the future tense is, once again, memory. For when the red light goes on, the learner must remember the teacher's having said 'red'. The difference between the cases of learning the past tense and learning the future tense resides above all in the possibility of one's pointing to the relevant fact itself, in the case of the future-tensed statement: when the teacher says 'You see?', she is getting her pupil to see exactly what it was that was predicted. The fact that this is impossible when it comes to the past tense may help to explain the temptation that exists to insist that it is a memory that gives 'was red' its sense: in lieu of the fact itself, the memory of it seems a good proxy. But this invocation of memory, as we have seen, produces circularity. A good way of seeing what kind of circularity is in play is by comparing 'was' and 'will be', and how they might be taught. The circularity at issue affects 'was', but not 'will be':

> (P) **B** sees a red light on, which then goes off. **A** says to **B**, 'A red light was on'. **B** hears **A** say this, and remembers the red light being on.

> (F) **A** says to **B**, 'A red light will be on'. The red light comes on, and **A** says 'You see?'. **B** hears **A** say this, sees the red light, and remembers **A**'s having said 'A red light will be on'.

(More could be included in (P) and (F), of course, concerning **B**'s subsequent use of the sentences, **A**'s responses, etc.) It is the clause '**B** remembers the red light being on', in (P), that produces the circularity, since it amounts to (or involves) '**B** knows that *the red light was on*'. To use this clause when attempting to explain the condition on which 'A red light was on' may be usefully uttered by **A**, or correctly uttered by **B**, is like using the following to explain how the sense of 'deipnosophist' may be taught:

> (D) **A** introduces Nigel to **B**, and says 'Nigel is a deipnosophist'. **B** hears **A** say this and (already) knows that Nigel is a deipnosophist.

It isn't just that (D) is applicable to **B** only if **B** happens to know what a deipnosophist is. (P) and (F) apply only to people who can remember things, after all. Rather, (D) cannot help us see what the sense of 'Nigel is a deipnosophist' consists in, how it is possible for a person to grasp that sense, what their grasp of it consists in, and so on. As Anscombe puts it:

If [the learner] said 'red' *remembering*, then his behaviour was intelligible and intelligent; his use of 'red' in (2) was not a misuse [. . .] But now it appears that I cannot understand what it means to say he said 'red' *remembering*, without understanding what it means to say that he meant the past event [. . .] I am saying that the learner acted intelligently if his saying 'red' in (2) was an expression of knowledge of the past showing of the red light; I am not stating an independently intelligible *condition* on which his utterance would express such knowledge.   (*RP*, 109)

It is not just that we have to use the past tense in explaining what it is for someone to (come to) grasp the past tense. As stated above, that would only show that a philosophical explanation of the past tense can be comprehended only by those who can already use the past tense. The problem is that in explaining what it is for someone to (come to) grasp the past tense, we have to ascribe an implicit grasp of the past tense *to the person*.

1.2. 'The Past Cannot Change'

Well, maybe the past tense is such a basic feature of language that a philosophical explanation of a person's grasp of it is impossible. This indeed is Anscombe's conclusion, if by 'philosophical explanation' one means the kind of explanation that shows us a foundation for, or a justification of, the way we think and talk (*RP*, 118). Such a justification cannot be given if no 'independently intelligible condition' of a person's grasp of the past tense can be given—which, as we have seen, it cannot. The alternative to such a philosophical explanation is a description of use, but especially a description of use that is wide-ranging enough to include those uses of the past tense that are not made on the basis of personal memory. Anscombe mentions receiving and using testimony, story-telling, deductions and guesses, counterfactual conditionals, historical statements, and more; and she writes:

If we were to describe the uses of words made in these cases, our descriptions would all lack one particular feature. The descriptions would not in these cases include any mention of actual events corresponding to the past-tense sentences or clauses, such as is made in any description of the personal-report use of the past tense. This would not seem to be of any importance except as regards those uses which are supposed to be statements of actual fact. But in these cases one has the idea that a philosophical description of what it is to know the facts necessarily tells one *what* one knows in knowing them; i.e. what the facts themselves consist in. If then the description does not bring in the facts themselves, it seems that what our knowledge really consists in must be considered as reduced to what the description does bring in.   (*RP*, 118)

If I report seeing the red light on, in virtue of what is my report to be deemed intelligent and intelligible—or as Dummett would say, warranted? In virtue of the fact that I remember the light's being on, or take myself to. Now if I merely take myself to remember the light's being on, a description of my personal-report use of the past tense will not mention the light's actually being on. Anscombe refers to 'actual events corresponding to the past-tense sentences or clauses, such as is made in any description of the personal-report use of the past tense'; isn't she forgetting false personal-report uses? I don't think so. Her point is presumably this: a description of someone's general grasp of the personal-report use of the past tense must include a sufficient number of true memory-reports at its heart. If someone's memory fails to achieve a certain level of reliability, she will not count as having grasped the past tense.[3] So past facts must be included in a description of someone's grasp of the personal-report use of the past tense; for as we have seen, the memory that the light was on *involves* the fact that the light was on. But if I claim that Anthony Eden suffered from gallstones, that in virtue of which my claim is to be deemed intelligent and intelligible will not be memory, either real or apparent, of the fact in question, but rather memory or perception of books read, or conversations had (plus my capacity to make relevant inferences, etc.). Such memories or perceptions are not foundational, in the sense of being required of me. I do not have to be able to supply them, either as reasons for my belief, nor in order that my utterance of 'Anthony Eden suffered from gallstones' be counted as intelligent; for the burden of proof of such things may not lie with me. But it is *at best* by appeal to there being or having been some memories or perceptions of books, etc. that such a past-tensed utterance gets to count as intelligent or warranted. The past fact itself is not involved in the description of my grasp of the sentence's meaning. And the same goes for all such uses of the past tense.[4]

But then doesn't it follow that such past-tensed sentences are not really about the past events they seem to be about? (The 'aboutness' picture of meaning once again.) At any rate, they are not about those events in the way that personal-report statements are about past events. However, it sounds perverse to say that 'Anthony Eden suffered from gallstones' isn't about a past event—for surely it must be about Anthony Eden's suffering from gallstones? To this it might be replied that ' "p" is about the fact/event that p' may indeed serve as a 'grammatical note'—as a disquotational truism—but that there is a stronger sense of 'about' in which 'Anthony Eden suffered from gallstones' really *isn't* about a past event. This sense of 'about' is connected with truth, and what it means to say that a sentence is true. And it is connected with knowledge: a true sentence is about a fact in the same way that a piece of knowledge is about its object. But, as the last sentence of the above-quoted passage has it, our non-personal knowledge that an event occurred seems to be reduced to knowledge of such things as books and conversations.

The anti-realist might not make his point using the word 'about'; he may be content with a disquotational approach to that term, whereby ' "p" is about the

---

[3] Someone may have acquired a grasp of the past tense and later on suffer a progressive deterioration in memory, both long-term and short-term. In that case, there may come a point when we can no longer interpret her utterances as being truly past-tensed.

[4] 'But if the past event was a cause of people's reporting it, which was a cause of a book being written about it, etc... won't my present utterance have the past event as its original cause? And won't the event then be involved in the description of my grasp of the sentence's meaning, just as in the case of personal memory?' The causal theory of meaning suggested by this objection divorces grasp of meaning from its manifestation; for whether a person means one thing rather than another by a sentence becomes a matter to be settled (if it can be) by historical investigation, rather than by observation of the language-user. This is admittedly a large topic, unfortunately beyond the scope of the present discussion.

fact that p' is simply true by definition. Instead, he may use the word 'criteria'. But according to anti-realism, the criteria for use of a past-tensed sentence are to be identified with its meaning, in such a way that the truth of the sentence is tied to the obtaining of its criteria—in just the way that it would be if the sentence were really *about* the criteria. But surely

a statement about the past cannot possibly have present criteria, it can only have present evidence. For if I think that a statement about the past has present criteria, must I not suppose that it is possible for the past to change; will not a change in the things that serve as criteria involve a change in the truth of the statement for which they are criteria?   (*RP*, 112)

'The past cannot change' can be interpreted in more than one way (*RP*, 112). What sense does it have when it constitutes an objection to the anti-realist, to the philosopher who ties the meaning and truth of past-tensed statements to their present criteria? One might think that the only available answer here is the one given by the Dummettian *realist*, according to whom the grasp of a statement's sense consists in a grasp of what it would be for it to be true—a grasp, in short, of its truth-conditions.[5] For the realist, I know the sense of 'Anthony Eden suffered from gallstones' in virtue of knowing what fact needs to obtain for it to be true, namely that Anthony Eden suffered from gallstones; and such a fact holds independently of the vicissitudes of subsequent memories, documents, and the like. However, Anscombe is no more of a realist (in this sense) than she is an anti-realist, as is evidenced by the following:

The situation which verifies a remark and that in which the sense of the remark is shown may be identical; and one is strongly inclined to think that in understanding a sense one grasps a fact or an apparent fact. But if one says this, one's problem 'What is it to understand this sense?' reappears for the sense of *that* fact or apparent fact.   (*RP*, 117)

Her phrase, 'sense of a fact', is quite justified in the context. For anything I can simply grasp (now) will be something about which we can ask, 'But what is its sense?'—as, a mental image, or a bit of Mentalese. If on the other hand my 'grasp' is explained in terms of things that I can *do*, such as identify, re-identify, verify, and so on, then I cannot be said to grasp the truth-condition for 'Anthony Eden suffered from gallstones' except insofar as I can assess the evidence for it, etc. But that is anti-realism, not realism.

So what sort of impossibility is asserted by 'The past cannot change'? Anscombe's treatment of this question constitutes the section of her paper most clearly influenced by her discussions with Wittgenstein, something which she freely acknowledges in a footnote (*RP*, 114 n. 3). For Anscombe, 'The past can change' is connected with certain kinds of nonsense, which are nonsense (roughly) because they are ruled out by the language-game, and not because

---

[5] Dummett, 'The Reality of the Past', in *Truth and Other Enigmas*, p. 358.

they have, as it were, a nonsensical meaning. But the feeling is strong that there must be some impossibility that corresponds to the nonsense in the way that a physical impossibility corresponds to 'You can eat a cake twice' (*RP*, 114)—and that it is *because* this thinkable, specifiable impossibility *is* an impossibility that the language-game rules the nonsense out, not *vice versa*. Once we have seen this feeling for what it is, and jettisoned it, we shall be in a position to appreciate why a description of our use of past-tensed sentences is philosophically adequate for understanding our knowledge of the past.

One of the aims of this description of use is to stop one from asking 'What do I know?' except as one asks this question in daily life, i.e. unphilosophically; and if one says: 'But now it seems to me as if I did not really have any knowledge about the past; all that I can say is that I use words in such and such a way', the reply is that 'I have no knowledge about the past' has a sense (e.g. in the mouth of someone who has lost his memory) which is certainly not that according to which one is using it here, and that one has not yet given it a sense as one is now using it.   (*RP*, 119)

'The past can change' is connected with certain kinds of nonsense. The piece of nonsense that Anscombe invites us to consider is: 'When was the Battle of Hastings in 1066?'—where this isn't simply tantamount to 'When in 1066 was the Battle of Hastings?'. Such a question would be allowable, as would answers to it, if 'The past can change' were allowable: for 'if a change occurs we can ask for its date' (*RP*, 112). The Battle of Hastings took place in 1066—this is (now) a past fact; and if the past can change, that means that such a fact can change. The fact that the Battle of Hastings took place in 1066 would be at one time true (e.g. given the existence of certain documents) and at another time false (e.g. given their replacement by other documents). But if it were sometimes true, sometimes false, we could ask when it was true. That is, we could ask, 'When was the Battle of Hastings in 1066?'.

The fact is that such a question *can* be given a sense, i.e. can be given a sense within the rules of the games we have at our disposal. Thus, it could be taken as asking after the date of a change in the calendar (*RP*, 112). These cases, however, do not interest us. We want to say that the question is ruled out, not *tout court* (for this is false), but *when it has a certain sense*. The Wittgensteinain rejoinder, of course, is: What sense? For after all it is nonsense.

A child can learn items of historical knowledge, such as 'The Battle of Hastings was in 1066', 'The Battle of Waterloo was in 1815', and so on; and then learn a use for the word 'when', by learning to say (e.g.) '1066' when the teacher says 'When was the Battle of Hastings?'. If the teacher then asks, 'When was the Battle of Hastings in 1066?', it is clear that the child hasn't been taught what to do.

The teacher *could* teach him something to do in response to this new question, but, until he does, the question does not belong to the exercise. This exercise as I have described it has no point. But the *actual* senselessness of 'When was the Battle of Hastings in 1066?' seems to be like its senselessness in this exercise.   (*RP*, 115)

This last sentence is the nub of the matter. All we have in the end is a grammatical sentence for which no role has yet been determined.[6] No amount of metaphysical explanation can illuminate for us why 'The past can change' is absurd, nor why we couldn't determine a role for it if we wished to—all such 'explanation' will beg the question in some way. Instance: 'If a past fact, dated at t, can change at time t1, then there must be a cause at t1 of a change at t—which is impossible, since causes are prior to their effects.' But why must the change have a cause? And why must all causes be prior to their effects? Mere definitions are clearly of no avail here—as, 'By *cause* I simply mean an event prior to and contiguous with, etc.'. But the relevant 'musts' will be hard otherwise to justify without going round in a circle.

And yet isn't the anti-realist *proposing* a sense and a role for 'The past can change', and hence for such a question as 'When was the Battle of Hastings in 1066?'? Well, if he is, he is not doing so in the way in which one can always stipulate a new use. The teacher in the above example could *make up* a right response to 'When was the Battle of Hastings in 1066?'—for example: 'In 1067'; or, in the style of the 'tenseless' theory of time: 'Always'. By contrast, what the anti-realist is doing is deriving a new use from what he takes to be the rules of the game as we already play it. The fact that we baulk at this new use should, for the anti-realist, be a sign, as it were, of false consciousness on our part—of our playing by an incoherent set of rules.[7] The idea that a linguistic practice could in this way be fundamentally incoherent is a deeply problematical one. But an alternative, and less drastic, solution is available.

Present criteria for past statements seemed to entail the possibility of a change in the past. The reason for thinking this is that if one states the criteria for saying something one may be claiming, or may seem to be claiming, to give a translation or analysis. [. . .] But if one gives up the idea that to give the criteria is to give a translation, then this no longer follows.   (*RP*, 116)

---

6 Cf. Wittgenstein, *Tractatus Logico-Philosophicus*, 6.53.

7 In *Truth and the Past* (New York: Columbia University Press, 2004), Dummett points out that an anti-realist is committed to the truth of 'The past changes', and writes that 'such a conception is not self-contradictory, but it goes very strongly against the grain' (p. 76). Anscombe would associate 'The past changes' with a species of nonsense, as exemplified by the question 'When was the Battle of Hastings in 1066?'. She may thus agree with Dummett that the anti-realist's 'conception' is not self-contradictory, on the grounds that it is something worse than that: nonsense.

I have presented the anti-realist as purporting to derive a role for the Battle of Hastings question from the rules of our actual linguistic practices; it is this feature of anti-realism, I think, that makes the matter more stark than one of merely opposing conceptions of time. The linguistic rules in question are those (allegedly) relating to the justifying grounds of past-tensed statements not based on personal memory. These grounds are present criteria—which for the Dummettian anti-realist go to determine the *meanings* of such statements. Hence the anti-realist must say that we are in fact committed by our own practice to the truth of 'The past can change', and that our denial of this proposition is irrational.

Dummett's anti-realist does not talk of translations or analyses. Nevertheless, the motive for the anti-realist assimilation of warranted assertibility and truth would appear to reside in the thought that the meaning of a statement must be exhausted by its criteria for use, where by 'use' is especially meant 'assertive use'. But as Anscombe has pointed out, the past tense is used in all sorts of ways other than in simple past-tensed assertions. The idea that the central and governing use of some expression or system of expressions should be the assertive use surely has its roots in something like an ostensive account of meaning-explanation—'This is red', 'That's a sheep', 'He's kneeling', etc. What, to take two related examples, are we to make of unfulfillable past conditionals and wishes that the past had been otherwise (see *RP*, 116)? As Anscombe says in connection with our concepts of perception, they 'are built up by our having *all* these uses' (*IS*, 13; see Ch. 4, pp. 138–9). A description of use should include as much of the smorgasbord as will stave off the malnutrition that results from a restricted diet of examples. When it does, the pull of constitutive criteria will be lessened.

A description of our use of past-tensed sentences, including personal-report uses, supplies us in the end with the answer to our original question: 'How can we so much as think and talk about the past?' It seems that we *can* think and talk about the past, and thus that the past is real, in the only respectable sense of that phrase. But will analogous arguments go for the future tense? Will a thorough description of use show us how we can think and talk about the future, and thus how the future is real? This move would be too swift. For one thing, of course, the two 'uses', of past and future tense, are radically different. Moreover, only if we assimilate warranted assertibility and truth will we be pushed towards the view that a large number of future-tensed statements are true when made, and hence are about the future in just the way that past-tensed statements are about the past. Anscombe, as we saw earlier on (e.g. Ch. 2, p. 49), regards at least some future-tensed propositions as becoming true after being uttered, and so not yet true at the time of utterance, however well grounded. (This view is connected in Anscombe's writing with a certain incompatibilism about freedom and physical determinism.[8])

It is true that the considerations which go to show why 'The past can change' is nonsense seem to be reduplicable for 'The future can change'. 'When will the kick-off start at 3.30?' is in the same boat as 'When was the Battle of Hastings in 1066?'. But the latter piece of nonsense was brought onstage as evidence against the anti-realist view of present criteria as truth-determining; the former piece of nonsense can play the same role. Present criteria do not render a future-tensed statement true when uttered. Indeed, for Anscombe, nothing does; which latter fact (if it is a fact) would help explain why there is less inclination to insist that

---

[8] See *CD*, 146; and 'Aristotle and the Sea-Battle', in *FPW*.

the future cannot change than to insist that the past cannot. If 'The future is real' is an apt saying, then at any rate it is not apt for the same reasons that 'The past is real' is apt.

2. CAUSALITY

2.1. Exceptionless Generalizations

I have in this book mentioned Hume's philosophy on several occasions. Anscombe again and again found in Hume a starting point for her discussions; and we must not be misled by her frequent dissent from his views into thinking of her as 'anti-Humean'. Indeed, in her treatment of the topic of causation Anscombe can even be seen as continuing Hume's work—as out-Huming Hume. The author of *A Treatise of Human Nature* turned an astute and interrogating eye upon our belief in causal necessitation, necessary connection, and what he called 'efficacy'. Anscombe casts the net wider, to include some of the things that Hume himself seems to have found obvious—in particular, the idea that 'being caused is—non-trivially—instancing some exceptionless generalization' (*CD*, 133). This latter view can be attributed to Hume in virtue of his use of the notion of constant conjunction. And it is a view that has pervaded theories of causation right up to the present day.[9] Such pervasiveness may suggest that the conception of causation as involving exceptionless generalizations ('An A is always and everywhere followed by a B') is seductive in itself, and not only to philosophers: 'The truth of this conception is hardly debated. It is, indeed, a bit of *Weltanschauung*: it helps to form a cast of mind which is characteristic of our whole culture' (*CD*, 133).

It would have been interesting to see a genealogical examination of this 'bit of *Weltanschauung*', analogous to her examination of the historical roots of the legalistic conception of morality (see Ch. 3, §3); but Anscombe leaves that as an exercise for the reader. She does note, however, that the idea of causation as involving exceptionless generalizations and the idea of it as involving necessary connection share a common doctrine or assumption, namely: 'If an effect occurs in one case and a similar effect does not occur in an apparently similar case, there must be a relevant further difference' (*CD*, 133). That the two ideas should be thus linked might come as a surprise to a Humean; for did not Hume *replace* the dubious notion of necessary connection with the more respectable one of constant conjunction? Anscombe's point, of course, is that a belief in exceptionless generalizations looks as dubious as a belief in

---

[9] Mill, Mackie, and Davidson being three notable examples. Anscombe (*CD*, 147) mentions the last philosopher's influential 'Causal Relations', *Journal of Philosophy*, 64 (1967), 691–703; also in *Essays on Actions and Events*.

necessary connection.[10] Many acknowledged cases of the cause–effect relation are not backed up by known exceptionless generalizations, and the idea that there *must* be such generalizations lurking behind those relations is just the sort of statement of necessity that Hume himself taught us to be wary of. The kinship of this idea with the idea of necessary connection is manifest in the 'shared assumption'—itself a statement of necessity.

Something else that is common to the two ideas is this claim: you can't know that A has caused B from simply observing A and B, however closely. If causation involves necessary connection, then no inspection of the situation shows us *that*. You can perceive that A is prior to and contiguous with B, but not that B must follow A. And if causation involves exceptionless generalizations, then observation of a particular instance, A then B, is not enough: you need to experience a series of instances of things like A being followed by things like B. (And even that seems only to *lend support* to an exceptionless generalization, and hence to the original 'A caused B'.) But this view of causation as unobservable is another dubious idea, for Anscombe. As so often, she reminds us how the relevant concept is taught and learnt:

The truthful—though unhelpful—answer to the question: 'How did we come by our primary knowledge of causality?' is that in learning to speak we learned the linguistic representation and application of a host of causal concepts. [The answer is so far unhelpful because of its circular reference to 'causal concepts'.] Very many of them were represented by transitive and other verbs of action used in reporting what is observed. [. . .] A small selection: *scrape, push, wet, carry, eat, burn, knock over, keep off, squash, make* (e.g. noises, paper boats), *hurt.*   (*CD*, 137)

You can on the face of it *see* that someone has knocked a lamp over. A philosophical theory that denies this would appear either to suffer from a distorted (e.g. atomistic) model of what it is to see, or to have ruled out such cases of seeing in advance (e.g. because of adherence to the idea of necessary connection). In Hume, we find both factors at work:

Hume presumably wants us to 'produce an instance' in which *efficacy* is related to sensation as *red* is. It is true that we can't do that; it is not *so* related to sensation. He is also helped, in making his argument that we don't perceive 'efficacy', by his curious belief that 'efficacy' means much the same thing as 'necessary connection'!   (*CD*, 137–8)

Seeing that someone has knocked something over is not just like seeing that something is red. But then nor is seeing that something is a human face, or is a picture of one, or is a forgery, or is your brother Jack, or is angry ... or even *is moving*. Imitating Hume, Anscombe writes, 'When we "consider the

---

[10] Cf. *TBC* (151): 'Hume's observation [that causation does not as such involve necessary connection] ought to have been a very liberating one. But so far few people have been much liberated, for Hume himself, and almost everybody since, has been anxious to forge some substitute for the chains that he broke—to replace the logical necessity by another one just as universal as it.'

matter with the utmost attention", we find only an impression of travel made by the successive positions of a round white patch in our visual fields ... etc.' (*CD*, 137)—which is absurd.

'Strictly speaking, you only see such-and-such' is almost always said by one who insists that there must be a core notion of seeing (that 'must' again), and who has identified the core notion with one favourite example. The choice of favourite may be motivated by an 'implicit appeal to Cartesian scepticism' (*CD*, 137). Thus: something can appear to be red, but in fact be lit so as to look red when in fact white—or you might even be hallucinating. This may drive us to say that, strictly speaking, what you perceive is a red patch in your visual field. No chance of error there. Similarly, a lamp can appear to have been knocked over, when in fact a gust of wind blew it over just as Jones put his elbow right up to it; in which case, we'd better say that what you saw, strictly speaking, was Jones's movement followed by the lamp's downward plunge. But Cartesian scepticism is not a good basis for an account of perception, and the sense in which it's true that 'what is seen' is authoritatively describable (only) by the subject is adequately explained by adverting to the intentional object of seeing (see Ch. 4, §1). If a real doubt arises, about whether something really was red or was knocked over, one can always retreat to a more purely intentional description of the object or incident. But that does not make such a description the best or most proper description *tout court*.

If you see that someone has knocked something over, and are not deceived, then you may be said to have perceived causation, or efficacy. You haven't perceived necessary connection, but that is because causation isn't necessary connection. Have you perceived the instantiation of an exceptionless generalization? Not under that description, it would seem. But in any case—and this brings us to the 'bit of *Weltanschauung*' itself—what would the generalization be? 'Whenever someone comes into contact with a sufficiently mobile object, with sufficient force, and if there is nothing to prevent it, then the object will move downwards ... '—or something like that. The problematic expressions, of course, are: 'sufficiently', 'sufficient', and the phrase 'if there is nothing to prevent it'. If the first two terms are cashed out, they seem to render the whole statement tautologous, and a similar danger appears to attend the 'if'-phrase even as it stands. 'But there must be *some* specification of a range of masses and forces, and a list of negative conditions (to rule out preventing factors), such that a non-tautologous exceptionless generalization is the result.' Experience does not teach us this 'must'; nor does reason. It is an article of faith, at best.

The phrase 'if there is nothing to prevent it', however, is certainly useful, and can figure in our account of causal generalizations, so long as we are not in the business of providing an *analysis*:

Suppose we were to call propositions giving the properties of substances 'laws of nature'. Then there will be a law of nature running 'The flash-point of such a substance is ... ', and this will be important in explaining why striking matches usually causes them to light.[11] This law of nature has not the form of a generalization running 'Always, if a sample of such a substance is raised to such a temperature, it ignites'; nor is it equivalent to such a generalization, but rather to: 'If a sample of such a substance is raised to such a temperature and doesn't ignite, there must be a cause of its not doing so.'   (*CD*, 138)

The last-quoted conditional statement is connected with various things, such as our propensity to search for a preventing factor when ignition fails, and our reliance on the 'properly vague' notion of normal conditions (*CD*, 138). The conditional statement (with specific substance-name and temperature inserted) is one for which there can be empirical evidence—e.g. experimental reports of what happened when the substance was or was not raised to that temperature. Thus the statement is not like the 'common doctrine or assumption' mentioned above on p. 177. The latter is not so much a scientific hypothesis or theory as a metaphysical claim of necessity. It is certainly not needed to *justify* the conditional about ignition. Somebody might say that the propensity to search for a preventing factor indicates a belief in the truth of some exceptionless generalization, which could be framed once we had discovered *all* the possible preventing factors. But clearly it need not indicate this; and the task of discovering all possible preventing factors, as well as lacking the practical utility of searching for one such factor in a given case, is not obviously a task that could ever be completed. In that sense, it is not even clear that it is a *task*, any more than is counting all the rational numbers between 1 and 2.

We have already encountered preventing factors and normal conditions, in our discussion of Anscombe's 'On Brute Facts' (Ch. 3, pp. 91–4). In that article, Anscombe showed how the application of an institutional rule requires that conditions are taken to be normal unless a preventing factor is known or suspected. For an institutional rule, 'conditions are normal' just *means* 'there are no preventing factors'; and preventing factors do not have to be ruled out *before* I can say such a thing as 'You owe me £5', inferring this from the fact that I've supplied you with the potatoes you asked for. There are similarities between an institutional rule and a causal generalization, or 'law of nature'. In both cases, 'unless something prevents it' is a needed adjunct to the rule or generalization; and in both cases, this fact shows why it is impossible to give non-tautologous conditions that are necessary and sufficient for the application or truth of the rule or generalization—for possible preventing factors are not enumerable in advance. But as I said in Chapter 3 (p. 92), there is this difference between the two cases: if an institutional proposition fails to follow in the usual way from certain premisses, this will be in virtue of certain preventing factors holding—there is nothing more to its failing to follow; whereas if an event fails to follow another in the usual way, in the way predicted by some causal generalization, this fact does not simply consist in there being preventing factors.

---

[11] The dictionary definition of 'flash-point' is rather different from Anscombe's.

The failure is established independently of, and typically prior to, our establishing the presence of preventing factors.

This means that we once again face a pressing question concerning the status of a 'must'. What sort of necessity-claim is 'If it doesn't ignite at that temperature, there must be a cause of its not doing so'? It is not like the parallel necessity-claim that one finds with an institutional rule, quasi-conceptual in nature; but nor, according to Anscombe, is it a necessity-claim arising out of either necessary connection or a background exceptionless generalization. So what is it?

Anscombe does not explicitly address this question in 'Causality and Determination'. Her main concern, as evidenced in the above quotation, is to criticize the idea of exceptionless generalizations. Moreover, although she is clearly not averse to the invocation of 'laws of nature', she regards such laws as no more essential to the truth of causal statements in general than are exceptionless generalizations. But in considering what it *is* that she regards as essential to causal statements in general, we may find a clue as to what her account would be of such laws, and of their implied necessity-claims.

2.2. Derivativeness and Determination

Given her recognition of the multifariousness of cause–effect relationships, and her eschewal of systematic theorizing, it comes as no surprise that Anscombe's statement of what is 'essential' to causality is modest, its purpose being more to point the way for further investigation than to pretend to encapsulate the whole truth about causation:

There is something to observe here, that lies under our noses. It is little attended to, and yet still so obvious as to seem trite. It is this: causality consists in the derivativeness of an effect from its causes. This is the core, the common feature, of causality in its various kinds. Effects derive from, arise out of, come of, their causes.   (*CD*, 136)

There are a variety of ways in which the phrase 'derive from', and like phrases, can be taken. Anscombe mentions physical parenthood and travel. An animal is born of its parents; an object is at place P1 having come from place P2. 'How did this get to be here?' could be asked in both cases ('here' being stressed in the second case), and in both cases one could answer by pointing to the source or origin of the thing's being here—to the parents, or to place P1. These are paradigms of causation. A philosopher might insist that the process of conception, gestation, and birth has to be mentioned in the first case, and the process of travel between P1 and P2 in the second. But (a), the idea that only processes or events count as *bona fide* causes comes from inheriting the terms of a certain debate, one associated with Hume. For ancient philosophers, and for ordinary people, it is not only processes or events that merit the title of cause, in the sense of 'thing responsible': an object, person, or pair thereof can all be cited as the thing(s) responsible for some state of affairs. And (b), travel from P1 to P2 is indeed involved in the second case; but this amounts only to asserting that there was some continuous path followed between P1 and P2—as opposed to the object's getting from one point in space to another without traversing any intermediate points. To insist on inserting '*travelled* from P1 to P2' is thus to insist on ruling out something quite impossible. That is fine—but it rather confirms the thought that 'It came from P1' is primarily a remark about P1. (It is true that some flesh would need to be put on the bones of this example for any detailed discussion.)

The derivativeness of an effect from its causes is connected with the derivability (by us) of a cause from its effects. That we trace causes back from their effects just as easily as *vice versa*, if not more easily, is something that Anscombe stresses (*CD*, 136). Her examples here are often medical; but the following extremely simple example from Wittgenstein gives us a vivid illustration of what is meant by 'derivativeness':

There is a reaction that can be called 'reacting to the cause'. We also speak of 'tracing' the cause; a simple case would be, say, following a string to see who is pulling at it. If I then find him—how do I know that he, his pulling, is the cause of the string's moving? Do I establish this by a series of experiments? [12]

The answer to this last question is, of course: No. And like Anscombe, Wittgenstein is showing us how the notions of cause and of constant conjunction (inductive inference, etc.) are distinct notions—the first does not, as such, involve the second. We learn causal verbs—here, 'pull'; and in connection with such verbs and what they represent, there are various reactions and activities, such as *tracing a cause*—also *stopping something happening* and *getting something to happen*. These latter are manifestations of human agency; and Wittgenstein's and Anscombe's remarks on causation are part of an approach to that topic which emphasizes agency in place of, or as well as, observation—the latter being the typical starting point for empiricist philosophers and their descendants. [13]

Wittgenstein's remarks are in the context of a discussion of whether and how we might be said to be 'intuitively aware' of causation. He was very probably responding to what Russell had written in 'The Limits of Empiricism', [14] to the effect that one's knowledge that one is saying 'cat' *because* one has seen a cat (or perceived a 'feline visual occurrence') must itself be perceptual, i.e. non-inferential, knowledge. It must be non-inferential knowledge, for if it were

---

[12] 'On Cause and Effect, Intuitive Awareness', from MS 119 in von Wright's catalogue, trans. P. Winch; reprinted in *Philosophical Occasions 1912–1951*, ed. James C. Klagge and Alfred Nordmann (Indianapolis, Ind., and Cambridge: Hackett, 1993), 387.

[13] Accounts of causation which emphasize agency include Dummett's (e.g. 'Bringing about the Past', in *Truth and Other Enigmas*), and Douglas Gasking's ('Causation and Recipes', in *Language, Logic and Causation*, ed. I. T. Oakley and L. J. O'Neill (Carlton South: Melbourne University Press, 1996)).

[14] Russell, 'The Limits of Empiricism', *Proceedings of the Aristotelian Society*, 36 (1935–6), 131–50.

not, there would be no verbal empirical knowledge at all; one's application of some words must, at bottom, be directly warranted, or we should have an infinite regress of justification. Now Wittgenstein does not go along with Russell's assertion that 'I said "cat" because I saw a cat' amounts to: 'I willed to say "cat" because I saw a cat', with the 'because' understood as causal. Such 'willing' is the sort of thing of which Wittgenstein, and Anscombe for that matter, are rightly suspicious. But Russell was on to something—namely, what Anscombe was to label a mental cause (see Ch. 1, pp. 19–20). Wittgenstein changes the example accordingly: 'If someone says: "I am frightened, because he looks so threatening"—this looks as if it were a case of recognizing a cause immediately without repeated experiments.'[15] In 'Causality and Determination', Anscombe mentions perceptible causes, such as scrapings, pullings, and cuttings. But equally problematic for a Humean account of causation are those mental causes she had dealt with in *Intention*, and which supply the starting point of Wittgenstein's remarks of 1937. In both cases, we have causal statements not arrived at through induction or inference; and in both cases, constant conjunction and exceptionless generalization are just not in the picture.

Nothing Anscombe says rules out the idea of a necessitating cause. Indeed, she takes a necessitating cause to be one mentioned in a 'law of nature', understood in the sense already explained (above, pp. 179–80). She takes 'necessitating cause', that is, to be a term applying to a *kind* of cause, not to particular causes: 'A non-necessitating cause is then one that can fail of its effect without the intervention of anything to frustrate it' (*CD*, 144). Modern physics seems to teach us that there are at least some non-necessitating causes, such as the radioactivity of a substance, responsible for a particle's emission from a lump of that substance (*CD*, 144–5). A necessitating cause, by contrast, is one that cannot fail of its effect if there is nothing to prevent the effect. What of this 'cannot'? Anscombe explains the modality here by reference to an antecedent range of possibilities:

When we call a result determined [i.e. necessitated, in the case of an *effect*] we are implicitly relating it to an antecedent range of possibilities and saying that all but one of these is disallowed. What disallows them is not the result itself but something antecedent to the result.   (*CD*, 141)

As Anscombe points out, this notion of determination is broad enough to apply to non-causal as well as causal situations. Thus in a chess game, the antecedent possibilities are the powers of the pieces; and a certain chess position can exclude all but one of the antecedently possible moves (*CD*, 141). So what sort of thing is it that excludes causal possibilities?—and what determines the range of those possibilities in the first place? Anscombe's example comes from genetic biology:

In the zygote, sex and eye-colour are already determined. Here the antecedent possibilities are the possibilities for sex and eye-colour for a child; or more narrowly: for a child of

---

[15] 'On Cause and Effect', 371.

these parents. *Now*, given the combination of this ovum and this spermatozoon, all but one of these antecedent possibilities is excluded.   (*CD*, 141)

There is in fact no such thing as *the* range of antecedent possibilities; we can specify more than one such range, by reference (e.g.) to human children, or instead to children of particular parents. (Or again, to mammalian offspring, or to children born of these parents in their thirtieth year ... etc.) What we have are nested families of possibilities. A parallel phenomenon is that of the different grades of potentiality. [16] Consider the following three ways of understanding 'It is possible for Tom to walk': (a) Tom has learnt to walk and is not tied up, paralysed, etc.; (b) Tom has learnt to walk but is tied up; (c) Tom hasn't learnt to walk yet, but has normal limbs, etc. (The English sentence 'Tom can walk' would be appropriate for the first two only.) Clearly, this list is not exhaustive; and equally clearly, no one paraphrase gives *the* meaning of 'It is possible for Tom to walk'. You could think of both (b) and (c) as meaning: 'Tom could acquire the capacity to walk [by being untied, or by growing up a couple of years].' But the same is true of instances of (a), for instance: 'Tom could acquire the capacity to walk by standing up.' (You can't walk from a sitting position, unless very athletic.) Each way of taking 'It is possible for Tom to walk' relates the Tom in question to a different class, of which that Tom is a member. For (a), unrestrained normal adults; for (b) restrained normal adults; for (c), normal one-year-olds (say). These classes are mutually exclusive: there are three different Toms in (a), (b), and (c). A single person—Tim, say—will belong to more than one class, e.g. that of normal adults and that of restrained normal adults. *These* classes are non-exclusive (obviously); and the range of possibilities for the person is relative to what class is assumed. *Qua* normal adult, Tim can walk; *qua* tied-up adult, he can't.

The grounds for believing or asserting a statement of possibility, or a statement giving a range of possibilities, are typically inductive. Hume would have said that an inductively based statement of possibility is no more than the expression of a psychological preparedness to expect or predict something, given further information (as, that Tom now wants to leave the room). For him, the only other sense, and perhaps the stricter one, of 'possible' is: 'logically possible', alias 'conceivable'. There is just one level of logical possibility, such that it is equally possible for Tom to walk whether he's tied up, or is a babe in arms, or is a fish (he could sprout legs). We shall have more to say about Hume's views on logical possibility presently. For now, it seems fair to say that Hume would have wanted us to understand empirical possibility in terms of empirical necessity—i.e. in terms of what we *call* necessity, as a result of being conditioned by experience to expect certain things to follow certain others. 'Preparedness to expect or predict' means 'preparedness to regard as necessary'. Anscombe,

---

[16] See Aristotle, *Physics*, Bk. 3, ch. 1.

by contrast, does things the other way around. She explains empirical necessity (necessitation, determination) in terms of empirical possibility, plus a principle of exclusion.

But what is it that excludes the possibility that a child should be born with blue eyes? The DNA of the zygote, presumably; something that only comes into being at conception, before which the possibility of blue eyes is still there. But if such-and-such DNA rules out the child's having blue eyes, is not this in virtue of its being a normal cause of (say) brown eyes? Brown eyes can be explained by reference to that DNA. However, it is not enough for the DNA simply to be a normal cause of brown eyes, since that on its own cannot exclude all possibilities but one—for there is such a thing as a non-necessitating cause. We seem to be on the verge of saying that necessitation is exclusion of all possibilities but one, while exclusion of all possibilities but one is effected by necessitation. One way of avoiding this appearance of circularity would be to insist that we are not supplying a reductive account of necessitation. According to this line, necessitation is to be understood primarily in terms of the phrase 'if X failed to occur, there must have been something to prevent it', and our remarks about antecedent possibilities, etc. were intended to show up conceptual connections, not to provide a conceptual analysis of 'necessitating cause'. This would leave unaddressed the status of the 'must' in 'there must have been something to prevent it'. And it is in any case not consonant with Anscombe's own statements in 'Causality and Determination':

> [A] cause *C* is a necessitating cause of an effect *E when* (I mean: on the occasions when) if *C* occurs it is certain to cause *E* unless something prevents it. [. . .] If 'certainty' should seem too epistemological a notion: a necessitating cause *C* of a given kind of effect *E* is such that it *is* not possible (on the occasion) that *C* should occur and should not cause an *E*, given that there is nothing that prevents an *E* from occurring.   (*CD*, 144)

The second of Anscombe's two definitions of 'necessitating cause'[17] employs just that notion of (im)possibility which she had earlier explained by reference to a range of antecedent possibilities, all but one of which is excluded. Hence her emphasis of the present-tensed '*is* not possible', meaning 'is no longer possible'. So it does seem that she is attempting to explain empirical necessity in terms of empirical possibility plus exclusion. And as I have suggested, there is a feeling of circularity about this approach. At any rate, the suspicion would have to be somehow allayed that (for example) such-and-such DNA excludes all other eye-colour possibilities *in virtue of* its necessitating a specific eye colour—rather

---

[17] There is a striking parallel between Anscombe's two definitions and Hume's two definitions, natural and philosophical, of *cause*. (See the *Treatise*, Bk. I, Part 3, §14; Everyman's Library, 1911, p. 167.) Hume proffered his philosophical definition (in terms of constant conjunction) lest his natural definition (in terms of psychological association) be not to the reader's taste; in similar vein, Anscombe gives us a definition in terms of objective possibility lest her first definition in terms of certainty be found 'too epistemological'.

than *vice versa*. This is not to say that there aren't conditions which can be seen primarily as ruling things out, rather than in—conditions that have an effect on proceedings by excluding certain possibilities. A barred window would be a good example. But such cases rarely appear in the guise of necessitating causes, and such-and-such DNA doesn't look like a barred window. It looks more like a terrified cat, in a room with just one open and unbarred window.

To sum up this discussion of Anscombe's remarks on causality I will lay out what I take to be the five main elements in her positive account of that notion. First, there is the general idea of an effect's deriving from its cause; second, the stress made upon the unavoidability, and open-endedness, of the phrase 'unless something prevents it'; third, the attempt to show how the possibility of prevention or interference is compatible with something's being a case of causal necessitation; fourth, the claim that we do *perceive* causation in the particular case; and fifth, an appreciation of the variety of kinds of cause–effect relationship. This last is especially evident in Anscombe's writings on topics to which causality is relevant, such as perception and memory (see Ch. 4, §1.3). Anscombe is, as always, ready to follow Wittgenstein's injunction, 'Don't think, but look!', and it is in this spirit that she exhorts the reader to free his mind of all prejudices on the subject of causation (*MEC*, 127). In this respect she is like Hume; indeed, as I have said, she can be seen on occasion as out-Huming Hume, something which we shall see vividly illustrated in the next section, where one of Hume's most famous efforts to free us of a prejudice will turn out to rest on just the thing that Hume made it his philosophical business to debunk—namely, an inflated conception of what the human mind can accomplish unaided.

2.3. *Aliquid ex Nihil*

The question whether something can come to be out of nothing has perplexed thinkers for centuries. The standard form of the Cosmological Argument rests on the premiss that nothing can come to be out of nothing, i.e. that it is impossible for a thing to come into existence without a cause of its doing so. The argument presents us with a dilemma: either everything had a prior cause of existence, or something (the 'First Cause') did not come into existence, but always existed. Reasons are then adduced why the first horn of the dilemma is unacceptable, and the second horn is adopted, the First Cause being eventually identified with God. But the dilemma would not force itself upon us if we could show that it was possible for a thing to come into existence without a cause. This is what Hume set out to do. Of course, the interest of the question does not have solely to do with whether the Cosmological Argument is sound or unsound; the answer to it will have implications for various other metaphysical questions, such as those to do with space, time, and determinism. And as we shall see, the process of arriving at an answer may well cast light on more general issues concerning possibility, imaginability, and philosophical method.

In Hume's *Treatise* we find the following argument (quoted by Anscombe in *TBC*, 152):

As all distinct ideas are separate from each other, and as the ideas of cause and effect are evidently distinct, 'twill be easy for us to conceive any object to be non-existent this moment, and existent the next, without conjoining to it the distinct idea of a cause or productive principle. The separation, therefore, of the idea of a cause from that of a beginning of existence is plainly possible for the imagination; and consequently the actual separation of these objects is so far possible, that it implies no contradiction or absurdity.[18]

The first observation to make is that Hume appears guilty of a conflation—namely, of (i) it's possible to have an idea of A without having an idea of B, and (ii) it's possible to have an idea of A without B. He begins by asserting (i) and ends by asserting (ii), which is what he really needs for his conclusion: that A without B is possible. Anscombe notes the implausibility of (i), especially in its contrapositive form, 'If there can't *be* one thing without another, you can't *think* of the first without thinking of the second' (*TBC*, 152). She turns to (ii), which looks like a simple argument from imaginability to possibility. How are we to understand 'It's possible to imagine so and so'? Hume is notoriously psychologistic about such statements; but perhaps we can revamp his argument.

Certainly if we look at a thought as a psychological event, and, by the 'experimental method' as suggested on Hume's title-page, try what we *can* think without what, the argument lacks all force. But suppose we consider a thought, not as a psychological event, but as the content of a proposition, the common possession of many minds. As Aquinas remarks in *Summa Theologica*, 'Habitudo ad causam non intrat in definitionem entis quod est causatum'. (The relation to a cause does not enter into the definition of the thing that is caused.) (1a. 44, art. I)   (*TBC*, 152)

Anscombe goes on to look at this last claim; but as she says, it isn't quite what Hume needs, since it relates to the idea (concept, definition) of a thing of a certain kind, rather than to the idea (concept, definition) of such a thing's coming into existence. The Thomist version of what Hume needs for his argument is this claim: 'The relation to a cause is no part of the concept of a thing's coming into existence' (*TBC*, 153). Hume may still be allowed his argument from imaginability, so long as certain constraints on what counts as imagining something are recognized—constraints having to do with the logical or conceptual character of imagining. The key idea, which we have encountered before, is this: you can have all sorts of things going through your mind, but you are not an unimpugnable authority as to the *content* of those states of mind, i.e. as to what their intentional objects are. For present purposes, we have to be able to say what distinguishes imagining something's coming into existence *without* a cause from imagining something's coming into existence *with* a cause.

---

[18] *A Treatise of Human Nature*, Bk. I, Part I, §3.

There is an ambiguity that needs to be sorted out first, one that already appears in the above quotation from the *Treatise*. 'The separation, therefore, of the idea of a cause from that of a beginning of existence, is plainly possible for the imagination', writes Hume. By 'a cause' does he mean 'a particular cause', or 'any cause'? If the first, then his claim is that, of any given cause, one can always imagine something's coming to exist without that cause (e.g. in virtue of its having some other cause); if the second, then his claim is that one can always imagine something's coming to exist without any cause at all. The second proposition is a more ambitious claim than the first, and the first is open to objection: it is far from clear that I can imagine that the marks on this page are not being caused by the pen I am holding, but rather by something else. (If I am *that* mistaken about things, then mustn't I be hallucinated, or similarly at sea?—and imagining being hallucinated isn't the same as imagining there being a different cause for the marks.) Be this as it may, it is the second proposition that is our concern, that one can always imagine something's coming to exist without any cause at all. Now to imagine X happening without any cause cannot be the same as just imagining X happening. Nor can it be simply to imagine X happening while internally adding the title, 'X happening without a cause'. For the question would then be, 'Does that title describe something *possible*?' (I can draw a chair and add the title, 'Chair about to time-travel', but in a very obvious sense all I've drawn is a chair, and my drawing adds nothing to the debate about time-travel.)

For many A and B, I can imagine an A's causing a B—the reason being that I can, *pace* Hume, perceive an A to cause a B (see above, pp. 178–9). Here, to imagine is to imagine perceiving. I can also have good perceptual and other *evidence*, more or less indirect, for saying that an A has caused a B; wherefore I can imagine an A causing a B, in virtue of imagining a situation in which one would have good reason to think that an A caused a B. These remarks all apply when B is something's coming into existence—a chair from some wood, a baby from a sperm and an egg, a pudding from its ingredients, and so on (*TBC*, 161–2). One's claim to be able to imagine such caused beginnings is unproblematic, since we know about all these things. But in order to imagine a chair coming into existence without any cause, I must imagine being in a position to rule out all possible causes. For this it is not enough that I imagine watching a space and suddenly seeing a chair where before there was none—which I can indeed imagine. For couldn't the chair have arrived there from another place? To air this possibility is not *ipso facto* to claim that something can get to one place from another without traversing the places in between; for as Anscombe says, maybe the chair travelled from elsewhere in some other form, e.g. as a gas, resuming its chair-like form on arrival (*TBC*, 161).

And in any case, what is our basis for ruling out a thing's getting from one place to another without traversing the places in between? Physicists have claimed that such discontinuous travel is possible for certain particles (Anscombe mentions α-particles); but we should probably beware of assuming that physicists only talk sense. Even so, it is worth noting that we have here yet another necessity-claim, and it is entirely in the spirit of Hume to ask, 'Why *must* a thing traverse the points in between?' What if it became commonplace for us to see an object disappear, and at the same moment, or a bit later, see an object just like it appear in another place? (This seems to be quite imaginable.) Might we not then talk of there being a single chair, say, rather than two?[19] For that way of talking could be much more practical, in all sorts of ways, than the alternative: an inventory of possessions would be an altogether simpler and stabler matter, for example. And if in this scenario it would be allowable, and even warranted, to say such a thing as, 'My chair moved from the kitchen to the living-room without traversing any points in between', then mustn't we conclude that discontinuous travel is after all an *a priori* possibility? If such travel is impossible, it is only impossible *given* everything we actually know about physical things. One could of course say that in the imagined world, the concept of a chair, and that of a physical object, would differ from our actual concepts, thus hanging on to the idea that 'Chairs cannot get from place to place without traversing the intervening points' expresses a conceptual (and so necessary) truth. This move has an *ad hoc* feel to it; but in any case, as we have noted, the problem which Anscombe raises for Hume's argument does not relate simply to the question of discontinuous travel. It relates to the question whether one can imagine having determined when and where a thing came into existence, given only that one sees it suddenly appear before one. One cannot imagine doing such a thing because one could not ever do such a thing: 'The task is too much for me; and for all I have a right to judge in the matter, I am forced to conclude that this object may have come into existence in any place and at almost any time you care to mention' (*TBC*, 161). The task is too much because it involves excluding an unspecifiable set of possibilities. And similar remarks will clearly go for imagining having determined that a thing came into existence without any cause. To imagine this, I have to imagine having ruled out all possible causes. But there is no such procedure as 'ruling out all possible causes'.

Anscombe's treatment of this question may well put us in mind of her claims concerning institutional rules and causal laws. In each case, she makes reference to an unfulfillable task. The specification of all possible preventing factors is that task when it comes to institutional rules and causal laws; while for a thing's coming into existence, it is the specification of all possible causes (with a view to excluding them all). But the point of invoking the unfulfillable task in the last case is different from the point of doing so in the other two cases. Anscombe's critique of Hume on uncaused existence works by showing us what *can't* be

<hr>

[19] Cf. Wittgenstein, *Philosophical Investigations*, para. 80.

established by appeal to the imagination[20]—just as Hume had managed on more than one occasion to show us what can't be established by appeal to reason. Hume may have been right that reason cannot teach us that every beginning must have a cause; where he erred was in thinking that the imagination could teach us the contradictory proposition.

But *was* Hume right about reason's impotence here? It may depend on what is meant by 'reason'. We have had some inkling of the problems involved in imagining having determined when and where a thing began to exist. And it looks as if, when we do actually determine when and where a thing began to exist, we are able to do so because we understand the thing's origins (*TBC*, 162)—we are aware, that is, of the causes of its existence. It could be argued that the only way of knowing when and where something began to exist is by knowing the cause of its existence: the cause (not simply *qua* cause, but in virtue of certain of its features) will count as not being a part of the thing's history, and hence will give a point in time *ante quem non*. If that is right, and I suspect Anscombe is hinting as much in 'Times, Beginnings and Causes', the question arises whether it's possible that there should be things the beginning of whose existence could not in principle be dated and located. If such things are impossible, then the main premiss of the Cosmological Argument appears to be reinstated.

---

[20] We shall encounter another argument of Anscombe's that points out the limits of what can be established by appeal to the imagination in Ch. 6; the argument there—also *contra* Hume—concerns historical knowledge. See Ch. 6, p. 225.

6

Language and Thought

Elizabeth Anscombe's name will be known to many as that of the English translator of a good number of Wittgenstein's writings, in particular of the summation of his later philosophy, the *Philosophical Investigations*. Her translation of the latter is still the authoritative and standard English version. And it is probably the influence of Wittgenstein's later philosophy that most readers of Anscombe will detect, rather than of his early philosophy. But her most sustained direct discussion of Wittgenstein is of course to be found in *An Introduction to Wittgenstein's Tractatus*; and it is interesting how themes from the *Tractatus* crop up in various guises in her articles, throughout her career. True, some of these themes persist, if only in transmogrified form, in Wittgenstein's own later work, so that for these themes, 'Earlier or later?' cannot always be given a definitive answer: for example, those of the 'limits of sense' and of the nature of philosophical understanding/error.

The question what degree of continuity exists between Wittgenstein's earlier and later philosophies has been much debated. Wittgenstein himself famously said that his later thoughts could only really be understood in the light of the earlier ones, to which they were in many ways a reaction or response—which if true would neither confirm nor throw doubt on a thesis of 'continuity', by the way. Whatever full account of the matter is correct, one rough and ready observation that can be made is this: in the *Tractatus*, truth receives a good deal more attention than meaning, while in the *Philosophical Investigations*, the reverse is the case. It is true that use is made, in the *Tractatus*, of the notion of sense (*Sinn*); but (a) this notion has a more restricted role than the one Frege had given it, being effectively confined to propositions; and (b) propositional sense is understood in terms of 'saying that things are thus and so', i.e. in terms of the depiction of possible facts—i.e. in terms of *truth*-conditions. As for questions about meaning in the sense of what a competent speaker of (say) English grasps in connection with a given English expression, the young Wittgenstein took such questions to resolve into ones about convention and human psychology, which phenomena he regarded as lying outside the province of the philosopher. These phenomena are, in the later philosophy, recognized to lie within that province after all (though not in such a way as to make philosophy a handmaiden to science or anthropology). Remarks concerning truth, on the other hand, are relatively few in the *Philosophical Investigations*, and can seem at first glance to have a debunking, or minimalist, tone to them, a reading that appears confirmed in the *Remarks on the Foundations of Mathematics*; whereas in the *Tractatus*, of course, truth had been absolutely central, to the extent that the text is often taken as a classic expression of the correspondence theory of truth.

In Anscombe's writing, the two topics of meaning and truth, insofar as they can be separated, seem to enjoy roughly equal status, although her manner of dealing with each is not the same. Anscombe almost always invokes meaning—i.e. facts about linguistic training, usage, rules, etc.—in the course of dealing with some philosophical topic not belonging as such to the philosophy of language. We have already encountered several examples of this: her discussion of the first-person future tense (expressions of intention), of stopping modals (e.g. in connection with promising), of direct objects (intentionality), of the first-person pronoun (the self), of the past tense (memory and the past), and so on. In these different discussions, the influence of the later Wittgenstein certainly outweighs that of the earlier.

By contrast, Anscombe treats truth much more as a topic in its own right; and I have the feeling that in doing so, she shows more sympathy with the earlier than with the later Wittgenstein. An interesting example of this is her greater readiness than many followers of the later Wittgenstein to stick to the principle of bivalence for various classes of sentence, a principle which in the *Tractatus* is applied to all meaningful propositions. Certainly, she does not go as far as the *Tractatus*—witness her saying of future-tensed propositions that they have no truth-value when uttered, but *become* true or false subsequently.[1] But there is a species of future-tensed propositions, namely expressions of intention, to which a Wittgensteinian might well be loth to ascribe any truth-value at all, on the grounds of their being in some sense performative, but which Anscombe takes as unexceptionably true or false, albeit not when uttered.[2]

And when it comes to sentences containing empty names, Anscombe is all in favour of bivalence. In a passage of *IWT* in which she considers such sentences, she writes:

It is well known that Russell and Wittgenstein were on the other side of this fence [sc. the one separating them from Frege and Strawson]; for Wittgenstein 'having a sense' was one and the same thing with being true-or-false. [. . .] Wittgenstein remained on this side of the fence all his life . . .   (*IWT*, 58, 59)

---

[1] See Ch. 1, p. 28; Ch. 2, p. 80.
[2] See Ch. 1, pp. 17–18. A performative verb is a verb, 'to φ', such that a person φs simply by saying 'I φ . . .' (in the right circumstances). Examples are 'promise', 'give', 'name'. A performative statement is a statement 'I φ . . .', containing a performative verb; and it is natural to say of such statements that they are not straightforwardly true or false, but rather are successful or unsuccessful (depending on whether the 'right circumstances' obtain). This definition of 'performative statement' could not apply strictly to, e.g., 'I am going to make some tea', but the claim that such a statement is quasi-performative is still intelligible, if we focus on the seemingly equivalent statement 'I intend to make some tea'. The term 'performative' is J. L. Austin's.

It appears from the surrounding passage that the 'fence' separates views as to whether sensefulness is as such associated with bivalence, for indicative sentences. If that is right, Anscombe's assertion that Wittgenstein was always on the same side of the fence as Russell, which she backs up with a quotation from the *Investigations*, is a claim rather hard to sustain in the light of what Wittgenstein has to say, e.g. in the *Remarks on the Foundations of Mathematics*.[3] Be that as it may, she places herself, meanwhile, on the Russellian side of the fence, as the ensuing argument in *IWT* shows, an argument we shall return to in §1.2.

Another theme of the *Tractatus* which Anscombe always took very seriously was that of the relationship between thinkability and possibility. The issue of thinkability is linked in turn to that of sayability; and the question of what can or cannot be said, or said clearly, brings us to those *echt* Wittgensteinian themes of senselessness, nonsense, the mysterious (or mystical), and the ineffable. Philosophers have grappled since ancient times with the problem of how thinkability and possibility are related, and it is characteristic of Anscombe to have drawn such diverse figures as Parmenides, Plato, Hume, and Wittgenstein into a single discussion. In the Introduction to *FPW*, she writes:

It was left to the moderns to deduce what could be from what could hold of thought, as we see Hume to have done. This trend is still strong. But the ancients had the better approach, arguing only that a thought was impossible because the thing was impossible, or, as the *Tractatus* puts it, 'Was man nicht denken kann, das kann man nicht denken': an *impossible* thought is an impossible *thought*. (*FPW*, p. xi)

We have already seen how Anscombe criticizes Hume's 'deducing what can be from what can hold of thought'; see Chapter 5, §2.3. And the form of her criticism gives us a clue as to why she sides with the ancients on this question. When she says 'because the thing was impossible', she does not mean anything meatily external by 'thing'—she is not gesturing towards some sort of 'metaphysical impossibility'. Her point, roughly, is that impossibility is a logical, not a psychological, matter. And in this, of course, she is at one with the early Wittgenstein.

One form of the question how thinkability and possibility are related has to do with false thought. If thinking what is false is thinking what is not real, how can there be false thoughts? How are false thoughts thinkable? As Plato puts it: 'In judging, one judges something; in judging something, one judges something

---

[3] See e.g. *Remarks on the Foundations of Mathematics*, ed. G. H. von Wright, R. Rhees, and G. E. M. Anscombe, trans. G. E. M. Anscombe (2nd edn., Oxford: Blackwell, 1967): Part I, Appendix I, para. 1–4 (p. 49). Wittgenstein's position might be put like this: 'Say, if you like, that a sentence with a propositional sense must have a truth-value; but then you must recognise that to ascribe a propositional sense to some string of symbols may often constitute a *decision*. One might instead construe the same string of symbols, e.g., as a command.' Cf. Part IV, para. 13 (pp. 140–1). It would be at least misleading to say that this leaves the later Wittgenstein on the same side of the fence as the author of the *Tractatus*, given the radically altered conception of 'proposition', 'sense', etc.

real; so in judging something unreal one judges nothing; but judging nothing, one is not judging at all' (*Theaetetus*, 189 A). (The passage is quoted in *IWT*; see p. 13 n. 1.) If false thoughts are *not* thinkable, that would seem to mean that what is false, being unthinkable, is also impossible—Parmenides' position.

Clearly one cannot get far with the question 'What is truth?' without having to face up to its brother, 'What is falsehood?'. And it is to these two questions that we now turn.

1. TRUTH

1.1. Truth and Falsehood

In the *Tractatus* we find the thought that a proposition is a logical picture. It has elements (names) that are correlated with things in the world; and it is *true* when the arrangement of those things is as the proposition says—which is to say, when the names of the things are arranged (concatenated) in a certain way. That the names are arranged in that way means that the things are arranged in a certain way. Note that the use made in the last sentence of the verb 'means' is of a word connecting two sentence-clauses. Wittgenstein speaks of a proposition, and indeed any logical picture, as itself a kind of fact (2.141)—namely, the fact that such-and-such names are arranged in such-and-such a way. A proposition is not a mere name, of a truth-value or anything else, nor is it a mere list of names.

This last point is connected with the fact that a picture can both say how things are and how things aren't. In *IWT*, Anscombe gives us a picture of two stick men fencing, and writes: 'if I have correlated the right-hand figure with a man A, and the left-hand figure with a man B, then I can hold the picture up and say: "This is how things are." But I can just as well hold the picture up and say: "This is how things aren't." ' (*IWT*, 65). And she points out that a set of figures correlated with men which couldn't be used in these two opposite ways would be a mere set of figures, analogous to a mere list of names.

To hold a picture up and say 'This is how things aren't' is to produce a negative proposition: *not P*. To *P* and *not-P* there do not correspond two pictures, but only one; it is the very same thing that *P* says to be the case that *not-P* denies to be the case: 'We must be careful not to confuse what is not the case with what is the case instead of it; if you tried to make a picture of a situation's *not* existing [different from the picture of its existing] you would only make a picture of what did exist instead of it' (*IWT*, 69–70). A picture of the cat on the sofa is not a picture of the cat's not being on the mat. The only possible picture of 'The cat is not on the mat' is a picture of the cat on the mat—accompanied by 'This is how things aren't'.

Anscombe does not swallow the whole of the picture theory of propositions. But she sees what is probably the most illuminating thing about Wittgenstein's comparison of propositions and pictures; namely, this Janus-faced aspect of a proposition, an aspect that can be expressed in various ways—as, that 'Not' doesn't correspond to anything in reality, or that P and not-P (the symbols) could be systematically swapped, each assuming the function of the other.[4] In a lecture given at the University of Navarre many years later ('La Verdad', 1983), Anscombe returned, not for the first time, to this theme. She mentions Joan of Arc as having used a code in which propositions were all to be taken in their opposite sense if a discreet cross were marked on the message: an example of an actual systematic swapping of P and not-P.

The question Anscombe raises in her lecture has to do with the primacy of truth over falsehood. For if P and not-P are both pictures of the same thing, meaning by that that they are identical pictures, then it seems that they will both bear a depictive (internal) relationship to the actual fact, whatever it is:

we might say, e.g., that 'p' signifies in the true way what 'not p' signifies in the false way [cf. *Tractatus*, 4.061]. What is wrong with saying that? What is the inequality between truth and falsehood, where you have the sort of proposition which can be true *or* false, and which is now one, now the other? For the false proposition does not lack all relationship to the fact. [. . .] It isn't meaningless, it *contains* the description of the fact which makes the other one [its negation] true.   (*V*, 49; pp. 4–5 of the original English MS)

But there clearly *is* a sense in which truth has a primacy over falsehood, a sense in which there exists an inequality between truth and falsehood. So what is that inequality?

Note that we cannot say that the inequality resides in a false proposition's depicting nothing, as opposed to something—nothing *real*, that is. For if all we can say of a false proposition is that it depicts nothing, we must surely agree with Plato that a false judgement is not a judgement at all: it is like a blank sheet of paper. Moreover, a question or command would in the same sense depict nothing real. Something positive has to be said about what a false proposition is, e.g. to distinguish it from questions and commands. That 'something' would seem to have to do with the *capacity* of any proposition, true or false, to depict a real fact. We might say that a true proposition has a realized, and a false one an unrealized, capacity to depict a fact. But when we say that a false proposition has this capacity, how are we so sure that it does? We appear to know this in advance of the proposition's being put to the test, as it were. And this of course is because in saying that a proposition has the capacity to depict a fact, we are saying nothing more than that it is a well-formed logical picture—i.e. the sort of thing which can be used to say either how things are or how they aren't, and which thus bears an internal relationship to what is actually the case, a relationship that one can imagine being dubbed either 'signifying in the true way' or 'signifying

---

[4] Cf. *Tractatus Logico-Philosophicus*, 4.0621. We find the thought also in Wittgenstein's later writings; e.g. para. 429 of the *Philosophical Investigations*, quoted by Anscombe in *IWT* (p. 70 n. 1).

in the false way', depending. Which brings us back to the problem about the primacy of truth.

It is a problem that St Anselm raised in his *De Veritate*, and Anscombe's 'La Verdad' is in fact a discussion of Anselm, whom she describes as an 'intellectual brother' of Wittgenstein on this subject. Anselm's solution of the problem consists in ascribing a *purpose* to assertion, that of saying what is the case. In this sense, truth, and not falsehood, is the goal of assertion. But what is it to use a sign (a picture, a proposition) to say what is the case? One clue here resides in the answer to another question, namely: Could we adopt the rule of using propositional signs to say what is *not* the case? The question is posed and answered by Wittgenstein thus:

Can we not make ourselves understood with false propositions just as we have done up till now with true ones? So long as it is known that they are meant to be false. No! For a proposition is true if we use it to say things stand in a certain way, and they do; and if by 'p' we mean not-p and things stand as we mean that they do, then, construed in the new way, 'p' is true and not false.[5]

Anscombe quotes this passage and asks: 'Does the general impossibility [of exchanging the roles of true and false] contain the whole substance of the "not equally justified relations"?' (pp. 11–12). That truth and falsehood do not bear equally *justified* relations to the things signified or depicted is what she takes Wittgenstein to have said at 4.061; she recommends this translation of the German 'gleichberechtigte' over others,[6] and also endorses the thought behind it, for reasons we shall come to in a moment. Now if it were simply a question of *some* sort of primacy of truth over falsehood, then we could rest content with the general impossibility of exchanging the roles of true and false. But as far as this general impossibility goes, '[i]t may give a primacy to truth over falsehood in theory of meaning; but why should truth be called a more *justified* relation because of that?' (*V*, 53; p. 12 of MS).

A natural response to this question is to invoke the way the propositional sign is used, in the rich sense of 'used' that is explored in Wittgenstein's later work. How a sign is used in a community is a matter of such phenomena as agreement, correction, mutual (mis)understanding, and so on. It is in virtue of such phenomena that the sign can be seen as having correct or incorrect uses; and it is surely the *correct use* of a propositional sign that gives us the paradigm for truth in a statement. The criterial test for whether someone grasps the sense of a propositional sign is whether they can use it correctly in a 'standard' situation, and such a use will count as a true assertion. (This can be admitted without our having to make the reductionist move of identifying truth and warranted

---

[5] *Tractatus Logico-Philosophicus*, 4.062, trans. D. F. Pears and B. F. McGuinness (London: Routledge, 1961).

[6] For example, that of Pears and McGuinness: 'otherwise one can easily suppose that true and false are relations *of equal status* between signs and what they signify' (my italics).

assertability.) But what is the correct use of a propositional sign if not a justified use of it? In this way, truth does indeed seem to constitute a justified relation to the thing signified.

For Anscombe, this response would only concern 'justification' as that notion appears in theory of meaning. As far as that notion goes, an 'unjustified' assertion is simply an incorrect use of language. But, as the distinction between linguistic error and factual error makes clear, false assertions frequently lack justification in quite another way—for example, when they are mistakes or lies. The goal of aiming at the truth goes beyond the norm of using words correctly, and this point seems unaffected by the thought that a correct use gives a paradigm of truth.

In Anselm's account of how truth serves as the goal of assertion, he describes truth as 'rightness perceptible to the intellect alone' (*rectitudo sola mente percepti-bilis*), a rightness that is to be found not only in propositions, but also in thought, will, action, and the being of things. This conception of 'true' as applying non-equivocally to (e.g.) actions as well as to propositions is a conception we have already encountered in our discussion of what Anscombe has to say about 'practical truth' (see Ch. 2, §3.3). I argued there that it was difficult to see the force of her claim that 'true' applies 'strictly and properly' to actions as well as to propositions, etc. But even were we to reject Anselm's (and Anscombe's) tran-scendental conception of truth as a kind of rightness running through different categories of thing, we would still be left with a challenge: what sort of norm is truth, beyond the norm of using words correctly? How does truth, and not falsehood, bear a 'justified relation' to the thing signified?

The answer can be found, I think, by turning to Anscombe's own explanation of practical necessity. That explanation has two strands: (i) an account of the nature of stopping/forcing modals; and (ii) an account of the Aristotelian necessity of our going in for the practice within which those modals have force. (See Ch. 3, §2.2.) The first strand encompasses the norms which attach to the use of linguistic expressions—as: 'You're meant to call that a cow.' These are the norms that relate, as Anscombe would say, to theory of meaning. But the practice of using language, like any other human practice, is one about which one can ask: Why do we go in for it? (If language is a bundle of practices, we can still ask of each practice: Why do we go in for it?) It is certain that human life would be almost inconceivably different were there no such thing as language, to the extent that if there are any distinctively human goods at all, language is essential to many or most of them. More than this, one can cite such general ends as recording history, calculating, sharing personal information, providing recipes, producing laughter, etc.

These ends are so varied that one is reminded of Wittgenstein's question: What does man think for? (*Philosophical Investigations*, para. 466.) Wittgenstein points out that it would be absurd to say, quite generally, that we think because we have found it advantageous to do so. Thinking, of course, can hardly be called a practice, in the sense in which language(s) is (are). But despite this difference, it would no doubt *also* be absurd to say that we go in for language because we have found that it is advantageous to do so. The 'advantages' of using language will not have been consciously aimed at, either before or after language got going. Nevertheless, as with many other practices—marriage, rearing of children, funeral rites—one can speak of the reasons why human beings go in for this one, or in other words, why it is a good thing for human beings to go in for it. Insofar as these reasons concern sharing information, cooperating in various ways, etc., the norm that one's assertions should be true appears explicable; more than that, it appears essential—essential for speakers to adopt it *as* a norm, for familiar reasons to do with rationality and mutual knowledge. (If it were not a social norm, that would mean that people knew it wasn't, in which case they wouldn't have any reason to trust what others say—which in turn would mean that people would have little reason to say anything to one another.) This norm of aiming at the truth is connected with the norm which gives truth primacy over falsehood in theory of meaning, but it goes beyond it in this way: one who intentionally flouts the norm (who lies, that is) can be seen as wronging an individual or individuals, since those individuals have a default right to be properly informed simply in virtue of the communicative situation. A liar not only thwarts the general aims of human communication, he typically thwarts, or tries to thwart, another person's aims. (And we may include among such aims the simple one of knowing what is the case.)

Now although I have invoked Anscombe's own account of practical necessity in giving an answer to her question, 'How does truth, not falsehood, bear a *justified* relation to the thing signified?', I suspect that my answer would not in fact satisfy her. Her attitude to lying is not so much that it is a wrong against another (though of course it usually is), nor that it is the flouting of a norm necessary for human beings, as that it is an offence against truth itself. We must not forget that this issue is for Anscombe a religious, as well as a social or ethical, one. At the start of 'La Verdad', she writes: 'Looking at my title ['Truth'] I am sometimes awed by it, for what leaps out of the page at me is one of the names of God' (*V*, 47; p. 1 of MS).

God as Truth—this is Anselm's notion of the *summa veritas*. It is a notion that perhaps has something of the mystical about it. That Anscombe was not opposed to the idea of there being mysteries or mystical truths is something we shall be returning to in §2. But let us now turn to another lecture dating from around the same time as 'La Verdad', in which variety, not transcendental unity, is stressed: the variety of ways in which a proposition can be *made* true.

1.2. Truth-Makers and Truth-Conditions

As was said above, the *Tractatus* is often taken to be a *locus classicus* of the correspondence theory of truth. For Wittgenstein, a true proposition corresponds to a fact, this correspondence being in virtue of the logical form shared by fact and proposition. A special status is accorded those facts corresponding to elementary propositions, called *Sachverhalte* (which following Anscombe I translate 'atomic facts'): in a crucial sense, these are all the facts there are. For non-elementary propositions are simply truth-functions of elementary ones, and so their truth has to do only with what *Sachverhalte* exist (see 4.4: 'A proposition is an expression of agreement and disagreement with truth-possibilities of elementary propositions' and 4.41: 'Truth-possibilities of elementary propositions are the conditions of the truth and falsity of propositions').

With a true disjunctive proposition, 'P or Q', whose constituent propositions are elementary, we can ask: which atomic fact or facts make the whole proposition true? And the answer will be one of 'The fact that P', 'The fact that Q', or 'Both the fact that P and the fact that Q'. Of course a proposition, 'P or Q', may be a disjunction of non-elementary propositions; so if we ask what makes such a disjunction true, an answer such as 'The fact that P' will be a preliminary answer only, for Wittgenstein—for what makes 'P' true in this instance is certain further fact(s). The termini of the series of truth-makers will be certain atomic facts, and it is these facts that would have to be mentioned ultimately in answer to the original question: 'What makes "P or Q" true?'

The notion of *making true* applies very naturally to non-elementary propositions. In a lecture delivered to the Oxford Philosophical Society in 1982, 'Making True', Anscombe begins with such propositions; specifically, *either-or* propositions and *some* propositions (disjunctions and existential statements). She points out that one can say what makes a proposition true simply by giving, i.e. by asserting, a further proposition: 'if it is said that some elements have a certain property, the question may arise which do. Suppose someone says that iodine and chlorine do. He purports to have told us what makes the "some" proposition true' (*MT*, 1). 'Iodine and chlorine have such-and-such a property' is an ordinary statement. It is not a noun-phrase of the form 'The fact that P'. There is as yet no hint of a 'metaphysics of facts', nor yet of a general theory of 'making true' for all propositions. The question what makes a proposition true is so far pretty unmysterious. But one or two points need to be noted straight away. Anscombe mentions these: (a) several facts can, each one, make a single proposition true, and (b) to say what makes a proposition true will not *ipso facto* be to give the sense of the proposition; nor will to list all the facts or combinations of facts that could make it true be to give its sense.

As to (a), the person who cites iodine and chlorine 'wouldn't be contradicted by someone who gave other ones [sc. elements], but not iodine and chlorine' (*MT*, 1). The *some* proposition is made true by iodine's being F, by chlorine's being F, by their both being F, by other elements' being F—and so on. A similar thing goes for disjunctions. One could indeed say that the proposition in question is made true by all of its confirming instances; but 'all' could be replaced by 'all or any' here. If a person denies the truth of 'Someone's smoking in this building', then he is *completely* refuted by the observation that Sonia is smoking in the building—you don't have to mention any others who may also be smoking. The idea that a full and proper answer to 'What makes it true?' would mention all confirming instances is thus unjustified. And behind this idea stands a wrong picture:

If a disjunction is true because more than one of its elements is true, then more than one makes it true. Is this like more than one man hauling on a rope in the same direction? Each is strong enough to haul the weight that is hauled; so either they haul it quicker than either would alone, or they each have to do less work, the labour being shared. Perhaps we can answer questions about who really does the work or how much each does. But it can't be like that with two elements of a disjunction, both true. This warns us against the idea of a work done, or a force exerted, in making true.   (*MT*, 2)

What about (b)?—It is clear that you wouldn't give the sense of 'P or Q or R' by mentioning the single fact that P (say). But it may well be claimed that you can give the sense of the disjunction by listing all the *possible* ways in which it could be made true, by one or more elements from the set of possible facts: {P, Q, R}. This would be to give the truth-table for 'P or Q or R', and thereby the truth-conditions of 'P or Q or R'. Anscombe allows that to do such a thing may count as giving an explanation of the meaning of 'P or Q or R'. But in giving the truth-table for 'P or Q or R', does one in fact supply an *equivalent* proposition? 'Only if you form a disjunction of the whole set [of possible truth-makers] will you have an equivalent. But what's the good of that, when it was the sense of a disjunction that you wanted to explain? You could go on forever in that way' (*MT*, 1).

The sense of a proposition can be explained (elucidated, conveyed…) by means other than that of supplying an equivalent proposition. You could, for example, use the proposition in question in a suitable context—as: 'The book is the direct object' (cf. Ch. 4, pp. 132–3). And another approach is to list some or all of the proposition's truth-conditions, or possible truth-makers. But for a disjunctive proposition, listing the truth-conditions would only give us an equivalent proposition if the list were replaced by a disjunction. One who did not already understand disjunction would therefore not understand an explanation of the disjunctive proposition in terms of such an equivalent proposition.

Now Anscombe is not saying that an explanation of an expression's sense that could only be understood by one who already understood the expression (or an equivalent) is necessarily futile. For one thing, such an explanation may come in the course of a philosophical investigation of the expression; for example, an investigation of 'It was the case that' (and more generally, of the past tense). Anscombe's own account of the meaning of past-tense sentences is explicitly such as could only be understood by one who already grasped the past tense, as we have seen (cf. Ch. 5, pp. 169–71). So what is the point of her remark about one's needing already to have grasped disjunction in order to grasp any truth-conditional equivalent of 'P or Q'? The answer, I think, is that she is pointing out the emptiness of the claim that to give a disjunctive proposition's truth-conditions is to *give its sense*. There are two main sorts of context for a philosopher's claiming that in giving a proposition's truth-conditions, one gives its sense: (i) that of providing a philosophical account of that proposition (and/or ones like it); or (ii) that of saying what a grasp of that proposition consists in. In both cases, the statement of truth-conditions must amount to something *sufficiently independent* of the proposition in question. This independence, as I've said, need not be such that it must be possible for a person to understand the statement of truth-conditions who didn't already understand the proposition; but if the statement of truth-conditions is too close to the proposition itself, then the goal—either of (i) or of (ii)—will not have been achieved.

It is (ii), more than (i), that is Anscombe's concern in 'Making True'. A useful equivalent of 'P or Q' in terms of truth-conditions, she says, is impossible—useful, that is, for understanding what (a grasp of) the proposition's sense consists in. Once it is recognized that a statement of truth-conditions for 'P or Q' must be taken as a disjunction—for remember that the list of those conditions, as a mere list, *could* be taken as (converted into) a conjunction, say—once this is recognized, it becomes evident that not much light has been cast on what it is that someone grasps who grasps the sense of a disjunction.

The point is made again in connection with other kinds of proposition about which it is natural to ask, 'What makes this true?'—and hence of which it is natural to want to talk of the truth-conditions (possible truth-makers). With many such propositions, giving the truth-conditions will only be feasible if those truth-conditions are scarcely independent of the proposition itself—as with the disquotational device: 'P' is true iff P. For the *independently* stateable truth-conditions of such propositions will be open-ended, in a way that precludes listing them.

What does it consist in, that p?—in this case? or ever?

There are plenty of cases where we know there must be an answer to the first question, and plenty where we can give some 'for example' answers to the second, though it is obvious that there isn't a complete list of possible answers which could tell what it might consist in. (*MT*, 5)

The thought is familiar to us from 'On Brute Facts' (see Ch. 3, pp. 93–4). We saw in our discussion of that article how my owing the grocer £10 may consist in my having been to his shop, his having supplied me with potatoes, etc. In other words, 'I owe the grocer £10' would be *made true* by my having been to his shop, his having supplied me with potatoes, etc. One can describe the truth-maker(s) in terms independent of the original proposition, terms that are 'brute' relative to it. But one cannot list all the possible truth-makers of the sentence 'RT owes the grocer £10'—one cannot, that is, give its truth-conditions.

There are two lessons here. The first has to do with the open-endedness of the set of truth-conditions for 'RT owes the grocer £10'. The second is that sentences such as this pose a problem for the view that a truth-condition (possible truth-maker) for a proposition is a condition whose obtaining suffices for the truth of the proposition. For, as Anscombe shows in *BF*, only a condition that included indefinitely many negative conditions (as: that we aren't acting in a play) could entail the truth of 'RT owes the grocer £10'—and no such complex condition can be stated. Both of these lessons throw doubt on the view that to understand a proposition is to grasp its truth-conditions, unless 'grasp' is being used in a fairly eccentric and as yet unexplained way. And the second lesson indicates how knowing the sense of a proposition must *outstrip* knowing its truth-conditions: for to know the sense of an 'owes' proposition, I must be able to identify preventing circumstances (that we're in a play, etc.) when they crop up; while to know that a truth-condition actually obtains, I do *not* need to know, in any positive way, that there are no preventing circumstances. All I need to know is such things as that the grocer supplied me with potatoes, and so on. And it is because I only need cognisance of such things that they merit the title of *conditions that make the 'owes' proposition true*. But since truth-conditions are simply possible truth-makers, my knowing the truth-conditions of a proposition like 'RT owes the grocer £10', were it even possible, would still fall short of a full understanding of that sentence, which involves my also being able to identify preventing circumstances.

All in all, then, it seems that Anscombe is opposed to the view that the canonical way to give a proposition's sense is by giving its truth-conditions.[7] This is not to say that she would willingly sever the link between a proposition's sense and its truth-*value*—rather the contrary, as we saw above (pp. 192–3). The argument in *IWT* to which I there referred takes the following form: the models of sense that have been proposed when it has been mooted that propositions may lack a truth-value fail to justify the moot. Those models include, notably, the Fregean model of sense as determined by truth-conditions. But the Strawsonian model of sense as assertability-conditions[8] fares no better, according to Anscombe; and the problem, in both cases, lies with associating sense with a set of stateable *conditions* at all. The issue here is one of overall consistency, it is true: Anscombe's argument is not intended to refute either model of sense, merely to show how neither model justifies a departure from the principle of bivalence. But since, as we have seen, she *was* wary of these models (certainly at the time she wrote *MT*), her argument is worth recounting, not only as casting light on her attitude to

---

[7] In 'Sentences and Propositions' (in Teichmann (ed.), *Logic, Cause and Action*, 9–23), Michael Dummett interprets what Anscombe says in *MT* as showing that she endorses the view that '[A proposition's] meaning is given by giving a comprehensive account of the conditions under which it is true' (p. 18). The sentence quoted is used by Anscombe in an imaginary dialogue, whose purpose is to show up what she thinks is a bad argument for the view that a truth-conditional account of meaning is incompatible with a 'redundancy' account of 'It is true that P'. Since she explicitly endorses (at least one version of) the latter, it is perhaps tempting to take her here as also endorsing the former; but this is not her aim, as I think a careful reading of the relevant passage makes clear (ibid. 5).   [8] As expressed in Strawson's 'On Referring,' *Mind*, 59 (1950), 320–44.

bivalence, but as casting light on her attitude to truth-conditional accounts of meaning:

> The propositions embodying the truth-conditions, or describing the circumstances in which a sentence could be used to make a statement, must themselves be either true or false, or require explanation in terms of further truth-conditions, or further circumstances. In view of this, the Frege-Strawson position on the possibility of sentences without truth-value appears to be a waste of time: in such an account the concept of 'sense' is not [after all] divorced from those of truth and falsehood; it is merely determined that when certain of the truth-conditions of a proposition are false [e.g. when there is no King of France, the proposition being 'The King of France is bald'] we are to say that 'nothing either true or false has been said'.   (*IWT*, 60)

The passage is not intended as an argument for the principle of bivalence, since it more or less assumes that principle as the default position ('The propositions [. . .] must themselves be either true or false, or ... '). Rather, it is an attempt to undermine a kind of attack upon that principle. As such, it surely has considerable force.

Returning to the main topic of 'Making True': what of the thesis that every true proposition is made true by something? This thesis is a form of the correspondence theory of truth, and is no less popular today than when Wittgenstein wrote the *Tractatus*. Anscombe writes:

> If what makes something true is something else—that is to say, the truth of a proposition which is not equivalent to the first—then it looks as if we had to say: 'This can't go on forever: we must come at last to the case where what makes "p" true is just that p.' Now I want to say that this is not right.   (*MT*, 7)

We began by describing cases of certain propositions' being made true by others—*either-or* propositions and *some* propositions. There are other cases, too; Anscombe mentions two main kinds, exemplified by (a) 'That is the French flag' and (b) 'That behaviour was hypocritical' (*MT*, 2–3). In answering 'What makes (a) true?', we would give a formal cause—roughly, a definition—along the lines of: 'That it's 3 vertical stripes, that sort of width, of red, white, and blue'. In answering 'What makes (b) true?', things are somewhat more complicated, relying as they do on an extra step, of *interpretation*. An interpretation may lead us to a description of events that is definitionally connected to the concept of hypocrisy: 'I recount events and imply an interpretation apparently amounting to hypocrisy. This description would be of a formal cause' (*MT*, 2–3). The interpretation presumably allows for the possibility of further defeating evidence, and in this respect (b) will be similar to 'RT owes the grocer £10'—which last, with other institutional propositions, could form a third class of propositions that are 'made true'. And there may be yet others. To these different classes of proposition there correspond different ways, or senses, in which a proposition is made true. And this point is crucial: for it can't be said that we have a clear and univocal concept of *making true* prior to explanations in terms of these various cases. If one began with 'making true' as it applies to 'P or Q', it is obvious that one could not just say: 'Take *that* sense of "making true"—it's in that sense that I want you to understand the thesis that every proposition is made true by something.' If it is claimed that every proposition is made true by something, we may ask *both* what sense of 'make true' is meant, *and* how this applies to any given proposition.

The general principle, that what is true must be made true by something, can't be rebutted by calling in question *any* idea of making true, but it is rebutted if we demand that the particular manner of making true be given for the question that is being asked when one asks what, if anything, makes a certain proposition true.   (*MT*, 8)

Anscombe's philosophical method here is essentially the one characterized in the *Tractatus* as appropriate 'whenever someone else wanted to say something metaphysical': 'to demonstrate to him that he had failed to give a meaning to certain signs in his propositions'.[9]

The problem for the correspondence theory is acute because of the need for a terminus of any series of truth-makers. ('P or Q' is made true by 'P'; 'P' is made true by 'R', etc.) As we have seen, the canonical way of answering 'What makes P true?' is by giving, i.e. by asserting, some proposition. And to assert P itself, in answer to 'What makes P true?', is evidently futile. Truth-makers, like truth-conditions, ought to be independently stateable. So it seems that the propositions that are the termini of series of truth-makers must themselves be true without being made true. The only way to avoid this, Anscombe argues, is by adopting 'a Tractatus-like metaphysic of facts', with elementary propositions being made true by the existence of atomic facts (*MT*, 8). This might seem to offer solace to a latter-day correspondence theorist. But (though it's not clear whether Anscombe meant this) the requisite Tractatus-like metaphysic would surely have to be one whereby the role of facts as truth-makers is *unsayable*. For if you say or report an atomic fact, you do so simply by asserting the corresponding elementary proposition; and we have just seen that saying 'P' in answer to 'What makes P true?' achieves nothing. Thus if an atomic fact makes an elementary proposition true in any non-trivial way, this isn't something that can be said. Whether the average friend of truth-makers would be happy with this state of affairs is an interesting question.

2. SENSE, NONSENSE, AND MYSTERY

2.1. Saying and Showing

That an elementary proposition is made true by an atomic fact was indeed, for Wittgenstein, something that could not be said. It is well known that the *Tractatus*

---

[9] *Tractatus Logico-Philosophicus*, 6.53, trans. Pears and McGuinness.

restricts quite severely the range of what can be said, of what is meaningful. But Wittgenstein speaks also of what can be shown (to show = *zeigen*). Attempts to say what can only be shown result in nonsense; and Wittgenstein includes the propositions of the *Tractatus* itself among such attempts. Why then write down those propositions? The answer is that nonsense of this kind can be illuminating:

My propositions serve as elucidations in the following way: anyone who understands me eventually recognises them as nonsensical, when he has used them—as steps—to climb up beyond them. (He must, so to speak, throw away the ladder after he has climbed up it.)

He must transcend these propositions, and then he will see the world aright. [10]

A piece of nonsense can be philosophically useful for the following reason: if a philosopher, bewitched by language, propounds something that is not so much false as nonsensical, then to oppose him by negating what he has said will be to produce more nonsense. For the negation of gobbledygook is itself gobbledygook. This might just seem to be a consequence of the picture theory of propositions, with its insistence that a meaningful proposition have true–false poles. And anyway, aren't there other ways of opposing philosophical statements than by negating them? Despite the fact that the answer to this last question is assuredly Yes, and independently of the merits or otherwise of the picture theory, it is difficult to give an account of what the rejection of philosophical confusion consists in that does not provide for the possibility of illuminating nonsense. Anscombe is clearly aware of that possibility, and goes so far as to refer to the corollary of illumination here as 'philosophic truth'. In the light of her endorsement of Anselm's conception of truth as 'transcendental', and hence as applicable not only to meaningful propositions, this may not surprise us; see §2.1 above.

This idea of philosophic truth [expressed at 6.54 of the *Tractatus*] would explain one feature of philosophy: what a philosopher declares to be philosophically false is supposed not to be possible or even really conceivable; the false ideas which he conceives himself to be attacking must be presented as chimaeras, as not really thinkable thoughts at all. Or, as Wittgenstein put it: An *impossible* thought is an impossible *thought* (5.61)—and that is why it is not possible to say what it is that cannot be thought; it can only be forms of words or suggestions of the imagination that are attacked.   (*IWT*, 163)

An example of philosophic truth in the form of nonsense might be 'The past cannot change'. We saw how Anscombe approached that proposition in Chapter 5 (pp. 174–5): by such methods as pointing out the senselessness of questions like 'When was the Battle of Hastings in 1066?'. The temptation to be resisted was that of imputing to 'The past can change' a sort of nonsensical sense. At best, the proposition is just a 'form of words', conveying only 'a suggestion of the imagination'—such as the sort of imaginings that H. G. Wells's *The Time Machine*

---

[10] Ibid. 6.54, trans. Pears and McGuinness.

might induce in a reader. 'The past cannot change', then, does not state a truth in any straightforward sense—for its negation is not false, but rather senseless.

But of course Anscombe does not simply state 'The past cannot change' in opposition to 'The past can change'. Rather, she examines such things as our use of the past tense, how it might be taught and learnt, how 'When ... ?' questions are taught and used, and so on. These investigations are what appear to bring enlightenment, not pieces of illuminating nonsense. And a philosopher might set up as a contrast with the doctrine of 6.54 that of para. 90 of the *Philosophical Investigations*: 'We remind ourselves[...] of the *kind of statement* that we make about phenomena'—this, despite our initially feeling 'as if we had to *penetrate* phenomena'. Cannot the whole saying/showing distinction be done without? Isn't the right method in philosophy in fact to say what's sayable, and specifically what's sayable about language and the role it plays in our life and thought?

The problem is that assembling reminders of how we talk may not persuade. What will actually persuade a person depends on the person. (If we follow Wittgenstein, of course, we will gloss 'persuade X' as 'turn X from wanting to say those things'.) It may, for example, be persuasive if you treat the person's philosophical utterance as if it *were* a substantive claim. But still, 'Even if for purposes of argument you bring it into contempt by treating it as an hypothesis, what you infer from it is not a contradiction but an incoherence' (*IWT*, 163). And this is certainly part of the later Wittgenstein's armoury, as we find at para. 464 of the *Investigations*: 'My aim is: to teach you to pass from a piece of disguised nonsense to something that is patent nonsense.'

However, such patent nonsense is not itself illuminating, even if the process of being induced to look it in the face is. (Not: 'of being induced to recognize it as following from what one has said', since mere nonsense doesn't follow from anything, strictly speaking.) The same would appear to go for the negation of patent nonsense. So we are still left with the query about the possibility of illuminating nonsense, as also about the pointfulness of the saying/showing distinction. Many of the logical positivists upon whom the *Tractatus* had an influence were unimpressed by these aspects of Wittgenstein's thought, particularly where they led on to remarks about the mystical (e.g. 6.522). In a footnote, Anscombe records that 'I once had occasion to remark to Wittgenstein that he was supposed to have a mystical streak. "Like a yellow streak", he replied; and that is pretty well how the Vienna Circle felt about certain things in the *Tractatus*' (*IWT*, 82 n. 1).

Mere disdain, however, could never be an adequate response; for the saying/showing doctrine is actually put forward as a solution (if that is the word) of certain intractable-seeming paradoxes and difficulties. Those difficulties arise when trying to speak on the most general logical topics, e.g. concerning names and predicates, objects and concepts. For Wittgenstein, such attempts were attempts to speak of 'the logic of the world', or 'of the facts' (the world being the totality of facts).

'Sentences [. . .] cannot represent, and nothing in them can stand for, "the logic of the facts": they can only reproduce it. An attempt to say what it is that they so reproduce leads to stammering' (*IWT*, 164). Perhaps the most salient example of such stammering is that of Frege, in connection with the distinction between objects and concepts. Frege introduces concepts as the referents of predicates. But if you try to say what the predicate 'is a horse' refers to, you end up referring to an object—for you can only say, 'It refers to the concept *horse*', and 'the concept *horse*', being a singular term or Fregean name, must refer not to a concept but to an object.[11] Still (Frege thought), a predicative expression does refer. So it seems that what it refers to cannot be said, but only shown—shown in the use of the expression *as* a predicative expression. 'The expression "is a horse" refers to a concept' appears to be an attempt to say what can only be shown.

A positivist, unhappy with the saying/showing distinction and all that with it goes, would have to suggest some alternative way of dealing with the paradox of the concept *horse* and similar paradoxes. And one of them did indeed do so—Carnap. His idea was to translate what Wittgenstein regarded as attempts to say what can only be shown into 'the formal mode of speech', i.e. into statements about expressions. '*Horse* is a concept' would be replaced by ' "is a horse" is a predicate'; 'Gottlob is an object' by ' "Gottlob" is a name'; and so forth. This is a version of the idea just mentioned, that philosophical problems are to be solved by talking about our language. The statements in formal mode avoid the problems like the one encountered by Frege, and count, by the criteria of the *Tractatus*, as meaningful propositions with true-false poles: for 'Gottlob', considered just as a noise or shape, might have been an adverb and not a name.

Anscombe discusses Carnap's view, and writes: 'It is an essential part of Carnap's view that the convention of forming the name of a word by writing it in quotes is *wholly* arbitrary [. . .] "red" *as a word* no more occurs in its name ' "red" ' [NB. double quotes for the name of a name] than it does in "predatory" ' (*IWT*, 83). Why is Carnap committed to this view concerning the names of words? The reason is that only on such a view will the relevant propositions have true–false poles. But consider the sentence ' "Someone" is not the name of someone':

This is obviously true. But it does not have the bipolarity of Wittgenstein's 'significant propositions'. For what is it that it denies to be the case? Evidently, that 'someone' is the name of someone. But what would it be for 'someone' to be the name of someone? Someone might christen his child 'Someone'. But when we say ' "Someone" is not the name of someone', we are not intending to deny that anyone in the world has the odd name 'Someone'. (*IWT*, 85)

We are not, that is, talking about the noise or shape, 'Someone', but about the word—or as Wittgenstein would put it in the *Tractatus*, about the symbol: that

---

[11] See Frege, 'On Concept and Object', in *Translations from the Philosophical Writings*, ed. Geach and Black, 42–55.

is, about what is common to all signs with the same logical function as the English word 'Someone'. But as far as the *symbol* 'Someone' goes, it could not be the case that *it* functioned as the name of somebody. There is, however, a point to saying ' "Someone" is not the name of someone', meaning thereby to talk of the symbol. For a philosopher might want to say, *of the symbol,* that its function is to refer to somebody; this would be a species of philosophical error, one actually committed by some logicians when struggling to explain, e.g., the difference between 'Someone' and 'No-one' (*IWT*, 85). (Such logicians may betray the muddle they are in by calling to their aid signs to which no proper meaning has been attached, as: 'refer indefinitely to'. Cf. *Tractatus Logico-Philosophicus,* 6.53.) Whereas the assertion that no child has been baptized 'Someone', were it even worth making, would not count as a philosophical or logical assertion at all.

Now Carnap could of course respond that ' "Someone" is not the name of someone' can be called illuminating nonsense, if that means only: (a) that it's nonsense, and (b) that it's the syntactic negation of a piece of nonsense typical of philosophers. And if someone wanted, confusedly, to say of the symbol 'red' that it is not a predicate, then our assertion ' "Red" *is* a predicate' might have to count as a piece of counter-nonsense after all. This would still leave untouched the meaningful proposition ' "Red" is a predicate', interpreted as a proposition about a noise or shape; and it is surely facts about how actual people use the noise/shape which underlie the classification of 'red' as a certain sort of logical symbol—as a predicate, in fact.

As Anscombe says, Carnap is committed to the view that 'the convention of forming the name of a word by writing it in quotes is *wholly* arbitrary'. Only thus will ' "Red" is a predicate' have true–false poles. And this will have to go also for the following proposition:

(S) 'Smith' is the name of Smith.

On the Carnapian view, another convention could exist, according to which (S) was replaced, say, by:

(S′) Plonk is the name of Smith.

Just as 'Smith' is the name of a man, so 'Plonk' would be the name of a name (Smith's name).

The idea that such a convention could exist, however, leads to a paradox, the discovery of which Anscombe attributes to the Czech logician K. Reach.[12] She states the paradox thus:

It is impossible to be told anyone's name by being told 'That man's name is "Smith" '; for then his name is named, not used as a name, in that statement, and so what I hear is the name of his name and not his name; and I can only learn his name if I know what

---

[12] K. Reach, 'The Name Relation and the Logical Antinomies', in *Journal of Symbolic Logic,* 3 (Sept. 1938), 97–111.

name this name-of-a-name is a name of, just as I can only obey the order 'Fetch a red one' if I know what colour the colour-word 'red' is a name of. (*IWT*, 84)

Could a person know what the name-of-a-name ' "Smith" ' was a name of? Not if the relation between the name of a word and the word is wholly arbitrary. To see this, we can suppose (S') to be the case. Jill asks what that man over there is called, and the reply comes: 'His name is Plonk.' For Jill to understand this, she must understand the expression 'Plonk'—she must, that is, have had it explained to her at some time. And she could not have had it explained to her by someone's answering her question 'What is the name of that word?', asked of (what *we* would call) the word 'Smith', as it occurs on a piece of paper, say; for the answer to such a question would consist in uttering a name of 'Plonk', related to 'Plonk' only arbitrarily—as it might be, 'Jimbo'. And so on and so on. Of course, the meaning of a word can in fact be explained by using it, so that one can explain 'Smith' by saying 'That man is Smith' (as opposed to ' "Smith" is the name of that man'). But this does not impugn Anscombe's point, which can be put thus: if there is to *be* such a thing as a name of a name of X, it must be an expression that may be informatively used when answering the question 'What is X's name?'. And such a condition can only be met if the relationship between name and name-of-name is not arbitrary.

The lesson is that if I am to be told what Smith's name is, I must in a certain sense be *given his name*, and not the name of something else (e.g. a word). It is necessary for the convention by which we talk about names to be such as to yield sentences like (S), and not (only) sentences like (S'). Sentences that are like (S) in the relevant respect come in more than one variety, to be sure.[13] Anscombe explains matters thus:

there must be a systematic connection between a name and its name such that a person can form the name of the name from mere acquaintance with *it* [the name], and know what name the name of a name is a name of on hearing it. This contrasts with what ordinarily holds for objects and their names. (*ACTP*, 222)

The proposition (S), in fact, has a quasi-necessary status: anyone who understands it knows it must be true. Whether 'understanding' is here taken to include knowing that 'Smith' is a non-empty name is a further question, which we need not go into. What is worth noting is that the quasi-necessary status to which I have alluded is compatible with there being *a* sense in which (S) is non-necessary: for of course (as Kripke would remind us) Smith might not have been called 'Smith', for instance if he had changed his name to 'Jones' by deed poll. This interpretation of (S) corresponds to the interpretation of ' "Someone" is not the name of someone' as meaning that nobody has been christened 'Someone'.

---

[13] e.g. the convention could be that Smith's name was given by spelling it out, 'S-M-I-T-H'. All that would then be needed would be 'a preliminary training in stepping from a letter-by-letter presentation of a word to the ordinary (continuous) reading of the word', as the winner of Anscombe's *Analysis* problem, the so-called Al Tajtelbaum, puts it. See *ACTP*, 223.

Our discussion of Reach's puzzle has focused on names, and the form of it presented by Anscombe relates only to names ('How is it possible to be told someone's name?'). But the nature of the puzzle is quite general, as is its solution: the name of any expression must be non-arbitrarily connected with that expression. We begin with words; if we are to talk *about* those words, using names of them, then the form of question 'What word is N a name of?' becomes possible; but such a question, and the answer to it, will employ the name of the name of a word; so unless the connection between word and name-of-word (and between name-of-word and name-of-name-of-word) is non-arbitrary, we are never able to get back to the primary level of words, those things which we were actually trying to talk about in the first place.

What might be called the Reach–Anscombe thesis thus appears to block Carnap's proposal that adopting the formal mode of speech is an adequate response to Frege's paradox of the concept *horse* (and similar paradoxes). This does not in itself force Wittgenstein's saying/showing distinction upon us as the only available response to the paradox; a much simpler line to take would be that of denying that predicates refer to anything—the same going for number words, sentences, adverbs, and so on. But in her discussion of Carnap, who is a representative of a very natural urge to dissolve philosophical problems by 'going metalinguistic', Anscombe does show us how space has to be made for useful nonsense, in particular because philosophical error very often takes the form of *confusion*, not of *mistakes*. ' "Someone" refers to someone'; 'One might travel into the past'; 'The actual world is just one among a plurality of worlds'—such statements are not adequately countered by stating, or attempting to state, the negations of them. And rephrasing them as statements about words, i.e. about signs (not symbols), will yield contingent falsehoods that can at least appear to bypass genuine philosophical worries.

2.2. Mystery

For the Wittgenstein of the *Tractatus*, those things that are shown, or which show themselves, though they cannot be said (or thought), can nevertheless be seen or understood. The person who throws away the ladder of 6.54 'sees the world aright'. Into the category of things shown or made manifest, Wittgenstein puts ethical and aesthetic matters, writing:

It is clear that ethics cannot be put into words.

Ethics is transcendental.

(Ethics and aesthetics are one and the same.)[14]

What cannot be said cannot be thought; so there are no ethical or aesthetic thoughts, strictly speaking. But Wittgenstein clearly did not think that ethics and

---

[14] *Tractatus Logico-Philosophicus*, 6.421, trans. Pears and McGuinness.

aesthetics are *nothing*—and he was keenly interested in the desire to put into words what cannot be put into words, regarding it not merely as an aberration, but as a deep-seated tendency of the human mind. In his 'Lecture on Ethics' of 1929, he cites certain experiences, saying of them that their natural expression takes the form of utterances which can only count as nonsensical, as attempts to '*go beyond* the world and that is to say beyond significant language'. These experiences and utterances he takes to be at the heart of ethics, about which he writes: 'it is a document of a tendency in the human mind which I personally cannot help respecting deeply and I would not for my life ridicule it'.[15]

To ethics and aesthetics should be added religion. Anscombe mentions how, at a meeting of the Moral Science Club, Wittgenstein took St Augustine's assertion of God that he moves without moving 'as a contradiction in intent', wishing 'at the same time to treat it with respect'. She connects this respect for what is nonsensical or contradictory with Wittgenstein's 'dislike of rationality, or would-be rationality, in religion': 'He would describe this with a characteristic simile: there is something all jagged and irregular, and some people have a desire to encase it in a smooth ball: looking within you see the jagged edges and spikes, but a smooth surface has been constructed. He preferred it left jagged.' And she remarks: 'I don't know how to distribute this between philosophical observation on the one hand and personal reaction on the other' (*QLI*, 122).

It might be thought that a religious person who regards certain articles of faith as 'mysteries' is more or less bound to embrace nonsense or self-contradiction; for what *is* a mystery such as that of the Trinity, or of the Incarnation, or of Eucharistic Transubstantiation, if not something whose appearance of incoherence cannot be dispelled by reason? If somebody utters 'I believe' in connection with such mysteries, won't we be entitled to say, along with Wittgenstein: 'But is this a belief, a thought, at all? Perhaps there is a state of enlightenment, or an urge to find expression for certain experiences of life—but for there to be a belief, you would need to be able, at least in principle, to state that belief clearly and without contradiction'?

In 'Parmenides, Mystery and Contradiction', Anscombe considers the view that 'can be grasped in thought' amounts to 'can be presented in a sentence which can be seen to have an unexceptionable non-contradictory sense' (*PMC*, 8). She explicitly compares this view with that expressed in the Preface to the *Tractatus*, that 'whatever can be said at all can be said clearly'. Having in mind Wittgenstein's notion of what is shown or made manifest, she goes on:

Someone who thought this *might* think 'There may be the inexpressible'. And so in that sense think 'There may be what can't be thought'. But he wouldn't be exercised by any definite claimant to be that which can't be grasped in thought. *Mystery* would be illusion—either the thought expressing something mysterious could be clarified, and then

---

[15] 'A Lecture on Ethics', in *Philosophical Occasions 1912–1951*, ed. Klagge and Nordmann, 44.

no mystery, or the impossibility of clearing it up would show it was really a non-thought. (*PMC*, 8)

The issue is of what can or cannot be clarified or expressed clearly. Note that the candidate gloss on 'can be grasped in thought' is not 'can be presented in a sentence which *has* an unexceptionable non-contradictory sense', but rather 'can be presented in a sentence which *can be seen to have* an unexceptionable non-contradictory sense'. Could these two phrases be non-equivalent? One is tempted to say: 'If a sentence has a non-contradictory sense, then it can *in principle* be seen to have one—and *vice versa*.' The function of the phrase 'in principle' would be to indicate that a merely psychological or empirical inability to grasp something is irrelevant to our enquiry. A logical formula may be too long for any human being to calculate its sense in a lifetime; but for all that (the thought goes) the formula would, if well formed, have a determinate sense. Something like this view must, I think, be attributed to the Wittgenstein of the *Tractatus*. The later Wittgenstein would reject it; hence his remarks to the effect that an unsurveyable proof in mathematics is not a real proof.[16] It is an interesting question whether the later Wittgenstein can still be seen as committed to the equivalence mentioned by Anscombe, between 'can be grasped in thought' and 'can be presented in a sentence which can be seen to have an unexceptionable non-contradictory sense', given a reading of 'can be seen to have' which connects it with empirical human possibility. Whatever the answer to that question, the equivalence is rejected by Anscombe; or rather it is taken as wanting justification, as is shown by the closing words of *PMC*, which follow on immediately after the passage just quoted: 'The trouble is, there doesn't seem to be any ground for holding this position. It is a sort of prejudice' (*PMC*, 8).

Anscombe would certainly admit that 'can be grasped in thought' is incompatible with 'can only be presented in a sentence with a contradictory sense'. Just before her description of Wittgenstein's attitude to Augustine's 'He moves without moving', she writes: 'what [given what he says about following a rule] will Wittgenstein say about "illogical" thinking? As I would, that it isn't thinking?' (*QLI*, 122). An *impossible* thought is an impossible *thought*. What Anscombe is trying to make room for is the idea of grasping a thought which cannot be cleared up, i.e. cannot be shown to have a non-contradictory sense. And this means: cannot be shown *by us* to have a non-contradictory sense. She is raising the possibility of a person's grasping a thought, even though the sentence expressing it 'cannot be seen to have an unexceptionable non-contradictory sense'—seen by us, that is. It is this idea that lies behind her account of what a mystery is:

In the Catholic faith, certain beliefs (such as the Trinity, the Incarnation, the Eucharist) are called 'mysteries'; this means at the very least that it is neither possible to demonstrate

---

[16] *Remarks on the Foundations of Mathematics*, II, paras. 42–3 (pp. 82–3).

them nor possible to show once for all that they are not contradictory and absurd. On the other hand contradiction and absurdity is not embraced; 'This can be disproved, but I still believe it' is not an attitude of faith at all. (*QLI*, 122)

The departure from Wittgenstein consists in saying that *we* might be able to grasp a thought which *we* cannot clear up—cannot, because of our human finitude. The problem for Anscombe is how to distinguish a mystery from sheer nonsense. She imagines someone producing a sentence and saying 'This is true, but what it says is irreducibly enigmatic':

Of course if the sentence is mere abracadabra no one will take any notice. But suppose the sentence is not abracadabra but yet there are difficulties about claiming an unexceptionable sense for it? If that is the situation, can we dismiss the possibility that this enigmatic sense is a truth? (*PMC*, 7–8)

'Abracadabra' is not a sentence at all. But since she is imagining a sentence's having been produced, Anscombe presumably means her point to apply to certain strings of words that count, grammatically, as sentences. An example might be 'Green ideas sleep furiously'; maybe also 'It is five o'clock on the sun' and 'I can change the past'. The Protestants who ridiculed the doctrine of Transubstantiation coined the phrase 'hocus pocus' in imitation of the Latin 'hoc est corpus' ('This is the body'), and would no doubt have put hocus pocus in the same bag as abracadabra. Anscombe would reject the assimilation. How then are we to know when to 'take no notice', and when to take seriously?

One reason why the doctrine of Transubstantiation is not *mere* abracadabra is that you can teach it, explain it—or at any rate do something that looks like teaching and explaining. In a pamphlet published by the Catholic Truth Society, Anscombe describes how, at Mass, it is possible to teach a small child about transubstantiation, by whispering such things as 'Look what the priest is doing ... He is saying Jesus' words that change the bread into Jesus' body', and the like (*OT*, 107). The child will understand and learn. Only, of course, on the assumption that these sentences do make sense; which is why, in the context of distinguishing mystery from e.g. philosophical nonsense, the data about teaching are inconclusive: for whole schools of philosophy have been based on the promulgation of enigmatic nonsense.

You can show that 'I can change the past' is an absurdity. It may take some philosophical delving, but it can be done. For Anscombe, a (proper) Catholic will believe that this cannot be done for those articles of faith called 'mysteries'. After denying that 'This can be disproved, but I still believe it' expresses an attitude of faith, she continues: 'So ostensible proofs of absurdity are assumed to be rebuttable, each one in turn. Now this process Wittgenstein himself once described: "You can ward off *each* attack as it comes." (Personal conversation)' (*QLI*, 122). You cannot show once for all that the sentence in question has a non-contradictory sense, but you can rebut each attempt to prove that it lacks one.[17] (For those fond of scope distinctions, the difference is between 'It is possible that: for every proof P, you rebut P' and 'For every proof P, it is possible that you rebut P'.) But how do you know in advance that each ostensible proof can be rebutted? By what right does somebody 'assume' that this can be done?

The grounds for thinking that a mystery can always be defended from attack will not lie within the mystery itself. They will lie elsewhere: among the grounds for a person's religious belief. A Catholic will have been taught that the bread of the Mass is the body of Christ. She will believe what she has been taught as she believes, and as we all believe, things taught—not because we have established the reliability of the teacher, but because of the set-up of teaching and learning.[18] For a Catholic, part of what she is taught is that certain teachings are, for historical reasons, peculiarly authoritative. Among these teachings are mysteries. Of course it would be disingenuous to pretend that there hasn't been a long-standing and serious debate about whether the set-up of teaching and learning represented by the Church is in fact (as one might put it) well constituted. The pros and cons of the Catholic's position are to be gauged from the details of that debate. And perhaps the most important question that arises from a consideration of the debate is this: can a religious person make out that certain propositions are *bedrock*, in Wittgenstein's phrase?—that they serve to establish the credentials of propositions that impinge upon them, not *vice versa*? Questions like these do not only apply to religious belief, of course. They apply to all human belief and knowledge.

3. BEDROCK

3.1. Essence and Grammar

We touched earlier (pp. 196–8 above) upon an important distinction: that between a misuse of language and a factual error or lie. This distinction bore upon the question why truth, not falsehood, bears a 'justified relation' to the things signified by a proposition. The justification that attaches to a correct use of language, and which is relevant to theory of meaning, appears, as Anscombe says, to be distinct from the justification which attaches as such to telling the truth. Invoking Anscombe's account of practical necessity, I very briefly sketched a way by which to derive the norm of truth-telling from constitutive facts about linguistic meaning, i.e. a way by which to show how the two kinds of justification, which might be dubbed semantic and epistemic, are after all related.

---

[17] Cf. *OT*, 109.

[18] In a particular sense of 'because'. Cf. Ch. 2, p. 61. There is a fuller treatment of this issue in R. Teichmann, 'Authority', in *Modern Moral Philosophy*, ed. Anthony O'Hear (Cambridge: Cambridge University Press, 2004), 229–44.

That these two kinds of justification are more closely related than might be thought is a theme that appears in some of Wittgenstein's most searching and radical later writings, notably in *Remarks on the Foundations of Mathematics* and *On Certainty*. Wittgenstein invites us to view the rules governing the correct use of words as comparable to the rules governing the acceptance or rejection of beliefs (which are themselves of course paradigmatically expressed in words); a 'world view' is determined as much by our language and its attendant conceptual scheme as by what we would ordinarily term our knowledge of things. The two aspects of world view, the two kinds of justification, come together in the phenomenon of certainty. 'I am sure', 'I cannot doubt' are related to 'It must be', which expression can be prefixed to any statement of *conceptual* truth.

One direction in which these thoughts seem to take us is towards regarding certain world views, or sets of beliefs, or very general beliefs, as no more susceptible of rational justification or criticism than are concepts. 'This is just how we go on' looks to be the final answer to a series of 'Why?' questions; and a language-game or practice can appear to be sealed off from external assessment.[19] An appeal to the objective measure of Reality is empty in this context; we can of course 'cite reality' when giving reasons in justification of a belief or practice, but that our reasons count as good reasons is determined by norms or rules of reasoning whose status *as* rules depends on the existence of a surrounding language-game.

Anscombe examines some of these themes from Wittgenstein in 'The Question of Linguistic Idealism'. It is her most sustained direct discussion of the later Wittgenstein. (The article was written for a book of essays on Wittgenstein in honour of G. H. von Wright.) Although it is a penetrating discussion of Wittgenstein's thought, and as such an important contribution to Wittgenstein scholarship, there is much in it that can be said to belong to Anscombe's own philosophy, and which connects with things she says elsewhere. The essay is in two parts; these correspond roughly to the semantic and the epistemological aspects of the topic. The semantic aspect is heralded by Wittgenstein's dictum: 'Essence is expressed by grammar' (*Philosophical Investigations*, para. 371), and the variant on it which Anscombe ascribes to the linguistic idealist: 'Essence is *created* by grammar' (*QLI*, 112). 'Grammar' is a term familiar from Wittgenstein's later philosophy, relating, roughly, to linguistic or conceptual necessities that relate to particular concepts or concept-groups—such necessities as will typically be uncapturable in formal languages. Thus 'there is a crude grammar common to all [words in different languages for *horse*], by which each is e.g. a count-noun which is the name of a kind of whole living thing' (*QLI*, 112). And the following dichotomy presents itself:

it looks as if *either* the grammar corresponded to something of the object, its real essence, which it has whether there is a language about it or not, *or* the 'object' were itself

---

[19] A classic version of this view, one which explicitly assimilates semantic and epistemic norms, is to be found in P. Winch, *The Idea of a Social Science and its Relation to Philosophy* (London: Routledge, 1958).

dependent on language. The first is like the suggestion made by Plato in the *Cratylus*;[20] the second, if it applies through and through, I call 'linguistic idealism'.   (*QLI*, 113)

In the end, as we shall see, the dichotomy turns out to be a false one. And in showing how it is a false dichotomy, Wittgenstein finally succeeds 'in his difficult enterprise', of 'attain[ing] "realism without empiricism" ' (*QLI*, 133; cf. *Remarks on the Foundations of Mathematics*, 3rd edn., VI, 23).

So what is wrong with Plato's view? The key problem is this: neither a thing nor an experience can dictate what shall count as the *same* as it. Articulating some of Wittgenstein's best-known ideas, Anscombe reminds us that

it is not experiencing pain that gives you the meaning of the word 'pain'. How could an experience dictate the grammar of a word? You may say: doesn't it make certain demands on the grammar, if the word is to be the word for *that* experience? But the word is not just a response to that experience at that time: what *else* is the word to apply to? The experience can't dictate what is to be put together with it.   (*QLI*, 114)

Similar remarks go for concepts for 'public' things like horses. Whether or not we regard a horse as mediated by our experience of it, a horse can't dictate what is to be put together with it. Yes, a horse is similar to other horses, so can be put together with them; but (a) the resultant concept is not compulsory, since (b) other quite different concepts are imaginable, based on different standards of similarity, which concepts would equally apply to *that thing* (the horse). The thing/experience won't itself give us a standard of similarity, a criterion of sameness.

These thoughts do not on their own point towards linguistic idealism, for they so far allow the possibility that our concepts 'track' objective similarities between things:

someone might say 'I don't want to say that such-and-such concepts are absolutely *the* right ones; I only want to know if they are right ones at all.' [...] What we want to be assured of is that 'what we realize' [in the way of similarities between things] actually exists and is not a mere projection of the forms of our thinking upon reality.   (*QLI*, 113)

The discussion might at this point turn to putative ways in which a concept might be justified—shown to be a right one, if not the right one. For example, a causalist might insist that colour-concepts are justified by the causal explicability of our application of them, in terms of light frequencies and the stimulation-ranges of rods and cones, etc. An 'objective cause' would underwrite an 'objective concept'. An obvious objection could then be raised about the *concepts* of cause and effect: these are just as much our concepts as any others under discussion, and so will not bring on board any objectivity not already inherent in human

---

[20] That a word like 'horse' is a sort of tool, designed to catch hold of something in nature. See *QLI*, 112.

concepts generally.[21] Anscombe, however, does not pursue this tack. Rather, she leads us gradually towards what looks more and more like linguistic idealism, by first of all introducing a contrast, between things whose existence does not depend on human linguistic practice (e.g. horses) and things whose existence does so depend, and then showing how among the latter are the rules that govern concepts (e.g. *horse*), and also the rules that govern logical thought.

That horses and pains do not depend for their existence on there being certain linguistic practices is something that everybody can allow. 'Animals have felt pain' only *makes sense* as a sentence because there is a linguistic practice in virtue of which 'pain' means what it does; it does not follow that its *truth* depends on that practice, and hence that before that practice existed there was no pain. The sentence is after all not about the practice, but about animals and pain. Pain would have existed without the language of pain. And this point is not affected by the acknowledgement that alternative, or variant, concepts are conceivable:

'But which "pain" are we talking about—pain according to our concept or according to some other possible concept, say the one described [which applies only if there is visible damage, such as a wound]?' Well, we are talking our language. So it is pain as we mean 'pain' that we are saying would have existed anyway. (*QLI*, 114)

The point applies equally to objects, properties, facts. There would have been horses without us; they would have been herbivorous; their being herbivorous would have been the case.

Bernard Williams seems to go wrong here in his interpretation of Wittgenstein. In 'Wittgenstein and Idealism',[22] he writes that 'on some traditional views', the proposition 'Unless Q, "S" would not express a truth' does not entail 'Unless Q, not S'. (For the purposes of the discussion, 'Q' is something like 'There are linguistic practices' and 'S' is something like 'Animals feel pain'.) In other words, those 'traditional views' can accommodate the truism that animals would have felt pain whether or not language existed. They can allow that 'Animals feel pain' could only be a true sentence if it *were* a sentence (and so if language existed), while insisting that what it says to be the case would still be the case in the absence of language. Which traditional views Williams has in mind is a bit unclear; this doesn't matter much, though, since his purpose is to make a contrast with a Wittgensteinian approach: 'But it is not obvious that for later Wittgensteinian views, and in particular for the theory of justified assertion, we can so easily drive a line between the sentence "S" expressing the truth, and what is the case if S.'

---

[21] The point would be particularly pertinent if Anscombe's account of causality were along the right lines, according to which the 'essence' of causality can be stated only in such vague terms as: 'An effect derives from, flows from, its cause'—this fact being connected with the great variety of types of cause–effect relation. See Ch. 5, pp. 181–2.   [22] In *Moral Luck*, 162.

What is the theory of justified assertion? The answer comes a couple of pages earlier in the article, where Williams mentions the view 'which has been charted by Dummett in much recent work, to the effect that *truth* must be replaced by, or interpreted in terms of, the notion of *conditions which justify assertion*. This view I shall summarily call Wittgenstein's constructivism.'[23] It is none too clear that the kind of constructivism Williams means can in fact be attributed to Wittgenstein—certainly not any form of constructivism which would entail a general replaceability of 'S' by ' "S" is a true sentence'. I doubt if even Dummett's anti-realist would concur with such a general statement of replaceability: even if the notion of justified assertion is useful (or essential) in understanding the notion of truth, a true proposition need not be asserted at all, e.g. if it occurs in a conditional proposition or as a supposition. (Geach has dubbed this the 'Frege point'.) And that goes for 'S' as it occurs in 'Unless Q, not S'. There is no reason to think that the *assertion-conditions* of 'S' will bear directly upon the role it plays in this complex proposition, given that 'S' is not asserted in that proposition.

Even if Dummettian anti-realism could be hooked on this line, Anscombe's brand of Wittgensteinianism—and Wittgenstein according to her interpretation—could not be. As we saw in Chapter 5 (p. 176), her recognition that by 'use' we should not only understand 'assertive use' helps her to avoid the assimilation of truth to warranted assertibility. It also helps her to avoid the sort of anti-realist reductivism which threatens to reduce (e.g.) past-tensed statements to statements about present criteria. In fact, the evident non-replaceability of 'S' by ' "S" is a true sentence' is surely more of a problem for philosophers like Tarski and Davidson than for a philosopher like Wittgenstein. Williams cites the following, from the *Philosophical Investigations* (para. 381): 'How do I know that this colour is red? It would be an answer to say: "I have learnt English".' But this reference to 'an answer'—not even 'the answer'—hardly suggests a wholesale assimilation of 'This is red' to 'This is called "red"', nor yet to ' "This is red" is assertible'. Wittgenstein is surely bothered by a completely different question here; his concern is to eschew a model of knowledge as a certain sort of grounded belief in favour of a model of it as a practical (here, linguistic) ability—for this kind of 'knowledge'.

It seems, then, that nobody, including the linguistic idealist, need deny that many things exist independently of human linguistic practice. For the linguistic idealist, it is essence that is created by grammar, not existence. Having stated this, Anscombe goes on:

But there are, of course, a great many things whose existence does depend on human linguistic practice. The dependence is in many cases an unproblematic and trivial fact. But in others it is not trivial—it touches the nerve of great philosophical problems. The cases I have in mind are three: rules, rights and promises.   (*QLI*, 118)

---

[23] In *Moral Luck*, 157.

The theory of stopping and forcing modals, which we have already encountered,[24] now makes its appearance once again. A modal expression like 'You must' is the basic linguistic move through which both the ability to play a game, and the concept of a rule of a game, are learnt. 'You must φ' cannot informatively be justified or explained by saying 'The rules dictate it', since the idea of a rule (as opposed, e.g., to an imperative, or a statement of human regularity) is dependent on the force of the modal expressions, not *vice versa*. Within a game, of course, reasons can be given for 'You must φ'—for instance, 'Because you were bowled out'. The key point is that 'You must φ' is in no way an abbreviation of any hypothetical imperative, such as: 'You must φ if you want to win', or 'You must φ if you want to do what is called "playing cricket"', or even 'You must φ if you want to avoid others' displeasure'. What goes for games goes for rule-governed practices generally. A justification for a 'You must' will not come from outside the practice, but from within it.

Anscombe takes it that for Wittgenstein, conceptual and logical necessity are both expressed by means of this 'You must'. Roughly speaking, 'A thing cannot be both red and green' becomes 'You cannot call a thing red and call it green'. The 'cannot' is not to be justified by reference to something outside the language-game of colour words. The passage from Wittgenstein quoted by Williams is indeed relevant here: if asked 'Why won't you call that thing red and green?', an answer would be 'I can speak English', or 'I have learnt English'.[25] The answer would not in fact give a justifying reason at all; rather, it would let the enquirer 'see what the situation is' (cf. Ch. 2, pp. 60–1). Similar remarks go for the logical concepts: *not, if... then..., or,* and so on. These too have a grammar; these too are governed by 'You must'.

Valid inference, not logical truths, is the subject matter of logic; and a conclusion is justified, not by rules of logic but, in some cases by the truth of its premises, in some by the steps taken in reaching it, such as making a supposition or drawing a diagram or constructing a table. If someone invents variant rules, e.g. a system with more than two truth values, there is the question whether these rules have been followed in some exercise. According to what rules is the deduction, the transition, made from given rules to particular practice? Always there is the logical *must*: you 'can't' have this *and* that; you can't do that if you are going by this rule; you must grant this in face of that. (*QLI*, 121)

An inference is just as much an action as a move in chess. When it is said that logical rules depend upon human linguistic practice, 'this does not mean just the

---

[24] See in particular Ch. 3, §2.2.

[25] Hugh Mellor has cited shot silk as a counter-example to 'A thing cannot be red all over and green all over' (in conversation). The possibility of experiences that lead us to deny what we had regarded as necessary truths—or simply what we had unthinkingly called necessary truths—is grist to Wittgenstein's mill: when a language-game changes or evolves, and what is called necessary changes with it, this will not in general be because of reasons that compel, but because certain things *strike* us a certain way. Whether Mellor has in fact come up with such an experience I leave to the reader's judgement.

practices of arranging words together and uttering them in appropriate contexts. It refers e.g. to *action* on the rule; actually going *this* way by the signpost' (*QLI*, 122).

I spoke earlier of the dichotomy between Platonic realism and linguistic idealism as being a false dichotomy (p. 216). This is because the linguistic idealist applies the notion of an object's being dependent on language 'through and through'. To really apply this notion through and through would perhaps be to embrace the quasi-Berkeleyan view, that objects (properties, facts) do not exist independently of human linguistic practice. We have already rejected that view, and found it absent from Wittgenstein's thought. But there is a lesser mode of applying the notion of 'dependence' through and through: one by which logical and conceptual necessities are made out to depend on practices that are essentially *arbitrary*. If essence is created by grammar, and if grammar is not only autonomous but arbitrary, then the cloud that is metaphysics has apparently been condensed into a droplet of no significance, and the overview of our language which philosophy brings us is an overview of random human action. But if the rules of a linguistic practice cannot be justified from without, and rest ultimately on the brute fact that human beings learn to respond to 'You must' in a way that produces agreement in response, then surely just this is the true picture? Can a path be steered between the *Cratylus* and *this* species of idealism?

It can. The dichotomy is indeed false. Anscombe (*QLI*, 123–4) quotes the following passage from *Philosophical Investigations*, para. 520:

'So does it depend wholly on our grammar what will be called (logically) possible and what not—i.e. what that grammar permits?' But that is surely arbitrary [willkürlich]! Is it arbitrary? It is not every sentence-like formation that we know how to do something with, not every technique has its application in our life; and when we are tempted in philosophy to count some quite useless thing as a proposition, that is often because we have not considered its application thoroughly.

That a technique, a rule, has or is capable of having a real application in our life is what prevents the essence created by grammar from being arbitrary. In virtue of what does a rule have such a real application? In our being the sort of creatures who find it natural to *give* it certain applications in our lives, and who agree in so finding it. But this doesn't mean: a description of the sort of creatures we are (say, in terms of biology, or evolution, or empirical psychology) will provide a justification of the rule. Will such a description at any rate provide an explanation of why we have the rule? Well, an explanation is something that succeeds in answering the question 'Why?', and the criteria for success here depend on what we are after when we ask the question. Presumably *not* just: a redescription of the phenomenon in scientific vocabulary. If it is said that a true account in terms of efficient causes (say) is self-evidently explanatory, the question would arise: what descriptions of the causes present them *as* explanatory? A description of what led up to human language in terms of movements of atoms would, for instance, hardly count as an explanation. Something more *like* justification, if not justification itself, is wanted.

One candidate here is explanation in terms of what is good for us, of what helps us *qua* human beings. An explanation of why we have the rules constitutive of the promising game can be given: 'such a procedure as that language-game is an instrument whose use is part and parcel of an enormous amount of human activity and hence of human good; of the supplying both of human needs and of human wants so far as the satisfactions of these are compossible'. This of course is Anscombe's explanation of how the 'technique' of promising comes to have application in our life (*PJ*, 18; see Ch. 3, p. 100). The question 'Why do we have these rules?' may well be asking after an explanation of this type, an explanation in terms of what is good for us, of what we need—an explanation in terms of Aristotelian necessity. I invoked such a form of explanation when sketching how the norm of truth-telling might be thought to arise out of constitutive facts about human language (above, pp. 197–8). Such explanation makes mention of empirical facts—as, that we cannot rely on others' love or on tit-for-tat arrangements if we are to achieve many wanted or needed things; that many human aims need cooperation for their achievement; and so forth. More obviously 'scientific' facts might throw yet more light—say, that human beings can remember what they have done over a considerable period (e.g. remember having said 'I undertake to ... '). The explanation being proffered need not have a definite terminus. But for it to be an explanation of the kind I am taking the 'Why?' question as asking after, it will, implicitly or explicitly, rely on notions such as *good for* and *need*. That 'It is good for us', 'Human beings need it', etc. should be explanatory here is connected with the fact that such statements also, in the context of practical reasoning, count as supplying desirability-characterizations. None of this prevents the explanation from being one that alludes to those very general facts of nature which Wittgenstein speaks of as underlying our concepts (*Philosophical Investigations*, II. xii; cf. *QLI*, 112). But it is Anscombe, rather than Wittgenstein, who has demystified such notions as *good for*, as well as reinstating that notion of non-logical necessity which has been dubbed 'Aristotelian necessity'. If these notions are ethical, or have an ethical aspect, then ethics is not, as Wittgenstein thought, a matter of what is shown and not said—or not only that.

To be sure, the concepts of *good* and of *need* are just as much our concepts as any others: so they are in that sense incapable of providing justification for our linguistic practices. But when Wittgenstein invites one to imagine concepts different from ours, it is often by imagining people or creatures with interests and aims different from ours that we are to do so; that is how the alternative concept-scheme is made intelligible. 'Interests and aims': roughly speaking, what is needed and what is wanted. And our wants are not a source of arbitrariness, for in the end they cannot be completely hived off from our needs, as Anscombe recognized (see Ch. 2, p. 70).

3.2. Certainty

I began the last section by mentioning the distinction between a factual error and a misuse of words. Corresponding to this distinction is another: that between two kinds of disagreement. A factual disagreement is to be addressed by 'looking to the facts'; a semantic disagreement, by 'looking to the meanings of words'. I mentioned Wittgenstein's view that the two species of justification, semantic and epistemic, are not sharply separated; the same will go for the two corresponding types of disagreement. Part of the reason for this is the existence of a third category of disagreement, one which in effect lies in between the first two, but which it is most tempting to assimilate to (and therefore most important to distinguish from) that of factual disagreement:

I can be accused of making a mistake when I know what it is for a given proposition (say) to be true, and things aren't like that but I suppose that they are. [. . .] This means that I have to be actually operating the language. My proceedings with it have to belong in the system of thought that is in question. Otherwise such an utterance may be nothing at all; it may be 'superstition' (*PI*, I, para. 110) or a 'queer reaction' or a manifestation of some different 'picture of the world', or of a special form of belief which flies in the face of what would be understood to falsify it but for its peculiarity; it may be some strange secondary application of words; it may be a mere manifestation of ignorance like a child's. It may be madness. But in none of these cases is Wittgenstein willing to speak of a 'mistake'.   (*QLI*, 124)

For a disagreement to be purely factual, the parties to it must be in some measure of agreement about what kinds of evidence, observation, or consideration could support either side. But there are disagreements, actual and hypothetical, where what is lacking is just this background agreement as to what count as reasons *pro* and *con*. That P counts as evidence for Q is not always a matter of a background empirical theory (e.g. one based on past experience). We may be tempted to say that in such a case P is a constitutive criterion for Q; but there is a danger that the term 'constitutive' will lead us too quickly to count any disagreement about whether P does in fact show that Q as a simple disagreement about concepts—and hence as a mere talking at cross-purposes. As is indicated by the examples which Wittgenstein comes up with, some of which Anscombe lists above, we are not dealing with disagreements of the sort that might end by either side simply saying 'Oh, well if *that's* what you mean by X, then I suppose you're right; but that's not how I would use the word'.

One sort of disagreement that could arise about possible reasons for or against some assertion is the sort where one party takes an assertion as not *requiring* any reasons. This attitude need not go with a belief in the sort of self-evidence that Descartes took to be perceptible by the light of reason. The assertion in question may be one the acceptance of which appears (to one party) to be a presupposition for going in for reasoning and investigation at all. In her discussion of *On Certainty*, Anscombe writes:

Finding grounds, testing, proving, reasoning, confirming, verifying are all processes that go on *within*, say, one or another living linguistic practice which we have. There are assumptions, beliefs, that are 'immovable foundations' of these proceedings. By this, Wittgenstein means only that they are a foundation which is not moved by any of these proceedings. (*QLI*, 130)

The 'immovable foundations' could be moved, e.g. by extreme experiences, or by the development of wholly new techniques (such as mathematical techniques). It is this fact which lies behind the possibility that, within some practice, I may be quite justified in saying 'I can't be making a mistake about this', while at the same time admitting that given certain changes, I could come to deny the truth of what I am now saying (*QLI*, 132; cf. *On Certainty*, paras. 643–5). Within the practice, I can't see how P could be doubted without this disrupting the whole practice (e.g. maths, or ancient history); so I can say, 'I can't be mistaken that P'. But I can simultaneously admit the general possibility of experiences or developments that would radically alter the practice, and so alter what counted in it as bedrock, while leaving enough of it intact for 'P' still to count as making the same claim as before—a claim, however, that no longer enjoyed its status as 'immovable', but on the contrary counted as false.

If (given certain changes) I were to disagree with my former self, and that disagreement had to do with a change in what I took to be bedrock or immovable, then it seems that by Wittgenstein's lights I shouldn't call my former assertion a *mistake*. Rather, I should think of that assertion as a 'queer reaction', or 'manifestation of a different world-picture', or the like. And in fact the relevant sentence is: 'I can't be making a mistake—but I may indeed some time, rightly or wrongly, believe I realize that I was not competent to judge' (*On Certainty*, para. 645). As Anscombe says, 'the distinction between *mistake* and something else that can't be called "mistake" just rescues us from the contradiction' (*QLI*, 132). The 'something else' would be: not being competent to judge. On the face of it, this doesn't look very like the diagnosis of anything as radical as a difference of world-picture, as Wittgenstein seems to regard the latter when imagining cases of disagreement between two parties; for in the end, *such* disagreement (he says) is only resoluble, if at all, by persuasion or conversion. Still, perhaps it could be made out that a possible expression on the part of one persuaded or converted is 'I wasn't competent to judge'. The matter need not detain us long, however, for as Anscombe says, the crux of the matter comes with Wittgenstein's next remark: 'If that always or often occurred [i.e. one's coming to think that one wasn't competent to judge], that would indeed completely change the character of the language-game.' In Anscombe's words: 'the "language-game" of assertion, which for speaking humans is so important a part of the whole business of knowing and being certain, depends for its character on a "general fact of nature"; namely that that sequence of phenomena is rare' (*QLI*, 133).

It is for this reason that she takes Wittgenstein to have avoided linguistic idealism in its epistemological form, attaining instead 'realism without empiricism'. For Wittgenstein, 'that one knows something is not guaranteed by the language-game' (*QLI*, 133)—for there is such a thing as radical change of view, however rare, and the natural expression of this is 'I was wrong'. The possibility of radical change of view is compatible with the fact that, in the absence of such change, 'I know' and 'I am certain' are justifiable forms of expression within the language-game.

'But we don't want to know about forms of words! We want to know when a person really *knows* something. And knowing is a mental state.' Wittgenstein's strictures against a too easy reliance on the idea of a 'mental state' are well known, and in this context quite justified. Consider the complaint: 'Why did you say that if you didn't really know it?' In many contexts, simply to assert that P counts as laying claim to knowledge that P; and this has to do with the function of assertion. Hence Anscombe's specification of the language-game of assertion, in the above quotation; and hence Wittgenstein's remarks, concerning radical change of view: 'such a case, or its possibility, does not discredit the sentence "I can't be making a mistake". Otherwise wouldn't it discredit all assertion?' (*On Certainty*, paras. 643–4).

That assertion can have the function or purpose ascribed to it by Anselm (see above, p. 196)—i.e. that there can be such a thing as assertion—depends on the empirical fact, among others, that people don't generally reject their earlier assertions as unfounded. It is 'by favour of Nature' that assertion and knowledge are possible (*On Certainty*, para. 505); for Anselm and for Anscombe, it is (also) by the grace of God.

Wittgenstein's views are subtle and complex, and it is important that one not reduce them to a formula or two. I have mentioned 'immovable foundations' and 'world-pictures'; but what Wittgenstein has to say about certainty, doubt, disagreement, and so on encompasses more than these. As Anscombe warns us,

we should not regard the struggling investigations of *On Certainty* as all saying the same thing. Doubts whether this is a tree or whether his name was L.W. or whether the world has existed a long time or whether the kettle will heat on the fire or whether he had never been to the moon are themselves not all subjected to the same treatment. Not all these things, for example, are part of a 'world-picture'. And a world-picture is not the same thing as a religious belief, even though to believe is not in either case to surmise. (*QLI*, 130)

In philosophy, each case should be considered on its merits. Relatedly, each case should be described in sufficient detail. This last maxim is particularly relevant when the question concerns whether we can conceive of certain of our beliefs being refuted or undermined. In 'Hume and Julius Caesar', Anscombe applies some of the lessons of *On Certainty* to historical knowledge, arguing that the mere statement that we can conceive of evidence turning up which showed there had never been such a person as Julius Caesar is no good until details are given of what sort of evidence that might be. If we try to do this, however, we are likely to fail. Wittgenstein himself appears not to have noticed this—see *Philosophical Remarks*, IV. 56, to which Anscombe alludes before asking:

> What would we *think* for example of an inscription saying 'I, Augustus Caesar, invented the story of the divine Julius so that Caesars should be worshipped; but he never existed'? To ask a question Wittgenstein asked much later [in *On Certainty*]: what would get judged by what here? (*HJC*, 89)

The proposition that Julius Caesar existed may in fact be an 'immovable foundation' within the practice called history. This shows up in the fact that, if one has the sort of education Anscombe assumes that we in the West have,[26] one cannot *check up* on whether Caesar existed, as one can check up on the actual date of his arrival in Great Britain (cf. *HJC*, 91). In the face of the hypothesis that Caesar never existed,

> either I should start to say: 'How could one explain all these references and implications, then?... but, but, *but* if I doubt the existence of Caesar, if I say I may reasonably call it in question, then with equal reason I must doubt the status of the things I've just pointed to'—*or* I should realize straight away that the 'doubt' put me in a vacuum in which I could not produce reasons why such and such 'historical facts' are more or less doubtful. (*HJC*, 91)

It is essential for Anscombe's argument that we take seriously the requirement that a hypothesis be fleshed out in proper detail. And this requirement holds more generally of those 'thought experiments' that are the bread and butter of many philosophers. Even if we allow ourselves, in the course of constructing some fanciful scenario, to suspend the laws of physics, say, we should (first of all) be quite clear that we are doing so, and (second) still and always ask ourselves: 'What would one REALLY have grounds for saying or thinking, in such a case?'

In many of her articles, Anscombe refers to some view as a prejudice, or apparent prejudice. When is a belief a prejudice, and when is it bedrock? When is it a questionable 'bit of *Weltanschauung*', and when a 'hinge proposition'? The answer to these questions must in large part have to do with how much, and what sort of, detail can be plausibly put into counter-examples to, or cases against, the belief in question. The hypothesis that Julius Caesar might turn out never to have existed can be rejected, once the details of that hypothesis have been demanded. (Needless to say, the hypothesis comes under more scrutiny in *HJC* than it has in this chapter.) If a similar thing can be said about the 'hypothesis' that a certain

---

[26] An important qualification. If classical education is not what it was, the example may need changing—say, to 'Adolf Hitler never existed'.

religious mystery is a contradiction, then that hypothesis, too, can be rejected—if not, not. In other words: the proposition that 'each attack can be warded off in turn' must be falsifiable-in-principle even if it is not verifiable-in-principle. As far as the philosophy of religion goes, this is entirely in keeping with Anscombe's view of religious belief as answerable to reason.

Conclusion

There are some large gaps in this book, as there were bound to be given the subject. I have merely touched on Anscombe's discussions of other philosophers; these include articles on Plato, Aristotle, Anselm, Spinoza, Hume, and others, in all of which she gives evidence of her considerable capacity for scholarship and textual criticism, while never failing to treat the questions raised by her predecessors as live ones. And there are numerous pieces on concrete ethical questions—those questions to which Anscombe says she was always more drawn than to meta-ethics, and which include writings on warfare, euthanasia, contraception, abortion, medical trials, and more.

In a way, Anscombe's interest in these two areas—history of philosophy and first-order ethics—gives an indication of one of her main strengths as a philosopher. And that is her recognition that philosophy is not a set of arcane puzzles to be picked over by professional academics, nor yet a research programme in which the latest 'results' render previous work obsolete. Rather, it is in an important sense a subject for everybody—for everybody, that is, who wishes to follow Plato's advice and eschew the unexamined life. As an undergraduate at Oxford, Anscombe studied Literae Humaniores (classical literature, philosophy, and history), and it came naturally to her to see philosophy as part of the culture in the same way as literature and history—and science too, for that matter. Her versatility as a philosopher was connected with a generous curiosity and a sense that philosophizing was one of the activities of life, continuous with its other activities.

Hume writes of his philosophical speculations:

I dine, I play a game of backgammon, I converse, and am merry with my friends; and when, after three or four hours' amusement, I would return to these speculations, they appear so cold, and strained, and ridiculous, that I cannot find in my heart to enter into them any further.[1]

And of abstruse reasoning in general he says: 'When we leave our closet, and engage in the common affairs of life, its conclusions seem to vanish like the phantoms of the night on the appearance of the morning ... '.[2]

---

[1] *A Treatise of Human Nature*, Bk. 1, Part IV, §7.
[2] Ibid., Bk. 3, Part I, §1.

Hume's thought can, of course, figure in a philosophical defence of common sense, the aim of which would be to bring the closet or study more into line with the outside world, at any rate when it came to scepticism and certainty. In other matters, it might be needful to bring the outside world into line with the study. What surely is to be avoided is a divided existence, in which the two domains are insulated from one another—in which philosophy is a profession like any other, offering the usual perks of money and status, whose practitioners clock off at the end of the day. If philosophy brings any sort of enlightenment, it is the sort that imbues a person's whole life. This was something that Anscombe understood, and of which professional philosophers need more and more to be reminded.

In fact, if I were asked 'What can we learn from Anscombe?', I would probably not start by listing her main thoughts and ideas, but would instead answer: 'A certain approach, a certain attitude, to philosophy'. Thoughts and ideas there are aplenty, and this book is intended as an introduction to them. But in thinking your way through what Anscombe has to say, whether it be about intention, self-knowledge, causality, happiness, truth, or God, what you bring away is to some extent independent of the claims she makes, in the sense that it is possible to disagree with a lot of what she says and yet still to benefit from it. (That one should be able to say this about a philosopher shows one of the ways in which philosophy is unlike natural science.) Bernard Williams, whose intellectual relationship with Anscombe was hardly free of friction, had this to say (he is speaking here about his experience of Oxford in the 1950s):

Another person who had *one* kind of influence on me—though I'm glad to say I think she didn't influence me in other ways!—was Elizabeth Anscombe. One thing that she did, which she got from Wittgenstein, was that she impressed upon one that being clever wasn't enough. Oxford philosophy, and this is still true to a certain extent, had a great tendency to be clever. It was very eristic: there was a lot of competitive dialectical exchange, and showing that other people were wrong. I was quite good at all that. But Elizabeth conveyed a strong sense of the seriousness of the subject, and how the subject was difficult in ways that simply being clever wasn't going to get round.[3]

The tribute is as perceptive as it is generous. A 'sense of the seriousness of the subject': that is one of the main things we can learn from Anscombe.

Another way in which we can learn from Anscombe is by seeing *how* she does philosophy, and understanding why she does it the way she does. Here is the point where it might be useful to consider whether Anscombe can be called a 'linguistic philosopher', and if so, in what sense. A distinction worth making straight away is that between (a) philosophers who direct our attention to what we actually say, and to features of our actual language (or group of languages), and (b) philosophers who ask us to think about possible, as well as actual, languages or language-games. The first group of philosophers might be

---

[3] From an interview in the *Harvard Review of Philosophy*, 2004.

called ordinary-language philosophers. Anscombe quite clearly belongs to (b), not to (a); examples of her imaginary languages include the language containing the self-referential 'A',[4] the language containing the verb to REMBER (see Ch. 4, pp. 146–8), the language containing the verb to blip, analogous to 'promise' (*RRP*, 100), and the language containing the primitive past-tense report 'red' (see Ch. 5, pp. 167–71). The purpose of presenting these imaginary languages is of course to cast light on our actual languages and conceptual schemes. By seeing how 'I' differs from the imaginary 'A', for instance, we are helped to understand what is meant by the claim that 'I' does not refer; by considering how 'red' could be taught and learnt, we come to appreciate the limits of the 'aboutness' model of meaning, and also get an idea of what sort of appeal to human memory can usefully be made in the course of explaining how we can so much as think about the past. Of course, there is also in Anscombe's work much close examination of our actual language; as we have seen, one form of question to be posed by Anscombe goes, 'Is such-and-such an *intelligible* thing to say?', where 'such-and-such' belongs, or is meant to belong, to our actual language. This is not just a version of the 'bad grammar' gambit, a way of saying 'I don't see what you mean'—as we can see from how it is used, e.g. when the sentence in question is 'I just want it'. That this assertion is not intelligible in all circumstances points towards the need for desirability-characterizations (see Ch 3, pp. 66–7), which in turn shows how wants are no more Humean 'original existences' than are beliefs.

These methods are certainly linguistic, even if they are not those of an ordinary-language philosopher. And there is still a great deal of misunderstanding of the point of linguistic methods in philosophy, despite the fact that the so-called linguistic turn took place a hundred years ago. It is perhaps not surprising that a writer like Ernest Gellner should have thought that the philosophers of his day were simply talking about words, not things;[5] that many professional philosophers should still see matters much as Gellner did would appear to betoken intellectual laziness, as well perhaps as wishful thinking (the wish being that we should sit at the same table as the scientists). Gellner saw linguistic philosophers as living in a sort of ivory tower of their own making. But the author of 'Mr. Truman's Degree' and 'Were You a Zygote?' is the last person to be accused of that species of superfluity. If we are hunting for ineffectual dons, they will not be hard to find, probably at a conference near you. On the face of it, the methods of linguistic philosophy are less inimical to connection with reality than the methods of, say, contemporary 'analytic metaphysics'.

In any case, of course, Anscombe can hardly be said to employ one method, the 'linguistic', any more than can Wittgenstein, who wrote: 'There is not *a*

[4] See Ch. 4, p. 159 n. 26.
[5] Gellner, *Words and Things: A Critical Account of Linguistic Philosophy and a Study in Ideology* (London: Victor Gollancz, 1959).

philosophical method, though there are indeed methods, like different therapies' (*Philosophical Investigations*, para. 133). (For the point of this comparison, see Ch. 6, p. 206. Different methods work on different people.) Other styles of philosophizing than the linguistic include: invoking similes and analogies; introspection; genealogical explanation; using historical, scientific, or other empirical data; *reductio ad absurdum* ... The list is open-ended.

One of the main aims of this book, as I said in the Introduction, has been to bring out the interconnections in Anscombe's philosophy. These interconnections signal a unity in diversity; they are the fibres that bind together the substantial whole, the corpus, of Anscombe's work. The achievement represented by that corpus of work is enormous, including as it does some of the most important contributions to modern philosophy over four or five decades, in philosophy of action, ethics, mind, metaphysics, and more. To read and reread her work is to take advantage of one of those rare opportunities, that of becoming acquainted with a great mind.

Bibliography of Works by Elizabeth Anscombe

The following list of published writings by Elizabeth Anscombe is based upon one that was prepared in January 2007 by Luke Gormally, Christian Kietzmann, and José Maria Torralba.[1] Items are listed in order of date of first publication. (The dates given in Anscombe's *Collected Philosophical Papers* are not always accurate.) Where a piece was reprinted in one or more of the collections of Anscombe's writings, reference is given to the relevant collection(s) in square brackets; abbreviations are explained in the key to title abbreviations at the beginning of this book. The version of an article as it appears in a collection is sometimes a revised version, different from the original. NB Some of Anscombe's articles appeared for the first time in one of these collections; these are typically texts of lectures or planned lectures. I have not included reference to other anthologies in which various of Anscombe's articles have been reprinted. I have, however, included details of the foreign translations of *Intention*.

For updated versions of this list, see <www.unav.es/filosofia/jmtorralba/anscombe_bibliography.htm>.

1939. (with Norman Daniel) *The Justice of the Present War Examined* (Oxford, 1939) (published by the authors). [*ERP*, 72–81].

1948. 'A Reply to Mr. C. S. Lewis's Argument that "Naturalism" is Self-Refuting', *Socratic Digest*, 4/2 (1948), 7–16. [*MPM*, 224–32].

1950. 'The Reality of the Past', in Max Black (ed.), *Philosophical Analysis* (Ithaca, NY: Cornell University Press, 1950), 36–56. [*MPM*, 104–19].

1953a. 'Note on the English Version of Wittgenstein's *Philosophische Untersuchungen*', *Mind*, 62 (1953), 521–2.

1953b. 'The Principle of Individuation', in *Proceedings of the Aristotelian Society*, suppl. vol. 27 (1953), 83–96. [*FPW*, 57–65].

1953c. Translation: L. Wittgenstein, *Philosophical Investigations* (Oxford: Blackwell, 1953).

1954a. (with Peter Geach) Translation: R. Descartes, *Philosophical Writings (A Selection)* (London: Nelson, 1954).

1954b. 'Misinformation: What Wittgenstein Really Said', *The Tablet*, 17 Apr. 1954, p. 373.

1956a. *Mr. Truman's Degree* (Oxford: Oxonian Press, 1956). [*ERP*, 62–71].

1956b. '*Analysis* Competition—Tenth Problem', *Analysis*, 16/6 (1956). [*MPM*, 220–3].

1956c. 'Aristotle and the Sea Battle: *De Interpretatione*, Chapter IX', *Mind*, 65 (1956), 1–15. [*FPW*, 44–55].

1956 d. Translation: L. Wittgenstein, *Remarks on the Foundations of Mathematics* (Oxford: Blackwell, 1956).

1957a. 'Intention', *Proceedings of the Aristotelian Society*, 57 (1957), 321–32. [*MPM*, 75–82].

---

[1] A previous version was published in J. M. Torralba, *Acción intencional y razonamiento práctico según G. E. M. Anscombe* (Pamplona: Eunsa, 2005), 223–31.

1957b. *Intention* (Oxford: Blackwell, 1957). [First edition; see 1963a for second edition].

1957c. 'Report on "It is Impossible to be told Anyone's Name"', *Analysis*, 17 (1957), 49–51.

1957d. 'Does Oxford Moral Philosophy Corrupt the Youth?', *The Listener*, 57, no. 1455, 14 Feb. 1957, pp. 266–71. [*HLAE*, 161–8].

1957e. 'Letter to the Editor', *The Listener*, 57, no. 1457, 28 Feb. 1957, p. 349.

1957f. 'Letter to the Editor', *The Listener*, 57, no. 1459, 14 Mar. 1957, p. 427.

1957g. 'Letter to the Editor', *The Listener*, 57, no. 1460, 21 Mar. 1957, pp. 478–9.

1957h. 'Letter to the Editor', *The Listener*, 57, no. 1461, 28 Mar. 1957, pp. 519–20.

1957i. 'Letter to the Editor', *The Listener*, 57, no. 1462, 4 Apr. 1957, p. 564.

1957j. 'Names of Words. A Reply to Dr. Whiteley', *Analysis*, 18/1 (1957), 17 19.

1958a. 'Modern Moral Philosophy', *Philosophy*, 33/124 (1958), 1–19. [*ERP*, 26–42; *HLAE*, 169–94].

1958b. 'On Brute Facts', *Analysis*, 18/3 (1958), 69–72. [*ERP*, 22–5].

1958c. ' "Pretending" ', *Proceedings of the Aristotelian Society*, suppl. vol. 32 (1958), 279–94. [*MPM*, 83–93].

1959a. *An Introduction to Wittgenstein's* Tractatus (London: Hutchinson, 1959).

1959b. 'Mr. Copi on Objects, Properties and Relations in the "Tractatus" ', *Mind*, 68 (1959), 404.

1959c. 'Letter to the Editor', *Times Literary Supplement*, 29 May 1959, p. 321.

1961a. Translation: L. Wittgenstein, *Notebooks 1914–1916* (Oxford: Blackwell, 1961).

1961b. 'Aristotle', in Anscombe and Geach, *Three Philosophers* (Oxford: Blackwell, 1961), 1–63.

1961c. 'War and Murder', in W. Stein (ed.), *Nuclear Weapons: A Catholic Response* (London: Burns & Oates, 1961), 43–62. [*ERP*, 51–61].

1962a. 'On Sensations of Position', *Analysis*, 22/3 (1962), 55–8. [*MPM*, 71–4].

1962b. 'Authority in Morals', in J. Todd (ed.), *Problems of Authority: The Papers Read at an Anglo-French Symposium Held at the Abbey of Notre-Dame du Bec, in April 1961* (Baltimore: Helicon Press; London: Darton Longman and Todd, 1962). [*ERP*, 43–50].

1962c. 'Letter to the Editor', *Times Literary Supplement*, 25 May 1962, p. 373.

1963a. *Intention*, 2nd edn. (Oxford: Blackwell, 1963; Cambridge, Mass.: Harvard University Press, 2000).

In German: *Absicht*, intro. and ed. J. M. Connolly, T. Keutner (Freiburg and Munich: Karl Alber, 1986); in Spanish: *Intención*, intro. J. Mosterîn, trans. A. I. Stellino (Barcelona: Paidós, 1991); in French: *L'Intention*, intro. V. Descombes, trans. M. Maurice and C. Michon (Paris: Gallimard, 2001).

1963b. 'The Two Kinds of Error in Action', *Journal of Philosophy*, 60 (1963), 393–400. [*ERP*, 3–9].

1963c. Review of Paul Ziff, *Semantic Analysis*, in *Mind*, 72/286 (1963), 288–93.

1964a. ' "Substance" ', *Proceedings of the Aristotelian Society*, suppl. vol. 38 (1964), 69–78. [*MPM*, 37–43].

1964b. 'Before and After', *Philosophical Review*, 73 (1964), 3–24. [*MPM*, 180–95].

1965a. 'Thought and Action in Aristotle: What is Practical Truth?', in J. R. Bambrough, (ed.), *New Essays on Plato and Aristotle* (London: Routledge and Kegan Paul, 1965), 143–58. [*FPW*, 66–77].

1965b. 'The Intentionality of Sensation: A Grammatical Feature', in R. J. Butler (ed.), *Analytical Philosophy—Second Series* (Oxford: Blackwell, 1965), 158–80. [*MPM*, 3–20].

1965c. 'Retractation', *Analysis*, 26/2 (1965), 33–6. [*FPW*, 108–11].

1965d. 'Necessity and Truth', *Times Literary Supplement*, 14 Feb. 1965, p. 26. [*FPW*, 81–5].

1965e. 'Contraception and Natural Law', *New Blackfriars*, 46 (1965), 517–21.

1965f. 'Mechanism and Ideology', review of Charles Taylor, *The Explanation of Behaviour*, in *New Statesman*, 5 Feb. 1965, p. 206.

1965g. (with G. H. von Wright and R. Rhees) 'Letter to the Editor', *Times Literary Supplement*, 18 Feb. 1965, p. 132.

1966a. 'A Note on Mr. Bennett', *Analysis*, 26/6 (1966), 208.

1966b. 'The New Theory of Forms', *Monist*, 50/3 (1966), 403–20. [*FPW*, 21–33].

1967a. Translation: L. Wittgenstein, *Zettel* (Oxford: Blackwell, 1967).

1967b. 'On the Grammar of Enjoy', *Journal of Philosophy*, 64 (1967), 607–14. [*MPM*, 94–100].

1967c. 'Who is Wronged? Philippa Foot and "Double Effect" ', *Oxford Review*, 5 (1967), 16–17. [*HLAE*, 249–52].

1968. 'You Can Have Sex without Children: Christianity and the New Offer', in *Renewal of Religious Structures: Proceedings of the Canadian Centenary Theological Congress*, ed. L. K. Shook (New York: Herder & Herder, 1968). [*ERP*, 82–96].

1969a. (with Dennis Paul) Translation: L. Wittgenstein, *On Certainty* (Oxford: Blackwell, 1969).

1969b. 'On Promising and its Justice, and Whether it Need be Respected *in Foro Interno*', *Critica*, 3/7–8 (1969), 61–83. [*ERP*, 10–21].

1969c. 'Parmenides, Mystery and Contradiction', *Proceedings of the Aristotelian Society*, 69 (1969), 125–32. [*FPW*, 3–8].

1969d. 'Causality and Extensionality', *Journal of Philosophy*, 66 (1969), 152–9. [*MPM*, 173–9].

1969e. 'On the Form of Wittgenstein's Writing', in R. Klibansky (ed.), *Contemporary Philosophy: A Survey*, iii (Florence: La Nuova Italia, 1969), 373–8.

1970. (with G. H. von Wright and R. Rhees) 'Letter to the Editor', *Times Literary Supplement*, 9 Oct. 1970, 1165.

1971a. *Causality and Determination. An Inaugural Lecture* (Cambridge: Cambridge University Press, 1971). [*MPM*, 133–47].

1972a. 'Contraception and Chastity', *The Human World*, 7 (1972), 9–30.

1972b. 'Reply' (to the letter signed by Peter Winch, Michael Tanner, and Bernard Williams), *The Human World*, 9 (1972), 49–51. Revised and abridged in Michael D. Bayles (ed.), *Ethics and Population* (Cambridge, Mass.: Schenkman Publ. Comp., 1976), 162–3.

1972c. (with J. Feldman) 'On the Nature of Justice in a Trial', *Analysis*, 33/2 (1972), 33–6.

1973a. 'On Justice in a Trial', *Analysis*, 34/1 (1973), 32.

1973b. 'Hume and Julius Caesar', *Analysis*, 34/1 (1973), 1–7. [*FPW*, 86–92].

1973c. 'Letter to the Editor', *Times Literary Supplement*, 16 Nov. 1973, p. 1401.

1974a. 'Comments on Professor R. L. Gregory's Paper on Perception', in S. C. Brown (ed.), *Philosophy of Psychology* (London: Macmillan and New York: Barnes and Noble, 1974), 211–20. [*MPM*, 64–70].

1974b. 'Discussion', ibid. 231–44.

1974c. 'Memory, "Experience" and Causation', in H. D. Lewis (ed.), *Contemporary British Philosophy*, 4th ser. (London: Allen & Unwin, 1974), 15–29. [*MPM*, 120–30].

1974d. 'Times, Beginnings and Causes', *Proceedings of the British Academy*, 60 (1974), 253–70. [*MPM*, 148–62].

1974e. ' "Whatever has a Beginning of Existence must have a Cause": Hume's Argument Exposed', *Analysis*, 34/5 (1974), 145–51. [*FPW*, 93–9].

1974f. *On Transubstantiation* (London: Catholic Truth Society, 1974). [*ERP*, 107–12].

1974g. 'Comment', in S. Körner (ed.), *Practical Reason* (Oxford: Blackwell, 1974), 17–21.

1974h. 'Letter to the Editor', *Times Literary Supplement*, 4 Jan. 1974, p. 12.

1974i. 'Letter to the Editor', *Times Literary Supplement*, 18 Jan. 1974, p. 55.

1975a. 'The First Person', in S. Guttenplan (ed.), *Mind and Language: Wolfson College Lectures 1974* (Oxford: Clarendon Press, 1975), 45–65. [*MPM*, 21–36].

1975b. 'Subjunctive Conditionals', *Ruch Filozoficzny*, 33/3–4 (1975), 305–12. [*MPM*, 196–207 (with 'Prefatory Note')].

1975c. 'Ursprung und Grenzen der staatlichen Autorität', in G. E. M. Anscombe, P. Berglar, and C. Clark, *Globale Gesellschaft und Zivilisation. Lindenthal-Institut Colloquium. Köln 1975* (Cologne: Adamas-Verlag, 1975), 37–55.

1975d. 'Aussprache', ibid. 56–64.

1976a. 'Soft Determinism', in G. Ryle (ed.), *Contemporary Aspects of Philosophy* (London: Oriel Press, 1976), 148–60. [*MPM*, 163–72].

1977a. 'The Question of Linguistic Idealism', in J. Hintikka (ed.), *Essays on Wittgenstein in Honour of G. H. von Wright = Acta Philosophica Fennica*, 28/1–3 (1976), 188–215. [*FPW*, 112–33].

1977b. 'On Frustration of the Majority by Fulfillment of the Majority's Will', *Analysis*, 36/4 (1976), 161–68. [*ERP*, 123–9].

1977c. 'The Subjectivity of Sensation', in *Ajatus* (Yearbook of the Philosophical Society of Finland), 36 (1976), 3–18. [*MPM*, 44–56].

1977d. *Contraception and Chastity* (London: Catholic Truth Society, 1977). (Modified version of the 1972a *Human World* article.)

1978a. 'Will and Emotion', in R. M. Chisholm (ed.), *Die Philosophie Franz Brentano's* (Amsterdam: Rodopi, 1978) = *Grazer Philosophische Studien*, 5 (1978), 139–48. [*FPW*, 100–7].

1978b. 'On the Source of the Authority of the State', *Ratio*, 20/1 (1978), 1–28. [*ERP*, 130–55].

1978c. 'Rules, Rights, and Promises', *Midwest Studies in Philosophy*, 3 (1978), 318–23. [*ERP*, 97–103].

1978d. 'L'ambiente morale del bambino', in *I diritti del fanciullo e della famiglia* (Quaderni ICU; Educazione e Sviluppo, 7 (Rome, 1978), 33–42.

1979a. 'Chisholm on Action', *Grazer Philosophische Studien*, 7–8 (1979), 205–13. [*HLAE*, 89–108].

1979b. 'Prolegomenon to a Pursuit of the Definition of Murder: The Illegal and the Unlawful', *Dialectics and Humanism*, 6/4 (1979), 73–7. [*HLAE*, 253–60].

1979c. ' "Under a Description" ', *Noûs*, 13 (1979), 219–33. [*MPM*, 208–19].

1979d. 'Understanding Proofs, Meno, 85d9–86c2, continued', *Philosophy*, 54 (1979), 149–58. [*FPW*, 34–43].

1979e. 'What is it to Believe Someone?', in C. F. Delaney (ed.), *Rationality and Religious Belief* (Notre Dame: Notre Dame University Press, 1979), 141–51.

1979f. Review of Jenny Teichman, *The Meaning of Illegitimacy*, in *Philosophical Quarterly*, 29/117 (1979), 375–6.

1979g. 'Letter to the Editor', *The Times*, 17 Dec. 1979, p. 13.

1979h. 'On *Humanae Vitae*', in J. N. Santamaria and J. J. Billings (eds.), *Human Love and Human Life. Papers on Humanae Vitae and the Ovulation Method of Natural Family Planning from the International Conference, University of Melbourne, 1978* (Melbourne: Polding Press, 1979).

1980a. 'La filosofía analítica y la espiritualidad del hombre' (Address, XVI Reuniones Filosóficas, Universidad de Navarra, 13.3.1980), *Anuario Filosófico*, 13/1 (1980), 27–40. [*FAEH*, 19–33; in English: 'Analytical Philosophy and the Spirituality of Man', in *HLAE*, 3–16].

1980b. 'Matters of Consequence', review of Richard Sorabji, *Necessity, Cause and Blame: Perspectives on Aristotle's Theory*, in *Times Literary Supplement*, 20 June 1980, p. 701.

1981a. *From Parmenides to Wittgenstein: The Collected Philosophical Papers of G. E. M. Anscombe*, i (Oxford: Blackwell and Minneapolis: University of Minnesota Press, 1981).

1981b. *Metaphysics and the Philosophy of Mind: The Collected Philosophical Papers of G. E. M. Anscombe*, ii (Oxford: Blackwell and Minneapolis: University of Minnesota Press, 1981).

1981c. *Ethics, Religion and Politics: The Collected Philosophical Papers of G. E. M. Anscombe*, iii (Oxford: Blackwell and Minneapolis: University of Minnesota Press, 1981).

1981d. 'Events in the Mind', in *MPM*, 56–63.

1981e. 'Faith', in *ERP*, 113–20.

1981f. 'The Early Theory of Forms', in *FPW*, 9–20.

1981g. Commentary on Harris's 'Ethical Problems in the Management of some Severely Handicapped Children', *Journal of Medical Ethics*, 9 (1981), 122–3. [*HLAE*, 279–84].

1981h. 'A Theory of Language?', in I. Block (ed.), *Perspectives on the Philosophy of Wittgenstein* (Cambridge, Mass.: MIT Press, 1981), 148–58.

1982a. 'Medalist's Address: Action, Intention and "Double Effect"', *Proceedings of the American Catholic Philosophical Association*, 56 (1982), 12–25. [*HLAE*, 207–6].

1982b. 'Morality and Religion', in C. Marneau (ed.), *Pro Ecclesia et Pontifice* (Vatican City, 1982), 16–18.

1982c. 'On the Notion of Immaterial Substance', in M. L. O'Hara (ed.), *Substance and Things: Aristotle's Doctrine of Physical Substance in Recent Essays* (Washington, DC: University of America Press, 1982), 252–62.

1982d. Review of Gareth B. Matthews, *Philosophy and Young Children*, in *Philosophy and Phenomenological Research*, 43/2 (1982), 265–7.

1982e. 'Por qué la prueba de Anselmo en el *Proslogion* no es un argumento ontológico' (Address, XIX Reuniones Filosóficas, Universidad de Navarra, 9.3.1982), *Anuario Filosófico*, 25 (1982), 9–18. [*FAEH*, 35–46; in English: 'Why Anselm's Proof in the *Proslogion* is not an Ontological Argument', *Thoreau Quarterly*, 17 (1985), 32–40].

1982f. §§ 1–5, 7–9 of 'Murder and the Morality of Euthanasia: Some Philosophical Considerations', ch. 3 of Luke Gormally (ed.), *Euthanasia, Clinical Practice and the Law* (London: The Linacre Centre for Health Care Ethics, 1982). [*HLAE*, 261–78].

1983a. 'Opening Address', in Werner Leinfellner, Eric Kraemer, and Jeffrey Schenk (eds.), *Language and Ontology: Proceedings of the 6th International Wittgenstein Symposium* (Vienna: Holder-Pichler-Tempsky, 1982), 26–8.

1983b. 'On Private Ostensive Definitions', ibid. 212–17.

1983c. 'The Causation of Action', in C. Ginet (ed.), *Knowledge and Mind: Philosophical Essays* (New York: Oxford University Press, 1983). [*HLAE*, 89–108].

1983d. 'Sins of Omission: The Non-treatment of Controls in Clinical Trials: II', *Proceedings of the Aristotelian Society*, suppl. vol. 57 (1983), 223–7. [*HLAE*, 285–91].

1984. 'Some Reminiscences of Wittgenstein from Littlewood's Papers per Dame Mary Cartwright', *Cambridge Review*, July 1984, p. 129.

1985a. Review of S. A. Kripke: *Wittgenstein on Rules and Private Language*, in *Canadian Journal of Philosophy*, 5 (1985), 103–09.

1985b. Review of Saul Kripke, *Wittgenstein on Rules and Private Language*, *Ethics*, 95 (1985), 342–52.

1985c. 'Paganism, Superstition and Philosophy', *Thoreau Quarterly*, 17 (1985), 20–31.

1985d. 'Truth: Anselm or Thomas?', *New Blackfriars*, 66 (1985), 82–98.

1985e. *Has Mankind One Soul ... An Angel Distributed through Many Bodies?* (The Casassa Lecture, 1985, Loyola Marymount University) (Milwaukee: Marquette University Press, 1986). [*HLAE*, 17–26].

1985f. 'Were you a Zygote?', in A. Phillips Griffiths (ed.), *Philosophy and Practice* (Cambridge: Cambridge University Press, 1985), 111–17. [*HLAE*, 39–44].

1986a. 'Gradualness in a Law, and a Law of Gradualness', *Anthropos*, 2 (1986), 183–6.

1986b. 'Knowledge and Reverence for Human Life', in R. Hittinger (ed.), *Linking the Human Life Issues* (Washington, DC: Regnery-Gateway, 1986), 170–8. [*HLAE*, 59–66].

1987a. 'Twenty Opinions Common among Modern Anglo-American Philosophers', in *Persona, verità e morale. Atti del Congresso Internazionale di Teologia Morale (Roma, 7–12 aprile 1986)* (Rome: Città Nuova Editrice, 1987), 49–50.

1987b. 'Descartes and Anselm', in J. Perzanowski (ed.), *Essays on Philosophy and Logic. Proceedings of the XXXth Conference on the History of Logic, Dedicated to Roman Suszko* (Kraków: Jagiellonian University Press, 1987), 15–18.

1988a. 'Existence and Truth' (Presidential Address, Aristotelian Society, delivered on 12.10.1987), *Proceedings of the Aristotelian Society*, 88 (1987–8), 1–12.

1988b. *Private Ostensive Definition/Private hinweisende Definition.* (English text, facing German translation) (Hagen: Fern Universität, 1988).

1989a. 'Elementos y esencias' (Address, Universidad de Navarra, 25.1.1989), *Anuario Filosófico*, 22 (1989), 9–16. [*FAEH*, 75–84].

1989b. 'The Simplicity of the Tractatus', *Critica*, 21 (1989), 3–16.

1989c. 'Von Wright on Practical Inference', in P. A. Schilpp (ed.), *The Philosophy of Georg Henrik von Wright* (Chicago: Open Court, 1989), 377–404. [As 'Practical Inference', *HLAE*, 109–48].

1990a. 'A Comment on Coughlan's "Using People"', *Bioethics*, 4/1 (1990), 60.

1990b. 'Why Have Children?', *Proceedings of the American Catholic Philosophical Association*, 63 (1990), 48–53.

1990c. 'Truth, Sense and Assertion, or: What Plato Should Have Told the Sophists', in E. Zarnecka-Bialy (ed.), *Logic Counts* (Dordrecht: Kluwer, 1990), 43–6.

1991a. 'On a Queer Pattern of Argument', in H. A. Lewis, *Peter Geach: Philosophical Encounters* (Dordrecht: Kluwer, 1991), 121–35.

1991b. 'La esencia humana' (Address, XXV Reuniones Filosóficas, Universidad de Navarra, 31.8.1988), in R. Alvira and A. J. Sison, *El Hombre: Inmanencia y Trascendencia. XXV Reuniones Filosóficas*, i (Pamplona: Universidad de Navarra, 1991), 3–15. [*FAEH*, 63–74; in English: 'Human Essence', *HLAE*, 27–38].

1991c. 'Wittgenstein, Whose Philosopher?', in A. Phillips-Griffiths (ed.), *Wittgenstein: Centenary Essays* (Cambridge: Cambridge University Press, 1991), 1–10.

1992a. 'Embryos and Final Causes', in J. Fellon and J. McEvoy (eds.), *Finalité et intentionalité. Doctrine Thomiste et perspectives modernes. Actes du colloque de Louvain-la-Neuve et Louvain, 21–23. Mai 1990* (Louvain-la-Neuve: Éditions de L'Institut Supérieur de Philosophie, 1992), 293–303. [*HLAE*, 39–44].

1992b. 'Practical Truth', *Ruch filozoficzny*, 49/1 (1992), 30–3.

1992c. 'Verité et raisonnement pratique', in B. Cassin (ed.), *Nos Greques et leurs modernes* (Paris: Seuil, 1992), 393–401.

1992d. Review of Ruth Chadwick, *Ethics, Reproduction and Genetic Control* and Michael Coughlan, *The Vatican, the Law and the Human Embryo*, in *Philosophical Quarterly*, 42/166 (1992), 375–6.

1993a. 'On Wisdom', *Acta Philosophica*, 2 (1993), 127–33.

1993b. 'Knowledge and Essence', in J.-M. Terricabras (ed.), *Wittgenstein Symposium, Girona 1989* (Studien zur österreichischen Philosophie, 18; Amsterdam: Rodopi, 1993), 29–35.

1993c. 'The Origin of Plato's Theory of Forms', in R. W. Sharples (ed.), *Modern Thinkers and Ancient Thinkers* (Boulder, Colo.: Westview Press, 1993), 90–8.

1993d. 'Russell or Anselm?', *Philosophical Quarterly*, 43 (1993), 500–4.

1993e. 'Was heißt beraten?', in H. Thomas and W. Kluth (eds.), *Das Zumutbare Kind. Die zweite Bonner Fristenregelung vor dem Bundesverfassungsgericht* (Herford: BusseSeewald, 1993), 211–18.

1993f. 'Ausprache', ibid. 238–58.

1994a. *Practical Truth*, in Working Papers in Law, Medicine and Philosophy (Program in Human Rights and Medicine, University of Minnesota), no. 1, 1994. (Series Editor: John M. Dolan). [*HLAE*, 149–58].

1994b. Review of P. F. Strawson, *Analysis and Metaphysics*, in *Philosophical Quarterly*, 44/177 (1994), 528–30.

1995. 'Ludwig Wittgenstein (Cambridge Philosophers II)', *Philosophy*, 70 (1995), 395–407.

1998. 'Die Wahrheit "Thun"', in M. Crespo (ed.), *Menschenwurde: Metaphysik und Ethik* (Heidelberg: Universitätsverlag C. Winter, 1998), 57–60.

2000a. 'Making True', in R. Teichmann, *Logic, Cause and Action: Essays in Honour of Elizabeth Anscombe* (Royal Institute of Philosophy, *Philosophy* Supplement, 46; Cambridge: Cambridge University Press, 2000), 1–8.

2000b. 'Grammar, Structure and Essence', *Arete*, 12/2 (2000), 113–20.

2002a. 'Wahrheit, Sinn und Handlung', in *Aletheia: An International Yearbook of Philosophy, Volume VII (1995–2001)* (Bern: Peter Lang, 2002), 11–20.

2002b. 'How Can a Man be Free? Spinoza's Thought and that of Some Others', ibid. 21–30.

2005a. *La filosofía analítica y la espiritualidad del hombre. Lecciones en la Universidad de Navarra*, ed. J. M. Torralba and J. Nubiola (Pamplona: Eunsa, 2005).

2005b. 'Verdad' (Lecture, Universidad de Navarra, Oct. 1983), in *FAEH*, 47–54.

2005c. 'La unidad de la verdad' (Lecture, Universidad de Navarra, 14.10.1983), in *FAEH*, 55–62.

2005d. *Human Life, Action and Ethics*, ed. M. Geach and L. Gormally (St. Andrew's Studies in Philosophy and Public Affairs; Exeter: Imprint Academic, 2005).

2005e. 'The Dignity of Human Life', in *HLAE*, 67–74.

2005f. 'Good and Bad Human Action', in *HLAE*, 195–206.

2005g. 'The Controversy over the New Morality', in *HLAE*, 227–36.

2005h. 'Must One Obey One's Conscience?', in *HLAE*, 237–42.

2005i. 'Glanville Williams' *The Sanctity of Life and Criminal Law*: A Review', in *HLAE*, 243–8.

Bibliography

Altham, J. E. J., 'Indirect Reflexives and Indirect Speech', in Diamond and Teichman (eds.), *Intention and Intentionality*, 25–37.

Aquinas, Thomas, *Theological Texts*, selected and translated by Thomas Gilby (Oxford: Oxford University Press, 1955).

Austin, J. L., *Sense and Sensibilia* (Oxford: Clarendon Press, 1962).

Blackburn, Simon, 'Against Anscombe', *Times Literary Supplement*, 20 Sept. 2005.

—— *Ruling Passions: A Theory of Practical Reasoning* (Oxford: Clarendon Press, 1998).

Carroll, Lewis, 'What the Tortoise Said to Achilles', *Mind*, 4/14 (Apr. 1895), 278–80.

Castaneda, Hector-Neri, 'The Logic of Self-Knowledge', *Noûs*, 1 (1967), 9–22.

Davidson, Donald, 'Causal Relations', *Journal of Philosophy*, 64 (1967), 691–703.

—— *Essays on Actions and Events* (Oxford: Clarendon Press, 1980).

Diamond, Cora, 'Consequentialism in Modern Moral Philosophy and in "Modern Moral Philosophy" ', in David S. Oderberg and Jacqueline A. Laing (eds.), *Human Lives: Critical Essays on Consequentialist Bioethics* (Basingstoke: Macmillan, 1997), 13–38.

—— and Teichman, Jenny (eds.), *Intention and Intentionality: Essays in Honour of G. E. M. Anscombe* (Brighton: Harvester Press, 1979).

Donnellan, Keith, 'Reference and Definite Descriptions', *Philosophical Review*, 75 (1966), 281–304.

Dummett, Michael, *Frege: Philosophy of Language* (2nd edn., London: Duckworth, 1981).

—— Obituary of Elizabeth Anscombe, *The Tablet*, 13 Jan. 2001.

—— 'The Reality of the Past', in Dummett, *Truth and Other Enigmas* (London: Duckworth, 1978), 338–59.

—— 'Sentences and Propositions', in Teichmann (ed.), *Logic, Cause and Action*, 9–23.

—— *Truth and Other Enigmas* (London: Duckworth, 1978).

—— *Truth and the Past* (New York: Columbia University Press, 2004).

Fodor, J., 'Methodological Solipsism as a Research Strategy in Cognitive Science', *Behavioral and Brain Sciences*, 3 (1980), 63–73.

Foot, Philippa, 'Morality as a System of Hypothetical Imperatives', in *Virtues and Vices and Other Essays in Moral Philosophy* (Oxford: Blackwell, 1978), 157–73.

—— *Natural Goodness* (Oxford: Oxford University Press, 2001).

—— Obituary of Elizabeth Anscombe, *Somerville College Review*, 2001, p. 119.

Frankfurt, Harry G., 'Alternate Possibilities and Moral Responsibility', in *The Importance of What We Care About* (Cambridge: Cambridge University Press, 1988), 1–10.

Frege, Gottlob, 'On Concept and Object', in *Translations from the Philosophical Writings of Gottlob Frege*, ed. Peter Geach and Max Black (Oxford: Blackwell, 1960), 42–55.

—— 'On Sense and Reference', ibid. 56–78.

Gasking, Douglas, 'Causation and Recipes', in *Language, Logic and Causation*, ed. I. T. Oakley and L. J. O'Neill (Carlton South: Melbourne University Press, 1996).

Geach, Peter, 'Good and Evil', *Analysis*, 17 (1956), 35–42.

—— 'Intention, Freedom and Predictability', in Teichmann (ed.), *Logic, Cause and Action*, 73–81.

Geach, Peter, *Reference and Generality: An Examination of Some Medieval and Modern Theories* (3rd edn., Ithaca and London: Cornell University Press, 1980).

Gellner, Ernest, *Words and Things: A Critical Account of Linguistic Philosophy and a Study in Ideology* (London: Victor Gollancz, 1959).

Glover, Jonathan, *Humanity: A Moral History of the Twentieth Century* (London: Pimlico, 1999).

Harcourt, Edward, 'The First Person: Problems of Sense and Reference', in Teichmann (ed.), *Logic, Cause and Action*, 35–46.

Hare, R. M., *Freedom and Reason* (Oxford: Clarendon Press, 1963).

Hinton, J. M., *Experiences: An Inquiry into Some Ambiguities* (Oxford: Clarendon Press, 1973).

Humberstone, Lloyd, 'Direction of Fit', *Mind*, 101/401 (1992), 59–83.

Hursthouse, Rosalind, 'Intention', in Teichmann (ed.), *Logic, Cause and Action*, 83–105.

Kenny, Anthony, 'The First Person', in Diamond and Teichman (eds.), *Intention and Intentionality*, 3–13.

―――― 'Practical Inference', *Analysis*, 26/3 (1966), 65–73.

Kripke, Saul A., *Naming and Necessity* (Oxford: Blackwell, 1980).

―――― *Wittgenstein on Rules and Private Language: An Elementary Exposition* (Oxford: Blackwell, 1982).

Langton, R., 'Intention as Faith', in J. Hyman and H. Steward (eds.), *Agency and Action* (Royal Institution of Philosophy suppl. vol. 55; Cambridge: Cambridge University Press), 243–58.

Lewis, David, 'Mad Pain and Martian Pain', in Ned Block (ed.), *Readings in Philosophy of Psychology*, i (Cambridge, Mass.: MIT Press), 216–22.

Lovibond, Sabina, 'Absolute Prohibitions without Divine Promises', in Anthony O'Hear (ed.), *Modern Moral Philosophy* (Cambridge: Cambridge University Press, 2004), 141–58.

MacIntyre, Alasdair, *After Virtue: A Study in Moral Theory* (London: Duckworth, 1981).

Mackie, J. L., 'Causes and Conditions', *American Philosophical Quarterly*, 2 (1965), 245–64.

―――― *Ethics: Inventing Right and Wrong* (Harmondsworth: Penguin, 1977).

Martin, C. B., and Deutscher, M., 'Remembering', *Philosophical Review*, 75 (1966), 161–96.

Platts, Mark de Bretton, *Ways of Meaning: An Introduction to a Philosophy of Language* (London: Routledge and Kegan Paul, 1979).

Putnam, Hilary, 'The Meaning of "Meaning"', in *Collected Papers*, ii: *Mind, Language and Reality* (Cambridge: Cambridge University Press, 1975).

Reach, K., 'The Name Relation and the Logical Antinomies', in *Journal of Symbolic Logic*, 3 (Sept. 1938), 97–111.

Russell, Bertrand, 'The Limits of Empiricism', *Proceedings of the Aristotelian Society*, 36 (1935–6), 131–50.

Ryle, Gilbert, 'Pleasure', in *Collected Papers*, ii (London: Hutchinson, 1971), 325–35.

Searle, John, 'How to Derive "Ought" from "Is"', *Philosophical Review*, 73 (1964), 43–58.

Smith, Michael, 'The Humean Theory of Motivation', *Mind*, 96 (1987), 36–61.

Snowdon, P., 'Perception, Vision and Causation', in *Proceedings of the Aristotelian Society*, 81 (1980–1), 175–92.

Strawson, P. F., 'Freedom and Resentment', in *Freedom and Resentment and Other Essays* (London: Methuen, 1974), 1–25.

——— 'On Referring', *Mind*, 59 (1950), 320–44.

——— 'Perception and its Objects', in Jonathan Dancy (ed.), *Perceptual Knowledge* (Oxford: Oxford University Press, 1988), 92–112.

Teichmann, Roger, 'Authority', in *Modern Moral Philosophy*, ed. Anthony O'Hear (Cambridge: Cambridge University Press, 2004), 229–44.

——— (ed.), *Logic, Cause and Action: Essays in Honour of Elizabeth Anscombe* (Cambridge: Cambridge University Press, 2000).

Thomson, J. J., 'The Time of a Killing', *Journal of Philosophy*, 68 (1971), 115–32.

Thompson, M., *Life and Action* (Harvard University Press, forthcoming).

Torralba, J. M., *Acción intencional y razonamiento práctico según G. E. M. Anscombe* (Pamplona: Eunsa, 2005).

Tye, M., *The Metaphysics of Mind* (Cambridge: Cambridge University Press, 1989).

Velleman, Daniel J., 'The Guise of the Good', *Nous*, 26 (1992), 3–26.

Williams, B. A. O., *Moral Luck: Philosophical Papers, 1973–1980* (Cambridge: Cambridge University Press, 1981).

——— *Truth and Truthfulness: An Essay in Genealogy* (Princeton: Princeton University Press, 2002).

——— (with J. J. C. Smart), *Utilitarianism: For and Against* (Cambridge: Cambridge University Press, 1973).

Winch, P., *The Idea of a Social Science and its Relation to Philosophy* (London: Routledge, 1958).

Wittgenstein, Ludwig, *Culture and Value*, ed. G. H. von Wright and Heikki Nyman, trans. Peter Winch (Oxford: Blackwell, 1980).

——— 'A Lecture on Ethics', repr. in *Philosophical Occasions 1912–1951*, 36–44.

——— 'On Cause and Effect, Intuitive Awareness', from MS 119 in von Wright's catalogue, trans. P. Winch; repr. in *Philosophical Occasions 1912–1951*, 370–405.

——— *On Certainty*, trans. Elizabeth Anscombe and Denis Paul (Oxford: Blackwell, 1969).

——— *Philosophical Investigations*, trans. Elizabeth Anscombe (Oxford: Blackwell, 1953).

——— *Philosophical Occasions 1912–1951*, ed. James C. Klagge and Alfred Nordmann (Indianapolis, Ind., and Cambridge: Hackett, 1993).

——— *Philosophical Remarks*, ed. R. Rhees, trans. R. Hargreaves and R. White (Oxford: Blackwell, 1975).

——— *Preliminary Studies for the 'Philosophical Investigations,' Generally Known as The Blue and Brown Books* (2nd edn., Oxford: Blackwell, 1969).

——— *Remarks on the Foundations of Mathematics*, ed. G. H. von Wright, R. Rhees, and G. E. M. Anscombe, trans. G. E. M. Anscombe (2nd edn., Oxford: Blackwell, 1967).

——— *Tractatus Logico-Philosophicus*, trans. D. F. Pears and B. F. McGuinness (London: Routledge, 1961).

Index

Made in the USA
Lexington, KY
11 March 2019